Stalin

This new biography of Stalin offers an accessible and up-to-date representation of one of the twentieth-century's defining figures, as well as new insights, analysis and illumination to deepen our understanding of his actions, intentions and the nature of the power that he wielded.

Christopher Read examines Stalin's contribution to and impact upon Russian and world events in the first half of the twentieth century. The biography brings together the avalanche of sources and scholarship which followed the collapse of the system Stalin constructed, including the often neglected writings and speeches of Stalin himself. In addition to a detailed narrative and analysis of Stalin's rule, chapters also cover his early years and humble beginnings in a small town at a remote outpost of the Russian Empire, his role in the revolution, his relationships with Lenin, Trotsky and others in the 1920s, and his rise to become one of the most powerful figures in human history. The book closes with an account of Stalin's afterlife and legacy, both in the immediate aftermath of his death and in the decades since.

This concise account of Stalin's life is the perfect introduction for students of modern Russian history.

Christopher Read is Professor of Later Modern European History at the University of Warwick. His previous publications include *Lenin: A Revolutionary Life* (Routledge Historical Biographies, 2005) and *War and Revolution in Russia: 1914–22* (2013).

ROUTLEDGE HISTORICAL BIOGRAPHIES

Series Editor: Robert Pearce

Routledge Historical Biographies provide engaging, readable and academically credible biographies written from an explicitly historical perspective. These concise and accessible accounts will bring important historical figures to life for students and general readers alike.

In the same series:

Stalin

From the Caucasus to the Kremlin

Christopher Read

LONDON AND NEW YORK

First published 2017
by Routledge
2 Park Square, Milton Park, Abingdon, Oxon OX14 4RN

and by Routledge
711 Third Avenue, New York, NY 10017

*Routledge is an imprint of the Taylor & Francis Group,
an informa business*

British Library Cataloguing in Publication Data
A catalogue record for this book is available from the British
Library

Library of Congress Cataloging-in-Publication Data
Names: Read, Christopher, 1946–
Title: Stalin : from the Caucasus to the Kremlin / Christopher
    Read.
Description: London ; New York : Routledge, [2017] |
    Includes bibliographical references and index.
Identifiers: LCCN 2016015485 | ISBN 9780415519496
    (hardback : alkaline paper) | ISBN 9780415519502
    (paperback : alkaline paper) | ISBN 9781315527659
    (ebook)
Subjects: LCSH: Stalin, Joseph, 1878–1953. | Stalin, Joseph,
    1878–1953—Influence. | Heads of state—Soviet Union—
    Biography. | Soviet Union—History—1925–1953. | Soviet
    Union—Politics and government—1936–1953. | World
    politics—1933–1945. | World politics—1945–1955.
Classification: LCC DK268.S8 R393 2017 |
    DDC 947.084/2092 [B]—dc23
LC record available at https://lccn.loc.gov/2016015485

ISBN: 978-0-415-51949-6 (hbk)
ISBN: 978-0-415-51950-2 (pbk)
ISBN: 978-1-315-52765-9 (ebk)

Typeset in Sabon
by Apex CoVantage, LLC

In celebration of my mother's 100th birthday and in memory of my father who would have loved to read this book.

We cannot regard Stalin's acts as the behaviour of a mad despot. He believed it was necessary to act this way in the interests of the party and the toiling masses, in the name of defending our revolutionary conquests. That is the tragedy. (Nikita Khrushchev, Secret Speech, 25 February 1956)

Contents

Preface

Stalin was a colossus who towered over the first half of the twentieth century and whose influence can still be traced more than half a century after his death. He had several lives – dashing labour organizer in the wild west atmosphere of the Caucasus; local commander in the Russian Civil War; Lenin's executive assistant; party bureaucrat; leader of economic transformation; terrorist in chief; war leader and international statesman. It follows that to cram such an eventful life into a book of the present dimensions is an exercise in leaving things out as well as putting them in. A recent attempt to include as much as possible has begun to appear, written by Stephen Kotkin. The first volume is 1,000 pages long and only goes up to 1928. What the present volume attempts is to convey a picture of Stalin consistent with new evidence emerging from the former Soviet archives and to integrate it with the vastly burgeoning scholarship on Stalin and the era over which he presided. There are many biographies of Stalin. The classics, by the likes of Isaac Deutscher, Adam Ulam, Robert Tucker and Robert Service, still have value despite their wide differences and, for the earlier ones, a limited evidence base compared to today. They have been powerful forces shaping widespread ideas about Stalin. Most were written under the overarching and intertwining influence of two shaping factors – Trotsky's views of Stalin and the post-1945 Cold War. A picture of a malevolent, cruel, megalomaniac, pragmatic, somewhat slow-witted despot with no ideals apart from a ruthless patriotism developed during the war years held sway in the West. True, an even more imaginary Stalin as benevolent father of his people was portrayed by his supporters. However, since the opening of the Soviet archives there has been a now-slackening torrent of access to, and open publication of, reams of documents ranging from the contents of his annotated library to Politburo minutes and letters between him and his fellow leaders. The library showed a person more engaged with ideas than had previously been suspected, while the letters were surprising not least because of the circumstances in which they were written. They were produced to keep the leaders in touch when Stalin took his customary four- to six-week summer holiday in Crimea in the early to mid-1930s. The fact that the supposed hands-on dictator, surrounded by minions who feared for their lives, could leave them in charge of the shop for long periods at a time when communications were fairly poor in itself forced a rethink. Deeper study, especially of the 1930s, showed a less cowed and even supportive spirit abroad in the country – for instance, in pioneering work on diaries by Jochen Hellbeck. While new research did little to undermine many of the general contours of our map of who Stalin was, many details, large and small, were challenged. The totalitarian view of Soviet society was replaced by a picture of mobility and often disorder to the point of chaos. The state appeared far more ramshackle than the Cold War view, which often portrayed it as malevolently efficient. Stalinism, it seemed, lurched from one crisis to the next. Figures for and debate over the 1932–1933 famine intensified while the number of gulag victims came to be calculated at considerably lower levels than the wilder estimates of the 1970s and 1980s. They remained, of course, devastating. In foreign policy, new interpretations indicated that the Soviet drive for 'collective security' was backed by enough military force to have deterred Hitler instead of appeasing him at Munich. A better understanding of the decisive role of the USSR in the European theatre during World War II, and even in the Pacific according to some, has emerged from some magisterial studies of that event and its linked horrors of occupation, holocaust and nuclear bombing. The heroic image of the Red Army has been besmirched by revelations of extensive rapes, especially when Berlin was captured. As far as the post-war period is concerned, some scholars have proposed that the Cold War was not inevitable and that a form of, roughly speaking,

Finlandization might have emerged where, in return for international neutrality, key countries such as Poland and Germany could have remained much more independent and, in Germany's case, united than was to be the case. The role of the United States and its allies, especially Britain, in seeing the iron curtain as a containment system limiting Soviet expansion, like the '*cordon sanitaire*' of Versailles and 1919 (Stalin actually used the earlier term before the phrase iron curtain was coined by Churchill), has been suggested by some authors. The 'miracle' of Soviet post-war recovery and the complexity rather than totalitarian simplicity of Soviet society in Stalin's last years have been portrayed in a new burst of historiography of the period. The once-prevailing assumption of an anti-Semitic last phase of Stalin's rule, including the 'Doctors' Plot', has become a focus of intense debate about the USSR's relations with the newly established Israel and Stalin's final political and international manoeuvrings.

In the light of these developments it seemed to be a timely moment, since the debates have, relatively speaking, begun to plateau after such a cascade of revisionism, to draw some of the main points together and try to establish a new, accessible representation of Stalin more in line with the rich new scholarship. It is impossible to separate the man from his era but the emphasis in the present study is to focus on Stalin and then on the context. A study of the USSR from 1917–1953, for example, would have looked very different. The aim has been to look at Stalin's contribution to and impact upon that history and to try to understand what his ideas and principles were and where they came from and, thereby, to help update our understanding of Stalin. No such enterprise can encompass all the new thinking – hence the problem of leaving things out; but it is the author's hope that the present volume provides an initial guide to the new ideas based on primary sources, including the frequently and rather surprisingly neglected writings and speeches of Stalin himself, published and some unpublished archive materials and the vast swathe of recent scholarship. Needless to say, the debates remain intense and the background sombre and tragic. The present account, certainly compared to Kotkin's ongoing blockbuster, aims to be an introductory account rather than a definitive one; but at least readers will save some weeks of their lives by reading this one instead!

Of course, there is no depiction of Stalin which will say it all, or please everyone. Nonetheless, the present volume is offered in the hope it will please someone.

It follows from what has been said above that this study stands on the shoulders of giants. That includes the producers of the wonderful scholarship mentioned in the text and detailed in the chapter endnotes and further reading. I am obviously deeply indebted to all my fellow scholars. I am also, as usual, thankful for the support of the academic collectives to which I belong – my colleagues at Warwick; friends from BASEES, ASEEES and its very friendly Southern Conference; to those involved in the constantly stimulating and intellectually replenishing Study Group on the Russian Revolution; and to the editors and contributors to the extraordinary Russia's Great War and Revolution Project which, although it was in sharp competition with Stalin for my time, has been a welcome new lease of intellectual life. I do have special thanks for the generous colleagues who gave their precious time and attention to parts of my draft – namely, Eric van Ree, Chris Ward, Tracy McDonald, Mark Harrison and Christoph Mick. Geoff Swain and Dan Orlovsky read the whole thing. All of them made excellent suggestions which I have tried to incorporate in the finished product but even that collection of eagle eyes will not have been enough to eliminate all my errors and weaknesses for which I am solely responsible.

Finally, I need to thank Françoise Read for patiently sacrificing the family dinner table for long periods when I was writing on it, as I am now for the last time on this project, and for putting up with piles of books about Stalin and grim topics surrounding him scattered around the living room, also for much longer than should have been the case. Happily, these are the last words I will need it for and our house can now get back to normal.

Chronology

Year	Events in Stalin's Life	Russian/Soviet Events	World Events
1878	18 December. Stalin born in Gori, Georgia.		
1894	Enrols at Tiflis (Tbilisi) Seminary.	Nicholas II succeeds Alexander III as Tsar.	
1899	Expelled for political (probably nationalist) activities.		
1899–1904	Spends next few years in revolutionary work in Caucasus and South Russia, mainly among the predominantly Muslim oil-workers of Baku. Several spells in jail from which he escapes on several occasions.		
1905	Marries Ekaterina Svanidze.	Revolution in Russia. Tsarism barely survives.	
1905–1906	First steps up the Bolshevik Party hierarchy. Represents Georgia and South Russia at party conferences in Tammerfors (Finland) and Stockholm in 1905 and 1906.	Vicious repression of revolution.	

1906–1912	Resumes his career as activist in South Russia and Caspian area. Several arrests and exile to Siberia from which he quickly escapes.	
1907	March. Birth of Stalin's first child, a son named Iacob. October. Death of Ekaterina.	
1912	Passes through St. Petersburg after Siberian escape. Co-opted onto Central Committee of party at Lenin's initiative and becomes editor of *Pravda*, the party newspaper.	
1913	Publishes *Marxism and the National Question*. Arrested by the Tsarist authorities and once again exiled to Siberia where he remains until March 1917.	
1914		30 July. Tsar orders Russia to mobilize to protect Serbia from Austria. 2 August. Russia declares war on Germany. Outbreak of World War I.
1917	Active as organizer in Bolshevik central party bureaucratic apparatus. Specializes in nationalities questions. Becomes commissar for nationalities in first Soviet government.	February Revolution. Tsarism overthrown. October Revolution. Provisional Government overthrown. Soviet (in reality, Bolshevik) power established.

(continued)

(continued)

Year	Events in Stalin's Life	Russian/Soviet Events	World Events
1918	February. Marries Nadezhda Alliluyeva.	March. Russia adopts Western calendar. March. Treaty of Brest-Litovsk signed. Russia withdraws from the World War. June. Civil War flares up again after revolt by Czech Legion.	November. World War I ends in an armistice.
1918–1920	An active commander in the Civil War but recalled from Tsaritsyn by Lenin after a dispute with Trotsky in 1919.		
1919		Communist International (Comintern) founded.	Versailles and associated treaties end World War I. Russia excluded.
1919–1922	Resumes role as a key figure in party and state supervisory institutions such as the Worker-Peasant Inspectorate and the Central Party Control Commission.		
1920		November. Last major White Army driven from Soviet Russia.	
1921	Birth of his second son, Vassili.	January. Georgia invaded and incorporated into Soviet Russia. February–March. Kronstadt uprising. March. Tenth Party Congress closes down factions within party and establi shes the New Economic Policy (NEP).	

1922	April. Becomes general secretary of the party.	25 May. Lenin suffers his first stroke.
1922–1923	Dispute with Lenin.	Lenin amends his testament proposing transfer of Stalin from post of General Secretary to one for which he is better suited. Lenin describes Stalin and Trotsky as the most capable members of Politburo but fears there might be a split between them.
1923		7 March. Lenin suffers third and final stroke. Severely handicapped for the rest of his life.
1923–1925	Succession dispute with Trotsky and then with Kamenev and Zinoviev.	
1924	April: Publishes *Foundations of Leninism*. November: Publishes *Leninism or Trotskyism*.	21 January. Lenin dies.
1925–1927	Struggle against the United Opposition.	
1926	Birth of his daughter Svetlana.	
1927	Fifteenth Party Congress expels Stalin's principal rivals, Trotsky, Kamenev and Zinoviev, from the Communist Party.	War scare. Fear of renewed intervention in Russia by capitalist powers.
1928		First Five Year Plan begins.

(continued)

(continued)

Year	Events in Stalin's Life	Russian/Soviet Events	World Events
1929	Bukharin expelled from Politburo leaving it and the Central Committee dominated by Stalin loyalists. 21 December. Celebration of Stalin's 50th birthday is the occasion for the start of the cult of his personality. His actual 50th birthday was 18 December 1928. There is no definite explanation for the discrepancy.	Campaign to collectivize agriculture begins. Stepped up in autumn to propose 'liquidation of the kulaks as a class'.	Wall Street Crash leads to Great Depression of early 1930s.
1930	2 March. In his newspaper article *Dizzy with Success* Stalin blames grassroots operatives for the shortcomings of the collectivization campaign.	Pace of collectivization reduced.	
1931	In a speech to industrial managers Stalin exhorts the country to prepare to face its enemies or be crushed within ten years.		
1932	Stalin declares First Five Year Plan to be more or less fulfilled in 4.5 years. 8 November. Stalin's wife, Nadezhda Alliluyeva, commits suicide by shooting.		
1932–1933		Devastating famine in Ukraine, South Russia and Southern Urals kills approximately 4.3 million people, mainly in Ukraine.	

Year			
1933		November. United States recognizes USSR.	30 January, Hitler becomes Chancellor of Germany. Germany expelled from League of Nations. USSR joins.
1934	December. Stalin rushes to Leningrad to interrogate the murderer of Sergei Kirov.	1 December. Sergei Kirov assassinated in Leningrad.	
1936–1939	Show trials. Stalin has private room from which he occasionally observes them.	The Great Terror. 680,000 executions and up to 1.5 million deaths in camps. Show trial and execution of Kamenev and Zinoviev and others. Soviet military intervenes in support of government in Spain.	Popular Front in France. (1936–1937) Popular Front government in Spain attacked by fascist military uprising leading to civil war. Hitler and Mussolini send troops to aid rebels.
1937		Second show trial. Secret trial of military leaders. Execution of Tukhachevsky, Yakir and others.	
1938		Show trial of Bukharin and others followed by execution of defendants.	Munich Treaty hands Sudetenland to Germany.

(continued)

(continued)

Year	Events in Stalin's Life	Russian/Soviet Events	World Events
1939	*History of the Communist Party of the Soviet Union (Bolsheviks): Short Course* published under Stalin's editorship and partial authorship.	July–August. Battle of the Khalka River/Nomonhan. Soviet counter-attack repulses and destroys Japanese Sixth Army. USSR and Japan remain neutral towards each other after this until August 1945. 20 August. Nazi-Soviet Pact signed in Berlin. Secret clauses accept Soviet invasion of Baltic States and Eastern Poland.	September. Germany invades Poland. Britain and France declare war on Germany. World War II begins.
1939–1940		Winter War with Finland. USSR annexes Finnish territory adjacent to Leningrad.	
1940			23 August. Trotsky assassinated in Mexico by Soviet agent.
1941	July. Stalin addresses nation and calls on it to resist the Nazi invasion.	21 June. Germany invades USSR. Take Kiev, besiege Leningrad and are halted in front of Moscow.	December. Pearl Harbor bombed by Japanese. United States joins World War II.
1942	July. Stalin signs Order 227 'Not One Step Back'. August. Churchill and Stalin meet for the first time in Moscow.	German armies advance in the south, reaching eastern end of Black Sea.	August. Moscow Conference

Year			
1942–1943		November–February. Battle of Stalingrad. July. Battle of Kursk.	Allies invade Italy November–December. Tehran Conference.
1943	April. Stalin's son Jacob Dzugashvili commits suicide in Sachsenhausen Concentration Camp, Germany. Stalin had refused to exchange him for the German General Von Paulus who had been captured after his defeat at Stalingrad. November–December. Stalin takes his only recorded flights on his way to and from the Tehran Conference with Roosevelt and Churchill.		
1944	October. Churchill, Eden and Averell Harriman visit Stalin in Moscow.	Operation Bagration/Bielorussian campaign drives German forces out of USSR.	
1945	February. Stalin hosts Roosevelt and Churchill at Yalta. May. Stalin toasts the Russian People for their role in victory over Nazi Germany. July/August. Stalin meets Truman, Churchill and Attlee at Potsdam Conference.	April/May. Battle of Berlin. Third Reich destroyed. Soviet forces occupy Poland, eastern Germany, Czechoslovakia, Hungary, Romania and Bulgaria. 9 August. USSR invades Japanese-occupied Manchuria.	August 6. Hiroshima August 9. Nagasaki destroyed by nuclear bombs. 15 August. Japan surrenders. USSR excluded from official signature of surrender treaty on 2 September.

(continued)

(continued)

Year	Events in Stalin's Life	Russian/Soviet Events	World Events
1946–1949		Zhdanovshchina – the restoration of cultural rectitude as decreed by the Central Committee and led by Andrei Zhdanov – begins. Culminates in campaign against Formalism in the Arts in 1949.	
1947			Cold War begins. NATO founded. Marshall Aid set up.
1948–1949			June 1948–May 1949. Berlin Blockade.
1949	Cult of personality peaks around Stalin's official 70th birthday.	Leningrad Affair. Politburo member Nikolai Voznesensky, the chief planner of the war economy, is arrested and executed. 2,000 arrests	Victory of Chinese Communists led by Mao Zedong.
1950	June. Stalin's *Marxism and Problems of Linguistics* published.		Korean War begins.
1952	Stalin's *Economic Problems of Socialism in the USSR* published.		
1953	5 March. Stalin dies.	Doctors' Plot supposedly revealed in Moscow.	Korean War ends.

1956   February. Khrushchev launches attack on the Stalin Cult of Personality at the Twentieth Party Congress.

1961   Stalin's body removed from the Lenin Mausoleum in Red Square and re-interred in Kremlin burial plot. Stalingrad renamed Volgograd.

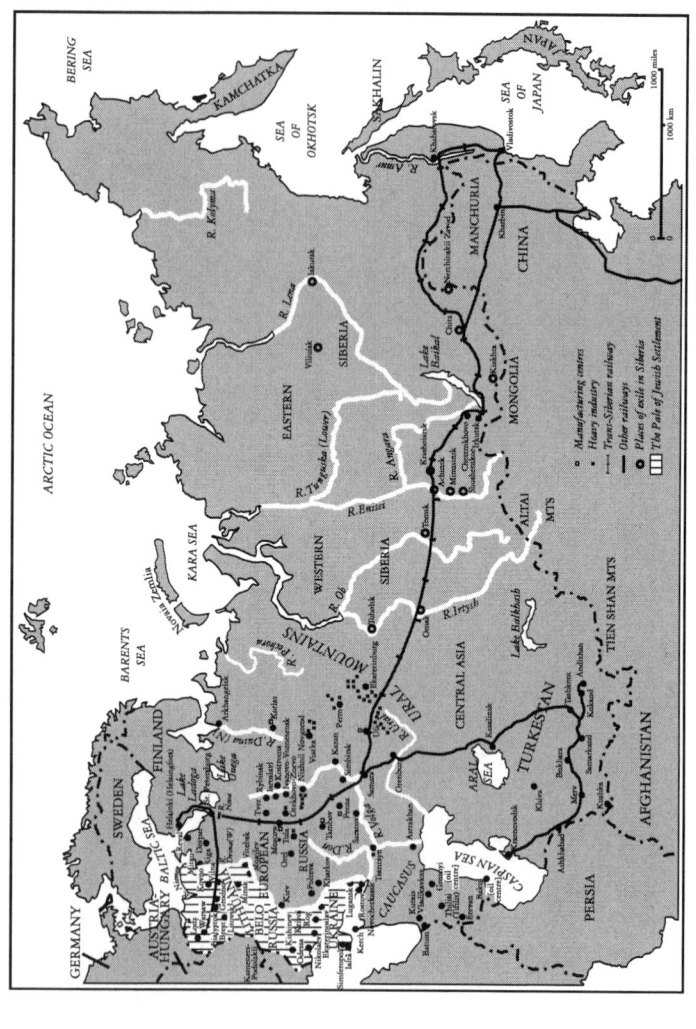

Map The Russian Empire/Soviet Union: main towns and regions (1914 borders). From William Simpson and Martin Jones (2009), *Europe 1783–1914*, 2nd edn, London, Routledge, p.395.

1 From Djugashvili to Stalin

'The child is father of the man.'[1] Many biographers have taken Wordsworth's insight to heart and spent considerable time and effort unearthing the character and actions of their subject when young. Stalin is no exception. Three large accounts of the 'young Stalin' have emerged since the year 2000.[2] However, even a cursory examination shows that all three books are longer than the total amount of reliable primary source material we have on the boyhood and youth of Soso (Joseph) Djugashvili – his family name before he adopted the conspiratorial name Stalin.[3] In the polarized, Cold War-dominated world of Stalin biographies, a variety of childhoods have been invented consistent with the authors' interpretations of the adult Stalin. At one extreme, the adult 'monster' has a monstrous childhood caused by a physically abusive drunken father, an escape into brigandage, notably armed robbery, dressed up as revolutionary activity and a side line in informing for the tsarist secret police. At the other, the adult beacon of humanity has an exemplary, 'heroic' childhood of hard work, devotion to his mother and a growing revolutionary conscience leading him inexorably into the Bolshevik Party and self-sacrificing commitment to the cause of liberating the working class. In neither case is there sufficient direct evidence to prove the majority of those judgements. However, what biographers at both extremes have done is to reverse Wordsworth's concept – the man has become father of the child. Not for the last time we enter a negative feedback loop in interpreting Stalin. Because he was considered to be, let's say, a 'monstrous' adult he must have been a monstrous child, and as a monstrous child, he obviously became a monstrous adult. The same lack of proof works for the opposite argument as well. There is also a tendency for absence of evidence to be taken as proof. In entering the murky and uncharted waters of the life of the young Djugashvili, care will be taken to minimize speculation and build as much as possible on the flimsy evidence. Much of the 'evidence' itself reflects the same negative loops. 'Memoirs' by 'friends' and 'acquaintances' of the young Stalin tend to recall a subject with characteristics very similar to the writer's own interpretation of the adult – that is, a young monster or a young hero.

The Georgian background

Despite these unpromising features, there are some points that can be made with a high degree of certainty. The basic contours of Stalin's early life are known and we also know a great deal about the background in which Soso grew up.[4] In the first place, had Georgia not been annexed to the Russian Empire in 1801, after its king threw off the rule of the Persian Empire, Russia (though not necessarily Georgia) might have been spared the travails of Stalin's rule. To cement the new relationship with Russia, an ancient route was used as the basis for the Georgian Military Highway. It passed through the Caucasus from the southern Russia city of Vladikavkaz (a name meaning 'Lord of the Caucasus'), continued under the shadow of the 15,000-foot (5000-metre) Mount Kazbek and descended to the Georgian capital Tiflis (today known as Tbilisi). Started in 1799 it was still not finished by 1860, not surprising given the scarcity of surfaced roads in Russia and the difficulty of the terrain. But it did symbolize and embody certain enduring features of the tangled relationship between Georgia and Russia. In the first place the alliance quickly turned into Georgia losing its brief independence and being sucked into the Russian Empire. At the same time this was not entirely regrettable for Georgia because Russia was a powerful Christian protector against the encroachment of Islam, notably in the form of Turkey and its Ottoman Empire. Georgia and its neighbour Armenia were the only Christian enclaves in the otherwise Muslim-dominated area south of the Caucasus.

But Russian rule did not wipe out other lasting features of Georgian history. As a mountain kingdom which stretched from the peaks of the Caucasus to the fertile shores of the Black Sea, Georgia was itself composed of a variety of ethnicities, not to mention a Muslim minority in Abkhazia. As a result, Georgia had the feel not only of a fighting frontier state where Christian confronted Muslim and vice versa, but also endured severe internal conflicts between its own inhabitants, one valley often turning against another. Banditry also thrived given the existence of the many high valleys and hideouts more or less inaccessible to outsiders. Conflict within and without has continued down to the present day. Two zones of historic Georgia – Abkhazia and South Ossetia – today remain outside Georgia's grasp. They, ironically, look to Russia for protection as Georgia itself once did. As recently as 2008, Georgia's rash attempt to regain South Ossetia by invasion rebounded spectacularly. In other words, Georgia has been a somewhat wild and unsettled country since its origin.

Within this troubled framework a fierce and independent culture continued to develop. Not surprisingly it had a warrior base. Male chauvinism and patriarchy were very strong. Sexual dual standards of male 'virility' and female virginity and fidelity were fundamental. Georgian men were brought up to be adept in martial skills. The gun, the dagger and horsemanship were highly prized. Lavish banquets accompanied by consumption of vast quantities of local wine (among other things the Georgians, like a number of other peoples, claim to have been the first to produce wine) marked clan, tribal and national festivals. Women were the mothers and providers. On ceremonial occasions their festive role was to dress elaborately, look beautiful (especially if young) and be adept at the traditional Georgian dance, the *kartuli*, which symbolized the gender roles. In such dances the men maintained a rigid upright back and circled the woman, gazing into her eyes but never touching her while women kept their eyes downcast and wore long, stiff dresses which reached the ground and concealed the feet, the movements of which were confined within the area covered by the skirt. The effect produced was that, instead of stepping, the dancers appeared to glide across the floor. Apart from drinking, eating and not infrequently fighting, the role of men at these festivities also included outdoing one another in singing and joining in all-male dancing, often in lines kept together by the dancers putting their arms on each other's shoulders. At the root of this culture was the family, better described as a clan, and the tribe, which associated clans together on the basis of kinship. Within the clan, like the very similar but more familiar Sicilian mafia culture, honour was the highest value. Duelling remained prominent well into the nineteenth century despite it being illegal. Stains on one's personal or family honour could lead to feuds which would never be forgotten if not avenged. Life itself had to be put on the line and a dishonourable man, or occasionally a wayward woman, would suffer its loss by unofficial execution or enforced suicide. Cowardice was the most despised of weaknesses. Within the informal laws of family and honour, state law, and even the much deeper and older laws of the Georgian church (an Orthodox church), had lesser significance so that technically illegal and sinful acts, including robbery and murder, were often sanctioned in the real, informal culture of feud and vengeance. As a result, what the modern state considered to be outlaw activity and banditry was rife throughout Georgia. As the modern, industrial, educated world gradually encroached, so the violent edge was taken off these fierce customs. Cities, like the capital, Tiflis, took on a veneer of bourgeois sophistication, but the violent undercurrents were not far away, even in 1900.

Soso's childhood 1878–1894: Gori

For the modern visitor as well as for earlier predecessors, visiting Georgia remains a fascinating activity. The remnants of its colourful history can be found not only in the life and activity of its contemporary inhabitants, but also in a vast legacy of objects, curiosities and monuments. One of the most curious and unique of all its monuments can be found in the provincial mountain town of Gori (the name is derived from the word for 'hill' in both Georgian and Russian). In this unlikely backwater the traveller is confronted not only with an unexpectedly vast town hall, a massive hotel and a giant museum, but also what looks like the misplaced colonnaded entrance to a Moscow metro station. Closer inspection reveals a single, modest, traditional, artisanal house beneath the archway. It was in this house that Soso was born to Beso (Vissarion) and Ketevan (Ekaterina) Djugashvili.

But even as simple a statement as this is not without contention. Some writers claim it is not the Djugashvili home at all but a neighbouring house or even a reconstruction. Others claim, with no evidence (but, as we shall see, that often makes little difference) that his father was the explorer Nikolai Przhevalsky or even Tsar Alexander III, not Beso Djugashvili. Even more bizarre, in his mature years Stalin changed his date of birth. Local parish records confirm that it was 6 December 1878. However, in the 1920s, Stalin, for reasons unknown but perhaps it simply amused him that he could, not only changed the date to 21 December, he also altered the year to 1879. From 1925 on this became his official birthday, stimulating national celebrations in his later years. As we progress through his life, we will find many similar complications. Welcome to the world of Stalin studies.

Very few firm facts about the young Stalin are known. Many others are contested. Legends, rumours, half-truths, outright lies and false propaganda abound. Picking through these thickets is a hazardous operation at all stages of Stalin's life but the empty canvas of his childhood and youth have been especially tempting for the conscious and unconscious elaborators of falsehood. What can we be reasonably sure of? His father was an artisan working with leather and usually described as a cobbler. At times he worked in a factory and was a genuine proletarian. At others he worked at home as a semi-artisan within the putting-out system.[5] He does not appear to have been a dominant influence in Soso's early life. By 1884, his father had retreated into alcoholism and separated from his mother. It was the latter who took Soso in hand. The couple had lost three children by the time Soso was born and even he had a near-fatal brush with smallpox when he was five. He also had two toes fused together and damaged his arm, probably in an accident involving a horse and carriage when he was ten years old. This resulted in his left arm being shorter and weaker than normal. His face also bore the marks of smallpox. All of this testified to the precariousness of life in poor, underdeveloped areas like the Georgian provinces. It may have contributed to Ketevan's apparent protectiveness and determination to make something of her son and ensure he escaped provincial obscurity. In this endeavour she was helped, first of all, by Soso's intelligence and dawning intellectual abilities. Second, there was the support of his local school, which, like most education for the ordinary inhabitant of Georgia, was under the influence of the church. Soso's talents were recognized and, at the age of nine, he made the first decisive upwardly mobile step in his career. He was accepted into the Gori elementary clerical school. On graduation from there in 1894 he passed the entry exam into the best educational establishment in Georgia, the Tiflis Theological Seminary, primarily dedicated to training priests for the Georgian Orthodox Church.

The Tiflis years 1894–1899: Soso becomes Koba

While these facts are mercifully uncontentious, we know little about Soso's specific talents, interests and personality.[6] Despite the lack of reliable sources, as we have noted, many writers have not resisted the temptation to build psychological profiles of the young Stalin. During the Cold War especially, Stalin's personality was often portrayed as psychopathic and efforts were made to trace the roots to his childhood. Leaning heavily on the unsupported account written in 1930 by Iakob Iremashvili,[7] a contemporary schoolmate of Soso who later became a political opponent, many commentators construct a narrative of paternal beatings and drunkenness. Iremashvili's remarks that 'terrible beatings' by his father made Soso 'hard and heartless'[8] have been enough to launch speculative psychoanalyses. Setting out from a paraphrase of Iremashvili, one such effort argued that 'undeserved, frightful beatings made the boy as grim and heartless as his father. Indeed, his suppressed hatred against his father transferred itself to persons in power and to all authority'.[9] Even more astonishing, as a leap from minimal information to maximum interpretation, is Daniel Rancour-Laferriere's approach:

> In adulthood, Stalin had to live with two affective extremes: he worshipped himself *and* he hated himself. The first he dealt with by promoting a narcissistic cult of personality. The second he dealt with by instituting a reign of terror, by

turning the hatred outward, especially toward objects that reminded him of his own latent homosexuality.[10]

While few historians have pushed the evidence so far into fantasy, many have felt the need to give some psychological explanation of Stalin. The most sustained and, to some extent, convincing approach is probably that of Robert Tucker who stressed Soso's tendency to identify with heroes such as Koba, roughly the Georgian Robin Hood, and later with Lenin. His adoption of the conspiratorial names Koba and Stalin, which is reminiscent of the name Lenin, are presented as testimony.[11]

In a determined rebuttal of the extremes of the psycho-historical approach, Ronald Grigor Suny reminds us that:

> Stalin is without doubt one of the least hospitable subjects for the psychohistorian. Not particularly introspective, he left no intimate letters, no secret diary, and few witnesses to his inner life. Moreover, Bolshevik political culture was hostile to open personal expression and imposed on Stalin and other adherents an enforced modesty. Denial of the importance of self was part of the Leninist tradition, and, even as a grotesque cult of Stalin's personality grew to gargantuan proportions, Stalin would continue, disingenuously, to claim that he disliked all the fuss.[12]

Not only that but we also have evidence refuting claims of childhood mistreatment. In a famous and important interview with the German historian and journalist Emil Ludwig in 1931, Stalin brushed off suggestions he had had an unhappy childhood. Despite being uneducated people, Stalin said, 'they treated me not badly at all'.[13] The testimony of his daughter, Svetlana Alliluyeva, partly confirms and partly confuses the issue. According to her, it was her grandmother who was the stricter and stronger parent who chastised her son. Svetlana, also unable to resist the call of amateur psychoanalysis, claims her grandmother's 'firmness, obstinacy, her strictness towards herself, her puritan morality, her masculine character – all of this passed to my father'.[14] While these testimonies also suffer from obvious potential bias it would seem reasonable to accept Suny's conclusion that 'the confusion in the sources about who actually beat the boy and the silence about young Djugashvili's feelings about the beating make it reasonable to doubt that the reported beatings had much of a determining effect on Stalin's later life'.[15]

However, even if we follow Suny's advice and set aside half-baked, under-evidenced psychohistories and turn to political, social and historical context, we are not entirely out of the wood. Two of the three most detailed studies of Stalin's youth and early years also present their own problems. One of the earliest, dating from deep within the Cold War era, was written by E. E. Smith.[16] Central to his interpretation is the view that, in his early revolutionary years, Stalin was an agent of the tsarist political police service, the *Okhrana*. The fact that no evidence and no files have been found to support such an interpretation is almost taken as proof of the theory rather than refutation. The absence of police files supporting it, so the argument goes, suggests there has been a cover-up and that Stalin himself was responsible, eliminating all trace of unsavoury elements of his past later on when he had the power to do so. While some speculative elements may suggest there is some truth in it – for example, the ease with which he escaped from detention on several occasions – it is also the case that the young Stalin was pursued by the police and spent the years 1912–1917 in Siberian exile: an odd way to treat an agent. The other, more recent, more popular and highly entertaining account,[17] based on archive and other sources which have become available since the collapse of the Soviet Union in 1991, takes an opposite line. It sees the central aspect of the young Stalin's life to be a swaggering youth of involvement with street gangs graduating into a leading role in bank robberies, masterminded and promoted by none other than Lenin and planned on the ground by Stalin. Such is the prominence of this opinion in the book that the dramatic opening pages describe the famous Tiflis armed robbery of 26 June 1907, which was accompanied by a shoot-out supposedly causing 40 deaths. So dramatic was the description that Hollywood is said to have purchased the film rights. If one adds that, in this interpretation, the young Stalin is irresistible to a chain of sultry, Georgian beauties and has an illegitimate child with one of them, it is easy to see the attraction of this approach for Hollywood. However, that is perhaps the best place for it. From the historical perspective the evidence behind the theories of tsarist agent on one hand and gangster on the other is sparse and suspect to say the least. In fact, even though they are largely self-contradictory, a number of writers claim both to be true.[18] Can we pick a way through the obfuscations and arrive at a better substantiated view of Stalin's crucial formative years?[19]

Before he became Stalin, Soso was Koba. This was his first revolutionary conspiratorial name.[20] Koba was a character in Georgian literature usually described as a heroic outlaw who robbed the rich and protected the poor, extracting vengeance on their behalf.[21] By now it will not surprise the reader that this, too, has been the basis of psychological analysis of the young Stalin. It is said to reveal a young man already having a grand idea of his own importance to take such a prominent figure as his role model. It also shows a Nietzschean element of living outside the law in order to be moral and just. In reality, we can only speculate on Soso's decision to select this name. However, we can throw some light on his activities in Tiflis.

It may seem ironic to say that Soso's first contact with the revolutionary movement came via the seminary. However, it is less puzzling if we recall that, perhaps wisely from their own point of view, the tsarist authorities had not permitted a university to be set up in Georgia, no doubt because they had enough problems with radical students in more stable parts of the empire. Establishing one in Georgia risked deep trouble so the only school anywhere near higher education standard was the seminary which functioned also as an elite secondary/high school. Soso entered it as a 15-year-old on 2 September 1894. It was, however, a path followed by many students. The main revolutionary socialist and nationalist party in Georgia the Mesame Dasi (Third Group) had been founded in 1892. Many of its leaders were seminarians or former seminarians. One of its members, Lado Ketskhoveli, who was a few years older than Soso but also came from Gori, appears to have introduced him to the writings of Karl Marx and the two of them set up a small left faction in the organization.

However, there is no really reliable evidence of his time there. The official account of his life claims he was expelled in 1899 for 'propagating Marxism'. It also states that he was part of a study group reading *Capital* and *The Communist Manifesto* and was even involved in spreading Marxist ideas among railway and other workers. The harmony of Mesame Dasi was, it says, disrupted in autumn 1898 by disagreement between its 'revolutionary minority' and 'the opportunist majority' over the issue of setting up a printing press. The final entry referring to the seminary is for 29 May 1899 which states laconically: J. V. Stalin is expelled from Tiflis Theological Seminary for propagating Marxism.[22] While this account improbably indicates that Stalin had a leading role in these activities it is quite likely that they do reflect his growing political involvement alongside numerous other radicals among the student body. We cannot say what specifically drew Soso to radicalism but the atmosphere of the seminary included profound anti-Russian and pro-Georgian sentiments stirred up by the domination of the seminary itself by Russian priests while the mood of the country was deeply affected by the centrally promoted policy of Russification associated with Konstantin Pobedonostsev. His plan was to swamp minorities with Russian values, religion, culture and, most contentiously, language. Such a confrontational approach was disastrously counter-productive. It resulted in resistance, unrest, demonstrations and an incentive to young revolutionaries like Soso and the Mesame Dasi. This point, as we shall see, was not lost on the young Soso. Later on the issue of nationalities concerned him deeply and he wrote one of his most significant articles on it, promoting cultural toleration in exchange for political co-operation between majority and minority nationalities. Whatever Soso got up to in his seminary days, 29 May 1899 was certainly a turning point. He was 20 years' old. His childhood and adolescence had passed and he had been cut loose from their institutional ties. He entered into a wider world of young adulthood. He was getting closer to becoming Koba. Let us examine more closely how he reached this point and where he went from there.

Confirmed evidence of this stage of Soso's life continues to be sparse, though it is interspersed with moments where his presence is recorded on a bigger stage. However, before trying to trace the detail of Soso's transformation into Koba we should note the obvious, which is so frequently overlooked by many biographers. The turn in the young Stalin's life was away from a career, profession and regular employment to full-time commitment to the cause of the poor and oppressed, initially of the Caucasus and Caspian region and later of the Russian Empire and the world. In his fine biography Robert Tucker was correct to entitle the early volume *Stalin as Revolutionary*,[23] though the implication that he was less revolutionary later on is at least arguable. The basic rock on which one can stand to assess Stalin is that he was a revolutionary and, in his own eyes at least, remained one until his death. Familiar characteristics attributed to Stalin – psychosis, paranoia, lust for personal power, cruelty and so on, whether true or not, and our enquiry is intended to examine them further – often distract attention from the vital, central fact of his revolutionary commitment. Even though the details are sparse, we can conclude that nowhere is that commitment clearer than in the activities of his immediate, post-seminary years. So how did his revolutionary commitment manifest itself?

The official record of his life at this time,[24] while unsurprisingly vastly overstating the young Stalin's prominence and leadership role at this early stage of his career, does tell us what he did in general. In addition, the unofficial first volume of his works published in Moscow in 2013 adds detail without revealing its source.[25]

While at the seminary Soso was introduced to the basics of underground revolutioneering. The young radicals in the seminary read illegal literature, almost certainly including Marx's *Capital* and *Communist Manifesto*. He is said to have read the former at the beginning of 1895, though no evidence has been brought forward to support this and it is unlikely he would have seen more than extracts of Marx's massive work. In addition to reading, some direct action was taken in the form of clandestine meetings with workers in Tiflis, of whom one of the most important groups was those who worked on the railway. In January 1898 he began to take part in a Marxist circle in the Main Tiflis Railway Workshop. By August of that year he was part of Mesame Dasi, which, like other evolving left-wing groups of that time in the Russian Empire, was falling into factionalism. One account says that the issue of setting up an illegal printing facility 'gave rise to the first sharp differences within Mesame Dasi between its revolutionary minority and its opportunistic majority'.[26] What this opaque language hinted at was that, even as the Russian Social Democratic Party was being born in Minsk in 1898, its future split into the 'revolutionary minority' of Bolsheviks and the 'opportunistic majority' of Mensheviks[27] was already being foreshadowed. Though there is no detail as to why he chose it, Soso's selection of the more active faction was, as we will see, crucial to his own, and thence to the world's, future.

Activities of this kind could not go unnoticed and unsanctioned within the seminary. Among charges and punishments brought against him at various times were that he was one of a group of students singing a forbidden song during a free period (21 January 1895); he was, unsurprisingly, refused a state grant for his studies (15 September 1895); had books confiscated, for example, on 3 March 1897, in connection with which the assistant inspector of the seminary commented that 'I. Djugashvili had already been reported three times for reading forbidden books'.[28] By autumn 1898 he was rebelling against the seminary regime in numerous ways including failing to attend prayers; disrupting the liturgy; a disinclination to greet his teachers; and arguing during searches.[29] Clearly this could not go on unchecked. For a month he was forbidden to leave his flat in his free time after dinner (19 January 1899). Finally, on 29 May 1899, he was formally expelled from the seminary for systematically being involved in concealing illegal literature and for challenging behaviour. Officially he was excluded for 'Failing to appear at examinations for unknown reasons'.[30] While official hagiographies tried to make mountains out of molehills by projecting a charismatic element of leadership into these activities, and those to come in continued semi-obscurity outside the seminary, in truth, there is little that is unusual in these activities. What can we glean from them? To repeat, the obvious point is that, for precise reasons we do not know, Soso took the option for the poor and oppressed and, most likely, for Georgian autonomy. He was prepared and did sacrifice his chances of a middle-class career, or even being a priest, for his developing radical vision. He was not alone and several other significant radicals followed a similar path. There was nothing exceptional, it seems, in the life of Soso beyond his self-sacrificing choice of the life of a professional revolutionary. By summer 1898 we was committed and associated with the more active radical factions. He may or may not have considered himself a Marxist at this point; we cannot know for sure. But we do know he had laid the foundations of his, as yet hidden, future. The next stage was the controversial phase of transition from Soso to Koba.

For the next five years or so the young Djugashvili underwent experiences which formed and perhaps hardened his developing persona. There is no systematic account of his activities and movements but there are, as it were, snapshots of moments in his life. He appears to have remained mainly in Tiflis with increasing forays into other parts of the Caucasus region and continued meeting and organizing workers in that area. The apparent concentration on factories, transport and the extractive industries and, in the main, ignoring of the peasants backs up his attributed institutional affiliation to the new, fragile Marxist-oriented Russian Social Democratic Workers' Party (RSDWP).

In these years he was living the life of a revolutionary activist. His contacts in radical circles helped him to find a place to live, sharing an apartment with fellow radicals at 102 Mikhailovskii Prospekt (Avenue) in the centre of the city. He also took a job to support himself at the Tiflis Observatory in December 1899, moving to its premises at 132 Mikhailovskii Prospekt. His real activity, however, was addressing meetings of workers in factories, talking to unions, getting involved in strikes, producing and handing out leaflets. He took part in the main working-class demonstrations associated with May Day, giving speeches and talking with workers. His official biography says he was, along with V. Z. Khetskoveli and A. G. Tsulukidze, a leader of the central group of the Tiflis RSDWP and supervised its transition from the status of a revolutionary circle (that is, in essence, a discussion group) to that of mass organization. His 'leadership' at this time is more a consequence of the fact that the organization was, as yet, very small and also the larger Marxist movement was divided.

This lifestyle continued up until March 1901; but during that month, there was a major change in his circumstances. His flat at the observatory was searched on 21 March and on 28 March he left his employment at the Observatory and went on the run, or, in other words, became an illegal underground revolutionary. He occasionally appeared in public – for example at the May Day demonstrations in Tiflis on 22 April where the official biography improbably suggest he was a leader. It is likely he was among the leaders but there is no evidence to suggest a special leadership role anywhere for the young Stalin as yet.

While Stalin, himself, seems to have remained in Tiflis, in September 1901 he is said to have written the opening editorial for the first issue of the underground newspaper called *Brdzola* in Georgian, meaning *Struggle* in English. Claims that the newspaper was his idea are unsubstantiated. In November, however, his growing status is easier to gauge in that he was elected to the Tiflis Committee of RSDWP. In December 1901 an unsigned article was attributed to him which appeared in the next issue of *Brdzola*. It was entitled 'Immediate Tasks of the RSDWP'. It was his first political article.

The Che Guevara of the Caucasus 1901–1912: Batumi, Baku, Kutais

At about the same time, in late November 1901, Soso Djugashvili was given the responsibility by the party, along with others, of setting up a branch in Batumi, some 10 kilometres (6 miles) from the Turkish border, where the city's first social-democratic circles were set up in the Rothschild, Mantashev and Sideris factories. Here he clearly did become a significant local leader of the small Leninist wing of the party. His initial action was, under the guise of a New Year celebration, to organize a meeting of representatives of the social democratic circles in and around Batumi. By January, he was organizing an illegal printing press. In conjunction with the comrades in Tiflis he requested that illegal literature be sent to him. Djugashvili himself wrote pamphlets and supervised the printing and distribution of proclamations.[31]

The Tiflis secret police had quickly noted, in December, that he was no longer in their city. He seems to have had a close shave with the authorities in Batumi in early February when the apartment he was living in was searched, causing him and the rudimentary printing equipment to move into another apartment rented under the name of two brothers named Darakhvelidze. From here, Djugashvili underwent the two most active months of his career so far. Everywhere, worker–employer and worker–state tensions were rising. The Caucasus region was one of the hotbeds. Djugashvili was deeply involved in strikes especially at the Rothschild factory. He made a risky journey back to Tiflis to get more printing equipment, and returned with a manifesto addressed to the authorities in Batumi to release 32 workers who had been arrested in the course of the strikes. The protests grew. On 8 March a demonstration resulted in a further 300 or so arrests. The situation escalated and on 9 March, there was a major protest with 6000 workers out on the streets. As the demonstrators marched on the jail where the prisoners were being held, they were fired upon by the police, resulting in 15 deaths and 54 wounded and 500 arrested.[32] Clearly this had vastly increased the tension and there were further demonstrations on 12 March in connection with the funerals of the victims of the shooting on the ninth. The authorities were also on their guard and were using whatever means they could to prevent the further development of the revolutionary tide. On 5 April, Soso Djugashvili and the whole of the Batumi party leadership were arrested at the Darakhvelidze apartment.

Oddly, and in deep contrast to the official Communist Party line that Djugashvili was a local leader of the Leninists in Tiflis and Batumi, the Gendarmerie (GZhU) in the administrative centre of Kutais concluded that there was no precise evidence of Djugashvili's exact involvement in revolutionary activity in Batumi. Charges against him were, it was said, based solely on supposition, hearsay and dubious overheard conversations.[33] If the authorities in Kutais were half-hearted in their prosecution of Djugashvili, their lack of zeal was more than made up for by that of their superiors in the capital. On 1 September his case was transferred to Tiflis prosecutors. Even so, it was only on 19 April 1903 that Djugashvili was transferred from Batumi to Kutais jail. On 9 June he was banished by decree to eastern Siberia. The first phase of Djugashvili's revolutionary career had come to an almost inevitable turning point.

It seemed that the same could be said for the Russian Empire itself. It was not only in the tiny region of Georgia that the political situation was hotting up. Across the whole of European Russia and into parts of Siberia, the Far East and Central Asia, the Russian Empire was stirring. It may or may not have been the case that the Minister for Education, Plehve, advised embarking on 'a small, victorious war' to distract the country from its internal divisions but one thing is clear. The war with Japan (1904–1905) was neither. Instead, it was a comparatively long, drawn-out series of humiliating defeats. The pivot of Russia's strategic position in Manchuria, the city of Port Arthur (today Dalian), fell on 2 January 1905. At sea, a fleet which had travelled around the world from the Baltic to try and relieve the blockade of the Far Eastern naval port of Vladivostok was obliterated at Tsushima on its arrival in the war zone on 27–28 May. A humiliating peace had to be concluded, all the more humiliating, in the almost universally racist ethos of the 'advanced' world around 1900, because it was the first time a non-white power had defeated one of the world's great white colonizing empires. Far from distracting attention, the disastrous war focused the eyes of the nation on the miserable misgovernment of the tsar and his cohort of ministers, administrators and war planners.[34] Historians have disputed the precise extent of the impact of the Russo-Japanese War but the bottom line is that it certainly worsened an already developing crisis. Through 1903 and 1904 strikes and peasant disturbances grew exponentially. The rising tide culminated in the so-called revolution of 1905, which lasted, in fact, from January 1905 into at least June 1907 and beyond in places. In addition, it was not a revolution in that the authorities and the elite got away with it, some would say, with key powers and property intact, though others argue there had been important concessions in the direction of constitutionality.

Be that as it may it is not our concern to tell the full story of 1905. That has been superbly done already from a variety of viewpoints.[35] However, we need to remember the main contours not least because these were the years when Soso Djugashvili's career moved out of its Georgian 'backwater' onto the national and international stage. The twin impulses in the escalation of the national uprising came on 8 and 9 January in the form of the breaking news of the Port Arthur calamity, followed the next day by the senseless shooting of hundreds, maybe a thousand, unarmed demonstrators in the capital St. Petersburg, earning the incident the name 'Bloody Sunday', which reverberated around the world not just as an atrocity and a piece of massive incompetence but as a symbol of the moral and political bankruptcy of tsardom.

Pressure mounted throughout the year. Strikes and demonstrations became commonplace. There was especial tension in some of the minority nationalities of the Empire already known as 'the prison house of nations'. Poland and Djugashvili's own Caucasus region were among the most combatant. The most fortunate was Finland which was granted autonomy within the Empire. The central point of the revolution, the crisis of the revolutionary fever, is universally acknowledged to be the October Manifesto, a document forced from Tsar Nicholas under extreme duress. Interpretation of its apparent concessions engaged activists at the time and historians ever since. Even the liberal Miliukov believed that, despite the promises of limited representation in a revived quasi-parliament known as the Duma, 'nothing had changed'. Others, like Peter Struve, thought it was the moment for all decent Russians to rally behind the tsar and the regime. It is not our task to follow this up in detail; this, too, has been done in many other places.[36] Suffice it to say that having used the divisions in the opposition opened up by the manifesto between those prepared to work with the tsar and those still opposed, the autocracy climbed back into the military saddle. In December, unlike October when it feared mutiny, the authorities sent in the Guards to heavily repress an attempted armed insurrection based on a working-class suburb of Moscow, Krasnaia Presnia. This was the bloody prelude to more than a year of military and police repression, made possible only by the remaining loyalty of the armed forces. In June 1907, the strong hand behind repression, Prime Minister Peter Stolypin, disbanded the Duma, tore up key clauses of the October Manifesto as it had been widely understood and replaced the relatively democratic Duma with a tame body largely, but not quite exclusively, elected by the propertied elites, especially the landowners. Although as late as 1909 the great novelist Lev Tolstoy was lamenting, in a key essay of 1909, that there were still 'Executions! Executions! Executions!',[37] the heat had gone out of the revolution and the autocracy had largely restored its power, although it had lost almost all its moral authority in the process. The autocracy governed, but the nation obeyed, largely in deference to its command of force. As we will see, by February 1917, it did not even have that and it crumbled into oblivion. But let us return to Georgia, where the battle between revolutionaries, intellectuals, parts of the middle class, workers and peasants on one side and the state with its police, army and judiciary on the other, was especially fierce.

Despite his sentence of banishment, Soso Djugashvili remained in Kutais jail. Official accounts even claim he continued his radical activities whenever he was in prison. In July 1903, the RSDWP group in Tiflis was indicted as a whole by testimony from police agents. In the official proceedings it was described as a 'circle', underlining the fact it had not broken out into the mainstream but remained very small and conspiratorial. Even though he was already in Kutais jail, Soso was not going quietly. He was said to have organized a successful riot by prisoners. On a more personal note he was also visited by his mother who made the journey through the mountains from Gori to see him in September. This had, no doubt, been allowed on compassionate grounds as a farewell visit since, at last, Soso's exile to Siberia was about to begin. On 8 October he was transferred back to Batumi jail and then on his long journey by train to Irkutsk, in eastern Siberia, travelling through Novorossiisk, Rostov-on-Don, Samara, where he crossed the massive Volga River, and Cheliabinsk, deep in the Urals where he crossed into Asia. From Irkutsk, beyond the range of the railway, he was taken to his tiny place of exile, a village called Novaia Uda in Balaganskii *uezd* (county) within the Irkutsk *guberniia* (province). He arrived on 27 November after a seven-week journey. Almost immediately he made a failed attempt to escape. On 5 January 1904, he succeeded and, in sharp contrast to his long, drawn-out official journey, he was able to get back to Tiflis within a couple of weeks and resume his residency, obviously as an illegal, in Batumi by the end of January. One of his first acts upon returning was the writing of a 'Credo' ('I believe') summarizing his views on the question of party organization which had been ripping through the RSDWP since the split into Mensheviks and Bolsheviks at the 1903 Second Party Conference in London. Unfortunately, this text has either not survived or remains unavailable. It is not included in the official or recent volumes of collected works.

What Soso Djugashvili got up to in the revolutionary years of 1904–1907 is, however, fairly clear in outline. He, despite his underground status, resumed his role as leader of the tiny party group in Batumi with visits to other proletarian centres in the Caucasus. His activities and interests in 1904 involved continuing to agitate among workers throughout the region, including contact with the desperately exploited oil-workers of Baku, writing his first article on the nationalities question but, mainly, organizing party cells throughout the region in Batumi, Kutais, Baku, Khoni, Kukhi, Gubi, Ianeti, Chiatura and Dzhikiashi. He spent most of his time in Chiatura. In Kutais, he helped to found the Imeretian-Mingrelian party committee, named after the two traditional regions of Georgia in which it operated. He also made contact with the peasants at this time who were an increasingly militant force in the rising revolution.[38] Crucially for the development of Djugashvili's future, these groups were Bolshevik and Leninist in orientation and much of Soso's activity was taken up in polemics with the much larger Menshevik organization which emerged under the influence of Noa Zhordania who returned from exile in January 1905. Thereafter, Menshevism dominated Georgian Social Democracy and continued to do so right down to the liquidation of the independent Menshevik government in Georgia by the re-expanding Soviet authorities on 25 February 1921. The official account of Stalin's life, written in the 1940s to accompany the *Collected Works*, naturally concentrates on this aspect of his life. We have no reason to doubt that it did occupy the young Stalin above all else as the establishment of a party and the continued publication of a newspaper (*Brdzola* continued to be published under the title *Proletariatis Brdzola* – that is, *Proletarian Struggle*) was, alongside agitation among worker and developing trade union groups, all one could expect from a tiny party with limited resources. Symbolically, the year 1904 ended dramatically, on 31 December, with the Bolshevik group in Tiflis, said to be 'under the leadership' of I. V. Djugashvili,[39] invading and dispersing a Menshevik-Liberal banquet.[40] The purpose of the banquet was to discuss the establishment of a constitution in the Russian Empire. After disrupting it, the Bolshevik group held a workers' meeting which adopted a resolution in favour of armed insurrection.[41]

The pattern continued through the revolutionary years. The tiny Bolshevik group remained committed to armed uprising though they were in no position to do much but talk about it.

The attack on the authorities opened up greater space for radical activity and the young Stalin and the party were able to take advantage and organize party and trade union groups. Soso continued to write for and edit *Proletaris Brdzola*. Not surprisingly, the activities of the fledgling Bolsheviks in the Caucasus came to the attention of the national leadership in exile. Lenin wrote to Soso during his brief exile in Siberia at the end of 1903.[42] In July 1905, Lenin's wife Krupskaya requested that the Caucasus Union Committee of the RSDWP send copies of Djugashvili's article on party disagreements and a regular supply of *Proletariatis Brdzola*. These were the first glimmers of Djugashvili's rise from the provinces to national significance within Bolshevism.

The struggles of 1905 in Georgia were as hard-fought and bitter as anywhere else in the troubled Russian Empire and we have no reason to doubt that Soso Djugashvili was in the thick of them. But we need to note one issue which gave them an especially distasteful tinge. As in other parts of the Empire, the increasingly desperate local authorities tried to turn the population against each other rather than have them unite against the government. In many regions Jews were subjected to vicious, violent attacks. This also happened in the Caucasus but there were few Jews in the area. Instead, in Georgia, it was violence against Armenians and Muslim minorities which stained the reputation of the local government. Djugashvili stood up unequivocally for freedom from racial and cultural domination and wrote several articles devoted to calls for equality and tolerance between national groups. These, too, were the first glimmerings of Djugashvili's development into one of the Bolshevik Party's leading specialists on questions of nationality.

There are also several key moments in the political life of Djugashvili which we need to note. In December 1905 and April 1906 Soso made two of his rare forays outside Russia. In December he was present at the First All-Russian Conference of Bolsheviks, held in Tammerfors in Finland (still technically in the Empire but enjoying a semi-independent autonomous status), and in April he visited Stockholm, Sweden, for the Fourth, so-called Unity, Congress of the RSDWP; in May 1907 he attended the Fifth Congress in London. On both occasions Djugashvili represented the Caucasus Union Committee of the RSDWP. He had been promoted to it in 1904 under the patronage of one of the most senior party figures in the Caucasus, Mikha Tskhakaia, who was, among other things, best man at Soso's wedding to Ekaterina Svanidze in 1906.[43] It was through Tskhakaia's mediation that Soso met Lenin at the congresses. Lenin was much impressed with his young warrior from the wild frontier. Stalin took an uncompromisingly militant and Leninist line, not for the last time appearing more Leninist than Lenin in his robust denunciations of Menshevism and his persistent admiration for armed uprising, a position Lenin himself was in the process of abandoning after its failure in Krasnaia Presnia in December 1905. One thing is crystal clear, however. At these encounters Djugashvili commended himself to Lenin as a rock solid supporter in the largely Menshevik-dominated Caucasus region. It was upon this rock that Lenin decided to build his South Russian and Caucasian party. Djugashvili was coming to prominence for his already fierce loyalty, his revolutionary zeal and courage, and the fortuitousness of him being one of very few options open to Lenin to build his movement in the Caucasus region.

Another key moment in this period came on 26 June 1907. Possibly in April the party had learned there would be a large shipment of cash from the Tiflis railway station to the Tiflis Central Bank some 2 miles away. Already, on 26 February 1906, a group of Latvian revolutionaries had succeeded in stealing the equivalent of nearly US$2 million from the Russian State Bank in Helsinki and passing it to a Bolshevik representative who was able to smuggle the massive amount of roubles to the United States to be, in modern terminology, laundered into usable funds for the party. 'Expropriations', as such politically motivated robberies were called, have been part of the armoury of many radical movements, including the IRA in Belfast in relatively recent times. However, their use among Social Democrats was officially condemned because they brought bad publicity and confused revolutionary struggle with baser forms of gangsterism. The wild situation of armed revolutionaries and semi-civil war in the Caucasus invited action of this kind. There are no clear details of the planning of the raid or of Djugashvili's part in it. What is known is that the raid took place on 26 June under the operational leadership of one of the most violent of the Caucasian revolutionary Bolsheviks, the Armenian Semeno Ter-Petrossian, better known by his revolutionary pseudonym, Kamo. Fighting and gun-running had appeared to be his staple activities during these years; but once the party leaders, including Lenin, were prepared to sanction expropriations, Kamo was the man for the job. It seems likely that Djugashvili was at the heart of the planning but did not take part directly on the day. The attack took place and, amid a welter of gunfire, the heist succeeded in relieving the Russian state of approximately US$3.5 million of its cash. The exuberance of the revolutionary robbers was tempered by the fact that much of the haul was in large denomination 500 rouble notes, the serial numbers of which were known to the police and the authorities. This created massive difficulties in laundering the money and several people were arrested in the United States and elsewhere when they tried to exchange them. Nonetheless, and despite the protests of the wider international socialist movement, substantial sums were transferred to the Bolsheviks. The precise number of victims of the shooting are, unsurprisingly, controversial. None of the robbers seems to have been killed and, at the time, it was announced that four people had died in the raid. More recently, it has been alleged that secret police documents stated that there were 40 deaths. It seems unlikely that such a large death toll, and presumably a corresponding number of wounded, could be concealed in an action which took place in the very centre of the city of Tiflis, in broad daylight under the gaze of the public bystanders and of the responsible and gutter press.

Be that as it may, the Tiflis bank raid was a significant escalation in hostilities in the Caucasus and the authorities resolved to catch those they held responsible as quickly as possible. That was easier said than done. Only on 25 March 1908 did they manage to arrest Djugashvili. Kamo was eventually arrested in Germany where he appears to have feigned madness so brilliantly that he was never brought to trial and almost fooled himself into thinking he was insane.[44] After a cameo to his career in the Civil War, where he undertook further gruesome operations supposedly including testing recruits through making them undertake fake executions and cutting the heart out of one executed white officer, Kamo settled down as a customs official only to suffer the fate of dying after being knocked off his bicycle by a passing truck.[45] Needless to say, the truck is said by some to have been directed to its target by Stalin, for reasons which remain obscure; but at least no one has claimed Stalin was actually driving the truck.

Apart from taking on new aliases (Djugashvili was arrested in 1908 under the name of Gaioz Nizharadze), one of the reasons Djugashvili was able to evade the police for so long was that he spent much of his ten months on the run in a relatively new sphere of operations, Baku, the capital of the Muslim region of Azerbaijan (today, like Georgia and Armenia, an independent state). The main economic activity was oil. The British company BP (British Petroleum) was the largest operator in the area. From June or July 1907 until his arrest the following March, Djugashvili was active in organizing the oil workers in this outpost of British imperialism.

The great metropolises of European Russia – St. Petersburg, Moscow, Kiev, even Warsaw – were relatively subdued following the fierce repression of 1906–1907. Not so in Baku and other parts of the Caucasus which retained their wild, violent character. They were at the margins of the Russian Empire, at one of its most contested frontiers with Turkey. Like many frontier areas, the authority of the central state was itself more violent, arbitrary and, often, weak compared to the more 'civilized' zones at the centre. This was certainly the case in Baku. Far from being sub-dued the city and its hinterland were the site of bitter struggles by oil workers for recognition of their developing trade unions and for improvement in the dire and dangerous conditions under which they worked. Much of the oil lay under the Caspian Sea and it was accessed by rickety jetties and platforms. The drilling rigs were themselves dangerous and unreliable. Working condi-tions were deplorable. Vicious, unrelenting heat at the height of summer, violent storms at any time of year, poor wages, no insurance for injury at work and a complete absence of job security made for an especially hostile work environment. Any injury caused by the spiralling drills or the shoddily constructed platforms would lead to dismissal. There was no comprehensive health service to which a sick or injured worker could turn. Along with mining, plantation work and railway construction in faraway places, the oil workers were exposed to capitalist exploitation at its most crude. Get paid little and lose your job if you were incapacitated or complained. In the rough, tough atmosphere of Baku, life itself was cheap, either through the appalling toll of industrial accidents or through street brawls or targeted assassinations of worker-activists. Fascist type groups, known as Black Hundreds – gangs supposedly loyal to God and Tsar – beat up and even killed those suspected of being leftists. On 29 September, Djugashvili himself, by then a member of the Baku City party committee, made a speech at the grave of one such murdered worker, Khanlar Safaraliyev. Though prone, as ever, to exaggerate the young Stalin's role, there is little doubt that, as suggested in official biographies, he threw himself into organizing political movements, newspapers and a trade union to protect the weak workers against the power of the oil companies backed by the state authorities. From late 1907 until his arrest, Djugashvili was one of the activists trying to get the oil employers to recognize the union set up by their workers and negotiate with it. In February 1908, the Baku party committee of the RSDWP set up a self-defence squad to protect itself and its followers from Black Hundred violence, a clear example of violence begetting violence as the Social Democratic workers became as fearsome as their adversaries. If bosses could take out contracts on troublesome labour organizers, so trade unionists ordered hits on their bosses. Without doubt, Djugashvili was exposed to the dirty, exploitative underside of 'liberal' capitalism and its selective values and deep hypocrisy. 'Civilized', even 'democratic' values were acknowledged in the home nations of Empire – France, Britain, Germany and the United States – but, at the super-exploitative work places at which much of the wealth was generated that supported the comfort, luxury and urbane values of the imperial upper classes, there was no law, no justice, no rights, no security and no support. The only law was that of survival.

Djugashvili's writings of the period burn with righteous indignation at this situation. His views of the time are encapsulated in a few sentences from one of his articles in which he argues that the continuing violence – described as 'economic terrorism' – comes not from the workers' side but from the viciousness of the employers against whom the workers are trying to defend themselves:

what is primarily needed is that the oil owners should drop their repressive measures, big and small, and satisfy the just demands of the workers. . . . Only when the oil owners abandon their *Asiatically* aggressive tactics of lowering wages, taking away the people's halls, reducing the number of schools and hutments, collecting the ten-kopek hospital levy, raising the price of meals, systematically discharging advanced workers, beating them up, and so forth, only when the oil owners definitely take the path of cultured European-style relations with the masses of the workers and their unions and regard them as a force 'on an equal footing' – only then will the ground for the 'disappearance' of 'assassinations' be created.[46]

It is perhaps not too much to suggest (though speculation is, as we have seen, the bane of Stalin studies) that the older Stalin continued to view the lords of imperialism, with whom he jousted as Soviet leader, through the image of capitalism's exploitative underbelly rather than its smiling, domestic countenance.[47] In a once influential lecture, the British novelist C. P. Snow not only complained about the growing gulf between the 'two cultures', arts and sciences, but he also made the shrewd observation that 'The Industrial Revolution looked very different according to whether one saw it from above or below. It looks very different today according to whether one sees it from Chelsea or from a village in Asia.'[48] Market-oriented imperialism was the form in which the Industrial Revolution presented itself to the wider world. It was the form in which the young Stalin first experienced the modern world in his almost Asian village and Asian frontier country. Indeed, it looked very different from there than it did from Chelsea.

From Baku to St. Petersburg via Vologda, Cracow, Vienna and Siberia: Koba becomes Stalin, 1908–February 1917

Koba's arrest in March 1908 was only one among many and they were to continue. The slow grinding of the tsarist legal system meant that only in early 1909 was Koba exiled to Solvychegodsk, a village in the Vologda province of northern Russia.

His transportation to this place of detention was interrupted by a fever ('relapsing fever') which kept him in Viatka for three weeks. He arrived at Solvychegodsk on 27 February 1909, but, predictably, escaped in June and by July he was in St. Petersburg on his way back south. On 23 March 1910, he was again arrested in Baku, this time under the name of Zakhar Grigoryan Melikyants, and taken back to the city's Bailov prison. In September an order was published banning him from the Caucasus for five years. He was returned to Solvychegodsk in September 1910, the journey taking a leisurely five weeks. This time he chose to sit out his relatively light sentence and was released in July 1911. He initially was only able to travel to the provincial capital, Vologda, where he remained under surveillance for six weeks before making his move and secretly travelling 650 kilometres/ 400 miles to St. Petersburg. Despite using yet more false documents, this time in the name of P. A. Chizhikov, he was picked up by the police after only two days in the city. In early December he was sentenced to three years in Vologda and was returned to the city. Once again he had no intention of sitting in obscurity for such a long time and escaped on 29 February 1912. Travelling more speedily than the northbound prison transport, he was back in Baku by the middle of March. He seems to have made a fleeting visit to Tiflis before leaving Baku on 1 April, this time permanently. He arrived back in St. Petersburg on 10 April but, again, the police in the capital were more efficient than their provincial counterparts and he was arrested on 22 April. On 2 July he was taken from St. Petersburg *en route* for the much more distant region of Narym in Siberia, to which he travelled via Tomsk on the railway and thence by horse-drawn carriage. It was not remote enough. Escaping on 1 September he was back in the capital by 12 September. The next five months, before his final arrest, were very intensive and important in the life of Koba. In addition to being part of the national party leadership he made two visits to Cracow, to make contact with Lenin who was residing there at the time. After his second visit to Cracow he was sent to Vienna during the second half of January to make contact with Marxist groups there with a view to studying their policy towards national minorities, the young Stalin's special area of expertise. The outcome was one of his best known writings, 'The

National Question and Social-Democracy', which was published in the magazine *Prosveshcheniye* in March–May 1913. By chance, his future rival and, at this moment, critic of Lenin, Lev Trotsky, was in the city at the same time, but they do not seem to have met.[49] On his return in mid-February, Koba helped set up and edit the crucial party newspaper, *Pravda*.

But this did not last long. On 23 February 1913, he was arrested once more; at last, the authorities got serious, perhaps because their captive was now a rising national figure in the revolutionary movement rather than an obscure agitator from the deep provinces. On 2 July he was escorted out of St. Petersburg on the Trans-Siberian railway, once again. The initial destination was Krasnoyarsk on the Amur River approximately 4600 kilometres/2800 miles from the capital. After a short stay (11–15 July 1913) he was moved by dirt road to Turukhansk county and the tiny hamlet of Kostino. In March 1914 he was moved to the even more inhospitable settlement of Kureika, situated beyond the Arctic Circle. There was to be no escape from this grim setting. Only revolution released him in February 1917. It was Koba who had been arrested in 1908, but it was Stalin who returned to European Russia in 1917.

It was largely in the years from 1905 to 1913 that Ioseb Djugashvili began to make his mark on the central leadership of the tiny Leninist Bolshevik faction. Initial contacts with Lenin went back to correspondence between them in December 1903. As we have seen, their first meeting was at the Tammerfors Party Congress and again in Stockholm and London shortly afterwards. He was warmly welcomed by Lenin because, in an important region with a significant working class, he was one of the few followers of Lenin in an otherwise Menshevik-dominated Caucasus. However, he was, initially, more an exotic decoration for the movement than an integral member of its leadership. Even so, he became a more important asset as time went on. Undoubtedly, his coup in helping plan, supposedly at Lenin's request, and execute the highly lucrative Tiflis expropriation certainly raised him in Lenin's estimation. Although Lenin himself returned to exile in early 1908, Ioseb, as we have seen, spent more time in the capital with the leaders Lenin left behind. Apart from his energetic work in Baku, there were two other aspects of his activity which particularly commended him to Lenin. In his brief stay in St. Petersburg he played a significant role in the complex task of setting up the newspaper *Pravda* which remained the central party journal (though it changed its name from time to time in 1917) until the end of the party and the Soviet Union in 1991.[50] Being an editor was one of the 'offences' which brought about his 1913 arrest.

As we have seen, by 1911–1912 he was sufficiently prominent on Lenin's radar to be invited urgently to visit him in Cracow, across the Russian border in Austrian Poland, on two occasions. After the second he made his significant journey to Vienna to elaborate the principles of party policy on nationality. Lenin was sufficiently taken with him at this point to describe him as a 'splendid Georgian' in a letter to the novelist Maxim Gorky.[51] Certainly, he was no longer simply an energetic provincial activist; he had become a significant component of the party leadership. This was formalized by his accession, as a partial member, to the most important party body, its Central Committee, in 1912. However, it must be emphasized that the party was still small and competition to be in its leadership was not especially intense. Anyone like Ioseb, with ability, total commitment, energy and unshakeable loyalty to Lenin, could go a long way and become a big fish in an, as yet, very small pond. Indeed, it was probably this increased bonding with Lenin which, also in 1912, motivated him to make permanent yet another alias, the one by which he is more or less universally known, 'Stalin', 'man of steel', which also had the advantage of sounding similar to 'Lenin'. The first known signature of 'Stalin' dates from December 1912. He continued to be known as Soso to those close to him and Koba to party comrades; but Stalin is how he became known to the world and that is the name we will use from this point on.

Stalin before the revolution: personality and values

So far, we have largely followed, as best we can, the political life and activities of the young Stalin. What do we know about his personality and values in these pre-revolutionary years? Obviously, at this point, there was no sign that he was destined to be the person who would carve his name across a whole epoch of

Russian history or make an indelible mark on world history, not least by playing the main role in destroying the greatest threat to Western civilization to emerge from within itself, Nazism. Nor could one foresee, pace the psycho-historians, that here was a ruthless leader prepared to send his own close comrades to execution and camps, let alone be responsible for the deaths of millions. All that we will examine later. If we set it aside for the moment we can, perhaps, get some reflection of who Stalin was before 1917.

As already noted, many interpretations have plunged into obscure and unsubstantiated sources to portray who Stalin was. He has been declared to be a gangster, a police informer, a serial womanizer, a case of psychiatric disorder from childhood and so on.[52] However, such interpretations often seem to have missed the obvious. The firmer facts of his life enable us to go a long way in forming a credible image of him. Some of these points we have already encountered, some we have not.

In the first place, Stalin was a Georgian, imbued with local culture. The mafia-style honour culture, of loyalty, betrayal and punishment, of warrior masculinity and loyal, supportive, faithful femininity was the atmosphere in which he grew up. The precise conditions of poverty and marginality in his own family are also significant. All three of his siblings failed to survive birth or infancy. Stalin himself had an infantile brush with death in the form of smallpox when he was four which left him with some lasting facial disfigurement. The difficult situation of his family, the precariousness of his father's work and the, perhaps defensive, drunkenness and domestic violence which followed, though normal for the epoch, may have had its effect though there is nothing to prove what effect that might have been. His relationship with the strong and enduring figure of his mother was also deep. Was it loving or based on filial duty? We cannot know for sure.

We do know the young Stalin was certainly capable of warm and close relationships. We have a little evidence of this from his brief and tragic relationship with Ekaterina Svanidze whom he married in 1906. Their son, Iakob, was born in 1907 and Ekaterina died of illness in 1908. While allowing for the Georgian custom of what outsiders might consider exaggerated expressions of grief, he was deeply affected by her death, as he was when his second wife committed suicide in 1932. Whether or not he said the words frequently attributed to him at Ekaterina's funeral – that with her died all his warm feelings for humanity – the effect was not permanent, shown by his later marriage and relationship if nothing else. We cannot be tempted into building a whole theory of his personality, as some have done, on the flimsy basis of an unsubstantiated comment. He left his son Iakob (Yakov in Russian form) to be brought up by his in-laws, a not uncommon practice in the circumstances of the time. He appears to have maintained good relations with his first set of in-laws throughout his life, though later praise of Stalin by them was subjected to the pressure of contributing, by the 1930s, to the cult of Stalin. While there are no lifelong friends from childhood in Stalin's life this is more likely to have been the result of the lifestyle of a professional revolutionary – clandestinity; mobility; imprisonment – than a personal character flaw. Most Bolshevik comrades were in the same boat, though Lenin, for example, was assisted actively by his family throughout his career and beyond. Stalin only had his mother and his in-laws, by comparison.

Though on a different level, further evidence of his 'normal' sensitivity comes from an unlikely source. It comes as a surprise to many to learn that Stalin's first published writings were poems.[53] He sent a notebook of poems to a leading local writer, Ilya Chavchavadze, and on 14 June 1895 (when he was 16) one was published in a newspaper called *Iveriia*.[54] It was entitled *Morning*. Four more were published in the same journal before the end of the year. Judging from the Russian translation from the original Georgian, they are competent and sensitive poems about the beauty and colours of nature in the Caucasus and imbued with love for Georgia. The support of Chavchavadze, a prominent Georgian romantic nationalist, also shows where Stalin was in terms of his developing world view at that time.

There is no significant evidence from his political life to suggest he domineered over his comrades or was unpopular or disloyal. On the contrary, he seems to have worked happily within the confines of the party and maintained reasonably good relations with other members and to have been respected by them. Certainly, he was entrusted with important duties, not least setting up a party organization in the tough context of working-class

Baku. Lenin's description of him as 'my splendid Georgian'[55] is not inappropriate for these years. That does not mean he was not abrasive. He was tougher than the average party leader and was more inclined to deal with opposition in a direct and heavy-handed manner. Tact and charm were not absent but they were not always his natural mode of inter-relating with his fellows, especially those who opposed him. This, in turn, led to complaints from party members about his behaviour but there is no reason to think this was any worse than the behaviour of a host of politicians, prominent and obscure, at the time and since.

This leads on to the most obvious and central point of Stalin's life which is often lost in the blur of images of gangsterism and police informing, and that is the centrality of his revolutionary commitment from his mid-teenage years. The one thing that focuses everything else in his life is that he was a totally committed revolutionary. We cannot say exactly why he turned in that direction but we have plenty of evidence of his political views and values in his writings of the period. By and large, biographers have made little of this obvious source where, one might say, the key features of Stalin's life were hiding in plain sight. Maybe this is because one of the repetitious themes in Stalin studies is that he was not an intellectual and had no real claims to be a theoretician in the class of Plekhanov, Lenin, Trotsky or Bukharin. This is so, but the great trio of writers were the exception. Other Bolshevik leaders – Kamenev, Zinoviev, Sverdlov – could turn their hand to a newspaper article, propaganda pamphlet or agitational manifesto but were activists first, writers and journalists second. The same was true of others on the left. Martov, leader of the Menshevik left, does not attract many readers to his theories today, even though he was relatively philosophical. Other Mensheviks – Chkheidze, Tsereteli, Chernov – wrote important contributions to party policy but are not seen as theoretical innovators. Stalin stood alongside this second rank of activists. His journalism of the period is imbued with hatred for the viciousness of the employers, full of admiration for the struggles of the workers and, despite the adverse circumstances after the failure of the 1905 revolution, optimistic about the future. It is also highly connected to the dreadful day-to-day struggles in the 'wild west' atmosphere of the Caucasus. If one wants to find a formative influence on Stalin why look beyond his time in Baku and Chiatura? There he lived and worked alongside some of the worst treated and most precariously employed workers in the dangerous oil fields of the Caspian Sea. Where the state's police failed to crush the nascent workers' movement, many employers would hire gangs of proto-fascist Black Hundred thugs to beat up workers and union organizers. Hits were carried out on a few of those who protested. The workers would fight back in kind and 'economic terrorism' would be directed at the most brutal managers and employers. Russian industrial relations in these years was a struggle everywhere but in Georgia and Azerbaijan it had a violent intensity unmatched elsewhere, not only in the Empire but in Europe. As we have seen, Stalin himself argued that the employers used 'Asiatic' methods of repression and he called on them to move on to recognition of unions and collective bargaining characteristic of the 'cultured', as Stalin described it, European model.[56]

Unsurprisingly, in this violent outpost, the temptation of armed struggle was almost unavoidable. Lenin himself had supported the idea of kicking off the revolution by means of armed insurrection in 1905; but in the face of the rout of the Moscow Armed Uprising in December 1905 (described as 'criminally premature' by Plekhanov, the 'father' of Russian Marxism) he had turned to more sober expectations of the 'democratic dictatorship of workers and peasants' instead.[57] In the Caucasus, however, violence continued. Kamo ran guns, ammunition, explosives and detonators across the Black Sea. The Tiflis Bank was robbed. Armed self-defence groups stood up to the Black Hundreds. Revolution in the Caucasus was not a tea party. It had more in common with 'peripheral' imperial struggles in India, Indo-China, China, Manchuria, 'the heart of darkness'[58] in West Africa, in the violent cities of Latin America and so on. Stalin, more so than any other Bolshevik leader, and herein lies his distinctiveness, was a front-line fighter in this battle. He did not discuss theory in the cafés of Paris and Geneva. He passed from safe house to safe house, from one illicit workers' meeting to the next. He did not, like Lenin, have a press handily available in the secure surroundings of the East End of London. He had to smuggle every last piece of type into a secret location under the nose of the authorities. Arrest, imprisonment, exile, escape were his routine for more than a decade. While we cannot say for certain, it would seem reasonable to speculate that it was his perception of the ferocity of the exploitative and inhuman processes of capitalist development and the bitterness of the class struggle in the south that brought him to Bolshevism in the first place, when most Georgian socialists were with the more 'moderate' Menshevik faction. In Stalin's eyes, the exploiters showed no sign of moderation so, in the Georgian tradition, violence had to be met with counter-violence. It is no coincidence that the concept of worker vengeance – a good old 'mafia' term – has prominence in these early writings of Stalin.

Even so, one should not make the mistake, visible in his later political opponents and many of his biographers alike, of underestimating Stalin's intellectual abilities. It is often pointed out he did not attend university, unlike most Bolshevik leaders. This is true, but there was no university for him to go to in Georgia at the time. The Tiflis Seminary was the closest there was. As we have seen, he had burned his educational bridges there before he was 20, thereby closing off any further educational opportunity in the Russian Empire. He had already chosen the path of the revolutionary. But that does not make him unintelligent or completely untheoretical. Like others in the second rank he did have ideas and could come up with policy initiatives even at this early stage. Not surprisingly, since he was himself from a national minority, he became the Bolshevik specialist in nationalities policy. The pamphlet he produced may not be brilliant but it is intellectually respectable. In essence, he argued that if a minority was given all it needed for the expression of its culture – its own schools, religion, language, presses – it would be content with autonomy within a larger framework.[59] Even before Stalin came to power, Soviet nationalities policy embodied a number of these principles, constituting what one leading historian of the issue has called an 'affirmative action empire'.[60]

To summarize, by February 1917, when he was 38 years' old, Stalin had earned his position in the Bolshevik leadership through his energy, practical ability, commitment to the cause and, from very early on, identification with and fierce loyalty to Lenin. Maybe his persistence with violence when Lenin had moved on was the first of a number of significant differences of opinion between the two – Stalin thinking Lenin was, perhaps, out of touch with the bitter realities of worker struggle in the south compared to the northern towns and cities – but that did not undermine his ultimate loyalty. From the age of 20 Stalin had been a professional revolutionary. He had gone underground in 1901 and only really emerged on his return from Kostino in March 1917. In some ways, he embodied the model of the revolutionary in Nechaev's *Catechism* published in the 1870s who was supposed to sacrifice family, friends, love to 'the single passion' – revolution. Lenin himself had called, in his early signature pamphlet *What Is to Be Done?* for a party of 'professional revolutionaries'. If there was one professional revolutionary in the party it was Stalin. However, he had, deviating from the celibate, monastic model advocated by Nechaev, become a devoted husband to Ekaterina Svanidze. True, he found little time for their son after her tragic death but there is no question the young Stalin could feel and inspire love and warm friendship from his wife and her relatives. Stalin was not a misfit or a loner still less a psychopath or monster. Nor was he a dull bureaucrat. In fact, his career up to the February Revolution, at least, belied all the favourite clichés. He was not a gangster, police informer or brooding madman. If anything, in his early career, he resembled an unarmed Che Guevara rather than Pol Pot. Was that about to change as the revolution unfolded?

Notes

1 Wordsworth, W. (1888) 'The Prelude', *Complete Poetical Works*, London.

2 In particular, the works of Montefiore and Kotkin and the much more succinct articles by Suny discussed below.

3 Galy, A. (2013) *Creating the Stalinist Other: Anglo-American Historiography of Stalin and Stalinism 1925–1990*, PhD thesis, University of Edinburgh, Edinburgh.

4 Kotkin, S. (2014), *Stalin, Volume 1: Paradoxes of Power 1878–1928*, New York, Penguin, is the most exhaustive.

5 Though there were many variants of detail, in the basic form of the putting-out system an owner would buy raw materials, in this case leather, and the worker would be given the materials and would work to fulfil the owner's orders at home. When the order was completed

the finished product, shoes and boots in this case, would be returned to the owner in exchange for pay.

6 Two articles project some sound and careful historical thinking on this area of Soso's life: Suny, R. (1991) 'Beyond Psychohistory: The Young Stalin in Georgia', *Slavic Review*, 50 (1), Spring, pp48–58; Rieber, A. J. (2001) 'Stalin, Man of the Borderlands', *The American Historical Review*, 106 (5), December, pp1651–1691.

7 Iremaschwili, J. (1932) *Stalin und die tragodie Georgiens: Erinnerungen von seinein langjahrigen Freund*, Berlin, Selbstverlag.

8 Ibid, p12.

9 Bychowski, G. (1971) 'Joseph V. Stalin: Paranoia and the Dictatorship of the Proletariat', in B. Wolman (ed) *The Psychoanalytic Interpretation of History*, New York, Basic Books, p125.

10 Rancour-Laferriere, D. (1988) *The Mind of Stalin: A Psychoanalytic Study*, Ann Arbor, MI, Ardis, p119.

11 Tucker, R. C. (1973) *Stalin as Revolutionary, 1879–1929: A Study in History and Personality*, New York, Norton, ppxvi, 76, 81, 82, 115, 120, 137, 140, 142.

12 Suny (1991), p48.

13 Stalin, J. (1946–1952) *Sochineniia*, 13 vols, Moscow, Gospolitizdat, p113.

14 Allilueva, S. (1967) *Twenty Letters to a Friend*, New York, Harper & Row, p204.

15 Suny (1991), p52.

16 Smith, E. E. (1967) *The Young Stalin*, New York, Farrar, Straus & Giroux.

17 Montefiore, S. S. (2007) *Young Stalin*, London, Weidenfeld & Nicholson.

18 Lack of evidence, of course, does not itself prove a theory is not true. Stalin may have been an *Okhrana* agent and/or a bank robber. The point is, we have no firm proof of either and other evidence suggests a more likely path of development. A thorough refutation of the notion that Stalin was an *Okhrana* agent can be found in A. Ostrovskii (2003) *Kto stoial' za spinoi Stalina*, Neva, St Petersburg.

19 Fortunately, in addition to the above-mentioned articles by Suny and Rieber we also have several deeply researched, balanced and penetrating articles by Erik van Ree to guide us: van Ree, E. (1994) 'Stalin and the National Question', *Revolutionary Russia*, 7 (2), December, pp214–238; van Ree, E. (2010) 'The Stalinist Self: The Case of Ioseb Djugashvili', *Kritika: Explorations in Russian and Eurasian History*, 11 (2), Spring, pp257–282; van Ree, E. (1994) 'Stalin's Bolshevism: The First Decade', *International Review of Social History*, 39 (3), pp361–381; and van Ree, E. (2008) 'Reluctant Terrorists? Transcaucasian Social-democracy, 1901–1909', *Europe-Asia Studies*, 60 (1), pp127–154. An exhaustive survey of Stalin's early career in the Georgian context can be found in S.

Kotkin's (2014) almost 1000 page *Stalin, Volume 1: Paradoxes of Power 1878–1928*.

20 In order to make life difficult for the police it was customary for revolutionaries to adopt false names to conceal their true identities and protect their families. This also involved various fictional birth dates which may have added to the confusion over Stalin's actual birth date.

21 Koba was the fictional hero of Alexander Kazbegi's 1882 novel in Georgian, *The Patricide*.

22 Stalin, J. V. (1954) *Collected Works*, vols 1–13, Moscow, Gosizdat; and Stalin, J. V. (1978) *Collected Works*, vols 14–16, London, hereafter abbreviated to *CW*. The present citation is *CW*, vol 1, p416, *Biographical Chronicle*. There is an online edition at Marxists Internet Archive: http://www.marxists.org/reference/archive/stalin/works/collected/volume1/biography.htm (hereafter MIA).

23 Tucker, R. (1973) *Stalin as Revolutionary 1879–1929*, New York, Norton.

24 *CW*, vol 1, *Biographical Chronicle*.

25 Stalin, J. V. (2013) *Trudy*, vol 1, Moscow, Rabochii universitet imeni I. V. Khlebnikova, Prometei Info, pp546–556. Hereafter *Trudy*, 1.

26 *Trudy*, 1, p548.

27 The term Bolshevik, of course, is derived from the Russian word for majority and Menshevik is derived from the word for minority. Despite the fact that, to all intents and purposes, his faction was smaller than the Mensheviks until August/September 1917, Lenin seized the name and the Mensheviks put up with their weaker 'brand' name.

28 *Trudy*, 1, p548.

29 Ibid, p549.

30 Ibid, p549.

31 Ibid, p552.

32 Ibid, p552.

33 Ibid, p553.

34 For a multifaceted account of the war and its consequences, see Wolff, D., Marks, S. G., Menning, B. W., Schimmelpenninck van der Oye, D., Steinberg, J. and Shinji, Y. (2005) *The Russo-Japanese War in Global Perspective: World War Zero*, 2 vols, Amsterdam, Heritage Amsterdam.

35 Harcave, S. (1964) *First Blood*, London and New York, Macmillan; Ascher, A. (1988, 1994), *The Revolution of 1905*, 2 vols, Stanford, CA, Stanford University Press; Smele, J. D. and Heywood, A. (2005) *The Russian Revolution of 1905: Centenary Perspectives*, Abingdon, Routledge; and Trotsky, L. (1972) *1905*, Harmondsworth, Penguin.

36 See, for example, Read, C. (2002) 'In Search of Liberal Tsarism: The Historiography of Autocratic Decline', *The Historical Journal*, 45 (1), pp195–210.

37 Tolstoy, L. (1948) *Essays from Tula*, London, Sheppard.

38 Accounts in English of peasant rebellion in Georgia during this period can be found in Theodore Shanin's book on 1905 where he gives a brief but graphic account of peasant activity in another Georgian region, Guria. Shanin, T. (1986) *Russia 1905–07, Volume 2: Revolution as Moment of Truth*, London, Macmillan; and Jones, S. (1989) 'Marxism and Peasant Revolt in the Russia Empire: The Case of the Gurian Republic', *Slavonic and East European Review*, 67 (3), July, pp403–434.

39 *Trudy*, 1, p556.

40 This apparently odd form of political protest had been adopted mainly by the liberals in 1904 to provide a thin disguise to enable what were actually political, anti-tsarist meetings to take place without being disturbed by the tsarist police.

41 *Trudy*, 1, p556.

42 CW, vol 1, *Biographical Chronicle*.

43 Tskhakaia was close to Lenin and, after the Congress, went into exile with Lenin in Switzerland, returning to Russia in 1917 on the same 'sealed' train. He became an important figure in the Soviet Union and lived until 1950.

44 Shub, D. (1960) 'Kamo – the Legendary Old Bolshevik of the Caucasus', *Russian Review*, 19 (3), July, pp227–247.

45 Ulam (1998), pp279–280, and Montefiore (2008), p362, add the colour to this story. Ulam, A. (1998) 'The Years of Waiting: 1908–1917', *The Bolsheviks: The Intellectual and Political History of the Triumph of Communism in Russia*, Boston, MA, Harvard University Press, pp279–280; Montefiore, S. S. (2008) 'Prologue: The Bank Robbery', *Young Stalin*, pp3–18.

46 Stalin, J. V. (1908) 'The Oil Owners on Economic Terrorism', *Gudok*, 21 April, 4 May, 18 May. Source: *Works*, vol 2, *1907–1913*, Moscow, Foreign Languages Publishing House, 1954. Retrieved from MIA, https://www.marxists.org/reference/archive/stalin/works/1908/04/21.htm

47 Laue, T. H. von (1983) 'Stalin in Focus', *Slavic Review*, 42 (3), pp373–389, argues that Stalin was, in part, created by the British Empire.

48 Snow, C. P. (1959) *The Two Cultures*, Rede Lecture.

49 It has also been pointed out that Hitler and Freud were also in Vienna at this time, though what that is supposed to tell us is unclear.

50 It survives today as paper of the successor Russian Communist Party.

51 Lenin, V. I. (1897–1916) *Polnoe sobranie sochinennii*, vol 48, Politizdat 1970 p162.

52 Montefiore, S. S. (2007) *Young Stalin*, is an exhaustively researched and wonderfully readable account of all that is improbable and unproven about Stalin's early life as well as what is more likely to be true. The problem is telling which is which. On the back of the

paperback edition there are nine photos of Stalin at different stages of his life, labelled Urchin; Choirboy; Student Priest; Poet; Lover; Pirate; Gangster; Killer; Commissar. None of them refers to him being a revolutionary.

53 Though, unsurprisingly, Stalin's authorship has been disputed and they were published under two pseudonyms, the transparent I. Djvili and Soselo derived from Soso; there is no hard evidence to lead us to think they are not his work.

54 Iveriia is the classical name of Georgia.

55 Lenin, 1970, vol 48, p162.

56 See note 46.

57 The issue is discussed in Harding, N. (1977) *Lenin's Political Thought*, vol 1, London, Macmillan; White, J. (2001) *Lenin*, London, Verso; and Read, C. (2005) *Lenin: A Revolutionary Life*, London, Routledge, pp83–86.

58 The title of Joseph Conrad's short dark novel about imperialism along the River Congo, framed by the thought that once the River Thames, where the narrator is situated when telling the story, was the Congo of its day. The novel became the basis for Francis Ford Coppola's film *Apocalypse Now* set during the Vietnam War. Both works chronicle the depravity inherent in colonial struggles of this kind.

59 Stalin, J. V., *Marxism and the National Question* in CW, 2, and MIA, https://www.marxists.org/reference/archive/stalin/works/1913/03.htm.

60 Martin, T. (2001) *Affirmative Action Empire: Nations and Nationalism in the Soviet Union 1923–1939*, Ithaca, NY, Cornell University Press.

2 The Grey Blur: Stalin in revolution and civil war

Return to Petrograd

In his brilliantly evocative memoir of 1917, the left-wing Menshevik-Internationalist activist Nikolai Sukhanov described Stalin as a 'grey blur'.[1] The memoir was published in 1922, long before Stalin became supreme leader of the party and the revolution. But it has stuck. For the acutely observant Sukhanov, Stalin was practically invisible in 1917. The mainstream view of Stalin in the Western world, in particular, is that he was part of the leadership of the Bolshevik Party, but he did not stand out. He made speeches, but they were of little importance, and he was no orator: not only boring but his flat delivery in Russian (his second language, remember) was made worse by a deeply provincial Georgian accent that was not easy to follow. He did not, so the accepted view continues, lead public meetings; he did not write key articles. In another cruel but emphatic phrase, Robert Slusser described him as 'the man who missed the revolution'.[2] Given his colourful, hands-on style of party activism before his long exile in 1913, these descriptions are very surprising. How justified are they? How far are they assumptions based, not only on Cold War influences but also yet another exercise in reading the supposed character of the older Stalin back into his younger self?

In actual fact Stalin was deeply involved in 1917. He was one of the first Bolshevik leaders to get back from exile. He remained at large in Petrograd[3] when Lenin was in hiding in Finland and Trotsky was in jail. He gave important reports to all the leading party convocations between February and October. He was once again on the editorial board of the party newspaper *Pravda*. If Stalin was a blur it might seem to be a result of his constant motion rather than indistinctiveness! Let us look more closely at his contribution to the rapid transformation of the Bolshevik Party from being a small sect with some 10,000 members to a party exercising a monopoly of power over one sixth of the planet and a population of 180 million.

The collapse of the Romanov autocracy was followed by the release of political and many other prisoners from the regime's jails. Stalin, focusing his formidable practical energy and revolutionary commitment, was one of the first Bolsheviks to return from exile. He had a head start in that, in its increasing desperation to resist the German invasion, the government had decided to conscript prisoners into the army. Stalin was summoned to Krasnoyarsk, where he was rejected for military service on medical grounds related to his withered arm. Since he was near the end of his sentence he was not returned all the way back up the frozen Yenisei so the February Revolution found him in Achinsk, on the Trans-Siberian railway, a much easier point from which he could return than Kureiko. However, although he was one of the most senior party members in the revolutionary capital, Petrograd, he was met with an insulting rebuff. The Bolshevik committee which had supervised party affairs within the country, the Russian Bureau, tried to prevent him from taking a leading role because 'of certain well-known character defects'. His reputation for abrasiveness had returned even more rapidly than Stalin himself.

Frustratingly, the exact characteristics to which his comrades were objecting were not specified. But what was Stalin's 'well-known' flaw at this point? The most obvious explanation, though that does not make it true, is that, in exile, Stalin was suffering a kind of log-cabin fever. Confined to an arctic wasteland he appears to have become morose and withdrawn according to fellow prisoners such as Kamenev, who were exiled to the same place. Political exile under the tsars was less of a burden than under the Soviet regime. Exiles could mix with one another up to a point. They could read books sent to them and circulated between them. They could have political conversations and engage in a limited amount of travel. In Stalin's case, he even had a good relationship with his chief guard which led him decades later to do the man a favour. Even so, it had mixed effects on the prisoners. The relative isolation and deprivation could drive people mad. Stalin's idol, Lenin, thrived in Siberia and was at his healthiest spending time walking, hunting and fishing in the somewhat less harsh and, for him, stress-free, conditions. Lenin even wrote his most detailed and longest book, *The Development of Capitalism in Russia*, under these circumstances. However, Stalin was cut from quite different cloth. For the young activist from the south, the lack of warmth, colour and company seems to have weighed heavily on him, even though he later claimed he had had a peasant woman companion with whom he had fathered a child in the frozen north who spent her or his life in obscurity even when Stalin was at the head of the country.[4] He also told tales of fishing in the wild Yenisei River and its tributaries, an activity that led the peasants who had showed him how to fish to think that he had magic powers because he was more successful: 'One day they came up to me and said "Osip, you know the magic word!" I was ready to burst out laughing! . . . The fact is they chose a place to fish and sat there whether the fish rose to the bait or not, whereas I waited for the fish to rise, and if not, I went to another place, and so on until I got a good catch.' The peasants apparently thought this was a ruse by him to avoid telling them his secret.[5] Despite this, in a plaintive message, he begged a friend to send him even postcards of the sunny, bright south because in Kureiko 'there was nothing but the river and the snow' . . . .'Nature in this cursed region is shamefully poor . . . I am crazy with longing for nature scenes if only on paper.'[6] Where his intellectual companions in arms could continue to read, to think, to plan, to write, to discuss the activities which Stalin engaged in, political agitation, organization, action, could not be carried on while in exile. Having said that, one of the examples we have of Stalin pulling rank on his fellow exiles, and possibly showing the personal arrogance which is another candidate for being the mysterious character flaw, Stalin claimed personal control of the meagre library at Kureiko for his personal use rather than, as was the custom, dividing the books up among the party members in the area. According to Stalin's first Soviet era historian, the dissident Roy Medvedev, there had been a gathering of Bolshevik exiles at Monastyrskoe, including Stalin who was on his way to a routine medical in Krasnoyarsk. Members of the Russian Bureau were among them. There are reports that he remained aloof and again pulled rank as a member of the Central Committee. Medvedev quotes an unpublished memoir by the Bolshevik Boris Ivanov who wrote, particularly of Stalin's ties with Sverdlov, another senior figure and future president of Soviet Russia, that 'the necessary reconciliation did not take place. Djugashvili remained as proud as ever, as locked up in himself, in his own thoughts and plans . . . As before, he was hostile to Sverdlov, and would not move toward reconciliation, although Sverdlov was prepared to extend the hand of friendship, and was willing to discuss the problems of the workers' movement in the company of the three members of the Russian Bureau of the party Central Committee'.[7] Whatever it was, Stalin had seriously annoyed some of his colleagues on the Russian Bureau.

In any case, the picture clashes with the best description we have of the young Stalin in the memoirs by members of the family of Sergei Alliluyev who had been closely acquainted with him in Baku and in whose home in Petrograd he lodged for part of the momentous year 1917. He even married his friends' youngest daughter, Nadezhda, in 1919 when she was 17 and he was 40. A much happier and humorous Stalin with a glint in his eye appears in the accounts of Anna Alliluyeva, Nadezhda's sister. His first visit upon his return to Petrograd is remembered with numerous details. Stalin 'never liked sitting down for a long time, and even when he was talking, he liked to pace up and down the room. His movements are calm and self-possessed'.[8] Something about him had changed since before the war: 'his face had become older, yes, considerably older. His eyes are the same, and that mocking smile never leaves his lips – it is still there.'[9] As the family gathers he entertains them: 'There are great gales of laughter . . . Stalin mimics the homespun oratory of the speakers who came out to greet the exiles returning from banishment at provincial railway stations. He imitates them to perfection. You can see them choking with bombastic phrases . . . We all collapse with laughter.'[10]

The first six months of the revolution

Whatever their roots, Stalin swept away the objections of the Russian Bureau and, along with other returnees, Kamenev, Sverdlov and others and threw himself into the heady atmosphere of the rapid and largely unexpected revolution. The initial instinct of almost all of those involved was that all the anti-dynastic forces should come together and prepare to resist the expected counter-revolutionary onslaught by the supporters of tsarism, presumably including the generals. The fact that no one had supported Nicholas II in his final hours as ruler was not generally known.[11] There was, initially, a national honeymoon even tinged, at first, with euphoria before the deep splits within the temporary coalition of forces – from army leaders to street demonstrators – began to emerge. The initial instinct of all participants was to stand together to support the reluctantly emerging Provisional Government, nudged into life by the radical Petrograd Soviet, supposedly a worker and soldier institution but led by intellectuals and party leaders on the spot like Stalin. The fact that the Soviet negotiated with the Provisional Government over the latter's proclamation of its governing principles and, in Army Order No 2, itself deferred to Provisional Government insistence that it prohibit the developing process of election of officers by the rank and file in the armed services, shows that the spirit of the moment was agreement with liberals, not opposition. There were even, as always happened when Lenin was absent, talks with the Mensheviks to see if, in the new situation, the two tiny wings of Russia Social Democracy could be brought together to make a larger and more influential force against the main left-wing party, the Socialist Revolutionaries.

Stalin was no exception. Resuming his leading roles including membership of the editorial board of *Pravda* from 15 March 1917, Stalin preached the same sermon as everyone else in the party. Revolutionary forces should unite to resist the anticipated suppression. To break up would invite the restorationists to divide and rule. The fact that the forces of restoration and counter-revolution were weak at this point was not truly perceived by the left. In fact, arguably, the potential counter-revolution from the right and the *ancien regime* was continually overestimated by the Bolsheviks and others right down to the decisive moments in the Civil War.

Trotsky, in particular, was scathing about these half-hearted, conciliatory revolutionaries. He wrote:

> Not one of those leaders of the party who were in Russia had any intention of making the dictatorship of the proletariat – the social revolution – the immediate object of his policy. A party conference which met on the eve of Lenin's arrival and counted among its numbers about thirty Bolsheviks showed that none of them even imagined anything beyond democracy. No wonder the minutes of that conference are still kept a secret! Stalin was in favour of supporting the Provisional Government of Guchkov and Miliukoff, and of merging the Bolsheviks with the Mensheviks. The same stand, or rather an even more opportunist one, was taken by Rykov, Kamenev, Molotov, Tomsky, Kalinin, and all the rest of the leaders and half-leaders of to-day.[12]

He left his readers in no doubt about who was really to blame: 'The Petrograd *Pravda*, which was edited by Stalin and Kamenev until Lenin's arrival, will always remain a document of limited understanding, blindness, and opportunism.'[13]

Trotsky's accusations about Stalin sound unlikely given what we have seen of Stalin in his early career. He was a street-fighting man from the backstreets of Baku and Tiflis, not a half-hearted conciliator. If we look at some of his writings of the time we will see that Trotsky's depiction is highly misleading. On 14 March, only two days after his return, Stalin wrote in *Pravda*:

> The pillars of the old power are tottering on their founda-tions and crumbling. Now, as always, Petrograd is in the forefront. Behind it, stumbling at times, trail the immense provinces.
>
> The forces of the old power are crumbling, but they are not yet destroyed. They are only lying low, waiting for a favourable moment to raise their head and fling themselves on free Russia.

Stalin asked what was to be done in this situation. His response is clear, unequivocal and combative, as we would expect:

> In order to *shatter* the old power a temporary alliance between the insurrectionary workers and soldiers was enough. For it is self-evident that the strength of the Russian revolution lies in an alliance between the workers and the peasants clad in soldier's uniform. . . . it is necessary that the alliance should be made conscious and secure, lasting and stable, sufficiently stable to withstand the provocative assaults of the counter-revolutionaries.

He also identifies the soviets as the engine room of this revolution:

> the more closely these Soviets are welded together and the more strongly they are organized, the more effective will be the revolutionary power of the revolutionary people which they express, and the more reliable will be the guarantees against counter-revolution.
>
> Workers, peasants and soldiers, unite everywhere in Soviets . . .
>
> Therein lies the guarantee that the fundamental demands of the Russian people will be realized: land for the peasants, protection of labour for the workers, and a democratic republic for all the citizens of Russia![14]

A few days later, on 17 March, an article was published in which Stalin totally rejects joining the Provisional Government:

> A few days ago resolutions on the Provisional Government, on the war, and on unity passed by the Yedinstvo group were published in the press. This is the Plekhanov-Buryanov group, a 'defencist' group. To understand the character of this group, it is enough to know that in its opinion:
>
> 1) 'The necessary democratic control over the actions of the Provisional Government can best be achieved by the

participation of the working-class democracy in the Provisional Government';

2) 'The proletariat must *continue* the war'—among other reasons, in order 'to deliver Europe from the menace of Austro-German reaction'.

In brief, what they are demanding of the workers is: Send your hostages, gentlemen, into the Guchkov-Milyukov Provisional Government and be so kind as to continue the war for—the seizure of Constantinople! . . . No, sirs, you have addressed your unity appeal to the wrong quarter! No, sirs, go your way![15]

On 18 March he expanded on that vision in terms which could in no way be interpreted as conciliatory. Indeed, he stated unequivocally that 'the ground is trembling under the feet of the Provisional Government'. As we would expect, he raises the flag of class struggle, not conciliation:

The revolution is on the march. From Petrograd, where it started, it is spreading to the provinces and is gradually embracing all the boundless expanses of Russia. More, from political questions it is inevitably passing to social questions, to the question of improving the lot of the workers and peasants, thereby deepening and sharpening the present crisis. All this cannot but arouse anxiety among definite circles of property-owning Russia. Tsarist-landlord reaction is raising its head. The imperialist clique are sounding the alarm. The financial bourgeoisie are extending a hand to the obsolescent feudal aristocracy with a view to joint organization of counter-revolution. Today they are still weak and irresolute, but tomorrow they may grow stronger and mobilize against the revolution. At all events, they are carrying on their sinister work incessantly, rallying forces from all sections of the population, not excluding the army.

Asking how this as yet weak but potentially dangerous counter-revolution should be confronted by revolutionaries he makes an interesting set of points which show something of his own background as a provincial activist. 'It is one of the peculiarities of our revolution that to this day its base is Petrograd . . . The provinces have confined themselves to accepting the fruits of victory and expressing confidence in the Provisional Government.' It is this provincial lag which, he argues, allows the Provisional Government and 'dual power' – incidentally one of the earliest uses of this term – to exist. Even at this early stage he declares that 'the Petrograd Soviet of Workers' Deputies is becoming inadequate for the new situation'. The solution is a militant one:

> What is needed is an all-Russian organ of revolutionary struggle of the democracy of all Russia, one authoritative enough to weld together the democracy of the capital and the provinces and to transform itself at the required moment from an organ of revolutionary struggle of the people into an organ of revolutionary power, which will mobilize all the vital forces of the people against counter-revolution.
>
> Only an All-Russian Soviet of Workers', Soldiers' and Peasants' Deputies can be such an organ.[16]

A number of features of these articles help us to understand Stalin's politics as the revolution gathered pace. Obviously, the tone is very militant, if anything more so than Lenin himself. Stalin thinks in terms of a workers' and peasants' revolution conducted by themselves. There are no references to the intervention of radical intellectuals let alone liberals. Soviets run by the masses for the masses are Stalin's dream at this point. It is yet another indication of Stalin's career and his closeness to the struggles of workers against employers. Underlying his ideas there is a foundation of proletarian chauvinism – the working masses can do whatever they need to do themselves without the patronizing assistance of educated intellectuals and other intermediaries.

A second key point is that, as Trotsky argued, Stalin does refer to 'revolutionary Social Democracy' rather than to Bolshevism. In some ways Stalin may have been ahead of the moment here in that, from early on, and even before 1917 with the breakup of the Second International and the peace conferences at Kienthal and Zimmerwald, it had become clear that the main differences were not *between* the left-wing parties but *within* them. The attitude to the war, the so-called defencist and internationalist positions, led to the formation of left-wing minorities in the Menshevik and Socialist Revolutionary (SR) parties which had more in common with the Bolsheviks than with the majority of their own party. Stalin was envisaging a restructuring of the left in which all those sharing the radical position would work together, as they had begun to do in the Petrograd Soviet. However, this was vastly different from allying with the defencist and conciliationist majorities in those parties, which is what Trotsky accused him of.

In at least one other respect, Trotsky's account is misleading. It is clear from the articles quoted that Stalin stood for a form of democracy, but it was clearly a revolutionary, soviet-based democracy. This is no different from what Lenin proclaimed in his April Theses. In fact, Stalin was already calling for something that never materialized, a strong national soviet. In the absence of such a soviet, the Petrograd Soviet took on this role and national Soviet Congresses were convened in June and October which spawned permanent Executive Committees to rule in their name. But no full-scale elected national soviet emerged before the October Revolution. There is no doubt that, as in his provincial years, Stalin was a class warrior above all and was instinctively repelled by the bourgeoisie.

Two final points. Another article in this period commented on the issue of nationalities, Stalin's speciality among the Bolshevik leaders. In it, he asserted some basic themes of nationalities policy, notably 'autonomy, not federation', linguistic and cultural equality – he particularly vilified attempts to impose Russian as the sole language of government – and the right of self-determination 'for such nations as cannot, for one reason or another, remain within the framework of the integral state'.[17] Stalin's style and method of thinking can also be discerned. While there are some acute ideas in Stalin's writing at this time, ideas which foreshadowed Lenin's *April Theses* in key respects like resisting being sucked into the Provisional Government, seeing the new authorities and their supposedly leftist supporters like Plekhanov as an unaltered form of imperialism and total support for soviets, their expression is ponderous, repetitive and, as we have seen, at times liturgical. He was not a brilliant writer, but his work showed competence and a fiery commitment to the masses.

We have dwelt extensively on Stalin's character and ideas as the revolution began. The next task is to examine his main activities in the revolution down to the victory in the Russian Civil War.

The Russian Revolution was a highly complex event about which historians have developed many interpretations. Although there had been a revolutionary movement since the 1860s the actual collapse of the autocracy came suddenly. Long-term and short-term factors reached critical mass and an explosion occurred. The deep structural roots of the revolution lay in the antiquated nature of the serf-owner state trying to rule a modernizing and industrializing society; peasant land hunger; worker resistance to crude, early capitalist exploitation and ever-increasing pressure from national minorities like, as we have seen, the Georgians. Combined with the stresses of a failing war and the fear of unrest from below, the elites deserted the tsar and turned him into a scapegoat, deflecting blame for war disasters from themselves and projecting it onto Nicholas II. When, in late February, unrest in the streets of Petrograd was threatening to boil over, the elites struck. Senior generals called for the tsar to abdicate. Politicians called for desperate reforms and when Nicholas finally agreed they told him it was too late. He was forced to abdicate by elites who believed that in securing this outcome they would end the incipient revolution. However, nothing could have been further from the truth. Lacking any clearly defined plans to deal with the outcome they had desired and precipitated, the unlikely revolutionaries of February – generals, landowners and the middle-class conservative and liberal politicians – only deepened the crisis. Far from saving their property and privileges at the tsar's expense, they actually kicked off the process by which they lost everything.

This is not the place to undertake a full analysis of the revolution and ensuing civil war but it is necessary to point out some of the main contours. Most important, unlike the French Revolution with which it is often compared, the collapse of the state led to the outbreak of mass revolution from below. The abdication sent a signal of weakness at the centre and the peasants, workers and soldiers and sailors began to assert their agendas. The result was a fluctuating battle for power. On one side there was the majority of the old elites, who formed the Provisional Government, committed, on paper at least, to democracy, constitutional rights and continuation of the war. A few anti-democratic forces also survived on the right and had their fateful moment in the historical spotlight in late summer. The masses began to organize around a bewildering array of organizations. Among the most important were soviets and a network of grassroots committees based on village, factory, mine, workshop, regiment and battleship. Political parties and trade unions added to the complexity. What Stalin referred to above as 'dual power' was the struggle between these right and left forces. The struggle oscillated back and forth up to the Soviet revolution of October and beyond and all, it must be remembered, with a critical defence against German invasion taking place.

For the centre and the 'moderate' right, defending Russia was the key. Democratic reform, land reform and all its great projects were put on hold supposedly until the end of the war, though sceptics on the left suspected forever was more likely. To greatly simplify the route from February to October, the main development on the left was that the dominant groups in February – the Socialist Revolutionaries and the Menshevik right who led the Petrograd Soviet – lost authority as the masses became impatient with the slow pace of reform. This was mainly brought about by the politics of 'defencism' – that is, prioritizing national defence and trying to avoid a fatal civil war which would deliver the country into the hands of traditional rivals Germany, Turkey and Austria. This tactic imprisoned these groups in critical support for, and eventual participation in, the Provisional Government. Those groups and parties on the left which had not supported the Provisional Government and called for salvation via revolution and revolutionary war, reaped the benefits. In the forefront were the Bolsheviks, plus left-wing breakaways from the SRs and Mensheviks and a handful of independent leftist and anarchist groups comprising the 'internationalist' wing of the soviets.

The progression of dominance on the left from 'defencists' to 'internationalists' was far from smooth. At first, the revolution deepened and radicalized. A multitude of committees were set up and asserted their rights. Wage claims were won. Peasants stopped paying rents and encroached on landowner pasture, fallow land and forests. The rank-and-file in the armed forces gained rights of representation, some of the worst aspects of discipline were abolished and unpopular officers were driven from their posts. The right was alarmed and set up a military offensive in Galicia in June to try to restore discipline in the army and in the country. Foolish at best, this policy exploded in the face of its enforcers when the offensive became a disastrous rout. In early July, disconsolate sailors and soldiers almost engineered the overthrow of the Provisional Government but were prevented from doing so by the failure of any party, even the Bolsheviks, to agree to lead them at this time.

This failure gave the right an unexpected chance to re-group. July and August saw the only serious attempt at national counter-revolution. But that, too, over-reached itself prematurely when Commander-in-Chief General Lavr Kornilov attempted a coup which threw Prime Minister Kerensky belatedly into the hands of the left. In fact, while Kornilov failed and was arrested, Kerensky and the Provisional Government were the most important victims. The left believed they had collaborated with Kornilov and the fear of losing the 'gains of February', as the phrase of the moment put it, galvanized peasants and workers into action. Land seizures began in earnest in September and worker control of factories spread rapidly – not least to stop employers closing them and dismissing their workforce. Not without some dissent within his party, this was the turning of the tide which Lenin perceived and took advantage of. From the defeat of Kornilov in early September until late October, the flood tide of revolution swept the country inexorably towards soviet and Bolshevik power.

For a street-fighting revolutionary like Stalin, this seemed to be the opportunity he was born for. Perhaps his romantic poetic side knew, or would have responded to, Wordsworth's joy at experiencing the French Revolution:

> Bliss was it in that dawn to be alive,
> But to be young was very heaven!

What we do know for certain is that he threw himself into the heart of things. As we have seen, revolution is not just an institutional change, it transforms the life of the individual. Stalin had been precipitated from exile in Achinsk to a share in the

Petrograd party leadership and editorial board of *Pravda* in a matter of days. Lenin's life was also about to be transformed through his return from exile. But his arrival at the Finland Station on 3 April (16 March OS) was not only a moment of personal significance. Arguably, the revolution, not to mention the twentieth century itself, was also about to change.

The extent to which Lenin's *April Theses*, which he read out for the first time as soon as he got off the train, were a new direction in Bolshevik policy has caused great debate among historians. They certainly caused uproar within and beyond the Bolshevik Party. Lenin was accused by Plekhanov, the founder of Russian Marxism, of being an anarchist. Lenin was described as 'raving' and was widely thought to be out of touch, having only been back in Petrograd for an hour when he dropped this bombshell. Even members of his own party, like Kamenev and Zinoviev who were the leading figures apart from Lenin and were already familiar with the Petrograd scene since they had returned earlier, had expressed opposition. What had Lenin said that provoked such rage and criticism? In the simplest terms, the *April Theses* were an attempt by Lenin to make a major adjustment in the party's orientation in the radically new conditions of post-autocracy and burgeoning democracy dominated by the middle-class. Instead of fighting under the rules of the autocracy it was time to lay a few ground rules for fighting bourgeois democracy. Three themes dominated the brief two-page list of theses. The future lay with the soviets as a basis for revolutionary government. Secondly, socialism itself was not on the immediate agenda, only a soviet supervised capitalist economy within a soviet democracy. This was in itself controversial but not very much noticed at the time (or since, by many commentators). Related to this were various comments about the need for 'patience' and prolonged preparatory work before the worker revolution could be envisaged, phrases which give the lie to the common interpretation that Lenin was calling for a rapid transition to the next stage of revolution.

But it was the third theme which caused the biggest reaction at the time. Lenin unequivocally defined the Provisional Government as being based on bourgeois imperialist principles and a force beholden to and imprisoned by Anglo-French capitalist interests. He pronounced that there should be 'No support for the Provisional Government.'[18] Not only defencists thought this was mad – after all, Russia would be open to invasion if the Provisional Government were to collapse – but so did close party colleagues. To dissolve the anti-tsarist alliance so soon, they argued, would give heart to the feared counter-revolution and endanger the revolution itself. As we have seen, Stalin's writings of the time foreshadowed Lenin's position in that he saw the new government as an imperialist successor fighting to obtain Constantinople as much as the Tsarist government. For his critics from within the party, however, it was nigh on impossible to oppose Lenin for any length of time and, at the party conference held three weeks later, it was Lenin's line that prevailed with some modifications.

Before turning to that it should be noted that the *April Theses* had a crucial, indirect impact on Stalin's life and career. They, in many respects, began the process of blurring the distinction between Lenin's policies and Trotsky's concept of 'permanent revolution'. By this, Trotsky meant that, in Russian conditions and with the support of an international worker revolution, it was possible to cut short or omit the capitalist stage of Russia's development. As such, this was an adaptation of Marx's view that capitalism had to exhaust itself before a society would be ripe for socialism. After February, while Lenin had not moved to accept Trotsky's basic premise, he was now planning for the socialist phase of the revolution and, as time passed, he shortened the period within which the socialist revolution might happen so that, in practical terms, the differences between the two of them were no longer relevant. In July, Trotsky finally adhered to the Bolshevik Party. The *April Theses* were the first step in this direction.

If the return of Lenin restored guidance to the party it certainly did the same for Stalin. Stalin had identified with Lenin and the Leninists since around 1904, largely on account of their more militant stance compared to the Mensheviks. He was not about to change now that, for the first time, it seemed he would be working alongside Lenin for a sustained period of time. Stalin's career, his promotions in the party and his brief, pre-war editorship of *Pravda* owed everything to Lenin. In the weeks after

Lenin's return, Stalin consolidated this key relationship, turning himself into Lenin's executive assistant, in effect. He was Lenin's go-to-guy for the demanding practical tasks of setting up and running a political party and press. Now that he was a leader and confidante of Lenin, Stalin began to move off the street and into the mode for which he is best known – that of bureaucrat and organizer. The fighter still had moments of influence to come, but the manager and organizer was developing fast. Almost inevitably, these changes have been attributed to Stalin's 'cunning', 'thirst for power', 'manipulativeness' and other supposedly key characteristics assumed to be embedded in his character in Cold War era interpretations. While Stalin certainly exhibited such characteristics at various points in his life, the same could be said to be true of most 'successful' politicians. We will examine later the degree to which Stalin took such characteristics to the extreme. For the moment, however, we should note that there is no evidence for giving them precedence at this time. There is nothing to suggest that Stalin was plotting a personal dictatorship at this point. Indeed, the Bolsheviks remained a tiny party and only fervent believers, like Stalin, really thought it might come to power. But that is what Stalin had been and remained – a fervent believer. Evidence from the Alliluyev memoirs, for instance, depicts a convinced Leninist working energetically and devotedly for the party and its leader. Though there were arguments, he also appears to have maintained working relationships with other leaders, including Trotsky. There was no repetition of anyone trying to bar Stalin for his 'well-known character traits', whatever they were. Either they had been the result of the stresses of exile or they had disappeared for the time being, or, at least, his colleagues had devised ways of working with him. Whatever the truth, in the revolutionary months of 1917 there were no signs of a Stalin issue in the party leadership. Stalin worked hard and effectively at his organizational tasks.

Stalin seems to have spent the revolutionary year of 1917 in committee rooms and offices. He had plenty to do. He addressed five party congregations of various kinds, giving the reports on the current situation to the delegates on several occasions. The first of these meetings was in late April when a party conference[19] was called largely to develop the policies outlined by Lenin in the *April Theses* and to resolve the issues that had arisen. Apart from a short intervention opposing an amendment to the main resolution supporting the Leninist position, Stalin's main interventions were on nationalities policy, where he continued to develop his role as the party's leading specialist. He summarized nationalities policy:

> The Party demands full equality of status in educational, religious and other matters and the abolition of all restrictions on national minorities; . . . our views on the national question can be reduced to the following propositions:
>
> a) Recognition of the right of nations to secession;
> b) Regional autonomy for nations remaining within the given state;
> c) Special legislation guaranteeing freedom of development for national minorities;
> d) A single, indivisible proletarian collective, a single party, for the proletarians of all nationalities of the given state.[20]

Two of these propositions caused some controversy. A number of delegates were reluctant to agree to a right of secession, fearing it gave too much ground to nationalism, the antithesis of the socialist value of internationalism. Stalin had been aware of this dilemma since he first became involved with the issue and, although he stood firmly for the right to secede, he had been reluctant to agree to it in practice. However, that was by no means the case here. The practical issue behind the theory was Finnish independence, which Stalin supported without prevarication: 'We must support every movement directed against imperialism. Otherwise what will the Finnish workers say of us? Pyatakov and Dzerzhinsky tell us that every national movement is a reactionary movement. That is not true, comrades. Is not the Irish movement against British imperialism a democratic movement which is striking a blow at imperialism? And ought we not to support that movement?'[21]

Of course, developments within Russia were more crucial and the turning point of June–July had its impact upon the party. Demonstrations in July brought the revolution to the brink of power. The impetus had come from below. It had been driven by the advance guard of the revolution, the sailors of Kronstadt who had already set up a form of soviet power in their island base in the Gulf of Finland. They were joined by soldiers facing removal from Petrograd in contravention of the agreement made between the Provisional Government and the Petrograd Soviet in the early hours of the revolution. Workers also came onto the streets. Without doubt they could have arrested the ministers of the Provisional Government and overthrown it. Whether they could have sustained such a move nationally was less clear and, nominally at least, the leaders of the left such as Lenin, who seem to have been caught by surprise, said that the move was premature in that conditions across the whole country were not ripe. What happened next suggests they were correct. In the face of left-wing hesitation the centre and the right took action. Police cleared the streets with bullets. The famous photograph of demonstrators fleeing on Nevsky Propekt, the main avenue in Petrograd, was taken at this time. The government itself blamed Lenin and the Bolsheviks for planning the attempted coup. They also claimed the events proved Lenin (who had, like many revolutionaries, been compelled by circumstances to return to Russia under German protection) was a German spy. A dossier of dubious documents was produced to back the claim. Right-wing street thugs, no doubt reminding Stalin of their equivalent in Baku, took to the streets. Suspected left-wingers were beaten up. Bolshevik presses were destroyed. The Bolshevik Party and its newspapers were banned. Arrest warrants were out for leading Bolsheviks.

Lenin considered it his duty to stay at liberty. This meant going into hiding which he did around 10 July. After a short time in the countryside near Razliv, around 6 August he crossed the Finnish border and moved to a safe house in Helsinki. All accounts agree that Stalin was a crucial link between Lenin and the party leadership in these difficult times. He had accompanied Lenin to the station and, from time to time, made secret visits to Finland to keep Lenin and the Central Committee in touch with each other. Not only that, but Lenin's absence left a hole at the heart of the *apparat* (the central bureaucracy of the party). Stalin was one of three or four people who filled it. Trotsky, who joined the Bolsheviks at this moment, handed himself over to the authorities, boasting, ultimately correctly, that they did not have a prison big enough to hold him. That left Stalin, Kamenev and Zinoviev as the leading figures left at liberty in Petrograd. They, too, were forced underground. So dire did the situation seem to Lenin that he claimed it had returned to the last years of tsarism when legal and illegal work had had to be combined.[22]

Stalin was, of course, no stranger to these conditions and he took to them like a duck to water. The banned *Pravda* reappeared almost immediately under a new title – *Rabochii i soldat* (*Worker and Soldier*)– under Stalin's joint editorship. He himself sought out the Alliluyevs and moved into their spare room, kept open for him since March. It was at this point that he and Nadezhda Alliuyeva came to know each other better, a relationship that resulted in their marriage in 1919, when she was 17 and he was 40, and the birth of their first child, Vassili, five months later.

In addition to his editorial duties, Stalin was also hard at work keeping the party together and even organizing an illegal party conference held from 26 July to 3 August. Not only that, but he played a significant role in its deliberations. He addressed it on several occasions including key reports of the Central Committee and 'On the Current Situation'.[23] In his own direct and unadorned style, Stalin made a number of interesting comments in the name of the Central Committee. He was not afraid to describe the outcome of the July Days in unequivocal terms as a defeat brought about, he stated, by armed repression on Nevsky Prospekt and elsewhere. He refuted Menshevik and SR assertions the Bolsheviks had acted alone by saying the 400,000 demonstrators – he gave a bourgeois newspaper, *Birzhevie vedemosti* (*The Stock Exchange Gazette*) as the source for the numbers – marched under a slogan of left-wing unity:

Our slogan was 'All power to the Soviets!' and, hence, a united revolutionary front. But the Mensheviks and Socialist-Revolutionaries feared to break with the bourgeoisie, turned their backs on us, and thereby broke the revolutionary front in deference to the counter-revolutionaries. If those responsible for the victory of the counter-revolution are to be named, it was the Socialist-Revolutionaries and Mensheviks. It is our misfortune that Russia is a country of petty bourgeois, and that it still follows the Socialist-Revolutionaries and Mensheviks, who are compromising with the Cadets. And until the masses become disillusioned with the idea of compromise with the bourgeoisie, the revolution will go haltingly and limpingly.

He also recognized that 'Overthrow of the dictatorship of the imperialist bourgeoisie – that is what the immediate slogan of the Party must be. The peaceful period of the revolution has ended. A period of clashes and explosions has begun.' Dual power, he stated, had come to an end because the Soviets had lost power: 'There is no longer any talk of dual power. Formerly the Soviets represented a real force; now they are merely organs for uniting the masses, and possess no power.' There was also, in one intervention, the emergence of a key Stalinist theme, that Russia might be at the forefront of the revolution, not dependent on Germany or elsewhere. Speaking to oppose a resolution (Preobrazhensky's) about proletarian revolution in the West being a necessary prelude to constructing socialism in Russia, he said:

> The possibility is not excluded that Russia will be the country that will lay the road to socialism. No country hitherto has enjoyed such freedom in time of war as Russia does, or has attempted to introduce workers' control of production. Moreover, the base of our revolution is broader than in Western Europe, where the proletariat stands utterly alone face to face with the bourgeoisie. In our country the workers are supported by the poorer strata of the peasantry. Lastly, in Germany the state apparatus is incomparably more efficient than the imperfect apparatus of our bourgeoisie, which is itself a tributary to European capital. We must discard the antiquated idea that only Europe can show us the way. There is dogmatic Marxism and creative Marxism. I stand by the latter.

In the course of the Congress Stalin spoke against Bukharin, Preobrazhensky, Manuilsky, Iaroslavsky, Angarsky, Nogin. Clearly he was able to go up against the big guns of left and right in the party. In a sense, in the absence of his mentor, Lenin, it was

Stalin's moment in the spotlight. It illuminates a number of Stalin's long-term characteristics – his simple and liturgical style which tends to lists and numbered points; his deep confidence in the workers as a revolutionary force; his belief in the Russian Revolution independent of revolutions elsewhere and his remarkable, very Leninist, claim to stand for creative rather than dogmatic Marxism. While the 'creativity' of his Marxism was to reach extremes later on, for the moment we do not need to resort to deviant psychoanalysis, half-baked theories of lust for power and deeply concealed, long-term thoughts of revenge to understand Stalin. He was a hardworking, effective and committed revolutionary with a circle of friends and opponents. Nothing in his career so far really projected what was to come.

The October Revolution

Trotsky had predicted the government's prisons could not hold him and on 4 September he was proven correct. As part of a deal between the Petrograd Soviet and the prime minister since July, Alexander Kerensky, all political prisoners were released, the Soviet was given access to weapons and the Bolshevik Party was no longer banned. The period of mixing underground and legal work was over almost as soon as it had begun, with the advantage that the period of persecution had made the small but rapidly growing Bolshevik Party look good. The turn of events had worked heavily to their advantage. What had created this miraculous transformation? Quite simply, in a curious mirror-image of the left over-reaching itself in July, the counter-revolution over-reached itself in late August and early September in the form of the Kornilov Revolt. The exact nature of this event remains obscure. At the heart of it was an operation by the Commander-in-Chief Kornilov who had been appointed by Kerensky in July.

From this elevated position Kornilov began to see himself as a military strongman and man of destiny. Fellow officers, fawning landowners, bankers and high society ladies took the opportunity of the Moscow Conference in August to indulge his dreams in the hope he could rescue their endangered property and social status. On the face of it, the military moves taken by Kornilov seemed to be aimed at suppression of the Petrograd Soviet – a logical outcome of the rising tide of reaction. But there were two problems that sank Kornilov's plans. First, Kerensky, who was worried about the effect of an attack on the Soviet, was persuaded by an intermediary that Kornilov aimed to overthrow Kerensky and proclaim himself head of government. Kornilov, when asked to confirm his plans by Kerensky, did so without asking Kerensky what plans he meant. Kerensky arrested him and thereby split the anti-Soviet action and was forced to take measures to conciliate and partially empower the Petrograd Soviet and the Bolsheviks mentioned above. Kornilov's second problem was that his attack was, like the July demonstrations on the left, premature. He did not have the force to carry it through. Buoyed up by Kerensky's belated and mistrusted support and by the weapons distributed to them, delegations from the Soviet were able to subvert Kornilov's troops under the noses of their own officers and the revolt melted away.

Despite that, again mirroring July, it was a game changer but in the opposite direction to that intended by its leaders. Instead of stamping on revolution it opened Russia up to its most extreme forms. The Bolsheviks began to gain important majorities in key soviets, not least Moscow and Petrograd. Peasants, spooked by the Kornilov affair into fearing the landowners might re-assert themselves decided they had to seize land while they still could and the rate of land seizure began to soar. Workers also feared the return of employers and, because of this and other reasons, especially fear they would be unemployed, began to take control of more and more factories and other workplaces with the aim of keeping them going and thereby preserving their jobs. Perhaps most important of all, the affair drove a renewed wedge between soldiers and sailors, on the one hand, and their officers, on the other. As if that were not enough a disastrous gap emerged between Kerensky and the military leaders who despised him and blamed him for the failure of Kornilov's enterprise on which they had pinned their hopes.

From his marginal vantage point in Helsinki, Lenin was quick to see the revolutionary potential of the developing conjuncture and began to bombard his comrades in the party leadership with urgent demands to organize the overthrow of the discredited government. Central Committee members in Petrograd and

Moscow were stunned by Lenin's furious insistence and, from their vantage point, they thought Lenin was vastly over exaggerating the revolutionary potential of the situation. The depth of the dispute is shown, in brief, by a number of points. First, there was a suggestion Lenin's letters should be burned; second, Lenin was so frustrated by the unenthusiastic response that he threatened to resign from the Central Committee and, finally, on 10 October, without breaking his underground status, he felt it imperative to attend a meeting of the Central Committee himself to ram his point home. Even that was not enough. At a second Central Committee meeting on 16 October, only nine days before the actual seizure of power, he was complaining that still nothing had been done. When the Petrograd coup actually came, on 25/26 October, it was engineered through improvisation and chance rather than any revolutionary blueprint. The leading institution behind the action was the Military Revolutionary Committee of the Petrograd Soviet, not the Bolshevik Party itself. However, this helped camouflage the takeover as an all-party action when, in actual fact, the Bolsheviks had seized power for themselves. While the action in Petrograd might be seen as a coup, it was enacted against the background of the rising social revolution of peasant land seizure, worker militancy and soldier/sailor resentment against officers. From Petrograd, the revolution spread quickly before encountering serious forces of resistance.[24] While the Kornilov affair might be considered the first campaign of the Civil War, since it was the first time organized groups of Russian citizens had fought one another, real resistance built up in late 1917 to be defeated in spring 1918. That was not the end. A second civil war erupted in June/July 1918.[25]

What did Stalin do to promote this revolutionary outcome? It was periods like this which Sukhanov was thinking of when he described Stalin as a 'grey blur'. To the outsider he was a distant, looming, background figure. He was not partial to great public occasions. However, he did address local party meetings in the city and attended many committees of many party and soviet bodies. He even attended meetings of the key Military Revolutionary Committee of the Petrograd Soviet which commanded the forces which overthrew the Provisional Government, though he does not appear to have played a very extensive part in its deliberations. He was energetically active in the Bolshevik engine room of a party, newspaper and revolutionary coup. Because of this he only rarely emerges into the light, leaving a reliable trace. A good guide at this time is provided by the minutes of the Central Committee for the crucial weeks before and after the October Revolution. Their publication in 1957 tells a story of its own. It was unique for such high-level party documents to be published at that time. The date, however, is crucial. In February 1956, Stalin's successor, Nikita Khrushchev, began a campaign of selective de-Stalinization. The publishing of the minutes was part of that campaign. How? The aim appears to have been to show, by the most reliable means available, that the myth of Stalin as co-leader of October with Lenin, one of many exaggerations promoted in the cult of Stalin's personality, had no basis in reality. Indeed, Stalin barely figures in the minutes. But they do show the main contours of Stalin's real role in the drama.

First of all, he was always present, always in the thick of it. He was appointed to every senior committee active at that time. When, at its 16 October meeting, the Central Committee appointed a Party Centre to oversee the preparations for the armed uprising, Stalin was one of its five members. Even though this body does not seem to have met, it unequivocally shows Stalin's stature within the party. The record also shows that Stalin was close to Lenin on most key issues. But he did not simply parrot his support. When Kamenev and Zinoviev went public with the Bolsheviks' plans and with their opposition to them after the 16 October meeting at which they had been outvoted, Lenin was incandescent with rage. His colleagues, however, including Stalin, were less hostile. Stalin allowed them to publish their views in *Pravda*, and when Lenin wanted to expel them for their betrayal, Stalin joined Sverdlov and others in trying to persuade Lenin to take lesser sanctions. In the end, they were expelled from the Central Committee but the decision was not implemented and they were playing a full part in Central Committee activities within two weeks. Finally, Stalin's interventions in Central Committee discussions were infrequent, terse and to the point. Stalin worked hard. If he was a 'grey blur' to outside observers it was not because he 'did nothing in particular and did it very well',[26] but because his work was behind the scenes. Though we do not have enough information to measure it precisely, it is clear that Stalin played a great part in the October Revolution. But taking power was the easy part. As one observer said, the Bolsheviks did not seize power, they found it lying in the street and picked it up.[27] Holding on to it was quite another thing. Was Stalin up to the challenges ahead?

From commissar to general secretary: Stalin's Civil War

The years from the October Revolution to the Tenth Party Congress, in March 1921, and the final wrapping up of all but the smallest pockets of armed resistance to Bolshevik rule in 1922 were a period of unparalleled complexity. At one time, Soviet historiography talked about 'The Triumphal March of Soviet Power' in the first few months and 'The Russian Civil War', kicked off by the actions of the Czech Legion and Trotsky's mistaken response in June 1918, and lasting until 1921/1922. There was also the highly important 'Russo-Polish War' of 1920. A large amount of attention was devoted to foreign intervention in these troubled times. Western historians were also fascinated by intervention, not least because it was an area of the revolution that could be studied from a sound source base. The archives of the intervening powers were available. Soviet archives, on the whole, were not. Over time, a less binary view emerged. Oliver Radkey talked of the 'Greens' in the Civil War, those who were neither 'Red' (pro-soviet) or White (anti-soviet and often described as 'counter-revolutionary').[28] During the 1980s and 1990s Vladimir Brovkin opened up the issue of conflict within the Soviet zone, not least between the Communist Party (as the Bolsheviks styled themselves from 8 March 1918) and its supposedly enthusiastic worker base.[29] Since the 1990s a whole wealth of scholarship has opened up many aspects of the topic – especially the peasantry,[30] the provinces[31] and the 'periphery' – and the course of events in areas which, permanently or temporarily, broke away from the Soviet Republic.[32] The result has been a greater understanding of the complexity of the events and the interweaving of a variety of revolutions – gender, nationality, political, economic and so on. In 1996, one synthesis described a 'kaleidoscope' of revolutions, a concept taken up by a group of leading scholars on the peasantry and the provinces.[33] In a similar vein, a superb new account of the military struggles of the period talks of civil wars in the plural and even of civil wars within the civil wars. In place of the 'Russo-Polish War' the author points to a fluctuating, six-sided conflict between several combinations of Russia, Poland, Ukraine, Belarus, Lithuania and the Jews of the region.[34]

Overall, the struggle was a desperate one. Some would argue that the Whites had little chance of winning because they had a very narrow basis of support. Others would argue the Bolsheviks' own survival was, at times, obtained by the thinnest of margins. It has also been argued that the outbreak of the second civil war in June 1918 saved the Bolsheviks from apparently inevitable disintegration and disunity. For two crucial years, the White threat created relative unity within the Communist Party and a degree of sympathy from the wider left, not to mention workers and peasants, who supported the Communist Party as the lesser of two evils. Former opponents from Mensheviks to a few Kadet liberals[35] came over to the Red side. Supporters emerged from within the interventionist armies themselves. As far away as the docks of Britain a 'Hands off Russia' campaign hampered supplies to the Whites.

The social and economic balance sheet of these years is unbelievable. Overall, there are thought to have been some 10 million deaths, largely from diseases such as cholera, typhus and the influenza epidemic which ravaged the exhausted bodies of postwar societies across the continent. A significant number died in battle. Perhaps the most horrific deaths, however, were the endless massacres which took place and the mind-numbing atrocities committed by all sides to eliminate 'enemies'. There were dozens of Srebrenicas.[36] At the top of the list were untold numbers of Jews, perhaps as many as 200,000 altogether. In all theatres, from the Caucasus, where mutual slaughter was especially savage, to the relatively 'civilized' environment of independent Finland, victories were followed by massacres of the defeated in thousands and, all too frequently, in numbers approaching and sometimes exceeding ten thousand. A precise accounting is impossible but the general picture is indisputable.

Economic collapse, though marginally less horrific, swallowed up even more lives. A famine, which first started to show itself in 1919, reached massive proportions by 1922. Recent calculations have scaled the death toll down to a million with many more suffering from hunger and non-fatal diseases. A superb measuring of economic life during the period of war and revolution has underlined the massive drop in economic output in these years.[37] Encapsulating the whole debate about the Lenin and Stalin eras, the authors put much of the blame for this on early Soviet experiments with state control of the economy but one could just as easily argue the collapse led to the desperate measures of state control leading to 'heroic' efforts at reconstruction. Whatever the reason the consequence is clear. The Russian economy was at an unimaginably low ebb in 1920/1921. Food supplies had collapsed. The vital railway network was hampered by numerous bottlenecks in the form of destroyed track and bridges and so on and breakdowns of ageing locomotives and rolling stock which could not be repaired for lack of spare parts. Without railways, the circulation of people, food, raw materials and the meagre supply of finished products could not take place. Industrial output was down to 18 per cent according to some calculations.[38] So disastrous were the figures that they have been described as being at fifteenth-century levels. Obviously, measures had to be taken and the New Economic Policy was what emerged. However, all the above indicates that the Civil War years were desperate beyond all imagining. There were battles on all fronts, not just military but social, gender, ethnic, economic and cultural areas. It was an age of fighters. One might have thought it was tailor-made for our fighting Georgian. What was Stalin's contribution to the Civil War? Or, maybe a more important question, what was the contribution of this desperate Civil War to the making of Stalin?

Unsurprisingly, when the moment came for Lenin to set up the first Soviet government – an event delayed by pressure from railway workers, non-Bolshevik Soviet politicians and even from within the upper echelons of the party itself[39] – Lenin named Stalin to the post of Commissar of Nationalities. The title of commissar prevailed over the supposedly bourgeois term 'minister' because, Lenin believed, it had a more revolutionary ring to it.

While it may sound obscure to our ears Stalin's responsibility was immensely important and pressing. The issue of nationalities was a massive one with a multitude of independence movements facing the new Soviet authorities.

Stalin set to work quickly. Already, in November, a Decree on Nationality was issued by the new government. The main practical issue was Finnish independence which had become an unrecognized reality even before the October Revolution. In November, Stalin went to Helsinki to announce the new government's agreement to Finnish self-determination and the link with Russia was broken. That, however, was not supposed to be a precedent for a massive rush of minority nationalities for the exit door. As we have already seen, the central ambiguity of Stalin's nationality policy was that the right to self-determination was recognized but the whole point of the policy was to ensure that no minority would want to exercise that right. The aim was that a maximum degree of autonomy would appease all the demands of the nation for cultural, linguistic and other aspects of independence but within the framework of the multi-national state. Within that framework, proletarian class solidarity would grow across national boundaries and eventually obliterate them, though no one thought that would happen soon. Such broad principles were all very well but, in the Soviet context, they barely helped with a multitude of primordial issues that needed resolution, the most primordial of which was what constituted a nation? What constituted a national administrative unit was also unclear. The dominant entities – Russia itself and Ukraine – had populations of some 100 million and 31 million, respectively. There were numerous small nationalities of 1 to 5 million and a whole host of ethnic groups down to only a few tens of thousands in size. There were also 6 million Jews with strong national bonds but no territorial base of their own.

With commendable rapidity, the Commissariat for Nationalities, Narkomnats as it was usually called, contributed to the emergence of the first Soviet constitution and the setting up of the Russian Socialist Federative Soviet Republic in July 1918. Stalin participated personally in the drafting of this document under the leadership of Iakov Sverdlov. In certain respects the hastiness with which it was produced showed. Some of its aspects, with respect to nationalities, exhibited a somewhat provisional, even cobbled together, nature. Sometimes antagonistic peoples were tied to one another in one and the same administrative unit. One of the most troubled was the area best known to Stalin, the Transcaucasus. The three dominant nations – Georgia, Armenia and Azerbaijan – were yoked together in a single Transcaucasian Republic. Nonetheless, the constitution held until it was replaced by a new one, reflecting the more permanent-seeming conditions of the time, at the end of 1922 when the Russian Socialist Federative Soviet Republic became the USSR (Union of Soviet Socialist Republics), a title it held until the end in 1991.

In part, the haste was occasioned by the need for the new government to explain what it stood for to its often bemused citizens. Lenin referred to the tactic as propaganda by decree and that is what the 1918 constitution and new party programme of 1919 were intended to be. In the area of nationalities, there was a particularly pressing reason for the party to define its position. It was competing against a host of nationalist movements in the minority areas. As Stalin himself put it at the time, the concept of autonomy had to be given a makeover by 'cleansing it of bourgeois filth' and converting it 'from a bourgeois autonomy into a Soviet autonomy'.[40] In other words, the middle class would not control the new institutions, the proletariat would.

But there was a second reason for haste. Precisely as the constitution was being proclaimed the country was sliding back into a major phase of the civil war. While there had been fighting somewhere almost continually, April to June had been a lull during which Lenin had claimed the Civil War was, by and large, over.[41] Nothing could have been further from the truth. In June, the Civil War flared up with a renewed and unprecedented intensity. Complications developed between the Soviet government and the Czech legion, who had fought on the Eastern Front alongside the Russians and against the Austrians. When the Treaty of Brest-Litovsk in March had ended the war between Russia and Germany they had been left stranded. They decided to withdraw from Russia by the only route possible, the Trans-Siberian railway. As they left they came into a series of abrasive conflicts with the Soviet authorities, notably Trotsky who, in a miscalculation enormous even by his standards, sent an unenforceable order that they should be disarmed. This meant the Czechs were in a state of conflict with the Soviet authorities and, since they were strung out along the whole Trans-Siberian railway and thereby controlled it, a vast area was lost to Soviet power in one, ill-conceived blow. Wanting only to leave Russia and rejoin the battle against Germany, the legion was unwillingly thrust into the whirlpool of Russian politics. In the vast political vacuum created, White and other anti-Bolshevik forces began to reform. Even in areas not directly connected with this turn of events, like South Russia, new opportunities arose. In addition, the ending of the war on the Western Front in November caused the withdrawal of Austrian and German troops from their occupation of Ukraine. A mad scramble of Soviet, anti-Soviet, nationalist and independent forces began to fill another vast political vacuum. To meet the massive crisis, the party and Soviet leadership went onto a war footing.

Stalin was no exception. The theory of nationalities was set aside for the time being. The practical issue of dealing with them, and other turbulent issues and enemies, came to the fore. Very quickly Stalin was sent to the front line. On 29 May he was put in charge of the key issue of food supply on the most critical of the fronts at that moment, the South-Eastern Front. He was given 'extraordinary powers' to deal with the issue in the decree of appointment signed by Lenin.[42] Stalin's relatively brief time in Tsaritsyn has often been seen as a highly significant moment in his life. Not only that, it became iconic. The city on the Volga was named Stalingrad in his honour in 1925 and became a model of Soviet development and it received worldwide renown as a symbol of Soviet resistance against the Nazis.

He arrived to take over his new task on 6 June 1918. His reports back to Lenin are terse but full of energy and action. He opened the first with the words: 'Arrived in Tsaritsyn on the 6th. Despite the confusion in every sphere of economic life, order can be established.' The words could serve as an epigram for Stalin's whole post-October career. His plans also reflected the essence of the 'Stalinist' method:

> In Tsaritsyn, Astrakhan and Saratov the grain monopoly and fixed prices were abolished by the Soviets; and there is chaos and profiteering. Have secured the introduction of rationing

and fixed prices in Tsaritsyn. The same must be done in Astrakhan and Saratov, otherwise all grain will flow away through these profiteering channels . . . Rail transport is completely dislocated owing to the efforts of the multiplicity of collegiums[43] and revolutionary committees. I have been obliged to appoint special commissars; they are already establishing order despite the protests of the collegiums. The commissars are discovering heaps of locomotives in places where the collegiums did not suspect their existence . . . Within a week we shall proclaim a 'Grain Week' and shall dispatch to Moscow right away about one million poods[44] with a special escort of railwaymen, of which I shall give you due notice . . . A line is already being laid from Kizlyar to the sea; the Hasav-Yurt-Petrovsk line has not yet been restored. Let us have Shlyapnikov, civil engineers, intelligent workmen, also locomotive crews . . . Chief Trade Agent Zaitsev will be arrested today for bag-trading and speculating in government goods. Tell Schmidt not to send any more scoundrels.

Here was a guy who got things done. A million poods of grain promised within a week! Even more astonishingly, the telegram was sent on 7 June, only one day after his arrival, which suggests there must have been no little exaggeration and wishful thinking in his description, although orders may have preceded his actual arrival. Nonetheless, a number of typically 'Stalinist' characteristics can be seen. The determination and energy; cutting through 'democratic' bodies, even revolutionary committees; the almost magical discovery of 'heaps' of hidden resources, in this case locomotives; the identification of profiteering as a key problem; the request for 'intelligent' workmen; the identification of corruption in the system in the form of a named speculator in a responsible position.

Later reports to Lenin were in the same vein. A month later (7 July) he had to write to Lenin to explain that the promised grain supply had been held up:

The railway south of Tsaritsyn has not yet been restored. I am firing or telling off all who deserve it, and I hope we shall have it restored soon. You may rest assured that we shall spare nobody, neither ourselves nor others, and shall deliver the grain in spite of everything. If our military 'experts' (bunglers!) had not been asleep or loafing about the line would not have been cut, and if the line is restored it will not be thanks to, but in spite of, the military.

Here was another Stalinist theme, lack of trust in the military specialists drafted in from the old regime to bolster the Soviet war effort. On July 10 he became more explicit. He asked Lenin to rein Trotsky in and stop him appointing people over the heads of the local officials as the practice was discrediting Soviet power. He also requested military powers for himself and claimed, in the absence of a reply or a piece of 'paper from Trotsky', he would take on such powers himself and 'dismiss army commanders and commissars who are ruining the work'.[45]

There were two other areas in which the Tsaritsyn experience was a landmark in Stalin's life and career. They were at opposite ends of the spectrum. On the one hand, Stalin married Nadezhda Alliluyeva, who was 17 at the time while Stalin was 39. Five months later Nadya gave birth to their first child, a son whom they named Vassili.

The second landmark was much grimmer. According to the memoirs of Stalin's long-time associate Voroshilov, Stalin, for the first time, ordered the execution of three suspected traitors, a father and two sons named Alexeev who thereby had the dubious distinction of being the first of many.[46] However, they were not alone, even at the time. Stalin, Voroshilov continued, instituted a 'ruthless purge of the rear, administered by an iron hand'. While a purge denotes dismissal rather than death, the escalation into terror was rapid, mainly as a result of events elsewhere. In July, a half-baked uprising against the Bolsheviks had been conducted by their former allies, the Left SRs. Lenin instructed Stalin 'mercilessly to suppress these pitiful and hysterical adventurers . . . Be ruthless.' Stalin's reply on 7 July was almost unnecessary: 'You may rest assured that our hand will not flinch.'[47]

However, things got incomparably worse in August. An attempt was made on Lenin's life which sent paroxysms of anxiety and a deep desire for revenge through the leadership of the party. Stalin was particularly affected by the near-destruction of the man he idolized. His reply to Sverdlov's telegram sending the news was to the point:

> Having learned of the villainous attempt of the hirelings of the bourgeoisie on the life of Comrade Lenin, the world's greatest revolutionary and the tried and tested leader and teacher of the proletariat, the Military Council of the North Caucasian Military Area is answering this vile attempt at assassination by instituting open and systematic mass terror against the bourgeoisie and its agents (Stalin, Voroshilov Tsaritsyn, 31 August 1918).

For the first time Stalin was getting his hands dirty in the bitterness of the Civil War.

He was not alone. There was not only a wave of Cheka terror but Trotsky had also shown his ruthlessness at the same time when he had ordered the decimation (execution of every tenth soldier) of a runaway regiment at Sviazhsk. In Trotsky's words: 'to a gangrenous wound a red hot iron has been applied'.[48] Not only Stalin but many other Bolshevik leaders were becoming accustomed to allowing the ends to justify the means. As S.I. Gusev put it at the time, 'Comrade Trotsky's harsh methods . . . were most expedient and necessary for that period of undisciplined and irregular warfare'.[49] 'Expedient', 'necessary', words frequently used by Stalin's apologists but here being applied to Trotsky. They were increasingly characteristic of the party as a whole, not just Stalin.

'Harsh methods' at this time worked for both Trotsky and Stalin and the Cheka. Enemies were overcome, for the time being at least, and Bolshevik authority, such as it was, was secured. On 6 September Stalin triumphantly reported to the Soviet government (Sovnarkom): 'The enemy has been utterly routed and hurled back across the Don. Tsaritsyn is secure. The offensive continues.'[50]

There was, however, one more twist for Stalin in his Tsaritsyn episode. Stalin's optimism and triumphalism were not shared by Trotsky. Once again it was the issue of *spetsy* (specialists) which had brought matters to a head. As we have seen, Stalin barely tolerated *spetsy*. He had maintained his forthright views and, in an interview published in *Izvestiia* on 21 September, he argued that the situation was improving because:

> First of all, Comrade Stalin said, two gratifying facts should be noted: one is the promotion to administrative posts in the rear area of working men with an ability not only for agitating in favour of Soviet power, but also for building the state on a new, communist basis; the second is the appearance of a new corps of commanders consisting of officers promoted from the ranks who have had practical experience in the imperialist war, and who enjoy the full confidence of the Red Army men.[51]

Stalin's hostility to *spetsy* even went as far as leading him to dismiss N. N. Sytin, Trotsky's appointee as head of the Southern Front. This enraged Trotsky who feared for the collapse of the whole front if matters were left to Stalin and Voroshilov. On 4 October he wrote to Lenin: 'I insist categorically on Stalin's recall. Things are going badly at the Tsaritsyn front despite the superabundance of forces. Voroshilov is capable of commanding a regiment, not an army of fifty thousand.'[52]

This is not the place for a full discussion of the role of *spetsy*, also known as 'specialists' or 'experts' in Soviet construction at this time but we should note they were developing under Lenin's patronage. In one of the few areas where there was a gulf between the ideas of Lenin and Stalin, Lenin had argued that it was necessary to recruit 'bourgeois experts' to help run the economy and the army, since workers lacked expertise. Alongside them, in the armed forces, political commissars were appointed to keep an eye on the *spetsy* and educate the ordinary soldier/peasants in party ideology. True to his immense trust in the workers alongside whom he, not Lenin, had worked, Stalin believed the proletariat could find the strength, energy and abilities it needed from within. It had no need to rely on potential traitors from an alien class who did not share the aims of the revolution. However, in challenging this principle, Stalin had bitten off more than he could chew. Trotsky complained to Lenin and Lenin stood in defence of his own policy and, instead of giving in to Stalin's attempt to rid his front of *spetsy*, Stalin was himself withdrawn from the area. The respected Sverdlov was sent to break the news to Stalin and to accompany him back to Moscow in October.

Even though, at a closed session of the next party congress in March 1919, Lenin apparently criticized the Tsaritsyn leadership for its errors in Stalin's time there, saying 'a regular army can only exist on condition that the most rational use is made of the work of specialists',[53] Stalin's career lost no momentum as a result. We might surmise it fed fuel to the flame of his resentment against Trotsky but we will also see that it did not lead him to revise his views that committed workers were better servants of the revolution than hired-in bourgeois specialists. It did, however, lead him to remain diplomatically silent about it. It was even the case that, in the Bolshevik manner, when the moment came, at the Eighth Party Congress in March 1919, to draft a decree on the structure of the Red Army, incorporating *spetsy* and political commissars, Stalin, as one of the dissenters, was elected to the drafting commission as a sign of his loyalty to a position with which he did not agree. He was even chosen to speak in favour of the decree. Only short extracts from his speech were published in the so-called *Collected Works*, grounds for thinking there were still nuances of dissent, but he did stand robustly in favour of 'a strictly disciplined regular army' because 'Six months ago, after the collapse of the old, tsarist army, we had a new, a volunteer army, an army which was badly organized, which had a collective control, and which did not always obey orders'. Uncharacteristically, he points to its volunteer worker composition as a root of its weakness, though he lays chief blame on the peasants who 'will not voluntarily fight for socialism' and must be 're-educated' and infused 'with a spirit of iron discipline, to get them to follow the lead of the proletariat at the front as well as in the rear, to compel them to fight for our common socialist cause'.[54]

March was a rare moment when Stalin was in Moscow. Despite the Tsaritsyn problem Stalin was still a leading, trusted trouble-shooter moving, in the course of late 1918 and 1919, to three key fronts to investigate failures and/or to prop them up for future offensives. He spent January, significantly in the company of the head of the Cheka (Secret Police) on the Eastern Front, mostly in Viatka and Glazov, the headquarters of the Third Army. In mid-May, as Iudenich's White Army approached from its

Estonian base, Stalin was sent to Staraya Rus to bolster the defence of Petrograd. Apart from important brief returns to Moscow to report on progress he remained on the Western Front until the end of September, by which time Iudenich's army was on the back foot. Stalin himself took credit for organizing the recapture of the forts at Krasnaia Gorka and Seraya Loshad after a counter-revolutionary uprising apparently by officers. The revolt was put down and was followed by severe reprisals.

No sooner was he back in Moscow on 30 September than he was sent to his home territory of the south where the situation was very complex. Azerbaijan was in Soviet hands, Georgia had a Menshevik, anti-Bolshevik government and Armenia was severely threatened by Turkey. South Russia itself, a land of Russians, Ukrainians, Cossacks, Tatars, Jews and Greeks, was the base for Denikin's anti-Bolshevik operations. Denikin's Volunteer Army had made major advances and was well on the road to Moscow, a fact underlined by the establishment of the Soviet headquarters of the Southern Front at Serpukhov, only 65 miles/100 kilometres from Moscow. The furthest White outpost was only another 65 miles/100 kilometres further south in Tula. Stalin arrived at this front on 3 October and moved to Serpukhov on 11 October. He arrived in time for the first major reversal in Denikin's fortunes, the loss of Orel on 15 October. A week later, Stalin's fellow Georgian and long-time associate, Budyonny, led his Red Cavalry to victory over their White counterparts and, shortly after, the city of Voronezh also fell. The Volunteer Army was in headlong retreat. The Stalin mythologizers claimed major credit for him but his role, though significant, was not decisive. As in the other areas of his activity his role was to be, ironically, a kind of super political commissar casting an eye over the whole scene and applying 'motivation' – physical and moral, coercive and exhortative – wherever it appeared to be needed. Stalin continued in the same vein into late 1919 and 1920, spending time on the Southern and South-Western Fronts, punctuated by important visits to Moscow for major events. By early January, the front headquarters had advanced to Kursk and Denikin's army was in headlong retreat. The recapture of his former base of operations, Rostov, on 10 January was the signal for Stalin to return to Moscow, no doubt to lap up praise for his contribution to this crucial turnaround in Red Army fortunes. Next time he forayed south Kursk had become the headquarters (HQ) for the South-Western Front though success there meant that, by 10 February, the Red Army had penetrated Ukraine and the HQ was moved to Kharkov. He had an immensely demanding schedule. He combined work in the Revolutionary Military Council with key troubleshooting roles in, perhaps surprisingly, the setting up of labour armies in Ukraine and militarizing the Donbas coalfield, initiatives normally thought of as aspects of 'Trotskyite' policies. The idea of labour armies was that military units, being less and less necessary for the war effort as the White threat diminished, could be transferred to key economic tasks to break through bottlenecks and get the economy moving again. The degree of control afforded to the state over its citizens and the labour process itself was subjected to severe criticism from workers, labour armies and party opponents and the policy, defended stoutly by Trotsky, was rejected by the party by March 1922. Stalin was also instrumental in calling a Ukrainian party conference from 17–23 March 1920 which concluded in time for him to return to Moscow for the full Ninth Party Congress from 29 March to 5 April. In February he had also been involved in drawing up revisions to the federal structure of Soviet Russia, a reminder of his ongoing responsibilities towards the nationalities. However, at the congress, he was involved in another drafting commission reflecting, this time, his closeness to the proletariat. There had been a deeply divisive dispute about the nature of trade unions under communism. Lenin argued that, since the state was the guarantor of workers' rights, unions were unnecessary. Trade union activists and leaders were only too well aware of the continuing grievances of workers against their managers and, ultimately, their employer, the proletarian state, and fought to preserve their independence. Predictably, the Lenin line won and, equally predictably, Stalin supported his views. When the Decree on Trade Unions was published, unions were, effectively, co-ordinated into management rather than worker representation against management, and were defined as 'schools of communism' in which workers would learn of the wonders which awaited them under the Soviet regime.

Shortly after, Stalin wrote a sycophantic, though probably heartfelt, article entitled 'Lenin as Organizer and Leader of the Russian Communist Party' which appeared in *Pravda*.[55] It was published on 23 April, Lenin's birthday, and marks a significant prelude to what became a crucial theme in Stalin's career, his status as originator and chief worshipper of the cult of Lenin. The article also indicates some other key Stalinist themes. In a simplified view of the world of Marxism, Stalin argued there were two kinds of Marxists, the dogmatists who refused to go beyond theoretical concepts and texts in developing policy – Mensheviks in Russia and opportunists in Europe – and a second type who, Stalin said:

> attach prime importance not to the outward acceptance of Marxism, but to its realization, its application in practice. What this group chiefly concentrates its attention on is determining the ways and means of realizing Marxism that best answer the situation, and changing these ways and means as the situation changes. It does not derive its directions and instructions from historical analogies and parallels, but from a study of surrounding conditions. It does not base its activities on quotations and maxims, but on practical experience, testing every step by experience, learning from its mistakes and teaching others how to build a new life. That, in fact, explains why there is no discrepancy between word and deed in the activities of this group, and why the teachings of Marx completely retain their living, revolutionary force. To this group may be fully applied Marx's saying that Marxists cannot rest content with interpreting the world, but must go further and change it. The name for this group is Bolshevism, communism.
>
> The organizer and leader of this group is V.I. Lenin.

Here, loud and clear, is the voice of the revolutionary activist for whom the current situation, not textual prescriptions, are the basis of action. More intellectual members of the party, with Trotsky in the forefront, pointed out that theory still had to be the root of action but Stalin persistently put the emphasis on the latter:

> In our time of proletarian revolution, when every Party slogan and every utterance of a leader is tested in action, the proletariat makes special demands of its leaders. History knows of proletarian leaders who were leaders in times of storm, practical leaders, self-sacrificing and courageous, but who were weak in theory. The names of such leaders are not soon forgotten by the masses. Such, for example, were Lassalle in Germany and Blanqui in France. But the movement as a whole cannot live on reminiscences alone: it must have a clear goal (a programme), and a firm line (tactics).
>
> There is another type of leader – peacetime leaders, who are strong in theory, but weak in matters of organization and practical work. Such leaders are popular only among an upper layer of the proletariat, and then only up to a certain time. When the epoch of revolution sets in, when practical revolutionary slogans are demanded of the leaders, the theoreticians quit the stage and give way to new men. Such, for example, were Plekhanov in Russia and Kautsky in Germany.
>
> To retain the post of leader of the proletarian revolution and of the proletarian party, one must combine strength in theory with experience in the practical organization of the proletarian movement. P. Axelrod, when he was a Marxist, wrote of Lenin that he 'happily combines the experience of a good practical worker with a theoretical education and a broad political outlook' [see P. Axelrod's preface to Lenin's pamphlet *The Tasks of the Russian Social-Democrats*]. What Mr. Axelrod, the ideologist of 'civilized' capitalism, would say now about Lenin is not difficult to guess. But we who know Lenin well and can judge matters objectively have no doubt that Lenin has fully retained this old quality. It is here, incidentally, that one must seek the reason why it is Lenin, and no one else, who is today the leader of the strongest and most steeled proletarian party in the world (Signed: J. Stalin).[56]

These paragraphs, apart from further underlining the black and white/good versus evil view of the world which Stalin had – one in which one might say, ironically, there were no grey blurs – separate Marxists into those who could implement Marxist ideas and those who could only theorize. The revolutionary epoch was one for the men of action. For the next key stages of his career this remained a central principle. Stalin gathered to himself colleagues whom he believed to be such men of action, people like himself who could 'get things done' without worrying about abstract niceties of theory and principle.

Stalin's own whirl of action continued without respite. The situation was radically changed by the onset of a conflict often described as the 'Russo-Polish War' in the summer of 1920. The struggle has been better described as a multi-sided conflict involving Russia, Poland, Lithuania, Belarus and the Jewish population all mixed together in an area memorably described as 'a 300 mile band of polyglot territories'[57] in which, even today and no doubt long into the future, there are no uncontested borders. There are many very different accounts of the war in which there is no consensus on who started it, why it evolved as it did or exactly why it ended as it did. By and large, Western accounts tend to blame Soviet Russia for invading Poland and praise Poland for resisting, not only saving itself but also constructing an impregnable roadblock on the Comintern's road to Berlin and revolutionary breakout into a volatile central Europe.

It is not our place to analyse these issues in detail but we do have to look at them to the extent they impinged on Stalin and he made a mark on them. Needless to say, this is one of the most contentious of all questions. As is frequently the case, the source of contentiousness goes back to Trotsky whose version of events has been absorbed deeply into the narrative of Soviet history, not least, ironically, by cold warriors. They found in Trotsky's writing a ready-made critique of Stalinism and purged it of its revolutionary base and recycled it as liberal and social-democratic truth. Of course, just because Trotsky wrote something does not mean it isn't true. Parts of his critique are very perceptive, others less so.

In so far as the wars of the western borderlands in 1920 were concerned, the question of who was to blame for the outcome was especially significant. Although the Soviet government did not pick the time and place of the war. It was Pilsudski's Poland which perceived a window of weakness with regard to its neighbours which its leader sought to exploit through military expansion. In Warsaw there were even dreams of an anti-Russian federation of Lithuania, Poland, Belarus and Ukraine which would stretch from the Baltic to the Black Sea. Nonetheless, Moscow took up the challenge of Polish invasion with relish. Appealing to the proletariat of the region would, they believed, undermine Pilsudski's landlord and rich peasant based government, spark a revolution, establish fraternal socialist powers in the region and open the road to a still unstable Berlin and middle Europe. In reality, having threatened Warsaw, the Red Army snatched defeat from the jaws of victory and the balloon of optimism burst. After six months of conflict the major parties were back where they started.

From that time until the present the reasons for the failure have been sharply contested. In Cold War times, Western historians put it down to the presence of French military commanders such as Weygand as the decisive element protecting Europe from the 'the plague bacillus'[58] that was communism and maintaining a founding version of the iron curtain of the Cold War in the form of the 'cordon sanitaire' designed at Versailles.[59] In recent years, resurgent Polish nationalism and its sympathizers have produced a version which emphasizes Poland's own contribution to defending itself against its expansionist neighbour.[60]

From our perspective, however, the issue is the debate from the Soviet side. Here three candidates have been blamed. Trotsky himself has been accused of encouraging a campaign which resulted in overstretching the real, available resources of a desperately weak post-civil war country. Stalin as political commissar to Egorov's army has been blamed for dallying too long in the ultimately unsuccessful attack on L'viv rather than diverting his troops to support Tukhachevsky's drive on Warsaw. Tukhachevsky has been blamed for seeking glory by pushing his army into a premature assault on Warsaw which became a rout, enshrined in Polish national mythology as 'the Miracle on the Vistula'. In truth, the mostly likely explanation is that Egorov, Stalin and Tukhachevsky all made crucial mistakes. On other parts of the front, another of Stalin's associates, Budyonny, who retook Kiev, not only lost much of the rest of what he and the Red Cavalry had initially obtained, but also added to the sad record of Soviet Cossack atrocities in their area of operations, of whom Jews were among the most prominent victims.[61] Whatever the reason, there was a sobering defeat and Stalin had shown he was far from infallible in military affairs. Although there was a ceasefire in October 1920, the aftershocks of the struggle rippled on into 1921. It was only on 18 March 1921 that a peace accord was concluded in the form of the Treaty of Riga. Poland regained territories in the east up to and including L'viv. However, Soviet Russia secured Ukraine and Belarus into its own federation. By 18 March, Stalin's, and the party's, attention had moved on. There was a crucial party congress and a dangerous rebellion at Kronstadt to be dealt with.

The Tenth Congress and after: Lenin's executive secretary

Once the main White bogeyman had been dispatched to the dustbin of history in 1920 the winding down of the Civil War did not bring stability and security to Soviet Russia. Quite the reverse. Internal tensions within Soviet territory, which had been held back during the fighting for fear of endangering the whole revolution, burst into the open as the White threat receded. There were pressures inside and outside the party. A series of peasant uprisings threatened the 'victorious' Soviet regime. Within the party, groups with a variety of agendas began to emerge. The conjuncture was still very dangerous. In Western Siberia and the province of Tambov serious peasant uprisings, largely protesting about the wartime policy of forced grain requisitioning, broke out. Serious military force was needed to repress them. Tukhachevsky was put in charge of restoring Soviet order in Tambov. His first campaign was repulsed but there was no underestimation of the peasants second time around and the uprising was ruthlessly put down.

Nonetheless, the peasants gained the political and economic victory in that, at the Tenth Party Congress (8–16 March 1921), grain requisitioning was abandoned and replaced by a tax on produce to be paid in kind, that is, by transferring a proportion of the produce to the state. This was an unpopular move for many within the party as it seemed to be a concession too far to the peasantry, who had few friends in the Communist Party. Stalin himself seems to have been sceptical but, not least out of loyalty to Lenin, he helped the key resolution to get through the Congress.

Much else was troubling certain members of the party. There was a debate about the militarization of labour and the nature of the new trade unions which pitted Stalin against Trotsky. A group who called themselves the Workers' Opposition were among the first to protest that the party was sacrificing working-class representation for bureaucratic control. There was also a radical wing reflecting the views of the earlier Left Communists who believed the revolution should be deepened in Russia and spread to the rest of Europe at all costs.

1921 brought peace, or, more precisely, silence and exhaustion, and a series of crucial decisions at the Tenth Party Congress, including a partial return to a market economy, the so-called New Economic Policy. It also brought consolidation of Soviet rule in the country by not only reinforcing the party monopoly of power but tightening up on dissent within the party. In the broad sense, 1921–1922 was a defining moment. The party suppressed all revolts, including the painfully symbolic rebellion in what had been a heartland of soviet revolution in 1917, Kronstadt, which broke out as the Congress was meeting. Delegates went directly from the conference hall in Moscow to participate in the suppression. The Congress adopted a new direction, the New Economic Policy. Discipline within the party was tightened through a Ban on Factions which meant members could not form groups to press for policy modifications. A series of new measures were adopted in the months after the Congress broke up. Cultural diversity was controlled more closely through expanding censorship, controlling publishing and other cultural outlets, ending the last vestiges of university independence and expelling some 250 intellectuals deemed to be incorrigibly opposed to the construction of socialism as envisaged by the party leaders.[62] The 'temporary' political police, the Cheka, became permanent under the first of several changes of name. It became the State Political Administration, known as the GPU from its acronym in Russian.

In many ways, this moment marks the end of the revolution to the extent that the party had defeated its immediate enemies, dispersed all other political organizations and was unchallenged in its one-party state. The revolutionary energies of the masses, despite their re-emergence in Tambov, Kronstadt and other strikes and rebellions, were spent. The protestors were worn out by struggle and the very economic exhaustion against which they were protesting, which had been brought on by the dreadful sequence of world and civil war, hunger, epidemics and industrial collapse. A period of recuperation was necessary all round.[63] This even applied personally to Stalin who, in late May 1921, was ordered by the party to take a convalescent break. He went off to the spa town of Nalchik in his beloved Caucasus. This was a tough assignment for the workaholic Stalin and he cut it short at the end of June to engage in local work in Tiflis, hoping to stay below Lenin's radar. In this he failed and through July Lenin persistently pursued the issue. He even threatened to write to Stalin's doctor to see if Stalin really was ready to resume work. At Lenin's insistence, Stalin returned, once more to Nalchik in mid-July, finally returning to Moscow on 8 August.

Lenin's concern clearly indicated how close he was to Stalin and how important it was to him to have a fit Stalin by his side in the struggle. Indeed, Stalin's actions had been invaluable, not least in ensuring a compliant Tenth Congress. With a variety of opposition groups eager to influence the meeting, Lenin feared he might not get the support he needed. It is unthinkable, looking back, that a party congress would fail to support him but the key insurance of his predominance came through Stalin. As a leading member of the party's Organization Bureau (Orgburo) he was able to supervise the processes of election of delegates and checking of credentials. We do not know directly how much he changed the complexion of the membership of the congress but it certainly helped Lenin, who had been doing back of the envelope calculations of his support in the run up to the main votes in the congress. Manipulative or not, it was the case that many of the most militant delegates were among the first to depart the congress for Kronstadt, even before the votes were taken on central issues like the tax in kind. This made the passage of such a controversial decree that much easier. Stalin was developing a new talent as Lenin's fixer. He soon began to use the same approach in his own favour.

In these early months of 1921 Stalin's own interests of nationalities and trade unions had absorbed his attention. Both areas had major significance for Stalin's continuing development. In the sphere of trade unions the main target of his wrath was Trotsky who was advocating the very thing Stalin himself had already utilized – the militarization of labour. Now, in late 1920 and early 1921, he argued that the whole concept confused peasant issues and proletarian issues. In an important article entitled 'Our Disagreements' Stalin outlined the correctness of his position and what he saw as the errors of Trotsky.[64] In Stalin's words 'Our disagreements are about questions of the means by which to strengthen labour discipline in the working class.' As he saw it 'There are two methods: the method of coercion (the military method), and the method of persuasion (the trade-union method).' Coercion was chosen because the peasants predominated in the party and peasants, in words portending the Stalinist future, 'can, and must, be compelled to fight for socialism by employing methods of coercion'. Trade unions were the preserve, by and large, of the working class and 'in contrast to the army, the working class is a homogeneous social sphere; its economic position disposes it towards socialism, it is easily influenced by communist agitation, it voluntarily organizes in trade unions and, as a consequence of all this, constitutes the foundation, the salt of the earth, of the Soviet state.'[65] Here is yet another re-statement of Stalin's deeply ingrained workerism and his profound mistrust of peasants. Though Stalin's own contribution to the debate is significant more for what it tells us about Stalin than it is for impact on the discussion, Trotsky, as so often, could not rouse sufficient support for his plan among party members. Lenin's opposition, rather than Stalin's, was crucial and Trotsky was forced to drop the issue.

When it came to nationalities it was, significantly, issues from the Caucasus which were the main focus of Stalin's attention at this time. As Soviet power was restored or extended to the area, so it became possible for Stalin to return to his old haunts. He was the natural choice for Lenin to send as an envoy to examine the situation at close quarters. On 16 October 1921 he set off for a month-long investigative tour of Rostov-on-Don, Vladika-vkaz, Baku and Temir-Khan-Shura (Dagestan). He was unable to return to Georgia or Armenia. The former was in Menshevik hands. Armenia, though, declared itself to be a Soviet republic in late November shortly after his return. He gave an interview to *Pravda* on 30 November in which he summarized the situation there. Perhaps surprisingly, Stalin analysed the situation in terms of the world revolution. The Caucasus, he argued, was vital to the revolution not only because of its oil but also because of 'its supremely important roads into the heart of Asia'. The Entente (Britain and France) still coveted the region and con-trolled Constantinople – 'the key to the Black Sea' – but its grip was weakening there and elsewhere. He was especially contemp-tuous of his old foes, the Georgian Mensheviks whom he described as 'bankrupt social-innkeepers'. 'Small wonder', he continued, that Kautsky, the chief opportunist, 'the putrefying leader of the moribund Second International, has found an asylum in this musty Georgia that is enmeshed in the net of the Entente'. Georgia, he concluded, was 'at its last gasp . . . It is scarcely to be doubted that the Entente will abandon Georgia at a moment of difficulty, just as it abandoned Armenia.' He ended with an internationalist flourish: 'one thing is certain, and that is that the struggle for the emancipation of the colonies, begun several years ago, will intensify in spite of everything, that Russia, the acknowledged standard-bearer of this struggle, will support those who champion it with every available means, and that this struggle will lead to victory . . . Testimony to this is the revolu-tion that is flaring up in the West and the growing might of Soviet Russia.'[66]

Just four days later, in another *Pravda* article, he was able to welcome Armenia into the Soviet family in extravagant terms:

> Neither the false assurances of Britain, the 'ancient protector' of Armenian interests, nor Wilson's celebrated fourteen points, nor yet the ostentatious promises of the League of Nations, with its 'mandate' for the administration of Armenia, had saved (or could save!) the Armenians from massacre and physical extermination. Only the idea of Soviet power has brought Armenia peace and the possibility of national

renovation . . . The age-old enmity between Armenia and the surrounding Muslim peoples has been dispelled at one stroke by the establishment of fraternal solidarity between the working people of Armenia, Turkey and Azerbaijan. Let it be known to all concerned that the so-called Armenian 'problem', over which the old wolves of imperialist diplomacy racked their brains in vain, only Soviet power has proved capable of solving.[67]

These were not the words of someone who had no interest in international affairs, quite the opposite. The local situation, as Stalin saw it, was only one aspect of a global struggle. It also showed that, in Stalin's mind, Soviet power and international revolution were not alternatives, they were parts of one process.

Although he was not directly involved, Stalin's old associate and fellow Georgian, Sergo Ordzhonikidze, led the political and military assault on Georgia's 'social innkeepers'. The struggle was bitter.[68] On 15 February the Red Army invaded Georgia. Tiflis was taken ten days later. In just over a month all but a few pockets of guerrilla resistance were overcome and the Menshevik government fled. Even so, Lenin was surprisingly conciliatory and shocked Ordzhonikidze and other leaders on the spot by warning them that it would be best to engage in compromise with any of the Georgian leaders, like Noi Zhordania, who might be favourable to working in the context of a Soviet Georgia and not to replicate the Russian model. He wrote:

> there is need for a special policy of concessions with regard to the Georgian intelligentsia and small merchants. It should be realised that it is not only imprudent to nationalise them, but that there is even need for certain sacrifices in order to improve their position and enable them to continue their small trade.
>
> . . . it is of tremendous importance to devise an acceptable compromise for a bloc with Jordania or similar Georgian Mensheviks, who before the uprising had not been absolutely opposed to the idea of Soviet power in Georgia on certain terms.

> Please bear in mind that Georgia's domestic and interna-
> tional positions both require that her Communists should
> avoid any mechanical copying of the Russian pattern. They
> must skilfully work out their own flexible tactics, based on
> bigger concessions to all the petty-bourgeois elements.

Perhaps Lenin had a soft spot for 'social innkeepers'! In any case
his words fell on deaf ears. When Stalin arrived in June for a
key party meeting he was, according to one eyewitness report,
heckled at a public meeting of the very railwaymen among whom
he had begun his political career. He was accused of being a
renegade and a traitor. A veteran Menshevik asked him 'Why
have you destroyed Georgia? How will you atone for it?'[69] Stalin
appeared to be shocked at the reception and was ushered away
by his Cheka security detachment. Obviously angry to have been
publically humiliated, he fiercely tore a strip off those who had
exposed him to it. Later at a party meeting on 6 July, he emphasized the need for the local party to 'stamp out the hydra of
nationalism'.[70]

It took several more years before full control was enforced.[71]
Even then the cost was high. The final uprisings in 1924 may
have cost 4000 lives in the fighting. More ominously, under the
authority of the rising star of Soviet repression, Lavrentii Beria,
there are said to have been 7000 to 10,000 prisoners executed
and some 20,000 deported.[72] The dreadful practice of massacre
as a political tool, which emerged on all sides during the Civil
War, was becoming institutionalized. The imprint of Caucasian
ferocity was seeping into regular Soviet practice.[73]

The harrowing of Georgia was not down to Stalin personally
but he does not appear to have objected although there were critics
in Moscow who suggested that maybe 'excessive' force had been
used.[74] However, had Lenin's advice to Ordzhonikidze been followed, there would probably not have been such a terrible outcome.
Though we do not know exactly why Lenin's words were ignored
(though we can speculate that those in the firing line in Georgia
not only had their own scores to settle but may have believed
Lenin was too far away to really know what was right) this terrible event was a forerunner of an important element in Stalin's
career. Stalin, as we have seen, could get things badly wrong, but

with Lenin around he had a guiding star to follow. The weaker Lenin himself became after his series of strokes began in 1922, the weaker his ability to haul Stalin back on track. Once Lenin died, Stalin had no respected higher authority to rein in his worst errors. But as far as Georgia was concerned, even after the 1921 campaign, it still had an important part to play in Stalin's career and in his relationship with Lenin as we shall see.

For the time being, however, Stalin's relationship to Lenin remained strong and it was no surprise when, on 3 April 1922, Lenin proposed him for the post of general secretary of the party. In effect, Stalin, although he had accumulated many responsibilities, had been performing a general function of this kind since the end of the main battles of the Civil War. He had been a key trouble-shooter in many areas from economic reconstruction, especially railways, to technical education. He had been Lenin's eyes and ears in far-flung outposts of the revolution like the Caucasus which Lenin could not personally visit. He had been Lenin's fixer when it came to controlling the party through its membership and meetings. In his appointment as general secretary, Stalin had reached the highest formal point of his career. Who, exactly, was Stalin by early 1922?

First of all, there had been no sign of a 'monstrous' Stalin by then. He had been, at times, fierce, opinionated, hard on himself and those around him but no more so than many others in the leadership. He was still a 'normal' Bolshevik. Second, the link to Lenin remained central to his advancement in the party and, clearly, Lenin was still pleased with the work of his 'splendid Georgian'.[75] Third, some basic alliances and enmities had emerged through these years. There is a famous cartoon by David Levine of Stalin as generalissimo in a group pose with his fellow leaders, but Stalin is the only one with a head. The rest have been decapitated. One of the darkest elements of Stalin's life and career is his acquiescence and initiative in the imprisonment and execution of former colleagues and acquaintances. But, contrary to popular belief, Stalin did not touch his immediate allies. By 1922, he had formed an entourage of like-minded, 'get-things-done-and-sort-the-niceties-out-later' Bolsheviks like himself. Two groups, in particular, had formed. One was based on his Civil War associates such as Budyonny, Voroshilov, Egorov and others.

Even though they were responsible for great errors, not least at the outset of World War II, none of them was touched throughout their lives. They were retired or kicked upstairs. The second group came from his Georgian allies such as Ordzhonikidze and, later, Beria. They, too, remained in his favour throughout. Others were added later – Kaganovich, Molotov and generals like Zhukov, Rokossovsky and Timoshenko.[76] At the same time, enduring enmities had already formed. Obviously Stalin and Trotsky detested each other and what they stood for, though working relationships were not as universally acrimonious as is often believed. Others, like Kamenev, Zinoviev and Bukharin, while not yet enemies, were certainly not associates of Stalin though he did work closely with Bukharin through the twenties and even beyond Bukharin's fall from leadership. Tukhachevsky's position was ambiguous. He appeared to be fairly close to Stalin but the Warsaw debacle seems to have created a wedge between them with Stalin blaming Tukhachevsky's egoism for the defeat. In this sense the code of Georgian honour held true. A chief was loyal to those loyal to him, but a betrayal, though it might be hidden for reasons of expediency, would never be forgotten. Indeed, in a famous quotation recorded by Trotsky on hearsay from Kamenev, he once made this explicit. Asked what he enjoyed most Stalin replied 'The greatest delight is to mark one's enemy, prepare everything, avenge oneself thoroughly, and then go to sleep.'[77] In quite what spirit Stalin said this, assuming he did, we do not know but, unsurprisingly, it has taken on the role of evidence for the prosecution in psychological interpretations of Stalin. According to Tucker, it was considered as 'a self-revealing confession' by 'Stalin's party comrades'[78] though no evidence is provided to back this up.

It should not be overlooked, however, that these relationships were not just personal but rooted in temperament and revolutionary outlook. Certain characteristics of 'Stalinism' were already visible. The workers were 'the salt of the earth' and intellectuals and bourgeois specialists untrustworthy and unnecessary. The Russian Revolution had to be defended at all costs but this was necessary for the international revolution as well. Like nearly all Bolshevik leaders, for Stalin, ends justified means and, increasingly, no means were too harsh for dealing with imperialism and capitalism because their utter ruthlessness could only be combated in kind. Like most Bolshevik leaders, including Lenin, Stalin had drifted into the 'administrative-command' style of government, as it was called later in the Gorbachev years. Complete power and authority were deemed to be in the hands of the party leaders and they simply gave orders to move people to achieve objectives. Should they refuse, threats of coercion and ultimately arrest and execution ensured compliance. Mass opinion was only taken into account if it presented problems and needed to be managed, when there were strikes or rebellions, for example. But the Bolshevik style of rule, with Stalin as a leading exponent, was comparable to the military model. The centre decided what was to be done. Officers gave orders. The lower ranks carried them out. During the Civil War the distinction between commanding the armies and commanding society became blurred. But it was not just the military environment which led to this. Bolshevik certainty that they were right and the masses should be educated, their consciousness raised, precluded listening to them to any great degree. Only the 'conscious' had valid opinions and the chief sign of correct consciousness was compliance. When Stalin went on a trouble-shooting expedition he assessed the situation, decided what needed doing and then ordered the appropriate people to do it. This was, however, exactly how Trotsky and the other revolutionary entrepreneurs operated.

Finally, we saw that, in Sukhanov's eyes, Stalin was a 'grey blur'. However, it is incontestable that Stalin was in the forefront of the leadership of the party from the first days of the revolution. While his 'informal' activities as fixer and trouble-shooter outweighed a number of his 'formal' appointments, his collection of posts held underlined his status. He was a member of all the highest party bodies of the period, including the Central Committee, naturally, but also the Politburo, the Revolutionary Defence Council and the Orgburo. He also had his state responsibilities as Commissar for Nationalities and head of the Rabkrin (the Worker-Peasant Inspectorate). In reality, these formal positions were secondary to what he actually did in that, as we have seen, he moved rapidly from field to field rather than spend all day every day dealing with a single portfolio. In fact, this whole style of activity, which was by no means confined to Stalin, was criticized within the leadership. In one instance, at the Eleventh Party Congress in 1922, Preobrazhensky complained that many higher party leaders spread themselves too thinly over a wide range of duties, neglecting their core responsibilities. He even named Stalin, and 'questioned whether any man could carry the work of two commissariats in addition to party responsibilities'. If this was a veiled attack on Stalin, as it may have been since Preobrazhensky was close to Trotsky, it backfired spectacularly in that Lenin came out in full support of Stalin, defending his role in Narkomnats at that moment – of the Caucasian crisis we have just examined – and challenging Preobrazhensky to name another person better suited to the task than Stalin. Similarly, Lenin said Rabkrin was 'a gigantic job' requiring 'a man with authority, otherwise we will bog down and drown in petty intrigues'.[79] This was a powerful show of support by Lenin for his protégé. In August 1918 Lenin had called for 'truly *hard people*' to be charged with the toughest tasks.[80] His admiration for Stalin was not least because he was one of the hardest. Stalin remained a determined revolutionary above all else.

Unsurprisingly, it has been argued that Stalin had been driven by personal ambition to accumulate posts and allies. For one distinguished analyst, where Trotsky devoted himself single-mindedly to his responsibilities, 'Stalin combined his war work with politics' so that this was 'the formative period of the Stalin faction . . . Trotsky emerged from the war with much glory and little power, Stalin emerged with little glory and much power'.[81] It would be naive to think Stalin ignored the question of power but it seems at least as likely to say that, in the incredible whirl of securing the revolution against a vast array of enemies, what stands out in Stalin's career is his devotion to Lenin and the cause of revolution, not personal dominance. It may be that, particularly once Lenin was forced by ill health to withdraw from the political front line and eventually die, in January 1924, the two elements, revolutionary commitment and personal power, began to coalesce. That is an issue to which we must now turn. But it seems likely that, at the moment he became general secretary in April 1922, Stalin certainly had a strong personality but had still not manifested any particular pathologies or strong psychological 'abnormalities'. From that point of view he was still a Bolshevik like any other. Stalin had not yet become Stalin. Would he?

Notes

1 Sukhanov, N.N. (1967) *The Russian Revolution: An Eyewitness Account*, vol 1, London, Oxford University Press, pp229–230.
2 Slusser, R.M. (1987) *Stalin in October: The Man Who Missed the Revolution*, Baltimore, MD, Johns Hopkins University Press.
3 The wartime name of St. Petersburg, which was changed to sound more Russian than German.
4 Svetlana, A. (1989) *Only One Year*, New York, Random House, pp381–382.
5 Alliluyev, S. and Alliluyev, A. (1968) *The Alliluyev Memoirs*, New York and London, G.P. Putnam, p190.
6 Montefiore, S. (2004) *At the Court of the Red Tsar*, Harmondsworth, Penguin, p31.
7 Medvedev, R. (1972) *Let History Judge*, New York and London, Oxford University Press, p7.
8 Alliluyev and Alliluyev (1968), p186.
9 Ibid, p187.
10 Ibid, p189. Although these memoirs were published in 1946 at the height of the Stalin cult and are overflowing with affection for him, they aroused the wrath of the ageing dictator. Anna, his sister-in-law, was arrested in 1948 and only released in 1954 after Stalin's death. It is not clear exactly why Stalin objected to them. Most likely the easy familiarity, some of the details – for instance, she quotes him saying his withered arm kept him out of the Tsar's army when, officially, it was his revolutionary ideals – or maybe perceived or real hidden barbs as in the descriptions above which show potential cruelty as well as humour. Or it may be that he simply thought she had betrayed him mafia-style by publishing without his knowledge or consent. In *Twenty Letters* Anna's niece, Stalin's daughter Svetlana, describes Stalin exploding with rage on reading Anna's writings.
11 There are many accounts of the February Revolution. See, for example, Read, C. (2013) *War and Revolution in Russia 1914–1922*, London and New York, Houndmills Press, which also has references to other accounts.
12 Trotsky, L. (1973) *My Life: An Attempt at Autobiography*, Harmondsworth, Penguin, p343, or MIA, http://www.marxists.org/archive/trotsky/1930/mylife/ch28.htm.
13 Ibid.
14 Stalin, J.V. (1954) 'The Soviets of Workers' and Soldiers' Deputies', *Pravda*, 14 March 1917, in *CW*, vol 3, or MIA, http://www.marxists.org/reference/archive/stalin/works/1917/03/14.htm.

15   Stalin, J. V. (1954) 'Bidding for Ministerial Portfolios', 16 March 1917, *CW*, vol 3, *Moscow*, or MIA, http://www.marxists.org/reference/ archive/stalin/works/1917/03/16–2.htm.

16   Stalin, J. V. (1954) 'Conditions for the Victory of the Russian Revolution', *Pravda*, 18 March 1917, *CW*, vol 3, *Moscow*, or MIA, http://www.marxists.org/reference/archive/stalin/works/1917/ 03/18.htm.

17   Stalin, J. V. (1954) 'National Disabilities', *Pravda*, 25 March 1917, in *CW*, vol 3, *Moscow*, or MIA, http://www.marxists.org/reference/ archive/stalin/works/1917/03/25.htm.

18   Lenin V, I., 'The Tasks of the Proletariat in the Present Revolution: The April Theses', *CW*, vol 24, p19, or MIA, https://www.marxists.org/ archive/lenin/works/1917/apr/04.htm.

19   Officially the Seventh Party Conference held in Petrograd from 24– 29 April.

20   *CW*, vol 3, 'Report on the National Question', or MIA, http://www. marxists.org/reference/archive/stalin/works/1917/04/24.htm.

21   *CW*, vol 3, 'Reply to the Discussion of the National Question', or MIA, http://www.marxists.org/reference/archive/stalin/works/1917/04/24. htm. Perhaps the Finnish workers regretted what they wished for. Separation from Russia opened them to repression from their own White generals and the outcome of the Finnish Civil War was a massacre of workers by the victorious generals.

22   Lenin V.I., 'The Political Situation: Four Theses' *CW*, vol 25, p180, or MIA, https://www.marxists.org/archive/lenin/works/1917/jul/10b.htm.

23   *CW*, vol 3, and MIA, https://www.marxists.org/reference/archive/ stalin/works/1917/07/16.htm.

24   The story of the October Revolution has been told many times and from many angles. See, in particular, Wade, R. (2002) *The Russian Revolution 1917*, Cambridge, Cambridge University Press; Daniel, R.V. (1967) *Red October*, New York, Charles Scribner's Sons; and Read, C. (2013) *War and Revolution in Russia 1914–22*, London and New York, Palgrave Macmillan.

25   Smele, J. (2015) *The 'Russian' Civil Wars 1916–1926: Ten Years That Shook the World*, London, Oxford University Press.

26   W. S. Gilbert's 1878 description of the British House of Lords in the comic operetta *HMS Pinafore*.

27   Mstislavsky, S. M. (1958) *Nakanune. 1917 God*, Moscow, Foreign Languages Publishing House.

28   See Radkey, O. H. (1976) *The Unknown Civil War in Soviet Russia: A Study of the Green Movement in the Tambov Region 1920–1921*, Stanford, CA, Stanford University Press; and Landis, E. (2008) *Bandits and Partisans: The Antonov Movement in the Russian Civil War*, Cambridge, Cambridge University Press.

29   Brovkin, V. (1994) *Beyond the Front Lines of Civil War*, Princeton, NJ, Princeton University Press; and Pirani, S. (2008) *The Russian*

Revolution in Retreat 1920–24: Soviet Workers and the New Communist Elite, London, Routledge.

30 Figes, O. (1989) *Peasant Russia, Civil War: The Volga Countryside in Revolution 1917–21*, Oxford, Oxford University Press; Raleigh, D. (2008) *Experiencing Russia's Civil War: Politics, Society and Revolutionary Culture in Saratov 1917–22*, Princeton, NJ, Princeton University Press; Badcock, S. (2007) *Politics and the People in Revolutionary Russia: A Provincial History*, Cambridge, Cambridge University Press; and Retish, A. (2008) *Russia's Peasants in Revolution and Civil War: Citizenship, Identity and the Creation of the Soviet State 1914–22*, Cambridge, Cambridge University Press.

31 Hickey, M. C. (1996) 'Local Government and State Authority in the Provinces: Smolensk, February–June 1917', *Slavic Review*, 55 (4), pp863–881. Hickey, M. C. (1996) 'Peasant Autonomy, Soviet Power and Land Redistribution in Smolensk Province, November 1917–May 1918', *Revolutionary Russia*, 9 (1), pp19–32. Karsch, S. (2006), *Die Bolschewistische Machtgreiferung im Gouvernement Voronez 1917–22*, Stuttgart, David Brown Book Company.

32 Several volumes of the emerging series *Russia's Great War and Revolution* touch on issues of the nationalities and civil war. One has already been published: Lohr, E., Tolz, V., Semyonov, A. and von Hagen, M. (eds) (2014) *The Empire and Nationalism at War*, Bloomington, IN, Slavica Publishers. The country's official title was the RSFSR, the Russian Soviet Federal Socialist Republic, until the name USSR, the Union of Soviet Socialist Republics, was adopted on 31 December 1922.

33 Badcock, S., Novikova, L. and Retish, A. (2016) *Russia's Home Front in War and Revolution, 1914–22, Book 1: Russia's Revolution in Regional Perspective*, in the *Russia's Great War and Revolution* series, Bloomington, IN, Slavica; and Read, C. (1996) *From Tsar to Soviets: The Russian People and Their Revolution 1917–21*, London and New York, Oxford University Press, p283.

34 Smele, J. (2016) *The 'Russian' Civil Wars, 1916–26* London and New York, Hurst/Oxford University Press.

35 For example, a group of former Kadet liberals became so-called National Bolsheviks.

36 Srebrenica marked the lowest point of recent European history. Over 8000 Bosnians, mostly men of fighting age, were massacred by Bosnian Serb 'neighbours' in 1999.

37 Markevich, A. and Harrison, M. (2017) 'The Economy' in *Russia's Home Front 1914–22: Book 3 National Disintegration and Re-Integration*, in the *Russia's Great War and Revolution* series, Bloomington, IN, Slavica.

38 Ibid.

39 Read, C. (2013) *War and Revolution in Russia 1914–22*, London, Palgrave Macmillan, pp124–126.

40 CW, vol 4, pp75–76.

41 In the final paragraphs of the first section of 'Immediate Tasks of the Soviet Government' Lenin makes it clear he believes the 'most acute phase' of civil war is over and the party has shown it has been 'able to win the civil war'. See MIA, https://www.marxists.org/archive/lenin/works/1918/mar/x03.htm.

42 CW, vol 4, MIA, http://www.marxists.org/reference/archive/stalin/works/1918/06/07.htm.

43 The Russian term for a board, here boards set up to direct the railways.

44 The standard Russian measure of weight equivalent to about 36 pounds.

45 CW, vol 4, MIA, http://www.marxists.org/reference/archive/stalin/works/1918/07/10.htm.

46 Voroshilov, K. E. (1951), *Stalin and the Armed Forces of the USSR*, Moscow, pp18–19, quoted in Tucker (1973), p191.

47 CW, vol 4, MIA, http://www.marxists.org/reference/archive/stalin/works/1918/07/07.htm.

48 Trotsky, L. (1975) *My Life*, Harmondsworth, Penguin, p418.

49 Ibid, p415. Gusev was a leading party figure on the Eastern Front with Trotsky but later came to support Stalin in the party disputes of the 1920s.

50 CW, vol 4, MIA, http://www.marxists.org/reference/archive/stalin/works/1918/09/06.htm.

51 CW, vol 4, MIA, http://www.marxists.org/reference/archive/stalin/works/1918/09/21.htm.

52 Trotsky, L. (1969) *Stalin. Volume Two: The Revolutionary in Power*, London, Panther History, p74.

53 Quoted by Medvedev, R. (1972) *Let History Judge: The Origins and Consequences of Stalinism*, New York, Alfred A. Knopf, p14.

54 CW, vol 4, MIA, http://www.marxists.org/reference/archive/stalin/works/1919/03/21.htm.

55 *Pravda*, 86, 23 April 1920. CW, vol 4, MIA, https://www.marxists.org/reference/archive/stalin/works/1920/04/23.htm.

56 Ibid.

57 Smele, Chapter 4.

58 This was Churchill's (1931) phrase from *The World Crisis, Volume 5: The Aftermath*, London, Hurst (2016), p73. Churchill applied it to Lenin in his 'sealed' train.

59 Historians such as Arno Meyer and W. A. Williams have seen the origin of the Cold War itself emerging at and around the Versailles Conference of 1919. A *cordon sanitaire*, originally a French term, is a boundary set up to contain a disease within an already infected area.

60 Smele is the soundest, most balanced, up-to-date account.

61 Memorably recounted in Isaac Babel's book of stories entitled *Red Cavalry*.

62 For more on this episode see Read (1990), pp.181–2 and Finkel (2007), pp.151–215.

63 For more on the politics of this moment see Read (1996), pp.278–282; Read, (2013), pp.195–217 and Pirani, S. (2008).

64 Stalin, J.V. (1921) 'Our Disagreements', *Pravda*, 12, 19 January, reprinted in *CW*, vol 5, and MIA, http://www.marxists.org/reference/archive/stalin/works/1921/01/05.htm.

65 Ibid.

66 Stalin, J.V. (1920) 'The Situation in the Caucasus', *Pravda*, 269, 30 November. *CW*, vol 4, and MIA, http://www.marxists.org/reference/archive/stalin/works/1920/11/30.htm.

67 Stalin, J.V. (1920) 'Long Live Soviet Armenia', *Pravda*, 273, 4 December. *CW*, vol 4, MIA, http://www.marxists.org/reference/archive/stalin/works/1920/12/04.htm.

68 Jones, Stephen F. (ed) (2014) *The Making of Modern Georgia (1918–2012)*, London and New York, Routledge. Excellent brief account in Tucker, R. (1974) *Stalin as Revolutionary 1879–1929: A Study in History and Personality*, London, Chatto & Windus, pp224–238.

69 Lang, D. (1962) *A Modern History of Soviet Georgia*, London, Weidenfeld & Nicolson, pp238–239.

70 Tucker (1974), p237.

71 An excellent and up-to-date account of these tragic struggles can be found in Smele (2016), Chapter 4.

72 Ibid.

73 According to Beria's biographer, Amy Knight, the episode 'served as Beria's final induction into the business of mass killing'. Knight, A. (1993) *Beria: Stalin's First Lieutenant*, Princeton, NJ, Princeton University Press, pp32–34.

74 Smele (2016), Chapter 4.

75 Lenin, V.I. (1913) *Letter to Maxim Gorky*, quoted in Trotsky, L. *Stalin*, New York (1941), p.158.

76 Fitzpatrick, S. (2015) 'V komande Stalina' ('On Stalin's Team') German Historical Institute, Moscow, *Soviet History Discussion Papers No 6*, 22 April 2015, http://www.perspectivia.net/news/soviet-history-discussion-papers-6–2015; Fitzpatrick, S. (2015) *On Stalin's Team: The Years of Living Dangerously in Soviet Politics*, Princeton, NJ, Princeton University Press, develops this theme.

77 Trotsky, L. (1963) *Diary in Exile: 1935*, New York, Athenaeum, p64.

78 Tucker (1974), p211.

79 Ibid, p208.

80 Pipes, R. (ed) (1996) *The Unknown Lenin: From the Secret Archive*, New Haven, CT, Yale University Press, p50 (Lenin's emphasis).

81 Tucker (1974), p209.

3   Filling Lenin's shoes

On the brink of catastrophe?

On 26 May 1922 the foundations of Stalin's life began to shift. On that day Lenin suffered his first stroke. It may be that Lenin had had some inkling that such a thing was likely,[1] but his colleagues were taken by surprise. At the personal level, there was great consternation among Lenin's comrades. Stalin and others were distraught at the thought of losing the great helmsman of the party. At the political level, Lenin's illness brought the question of succession to the very top of the agenda. The urgency was doubled in December when Lenin had another, more serious, stroke and withdrew from the public gaze for the remaining 14 months of his life.

It was in these crucial weeks and months of Lenin's twilight that relations between Stalin and Lenin hit their lowest ebb. Nothing prior to these weeks had signified a potential breakdown. Stalin had continued to be Lenin's most trusted go-between liaising between Lenin and the other party leaders. Stalin had the most frequent access to Lenin and it was Stalin whom Lenin approached with his most intimate request – that Stalin should bring him a phial of poison so that, when the moment came, Lenin could end his own life. Stalin refused and reported Lenin's request to the Central Committee.

However, a lifetime of adulation of Lenin and of dependence on his goodwill and direct support, which had brought Stalin up to the very summit of the party, was almost irreparably damaged. The crisis had three elements to it. First, the whole Central

Committee was concerned about Lenin, personally and politically. Second, stories of the misbehaviour of Stalin and his associates in the invasion of Georgia, which we encountered in the previous chapter, came to Lenin's attention. Third, an apparently trivial but almost fatal argument between Stalin and Lenin's wife Nadezhda Krupskaya brought a threat that Lenin would break off relations between himself and Stalin. As we have seen in other cases, the interpretation of key events by Trotsky has been taken up, in its main directions, by mainstream Western historians and became the consensus. In it, Trotsky maintains that Lenin was only prevented by a deepening of his illness from destroying Stalin's career and establishing Trotsky as his anointed successor.[2] As is frequently the case with Trotsky there is a core of truth embellished with exaggeration. Examining each of the three aspects in turn shows a more complicated picture.

Lenin's enforced withdrawal from the hurly-burly of daily political life developed gradually after his first stroke. Doctors kept urging him to take considerable amounts of rest and not to involve himself in political issues which could fatally overexcite him. Obviously, for a workaholic political animal like Lenin, these were grievously difficult injunctions to keep and he was forever going further than the doctors advised. Nonetheless, especially after his turn for the worse in December, he had good days, permitting a little work, and bad days when he could do none. By then, he was also plagued by headaches, forgetfulness and, as his secretary L. A. Fotieva put it on 10 February 1923, Lenin 'Looks tired, speaks with great difficulty, losing the thread of his thoughts and confusing words. Compress on his head.'[3] A Lenin in this state was recognized by his associates as a potential danger to them all. There was no knowing what he would say next and there was a fear that, since his prestige was still as great as ever, he could complicate the plans and policies of the Central Committee and the Sovnarkom. From his first convalescence after the 26 May episode, the Central Committee tried to control Lenin's access to information, limit his hours of work and vet his output. As his closest associate and assistant, Stalin was the chief intermediary. He had the difficult task of preventing Lenin from sabotaging the Central Committee. Lenin himself resented the controls and used various stratagems to subvert them. In particular, his household of Krupskaya, his sisters and his secretaries were all drawn into confidential arrangements to get him access to items the Central Committee wanted to keep away from him.

He also wrote key items he entrusted to them for secrecy, away from the eyes of his political associates. In this category the most important were his observations on the revolution – its strengths and weaknesses – and, more potentially explosive – his views on the personalities of those who would be likely to succeed him. Together these items are known as Lenin's last testament. Our task is to note how seriously they affected Stalin; but a few general points need to be made. Perhaps the most important is that the whole content of the testament is almost un-Leninlike in being imperceptive, tentative and contradictory.

The general prescriptions show almost a complacency about the state of the revolution. One of the elements of the testament is a review of Sukhanov's memoirs, the ones in which Stalin is described as a 'grey blur', which were hot off the Berlin émigré presses in 1922. Lenin ignores the detail but ridicules Sukhanov's main point, that the revolution was, in Marxist terms, premature – that is, it occurred before conditions were 'ripe' for the establishment of a Marxist version of a socialist society. The distortions of the revolution – identified by Lenin himself, in 1919, as 'bureaucracy and profiteering'[4] – arguably arose from this root. Lenin, however, would not hear of such things. Instead, he said, the Russian Revolution had produced preconditions for socialism like control of the state and from that basis the other economic and social preconditions could be nurtured. Lenin remained critical of bureaucracy in his last testament but did not equate it with this very issue identified by Sukhanov of having a revolution led by the state, in effect a revolution 'from above'. Lenin's solution, in his last ever article 'Better Fewer but Better' and in his comments about the Central Committee was that certain parts of the bureaucracy should be smaller, but the Central Committee should be much larger. Neither solution seemed to match the vastness of the problem. Trotsky, too, railed against bureaucracy but he, no more than Lenin, was prepared to identify or reform the real cause – what was coming to be called 'the leading role of the party'. This is an enormous debate but from our perspective, based on almost 100 years of hindsight, the weight of the argument lies with Sukhanov rather than Lenin and Trotsky. The forces for constructing socialism in the USSR were too weak, in the long run, and the basic Marxist prerequisites for a successful revolution, such as an advanced working class, a highly developed capitalist economy which was near to exhausting its potential and what Marx called 'an abundance of products', were all either weak or absent. Ironically, Marxism was essentially about distribution in a highly developed economy while the Soviet system from early on (March 1918) was centred on achieving the first stages of industrial growth – the primary accumulation of capital – through productionism, a concept to which we will return in greater detail below.

Lenin's testament was not, however, only about prescriptions for general policy. He also included more specific guidance about the burning issue of succession. Who did Lenin believe to be capable of filling his shoes? Lenin's initial comments, in the 'Letter to the Congress', meant to establish guidelines for the party when it had to face life without him, seem to reflect the blindingly obvious and omit any real solution. Fearing a split would arise out of the succession struggle he points to the differences between Stalin and Trotsky, 'the two outstanding leaders of the present Central Committee'. To say that 'I think relations between them make up the greater part of the danger of a split' is hardly original or perceptive. Anyone in the leadership would have said the same. Lenin's solution – 'increasing the number of Central Committee members to 50 or 100' – seems woefully inadequate and suggests that even then (24 December 1922), Lenin's brain was not firing on all cylinders.

Neither Trotsky nor Stalin emerge with Lenin's blessing as a successor. Both, despite being the 'outstanding' candidates, have serious flaws:

> Comrade Stalin, having become General Secretary, has unlimited authority concentrated in his hands, and I am not sure whether he will always be capable of using that authority with sufficient caution. Comrade Trotsky, on the other hand, as his struggle against the Central Committee on the question of the People's Commissariat of Communications has already proved, is distinguished not only by outstanding ability. He is

personally perhaps the most capable man in the present Central
Committee, but he has displayed excessive self-assurance and
shown excessive preoccupation with the purely administrative
side of the work.[5]

To say that 'These two qualities of the two outstanding leaders
of the present Central Committee can inadvertently lead to a
split, and if our Party does not take steps to avert this, the split
may come unexpectedly'[6] seems wholly inadequate to the potential crisis. However, events conspired to lead Lenin to tighten up
his criticism of Stalin when, under a degree of pressure and spin
from Trotsky, he heard of two more issues reflecting badly on
Stalin. These were the Georgian Affair and Stalin's argument
with Krupskaya.

Unsurprisingly, the realities of the so-called Georgian Affair
are rather murky from the point of view of what actually happened and from the point of view of what Lenin knew about it
and when.[7] At the heart of it were the supposedly overbearing
attitudes of Stalin and his associate Ordzhonikidze, both Georgian
themselves, at the time of the imposition of Soviet power in Tiflis.
We have already seen that Lenin's uncharacteristic call for restraint
and, if possible, compromise with the Menshevik left in Georgia
had fallen on deaf ears and a rapid and violent campaign of
military suppression had been conducted at Stalin and Ordzhonikidze's command. Tiflis had been taken in ten days (15–25 February 1921) but uprisings were still being cruelly suppressed in
1923 and 1924. As Georgians themselves, Stalin and Ordzhonikidze decided to settle matters for themselves in the 'traditional'
Georgian manner of direct confrontation and threat. Old scores
going back to Stalin's youth and early revolutionary career still
rankled. Why use kid gloves to treat Stalin's oldest and best-
known enemies – the Georgian nationalists and Mensheviks – and
to keep the lesser minions among Georgian Bolsheviks in order?

The underlying issue was nationalism, deemed by Stalin to be
alive and well in the local Bolshevik leadership, and 'Great Russian chauvinism' – the bullying attitude of officials in the tsarist
empire – which Lenin and others identified in the behaviour of
Ordzhonikidze and Stalin. This was ironic in that both of these
'Russian chauvinists' were actually Georgian. Politically, the issue

was about how much autonomy Georgia should have. Local Bolsheviks in Georgia supported the highest degree of autonomy while Stalin and Ordzhonikidze were determined to establish ultimate control from Moscow. Lenin soon realized this was no ordinary spat and set up a commission of enquiry consisting of Dzerzhinsky, the head of the Cheka, who was conveniently on holiday in Batumi at the time, and two other members of the Central Committee. In late November, just as the commission was about to arrive, Ordzhonikidze came to blows with A. Khobakidze, one of the local Bolshevik leaders, who had insulted him. Even though Dzerzhinsky's commission exonerated Stalin and Ordzhonikidze, the ailing Lenin was not convinced. In notes unpublished at the time he said: 'I think that Stalin's haste and his infatuation with pure administration, together with his spite against the notorious 'socialist-nationalism' played a fatal role here. In politics spite generally plays the basest of roles.' Even Dzerzhinsky did not escape censure: 'I also fear that Comrade Dzerzhinsky . . . distinguished himself there by his truly Russian frame of mind . . . and that the impartiality of his whole commission was typified well enough by Ordzhonikidze's "manhandling". I think that no provocation or even insult can justify such Russian manhandling and that Comrade Dzerzhinsky was inexcusably guilty in adopting a light-hearted attitude towards it.' Curiously, none of them was actually Russian but Lenin was not above cliché: 'it is common knowledge that people of other nationalities who have become Russified over-do this Russian frame of mind'.[8]

The accusation of 'spite' or 'malice' is a new one and was obviously very damaging at this delicate point in Lenin's relations with Stalin. It was to get much worse. On 22 December Stalin phoned Lenin's wife, Krupskaya. The issue at stake was that Lenin had made a significant intervention into a currently controversial, though dull-sounding, issue about maintaining the state monopoly on foreign trade even in the conditions of the New Economic Policy (NEP). Trotsky was intriguing with Lenin on this issue. Stalin exploded on the phone to Krupskaya and swore at her because he blamed her for allowing Lenin, so soon after his second stroke, to be involving himself in politics. Krupskaya informed Kamenev of what had happened in dignified terms. She asked to be protected from 'unworthy abuse and threats' and complained that 'I have no time to spend on this stupid squabble.'[9] Some time later Lenin learned of this. It is unclear how. His response, which only came on 5 March, was forthright. He accused Stalin of rudeness (*grubost*). Although, Lenin continued, Krupskaya herself was willing to forget the incident, 'I do not intend to forget so easily what was done against me' since 'what is done against my wife I consider to be against me also'. He demanded Stalin decide if he preferred to take back what he said and apologize 'or whether you prefer to break relations between us'.[10] Krupskaya tried to prevent the note from being delivered but failed. As soon as Stalin saw it he dictated a fulsome apology which was immediately communicated to Lenin.

Some authorities[11] have argued that Lenin had heard of the incident long before he sent the letter. According to one of them[12] Lenin sent the letter to get written confirmation of the incident to add to a dossier he wanted to present to the upcoming Twelfth Party Congress as part of a sustained campaign 'to crush Stalin politically'.[13] The campaign was said to have begun in December when he wrote the 'Letter to the Congress', the centrepiece of his testament. A decisive piece of evidence presented is that on 4 January he tightened up his criticism of Stalin, using the same term '*gruby*' in a postscript to the 'Letter to the Congress', stating:

> Stalin is too rude (*gruby*) and this defect, although quite tolerable in our midst and in dealing among us Communists, becomes intolerable in a General-Secretary. That is why I suggest that the comrades think about a way of removing Stalin from that post and appointing another man in his stead who in all other respects differs from Comrade Stalin in having only one advantage, namely, that of being more tolerant, more loyal, more polite and more considerate to the comrades, less capricious, etc. This circumstance may appear to be a negligible detail. But I think that from the standpoint of safeguards against a split and from the standpoint of what I wrote above about the relationship between Stalin and Trotsky it is not a detail, but it is a detail which can assume decisive importance.[14]

It seems more likely that Lenin, having used the term *gruby* when criticizing Stalin over the Georgian affair, simply repeated it when he heard about the swearing at Krupskaya. In any case, Lenin seems to have over-reacted on both counts. A slap in the face was highly undesirable but hardly unique in party relations and Krupskaya herself seemed to have thought it was not worth breaking relations with Stalin.

This last point also undermines recent interpretations which suggest Krupskaya actually forged the letter. A Russian historian largely favourable to Stalin, Valentin Sakharov, first questioned the authenticity of the testament along these lines. Kotkin has, more cautiously, adopted the view that Krupskaya's role in its production was decisive. However, he also points out that Krupskaya had no reason to favour Trotsky with whom she had had longer and deeper differences than the transient spat with Stalin. Also, why would Lenin's sister, Maria, close to Lenin, Krupskaya and Stalin, have gone along with such an attack? It is unlikely in the extreme. While there is no ultimate proof it seems the anomalies in the testament are most logically explained as a consequence of the conditions in which they were produced. In other words a sick Lenin was not at the height of his powers and his ideas were being filtered piecemeal through the intervention of his secretary, Fotieva, and Krupskaya, Maria Ulyanova and other members of his household. In fact, Kotkin agrees this might be possible – that 'someone knowing Lenin's thoughts, rendered some barely audible but genuine words and gestures into this form' – but favours the interpretation which emphasizes Krupskaya's intervention.[15]

Whatever the precise circumstances of their production, the measures themselves and Lenin's phraseology also seem tentative. Stalin's vulgarity was only a 'minor detail' which might become significant. The sanction, that Stalin should not be general secretary, was a limited one. His other positions, such as membership of Politburo and Central Committee, were not brought into question.

Does all this signify a ten week campaign 'to crush Stalin politically'? It seems most unlikely, not least because Lenin could have been more direct if it were that important. Nonetheless, Trotsky certainly interpreted it as an assault intended to end Stalin's career and we have one other piece of weighty evidence.

According to Trotsky, Fotieva told him Lenin was preparing a 'bomb', as Lenin is said to have called it, in connection with his Georgian policy. He does not mention the row with Krupskaya. He quotes a letter of 5 March, the same day as Lenin's letter to Stalin about the row with Krupskaya, asking Trotsky to present his, Lenin's, position at the Congress and 'take upon yourself the defence of the Georgian case' because 'I cannot trust their impartiality'.[16]

But this, too, seems quite mild and limited to the contentious issue of Georgia, not a general split with Stalin. Overall, the idea that Lenin was only prevented from destroying Stalin by the sad chance that on 9 March he had his third and most disabling stroke which deprived him of the ability to speak, is far from proven. The most likely explanation is that Lenin was very concerned over the Georgian issue, and the precedent it set for the formation of the Soviet constitution, but was not embarking on a belated, full-scale campaign against Stalin, Ordzhonikidze and Dzerzhinsky and their associates. It is also hardly likely that Stalin, who seemed oblivious to any great danger to his career, would not have heard from some source of what was afoot in the gossip-saturated 'village' of the Kremlin, where the shelf-life of 'secrets' could be measured in days rather than months.[17]

Inventing Leninism

After the third stroke Lenin was extremely frail and helpless. He was reduced to a wheelchair or sleigh most of the time but did manage to walk a few paces with the aid of a stick. His speech also returned. Poignantly, in October he felt well enough to take a final trip in his Rolls Royce from his *dacha* in Gorki, a village in the outskirts of Moscow. His destination was the Kremlin in order to make a nostalgic visit to his office. So changed was he that the guard would not let him in at first because he was not recognized and his pass was out of date. It was his last excursion from Gorki. On 21 January 1924, Lenin had a final crisis and died in the presence of Krupskaya, his devoted sister Maria and Bukharin, who just happened to be visiting at the time.

In this final phase of his life he had been protected from all direct political involvement and was kept in the dark about many issues including the growing feud between the Trotsky left and the Stalin centre of the party. His intervention had been too little, too late. Lenin's failure to ensure a smooth succession was one of his biggest errors. He had believed the party was mature enough to look after itself. In reality, events showed exactly how important he still was to the party. In many respects, loyalty to Lenin had been the glue keeping the party together since 1903. The essence of Bolshevism is often described in terms of its policies of being composed of professional revolutionaries, or its supposed rejection of waiting for the 'capitalist' or 'bourgeois' stage of social evolution to work itself out before a revolution was possible or its support for soviets. On all these issues policy changed over the years but the leadership of Lenin remained the rock on which the party was built. If Lenin called for armed insurrection, as in 1905, it became party policy. If he moved on, given the failure of that approach, to replace it with 'the democratic dictatorship of workers and peasants' then, inevitably, the party moved with him.[18] Even more foreboding for the issue of succession, however, was his role in the long series of splits which constituted the history of the party between 1903 and 1917 and even beyond. It was Lenin's leadership which managed those splits and, at times where he was physically remote from the rest of the leadership, during his 1917 strategic retreat to Finland for example, the party fell into disarray. It was only his dramatic return in October that resolved that crisis. After 1917 factiousness grew. Although there were numerous 'oppositions' – the Left Communists, the Workers' Opposition, the Trade Union opposition, the Military Opposition and others – the most powerful tension underlying them was between 'dogmatists' who wanted to implement party policy at all costs, and pragmatists who saw a need to compromise, supposedly for the short term in order to survive. For example, the Left Communists wanted to conduct a revolutionary war and spread the revolution across Europe. Pragmatists, led by Lenin, wanted a kind of 'socialism in one country' to defend the Russian Revolution first and spread it when possible.[19] Only Lenin had the prestige within the party to carry such things off. The Tenth Party Congress was a triumph for him. It adopted the key measure of NEP, namely the adoption of a 'tax-in-kind' which implied limited market restoration. It also banned factions, denounced the Workers' Opposition and, in the persons of many delegates, marched off to Kronstadt to crush the very sailors who had been a crucial support for soviet power in 1917. No one else could have performed such a dizzying series of U-turns. Lenin was the chief prop of party unity. It is no surprise that his declining influence and death was the prelude to the bitterest factionalism yet. How did Stalin navigate through this tempest?

If the loss of Lenin's leadership was devastating for the party it was personally devastating for Stalin. He had been devoted to Lenin from his first contacts – via reading his work – in the Caucasus to the instant apology to Lenin when he threatened to break off relations. Not only that. Stalin himself did not have the judgement and tactical and strategic sense of Lenin. He made big mistakes in Tsaritsyn, in Georgia and elsewhere. Lenin was the only one who could correct him, the only one whom Stalin respected enough to listen to and learn from. Without Lenin's corrective supervision, Stalin could get out of hand, as his forays to Georgia and Azerbaijan in 1921 and 1922 showed. Once Stalin became powerful, by the end of the decade, Stalin's proclivity to uncorrected mistakes became destabilizing. Lenin had not only been Stalin's mentor he had also been his patron and protector. Lenin had got Stalin into the leading circles of the party. How would Stalin fare without him?

Whether by accident or design, Stalin's response was to maintain the link, not only as Lenin's health deteriorated but also beyond the grave. This happened in stages and seems the natural outcome of his long-lasting devotion to Lenin rather than a complex Machiavellian plot. Once again, the Trotsky account needs to be modified. According to him, Stalin sent misleading information to ensure Trotsky would not be present at Lenin's funeral. Stalin, according to Trotsky, could thereby take the initiative in the succession struggle and Trotsky's absence would be interpreted as a snub to the deceased leader. This has been shown not to be the case in a short but detailed and comprehensive study of the incident by Ian Thatcher. Stalin, so the argument goes, did not lie to Trotsky about the date of the funeral. He passed on the information about Lenin's death and funeral arrangements rapidly and accurately to Trotsky who had just arrived on the Black Sea coast at Sukhumi in Georgia. He had been sent there by order of the Central Committee to recuperate from a debilitating illness. According to Trotsky, Stalin told him the funeral would be on 26 January which would not give him time to get back to Moscow. In the event, the funeral was on the 27th. In any case, it would have taken only three days to get back and the original message arrived early on 22 January. It seems likely that Trotsky was advised to remain in the south for his health, not to outmanoeuvre him. Far from being excluded from the official mourning for Lenin, a major article by Trotsky was given prominence in the first issues of the main newspapers, including *Pravda* and *Izvestiia*, the official newspapers of the party and the state, respectively. Trotsky's absence at the funeral itself was not, in itself, terribly significant. After all, another leader, Rykov, was also prevented by ill health from attending. No evidence has been found to vindicate either of Trotsky's versions of the incident.[20] Thatcher's careful account concludes that 'archival materials from the Soviet Communist Party's elite bodies, the Politburo and the Central Committee, do not provide clear answers, but they do suggest that Stalin acted honourably' and that 'in the absence of hard evidence it may be reasonable to assume that the story of Stalin's deception is precisely just that: a story'. Indeed, Thatcher even turns the issue on its head:

> One might conclude that this incident provides further evidence about why Trotsky lost to Stalin. Trotsky bumbles at a time when he is under the weather and makes what subsequently becomes clear is the wrong call – which he later tries to cover up. Stalin just acts according to the book, which is why he is in the job he is: the safe pair of hands. This explains why party members at the time would plump for Stalin rather than Trotsky, a man who makes bad decisions and then tries to put the blame on someone else.[21]

Stalin did, indeed, take the role of a chief mourner. In his thickly accented and slurred Russian he gave a liturgically influenced encomium at the Second All-Union Congress of Soviets on 26 January. Stalin praised Lenin's great achievements, first of all as founder of the Communist movement: 'Comrades, we Communists are people of a special mould. We are made of a special stuff. We are those who form the army of the great proletarian strategist, the army of Comrade Lenin. There is nothing higher than the honour of belonging to this army.' He then went on to praise Lenin for founding 'our party' which 'stood firm as a rock, repelling the countless blows of its enemies'. Third was his achievement in leading the first revolution in which the working people had come out on top: 'Ours is the only country where the oppressed and downtrodden labouring masses have succeeded in throwing off the rule of the landlords and capitalists and replacing it by the rule of the workers and peasants.' Next he praised Lenin for establishing the alliance of peasants and workers, the Union of Soviet Republics and, finally, world revolution and the Communist International which were praised in a typically Stalin balance of 'internationalism' and 'socialism in one country':

> The workers and peasants of the whole world want to preserve the Republic of Soviets as an arrow shot by the sure hand of Comrade Lenin into the camp of the enemy . . . and they will not allow the landlords and capitalists to destroy it . . .
>
> Lenin never regarded the Republic of Soviets as an end in itself. He always looked on it as an essential link for strengthening the revolutionary movement in the countries of the West and the East, an essential link for facilitating the victory of the working people of the whole world over capitalism. Lenin knew that this was the only right conception, both from the international standpoint and from the standpoint of preserving the Republic of Soviets itself.[22]

The speech has been the subject of frequent comment, often to point out the ecclesiastical and liturgical structure as a litany of vows to Lenin. As such it was not only a foundation stone of the cult of Lenin but Stalin was establishing his role as a (maybe the) high priest of the cult. It also shows many other interesting points. We have already noted that, for Stalin, world revolution and socialism in one country were not opposites but aspects of the same thing. Socialism in one country did not preclude world revolution, it was its key foundation. The points chosen also seem ironic. The great proponent of collectivization praising the worker-peasant alliance. The purger of the party and Comintern praising the quality of the activists and members in both. Stylistically, Stalin is brief and to the point but also repetitive and given to clichéd formulations and mixed metaphors such as being firm as a rock which repels blows. His audience of barely educated workers would not have noticed. Only the more refined intellectuals, such as Trotsky, would have winced at the roughness of Stalin's style.

In a memorial meeting on 28 January at the Kremlin Military School Stalin praised Lenin and his personal qualities, but the categories he chose are interesting, above all as features of Lenin on which Stalin modelled himself. Lenin was a 'mountain eagle', a somewhat more poetic metaphor reminiscent of the Caucasus and Stalin's early romantic poems. He praised Lenin's writing style: 'Only Lenin could write of the most intricate things so simply and clearly, so concisely and boldly, that every sentence did not so much speak as ring out like a rifle shot.' He was modest. In a rare personal reflection Stalin admitted disappointment when he first met Lenin:

I first met Lenin in December 1905 at the Bolshevik conference in Tammerfors (Finland). I was hoping to see the mountain eagle of our Party, the great man, great not only politically, but, if you will, physically, because in my imagination I had pictured Lenin as a giant, stately and imposing. What, then, was my disappointment to see a most ordinary-looking man, below average height, in no way, literally in no way, distinguishable from ordinary mortals . . .

It is accepted as the usual thing for a 'great man' to come late to meetings so that the assembly may await, his appearance with bated breath; and then, just before the 'great man' enters, the warning whisper goes up: 'Hush! . . . Silence! . . . he's coming.' This ritual did not seem to me superfluous, because it creates an impression, inspires respect. What, then, was my disappointment to learn that Lenin had arrived at the conference before the delegates, had settled himself somewhere in a corner, and was unassumingly carrying on a conversation, a most ordinary conversation with the most ordinary delegates at the conference. I will not conceal from you that at that time this seemed to me to be something of a violation of certain essential rules.

Only later did I realise that this simplicity and modesty, this striving to remain unobserved, or, at least, not to make himself conspicuous and not to emphasise his high position, this feature was one of Lenin's strongest points as the new leader of the new masses, of the simple and ordinary masses of the 'rank and file' of humanity.

This extract is also fascinatingly revelatory about Stalin's view of how a 'great man' should behave, a kind of Nietzschean assumption that such people were above ordinary mortals. Stalin, as we shall see, was able to accommodate both of these models – the superman and the modest 'man of the people' in his own cult of personality. The other characteristics of Lenin which Stalin picked out in this speech were the power of his logic, the absence of boasting (another Georgian nuance here, perhaps?), fidelity to principle, faith in the masses, his revolutionary genius. There was one other particularly interesting characteristic Stalin selected. If there was to be no boasting in victory there should be no 'whining' in defeat. Again, in an unaccustomed personal reflection on a moment in 1906 when the Bolsheviks had been defeated at the Stockholm Party Congress by:

> Plekhanov, Aksel'rod, Martov and the rest . . . the speeches of some of the delegates betrayed a note of weariness and dejection. I recall that to these speeches Lenin bitingly replied through clenched teeth: 'Don't whine, comrades, we are bound to win, for we are right.' Hatred of the whining intellectual, faith in our own strength, confidence in victory – that is what Lenin impressed upon us. It was felt that the Bolsheviks' defeat was temporary, that they were bound to win in the very near future.
>
> 'No whining over defeat' – this was the feature of Lenin's activities that helped him to rally around himself an army faithful to the end and confident in its strength.[23]

It has often been said that encomiasts, in praising the deceased, define their character in terms of the encomiast's own values.[24]

What Stalin was doing, probably inadvertently, was defining himself and the features of what was to become his own cult. The 'Lenin' depicted by Stalin was Stalin's own depiction of himself and his values. Confidence, faith in the masses, modesty, despising 'whining' especially from intellectuals, a touch of the Nietzschean superman, a detestation of the hypocritical and cruel liberal exploiters of capitalist society – these were all pillars of Stalin's personality. The policies he claimed were Leninist – socialism in one country as the basis of world revolution; the predominance of party and working class (not a word about the hated *spetsy*), the subsidiary but complementary role of the peasantry – were the foundations of Stalinism. Far from losing his link with Lenin after Lenin's death, Stalin was absorbing Lenin and recreating him in his own image at the same time.

It is not clear if this was mainly a 'natural' process arising from Stalin's long-time admiration of Lenin or if it was, even at this early stage, more manipulative, as it was later. What is certain is that Stalin built extensively on these foundations. In particular, he was quick to give a series of lectures on the topic at the Sverdlov University, the higher party school for training working class students to take on senior administrative and other responsible duties, mainly in the party but also in the state. In other words, he was talking to a rough and ready audience of people in his own mould. The lectures were published under the title *Foundations of Leninism*.[25] It was one of the very first times the term Leninism had been used. He was one of the first formulators of the doctrine. The main points developed, in a more discursive and systematic fashion, the policy initiatives and personal characteristics identified in his two, much shorter, pieces associated with Lenin's funeral. The discussion also shows that for Stalin, ideas were very important and they played a considerable role in his rise to power.

In order to develop these themes in context we need to turn to the conflict at the top of the Communist Party between possible successors to Lenin's leadership role. As we have seen, Lenin's final intervention in the area had been erratic and weak. What might have happened had he still been healthy we do not know. What is for sure is that his failure to make provision for a smooth succession was one of his most important failures. Initial skirmishing had begun even before Lenin's death but 1924 was a key moment in the expansion of the dispute and it is to the succession issue that we know turn.

Succession

There are a wide variety of interpretations of Stalin's rise. In some he is a lonely, brooding plotter, driven by a growing lust for personal power, carefully planning the stages by which he will eliminate his opponents. A popular interpretation, derived from Trotsky, has it that Stalin was the arch-bureaucrat who controlled the party administrative machine and was able to outmanoeuvre and double-cross his rivals in a decade long game of political chess. Trotsky who, as we shall see, accused the party in the mid-1920s of being 'degenerate' argued that Stalin was:

> needed by all . . . the tired radicals, by the bureaucrats, by the NEP-men, the upstarts, by all the worms that are crawling out of the upturned soil of the manured revolution. He knows how to meet them on their own ground, he speaks their language and he knows how to lead them. He has the deserved reputation of an old revolutionist, which makes him invaluable to them as a blinder on the eyes of the country. He has will and daring. He will not hesitate to utilize them and to move them against the Party. Right now he is organising himself around the sneaks of the party, the artful dodgers.[26]

However, better access to sources has enabled a more realistic and complex view of Stalin's emergence as leader to be put together. The main components of the 'new history of Stalin',[27] to quote the title of an excellent contribution to the debate, include situating the dispute in the broader context of party discussion and revolutionary dilemmas. Arising from this the intellectual and political positions of the competing leaders have to be taken into account. Third, the tactical errors made by the losing candidates played into Stalin's hands. In order to elucidate this process we need to look at the key debates within the party, especially about NEP and the future course of the revolution, then at the political positions and policy initiatives associated with the competing factions and, finally, at the stages by which Stalin came out on top.

The adoption of NEP in 1921 had been one of Lenin's last triumphs. In his testament writings he was full of praise for the new balance between state and market and between worker and peasant. In the fire of battle the party had stumbled across the formula for success which had eluded earlier generations.[28] NEP would create a dynamic of socialist construction in that the market elements would decline and the socialist elements grow. Crucially, Lenin thought, the peasants would realize that collective agriculture would benefit them more than traditional communal redistribution and private plots. Peasants would see that by combining their resources they would gain access to cheaper inputs of fertilizer, seed, machinery and other items which would otherwise be too expensive for an individual household to purchase or which could be bought cheaper in greater bulk. Seeing this, Lenin argued, the peasants would, voluntarily and happily, adopt collective forms of agriculture. 'All that was necessary' to fulfil this vision was, Lenin said, to promote a 'cultural revolution' among the peasantry.[29] By this he meant spreading advanced, Western methods of agriculture and a more literate, hygienic, disease-free, vodka-free village oriented to hard work and efficient production and accounting methods. In this way, peasant prosperity would flourish. The growing wealth would create a market for industrial goods, like farm machinery. Greater output would feed the cities, towns and army. Rising productivity (that is, output per person employed) as a result of mechanization and economies of scale would enable surplus labour to leave the village and take up urban industrial employment. In Lenin's optimistic view, this would create a benevolent cycle which would 'naturally' strengthen socialism and weaken private, individual and market instincts and interests.[30]

Lenin had the standing within the party to persuade his fellow members to adopt this new line but there were, from the outset, important problems. In the first place, many, perhaps most, party members were unhappy to 'retreat'. They had just wiped out their enemies through coercion in the Civil War and were straining at the leash to do the same socially. They were dismayed that the remaining 'enemy' elements – traders, *spetsy*, petty entrepreneurs – were to be encouraged. The turn towards conciliating the peasantry was also barely tolerated. Lenin's injunction that there should be an alliance between worker and peasant and that the state should never again coerce the peasantry into compliance was hard for many of the party militants to accept. It took all Lenin's authority and prestige to keep protest down to a minimum. In any case, as an insurance, party discipline was tightened at the Tenth Congress. Party factions were banned. Individual criticism of policy was permitted up to a point but no groups were to be allowed to coalesce as pressure groups around what were called 'platforms' – that is small or large political programmes. Wider coercion was also employed to limit intellectual dissent – expulsion of dissenting intellectuals; control of universities; a more rigorous and systematic censorship apparatus – and political dissent. The remnants of the SR party were put on trial, one of the earliest 'show trials' of the Soviet era.[31]

The second key problem of NEP was that it was not working in the smooth and beneficial way assumed by Lenin. Instead, it was producing a series of economic crises resulting in a series of concessions to the peasantry, which were deeply unpopular in the party. The growth of collective forms of agriculture was minimal. By 1928 the percentage of co-operative farms was around 3 per cent, the same as it had been under tsarism. Ironically, although they remained relatively poor and famine was never entirely absent, the 1920s was almost a golden age of the peasantry in general and the traditional peasant commune, in particular. During the 1920s the peasants were living the dream of landowner-free villages and a sovereign commune.[32] State and party institutions in the countryside were very weak. Even at the end of the decade there were only some 250,000 rural party members in a population of 120 million peasants.

The 'flourishing' of Russian agriculture at the expense of industrialization was very difficult for the party to take. At meeting after meeting from local to All-Union level, members complained bitterly of the increasing flow of resources from the state and industrial sectors – that is the growth points of socialism – towards the peasantry and the market. At one meeting a diagram was produced to show that agricultural prices were falling too quickly as production recovered and industrial prices remained high. The two lines on the graph resembled the blades of a pair of scissors moving ever further apart when the point was to close the blades, to bring them together. The process became known as the 'scissors crisis'. While the blades were wide apart the peasants would be reluctant to market ever-more grain to buy expensive industrial goods. This led to food shortages and the need, in 1928, to ration food supplies, an unprecedented measure in peacetime. NEP was not a smooth machine, whirring away building a harmonious, socialist society; it was a set of improvised measures proceeding in fits and starts. Its defenders, as we shall see, found it increasingly difficult to defend what appeared to be a continuous series of concessions, every one of which weakened the socialist elements of Soviet society and made the ultimate goal appear to be further and further away. The succession dispute was deeply entwined with proposed solutions to this fundamental problem.

There were, however, other serious issues confronting the party. These were bureaucratization and the spread of the revolution. The emergence of bureaucracy after the revolution was an issue which exercised the party's best minds. Lenin himself had complained about it and, as we have seen, hoped to deal with it through some astonishingly timid tinkering with the system proposed in his final writings. The issue became a major area in which the succession dispute was fought out at the level of policy and theory. But for all the attention lavished on it within the party, no one came up with the real source. If the party were to take on wide functions of social supervision and leadership of the transition to socialism, then the spreading tentacles of bureaucracy were an inevitable consequence. If the party believed, and there were no major dissenters on this, that it should run the economy, the military, the education system, trade unions, the judiciary and so on, how could it do so without massive bureaucratization? The alternative was to devolve decision-making and to open up space for genuine democratic discussion and opposition. Within the party, the only ones who supported the rights of the opposition were those in the minority who formed oppositions. These were not necessarily the same people. In 1921, Trotsky had not disagreed with the decree banning factions. Three years later, when accused by his opponents of forming a faction,

Trotsky bemoaned the lack of democracy within the party, an outcome he had done as much to create as anyone else.

As early as 1918, shortly before her death, the Polish-German Marxist Rosa Luxemburg expressed the fear that, despite their great work for the revolution, the growing dictatorship, promoted by Lenin and Trotsky, brought real risks. 'With the repression of political life in the land as a whole', she warned, 'life in the soviets must also become more crippled. Without general elections, without unrestricted freedom of the press and assembly, without a free struggle of opinion, life dies out in every public institution . . . only the bureaucracy remains as the active element.'[33] Her words were not heeded. At several points in his opening address to the Tenth Congress in March 1921, Lenin described debates within the party as a 'luxury' and even as 'an amazing luxury'.[34] His reason was that since the revolution was surrounded by powerful imperialist enemies abroad and the dangerous remnants of the enemy at home, the party had to maintain 'iron proletarian discipline'.[35] An authoritarian style of government was becoming second nature. The value of criticism in creating life and preserving health in the party as proposed by Luxemburg, was not one any Bolshevik leader subscribed to, at least while they were in charge. The prospering of enemies abroad, as successive waves of European revolution receded in 1919, 1920/1921 and 1923, not only provided cover for lack of internal democracy, it also opened up the question of how 'world revolution' should be achieved and what priority it should have. The Left Communists of 1918 and their successors believed it was vital to promote world revolution at all costs, even risking the Russian Revolution itself since it would, in their view, inevitably fail if it did not spread. By the time of Lenin's death, the right of the party, led by the former leftist, Nikolai Bukharin, believed it was necessary to be pragmatic in that no real prospect of revolution existed after 1923 and that had to be taken into account. Stalin, as we have seen, tried to square the circle by claiming, supposedly on Lenin's authority, that it was necessary to defend the Russian Revolution first as its survival was essential to any future revolutions abroad.

There were many major issues in play – how should socialism be built and at what pace? All parties agreed industrial development was essential but at what tempo and by what methods could it be promoted? Would the many-headed Hydra of bureaucracy overcome the revolutionary energies of party activists and sympathizers? The emergence of the Communist International (known, colloquially, as Comintern) was welcomed by all but what should its strategy be and what resources should it command? There were many vital issues at stake. But no clear reorientation of policy would take place on these issues while the party was divided into warring groups with different views on how to proceed. Not only was the wider context crucial to the dispute over the succession, resolution of the dispute was vital to the answers that would be applied to these questions.

The most influential and distinguished salvo in the dispute was fired by Trotsky in his role as brilliant analyst. In two major works, *The New Course* (1923) and *Lessons of October* (1924), Trotsky set out his vision of the future of the revolution; but also, perhaps more importantly, he criticized the way things were going during Lenin's twilight years and he attempted to undermine the reputation of those he held responsible.

He opened the barrage with a pamphlet entitled *The New Course*, which was devoted to a critique of the state of the party. It was falling away from its high, revolutionary standards:

> If we now take our Bolshevik Party in its revolutionary past and in the period following October, it will be recognized that its most precious fundamental tactical quality is its unequalled ability to orient itself rapidly, to change tactics quickly, to renew its armament and to apply new methods, in a word, to carry out abrupt turns. Tempestuous historical conditions have made this tactic necessary. Lenin's genius gave it a superior form.

However, difficulties were emerging and instead of the flexibility he claimed to see in the party's past it was now facing 'ideological petrifaction' arising from 'the relatively strong bureaucratization of the party apparatus' which 'is inevitably accompanied by the development of conservative traditionalism with all its effects'. It was easy enough to supposedly identify the problem: 'Democracy and centralism are two faces of party organization. The question is to harmonize them in the most correct manner, that is, the manner best corresponding to the situation. During the last period there was no such equilibrium. The centre of gravity wrongly lodged in the apparatus. The initiative of the party was reduced to the minimum.' Even worse, the dead hand of bureaucratism prevented the invigoration of the younger members joining the party. Trotsky agreed that 'It is incontestable that we must raise the ideological level of our party.' While Trotsky did not mention names no one could doubt who was being blamed for the heavy 'conservatism' spreading from the centre. He walked confidently but also naively deeper into the swamp. 'Bureaucratism kills initiative and thus prevents the elevation of the general level of the party. That is its cardinal defect. As the apparatus is made up inevitably of the most experienced and most meritorious comrades, it is upon the political training of the young communist generations that bureaucratism has its most grievous repercussions.' Not an easy passage to understand but what is clear is that blame for poor preparation of young members lay at the door of the party elite. He brought out some, in socialist circles of the time, frightening implications of what he was arguing:

> It is not necessary to speak of the immense authority of the group of party veterans, not only in Russia but internationally; that is universally recognized. But it would be a crude mistake to regard it as absolute. It is only by a constant active collaboration with the new generation, within the framework of democracy, that the Old Guard will preserve itself as a revolutionary factor. Of course, it may ossify and become unwittingly the most consummate expression of bureaucratism.
>
> History offers us more than one case of degeneration of the 'Old Guard'. Let us take the most recent and striking example: that of the leaders of the parties of the Second International. We know that Wilhelm Liebknecht, Bebel, Singer, Victor Adler, Kautsky, Bernstein, Lafargue, Guesde, and many others were the direct pupils of Marx and Engels. Yet we know that in the atmosphere of parliamentarism and under the influence of the automatic development of the party and the trade union apparatus, all these leaders turned, in whole or in part, to opportunism.[36]

Without naming anyone, Trotsky was accusing the party elite of the greatest Bolshevik sin – opportunism, meaning putting compromise ahead of principle. He also appeared to be talking as though he, himself, was not an integral part of that elite and it was Trotsky's semi-detached position from the first moment he linked up with the party in July/August 1917 that had surrounded him with suspicion from that moment on.

Trotsky's second major broadside came the following year, 1924, in the form of a pamphlet entitled *Lessons of October*. It was designed as an introduction to his great *History of the Russian Revolution* which, in fact, did not come out until 1932. At one level it was intended to outline what the party had learned in 1917 but there was another, much more immediate, theme running through it. In his testament Lenin, as we have seen, said the fact that Kamenev and Zinoviev had made serious mistakes in October 1917 should not be held against them. Ironically, by saying this, Lenin was himself drawing attention to the issue. It was too much for Trotsky to resist. With 'right-wing' Communism in the ascendant, in the form of NEP, Trotsky argued that a key lesson of October was that Lenin (and by implication) Trotsky himself, had only reached the seizure of power as a result of overcoming six or seven months of unrelenting opposition of 'the rightists' in the party to the seizure of power. Numerous damning quotations from Kamenev and Zinoviev were included. Incidentally, as Trotsky was himself to find out, selective quoting of past speeches and articles was a double-edged sword. There were many vigorous denunciations not only of Lenin but also of his key conception of the party and democratic centralism in Trotsky's own past. He was to find that the master of digging out such items was not himself but Stalin. Perhaps surprisingly, Stalin himself is not mentioned anywhere in this pamphlet. Was that tactical on Trotsky's part or was it that he still underestimated Stalin? There is no definitive way of knowing.

Trotsky was focusing on the bureaucratization of the party, the risk of opportunism among its leaders and denunciation of his apparently key rivals as dangerous and unreliable rightists; Stalin was to take a different line. Without any coyness whatsoever, he launched into the evils of 'Trotskyism', practically inventing the name, or at least popularizing it, as he had with the term Leninism.

In December 1923, some time after the appearance of *The New Course*, Stalin was responding vehemently to Trotsky's assault. Much of the fire is directed on lesser targets, Trotsky's associates in the 'left opposition', Rafail, Sapronov and Preobrazhensky. But, finally, Stalin turned his attention to Trotsky. He accused Trotsky, not incorrectly, of deception in having voted in favour of a key Central Committee and Central Control Commission resolution on 7 December 1923 and then publishing a letter critical of its major aspects. Stalin picked up Trotsky's point about the 'Old Guard' being susceptible to the risk of opportunism. First, with heavy sarcasm, one of his favourite literary stratagems, he claims he needs to 'protect Trotsky from Trotsky':

> First, I must dispel a possible misunderstanding. As is evident from his letter, Trotsky includes himself among the Bolshevik old guard, thereby showing readiness to take upon himself the charges that may be hurled at the old guard if it does indeed take the path of degeneration. It must be admitted that this readiness for self-sacrifice is undoubtedly a noble trait. But I must protect Trotsky from Trotsky, because, for obvious reasons, he cannot, and should not, bear responsibility for the possible degeneration of the principal cadres of the Bolshevik old guard. Sacrifice is a good thing, of course, but do the old Bolsheviks need it? I think that they do not.

Trotsky, he goes on, 'has adduced no evidence to show that the danger of degeneration is a real danger'. Why does Trotsky want to suggest a split between the older and younger elements in the party?

> Have not the youth and the old guard always marched in a united front against internal and external enemies? Is not the unity between the "old ones" and the "young ones" the basic strength of our revolution? What was the object of this attempt to discredit the old guard and demagogically to flatter the youth if not to cause and widen a fissure between these principal detachments of our Party?

Herein, for Stalin, lies Trotsky's duplicity: 'diplomatically to support the opposition in its struggle against the Central Committee of the Party while pretending to support the Central Committee's resolution. That, in fact, explains the stamp of duplicity that Trotsky's letter bears'.

In his second major response, this time to *Lessons of October*, Stalin poses the question, as the title of his piece emphasizes, *Trotskyism or Leninism?* He refutes charges, some of them not actually made as such by Trotsky, relating to the opposition to the October seizure of power. He also confronts Trotsky and his supporters' supposed exaggeration of Trotsky's role in October at the expense of other party members. Without mentioning his own role in events Stalin says that of course Trotsky played a significant role. 'I am far from denying Trotsky's undoubtedly important role in the uprising', Stalin says. And again, later in his speech, 'it cannot be denied that Trotsky fought well in the period of October'. He draws subtle but important attention to a key weakness of Trotsky's position in 1917 and 1924, saying one reason he could not have had a special role was that 'he was a relatively new man in our Party'. Stalin continues, the October uprising 'did have its inspirer and leader, but this was Lenin, and none other than Lenin . . . that same Lenin who, in spite of what Trotsky says, was not prevented by being in hiding from being the actual inspirer of the uprising'.

Stalin also lands two more hefty blows on Trotsky. Continuing the phrase quoted above about Trotsky fighting well in October, Stalin says that 'Trotsky was not the only one who fought well in the period of October. Even people like the Left Socialist-Revolutionaries, who then stood side by side with the Bolsheviks, also fought well. In general, I must say that in the period of a victorious uprising, when the enemy is isolated and the uprising is growing, it is not difficult to fight well. At such moments even backward people become heroes.' Stalin was moving ponderously to the sting in the tail. The point at which both Trotsky and the left SRs ceased to 'fight well' came in March 1918 with the Treaty of Brest-Litovsk. Trotsky, Stalin said, went into a funk:

> The Left Socialist-Revolutionaries did not fight badly in the period of October, and they supported the Bolsheviks. But

who does not know that those 'brave' fighters became panic-stricken in the period of Brest, when the advance of German imperialism drove them to despair and hysteria. It is a very sad but indubitable fact that Trotsky, who fought well in the period of October, did not, in the period of Brest, in the period when the revolution suffered temporary reverses, possess the courage to display sufficient staunchness at that difficult moment and to refrain from following in the footsteps of the Left Socialist-Revolutionaries. Beyond question, that moment was a difficult one; one had to display exceptional courage and imperturbable coolness not to be dismayed, to retreat in good time, to accept peace in good time, to withdraw the proletarian army out of range of the blows of German imperialism, to preserve the peasant reserves and, after obtaining a respite in this way, to strike at the enemy with renewed force. Unfortunately, Trotsky was found to lack this courage and revolutionary staunchness at that difficult moment.

This was, actually, a travesty of Trotsky's position at the time but the blow landed. Trotsky had, indeed, been out on a limb and had been reluctant to accept Lenin's insistence that a peace had to be concluded on any terms, a decision which, as we have seen, marked a great division between driving onwards to a possibly hopeless revolutionary war and adopting a kind of 'socialism in one country' doctrine. Trotsky's attempt to carve out an intermediate position – summed up in the phrase 'neither war nor peace' – was disastrous in that the bluff failed and the Germans acquired more territory and a stronger bargaining position. It also made Trotsky vulnerable to the accusation of disloyalty to Lenin who urged a settlement at any cost.

Another major theme of Stalin's attack was the primacy of party over individuals. One of the main reasons that Trotsky could not have had the special role supposedly suggested by him and his supporters was because Trotsky 'like all the responsible workers, merely carried out the will of the Central Committee and of its organs. Whoever is familiar with the mechanics of Bolshevik Party leadership will have no difficulty in understanding that it could not be otherwise'. It is very important to note that, throughout the campaign and the distorted polemics of all sides, Stalin purported to be the voice of the party. Where Trotsky accused the party leaders of weakness and opportunism, Stalin spoke with pride of 'our Party, which has made three revolutions, which routed Kolchak and Denikin, and is now shaking the foundations of world imperialism, a party which would not have tolerated the weaknesses alleged by the opposition'. The notion that it would tolerate such things was 'But a frightful dream, but thank God, only a dream.'

Stalin also showed an ability to turn his opponents' words and position against themselves. Stalin claimed that while the possibility of degeneration in the party could be no more disputed than the possibility of an earthquake, the fact the possibility existed did not mean the thing itself did. Stalin went on to add that 'Nevertheless, there are a number of elements within our Party who are capable of giving rise to a real danger of degeneration of certain ranks of our Party.' While Stalin refrained from spelling it out, his following assertion that the elements he had in mind were former Mensheviks would certainly have reminded many in the party that Trotsky was himself one such person. The degeneration argument had been astutely turned on Trotsky himself.

The main discussion and difference emphasized in these key polemics was bureaucracy and party democracy. There were other issues the most important of which was the future of NEP. As we have seen, Lenin had had high hopes for NEP. It was, if cultural revolution was added, 'all that was necessary' to achieve socialism. While some comrades had been against it from the beginning, denouncing it as a sell-out to peasants and petty-capitalism, others had gone along with it, some enthusiastically like Bukharin, others reluctantly. Stalin appears to have been in the latter group. Their support began to ebb away when Lenin was no longer around to boost it and when, as the 'scissors crisis' kicked in, Lenin's vision of a harmonious transfer of resources from private to collective interests appeared to be the reverse of the truth. The beneficiaries of NEP appeared to be non-socialist elements of Russian society, notably so-called kulaks (essentially understood to be peasants who employed other peasants) and market traders, given the name NEPmen.[37]

A third category also flourished, the *spetsy*, especially in the economic area. Because of lack of expertise among the working class, the state was still turning increasingly to former middle-class and even upper-class individuals who would work for it. Even former political enemies were recruited, including the memoirist N. N. Sukhanov who was a Menshevik Internationalist denounced, as we have seen, by Lenin himself for scepticism about the October Revolution and for claiming it was 'premature'. The former Kadet and adviser to Kolchak in the White government in Omsk, Iu Kliuchnikov, worked as an adviser and functionary in the Soviet Foreign Ministry and even had articles published in *Pravda*. Somewhere around 2 million Russians, mostly from the pre-revolutionary elites, had left Russia in the course of the years of turbulence from 1917 to 1921/1922. From the early 1920s efforts were made to recruit as many as possible to return. Obviously, active political enemies were not permitted but otherwise hundreds of thousands did return. Engineers and those with advanced clerical and managerial skills were a priority.

Many prominent non-Bolshevik intellectuals, some of whom returned from abroad while others had somehow survived the rigours of civil war, were also taken on as teachers and so on to help in the vast process of transferring skills from the pre-revolutionary generation to their proletarian successors. There was even a political movement set up among émigrés known as National Bolshevism. It had first stirred in the minds such as those of demoralized White officers in Siberia, such as Nikolai Ustrialov and Kliuchnikov, who saw they were being defeated. As Russian nationalists they had been uneasy over the degree of foreign support upon which the Whites practically depended. By contrast, the Bolsheviks were a purely Russian (in the Imperial rather than ethnic sense) force and they began to admire the vigour of Bolshevism compared to the increasing decrepitude of the crumbling White cause.[38] Conveniently, they developed a theory of 'normalization', according to which the socialist peculiarities of the Soviet system would fall away and the country would revert to European normality of democracy of some sort and capitalism. They interpreted the adoption of NEP as a major step in that direction.[39]

As a result, many Soviet institutions had significant layers of *spetsy* working within them. The Commissariats for Enlighten-ment (Education), Finance and Foreign Affairs and their sub-branches were hotspots of employment of specialists. Ironically, one of the pre-eminently Soviet-style institutions, the *Vesenkha* (Council for the National Economy), which was charged with supervising economic policy and preparing economic plans, was full of non-Bolsheviks. This was where Sukhanov turned up to work every morning. Numerous other former Mensheviks and SRs were on the payroll. Most surprisingly, the number included a truly remarkable person, one of Russia's most brilliant, original, multi-talented individuals, Father Pavel Florensky, a priest of the Orthodox Church. He was equally at home in sciences, mathemat-ics, languages, art, philosophy and theology.[40]

Stalin had not weakened in his mistrust of specialists and sniped at them from time to time in his speeches in the mid-1920s. In the dispute between Red and expert – that is, between political reliability and technical expertise, Stalin's heart was always with the former. Presumably this arose from the continuing effect of his background, his career and his closer knowledge of workers than any other Bolshevik leader, derived from his tough fights against imperialist employers in the oilfields of Baku while other leaders were arguing heatedly in the cafés of Vienna, Berlin, Paris, London and New York. He continued to side with rough, tough, proletarian boot boys from the south such as Frunze, Ordzhoni-kidze, Kirov and Budyonnyi, and characters like Molotov and Dzerzhinsky, all of them people who got the job done first and asked questions afterwards. While he maintained perfectly civil relationships with supporters of NEP, notably Bukharin who was a frequent weekend visitor for parties at the Stalin *dacha* in the 1920s, his instincts were elsewhere.

But what did 'elsewhere' consist of for those in the party who were most dissatisfied with NEP? It was the left of the party, including Trotsky, the great believer in the necessity and efficacy of specialists, and his close supporters, who were most vociferous in criticizing the way in which NEP was evolving and putting forward an alternative. Two closely inter-related issues were at the heart of the main critique of NEP. It slowed down the process of transition to socialism and the related process of industrialization. From early on, at least March 1918, the two had become fused in the concept of 'productionism'. It was related to the 'premature' status of the Russian Revolution. To simplify greatly, Marx had assumed that socialism would take over once capitalism had achieved its full potential and was choking on its own success, as it were. Capitalism would have exhausted the potential to expand so completely that it could only exploit its own employees. Since they would also be the main market for capitalist products a basic and fatal contradiction would occur. Capitalism would be trying to cut its labour costs and expand its markets and profits at the same time. Since its employees were its customers it could not impoverish and enrich them at the same time. Workers, being reduced to having 'nothing to lose but their chains', would rise up and seize the means of production and convert them to rational, human-need oriented use rather than producing for the market.[41] Russia, for all its pre-revolutionary progress, was far from fulfilling the condition of an exhausted capitalism. If anything, Russian capitalism remained in its infancy. That being so, one could either side with fatalists and say nothing could be done from the Marxist perspective until capitalism had exhausted itself or one could adapt. Lenin (and Stalin who was not much preoccupied with deep theory) chose the latter.

By 1923 Lenin had established several conditions under which socialism could evolve in Russia. Enthusiasm for 'world revolution' had peaked in 1917 but it was still the case that spreading the revolution to the advanced capitalist world was essential in the long run. 'Socialism in one country' was, for Lenin and Stalin, a step towards world revolution, a firm foundation for it, not a retreat from it as critics like Trotsky argued. Second, capture of the state meant that, from the commanding heights, the other preconditions could be nurtured. The most important of those were productionism and the need to raise class and socialist consciousness. Stalin did discuss the latter and we will return to it; but in the mid-1920s productionism was at the forefront of discussion.

What was meant by productionism? In theory it meant that since socialism could only be built on a potentially high-capacity industrial and economic base, the first step in internal socialist construction was to maximize economic output. Lenin even praised the adoption of the latest capitalist exploitative techniques of time and motion studies and the production line, developments hated by Western workers. Under capitalist conditions, he argued, such processes were super-exploitative. Under socialist conditions, however, they were emancipatory because the gains of output that resulted would benefit the whole community not just the shareholders. In any case, the lesson was clear. Socialism would only progress when industry progressed, therefore the number one priority was industrialization.

In fact, this proposition itself was not controversial in the party. Dispute began in attempting to suggest how such a vast objective could be realized. While we will look in more detail at the outcome of the debate in the next chapter, we need to note, at this point, that the party right, led by Bukharin who had some claim to being an economist as well as party activist, believed that although it was slow, NEP would eventually deliver industrialization. On the left, a more rapid promotion of industry by means of planning was thought to be the way forward. As we will see, the term planning had many shades of meaning. Economic planning was a widespread concept arising from the war economies of World War I, especially the German economy. Markets had been partially suspended in all the main combatant countries. The state had stepped in to supervise production of the most important war materials. Both capitalism and socialism had enthusiastically taken up the concept of planning after the war. In Soviet Russia, a plan for electrification had emerged in 1920. Trotsky claimed to have begun the implementation of a transport plan, number 1042, in the early 1920s. Since 1918, under Lenin's patronage, the *Vesenkha* had been looking at ways to plan and had been accumulating the necessary factual bases for planning to occur. However, without engaging deeply with the argument, it is evident that planning at that time had more in common with what today is called economic policy. It was aimed at creating the institutional and fiscal infrastructure for economic development. It did not necessarily imply what emerged in the 1930s, a command economy attempting to directly intervene down to factory and shop level. Thus, there was intense debate in the party about what direction should be taken in this vital area. Only the resolution of the struggle for power within the party would decide this issue. Therefore we need to look at how it was that Stalin and his associates came out on top in this complex world and Trotsky, Kamenev, Zinoviev and Bukharin were defeated.

The Stalinists takeover

One of the most popular interpretations of Stalin's final drive for power was that he had a crucial control over the administrative machine. This enabled him – by devious methods of appointing key officials, packing party committees, conferences and congresses and assigning unwanted figures to remote, but often comfortable posts[42] – to manipulate majorities for himself and his supporters. I apologize to the reader for once again pointing out what they may already have inferred – that this was, as so often, Trotsky's view of Stalin's rise. Trotsky's great admirer and biographer, Isaac Deutscher, is a subscriber to this interpretation. Even before Lenin's death Stalin had 'an amazing accumulation of power' in his hands. Before the fight with his rivals began, Deutscher argues, Stalin 'had firmly gripped all the levers of power' to the extent that his rivals, who 'voted and moved him into all his positions of power' found him to be 'immoveable'.[43] The result, for Deutscher, was that Stalin was 'the indisputable master of the party' which was in his 'grip'.[44] Tucker, also influenced by Trotsky at one point in his life, has a whole section in his biography devoted to 'the Stalin machine' which forms a 'formidable base' for him, but at least Tucker says the machine theory plus adroit manoeuvring 'do not suffice to explain the events' of the post-Lenin period.[45] This does not prevent him from talking of 'the Stalin political machine' or his 'machine politics of self-advancement' to build up 'a party clientele'[46] for 'the Stalin organization'.[47]

We have already seen that formal positions in the bureaucracy were very fluid. Commissars often paid scant attention to their commissariats (ministries), attending the most important meetings but certainly not attending on a daily basis, leaving the actual running of them to deputy commissars and permanent officials.[48] Stalin's accumulation of posts was certainly important but far from being the full story. A fine recent study has confirmed this and pointed out difficulties with the view that it was Stalin's control of the administrative apparatus which was decisive.

James Harris points out that:

> Stalin gave his own views on the subject in a conversation with his inner circle on the day of the twentieth anniversary of the October Revolution. [1937] Stalin observed that his victory over the oppositions, and Trotsky in particular, had been improbable. He had been an 'unknown', 'lacking talent as a theoretician' (*praktik*), a 'second-rater' (*zamukhryshka*). Trotsky was a great orator, and his closeness to Lenin was commonly acknowledged. How had he defeated him? Trotsky's mistake, according to Stalin, was to try to decide matters 'with a majority of votes in the Central Committee'. In contrast, Stalin attributed his victory to the mass of average Party members (*seredniatskaia massa partii*) who supported him for his concrete achievements. Stalin likened them to officers, who had shown loyalty not to the Generals who have the best training, but to those who bring victory in battle.

Such remarks, the author continues, 'make considerable sense in the context of what we know about the succession struggle'. The author comes to the conclusion that 'Some have argued that Stalin tipped the weight of the Central Committee in his favour by excluding his opponents from it and appointing his supporters. Yet there is little evidence to suggest that Stalin could control the slates of Central Committee members up for election at the party congresses in the 1920s, or overtly manipulate its expansion in his favour. Rather, it appears as though Stalin largely carried the Central Committee on the basis of his policies and, in time, on the concrete results they brought.'[49]

That being said, the senior party committees, like the Politburo and Central Committee, and major congresses and conferences of the party, state and trade unions, were the arenas in which the battles were fought out. The stages of the rise of Stalin and his allies has been charted many times. The first skirmishes came while Lenin was still alive. Trotsky's attempted intrigue against Stalin served only to alert the leading figures in the party to the dangers. His critique of the 'Old Guard', in which Stalin so generously included Trotsky himself, was a warning to all of them. It forced an unlikely 'triumvirate' – composed of Kamenev, Zinoviev and Stalin – to coalesce around a programme which was little more than a shared dislike of Trotsky and a concerted attempt to block him. Trotsky's strength and weakness at the time was that he was still Commissar for War which put him at the head of the armed services. This was an apparently strong position for him to hold. However, it opened him up to criticism. At many points, activists in the Russian Revolution, and not only Bolsheviks, had seen themselves repeating aspects of the French Revolution, replicating its liberal phase, then 'moderate' revolution (Girondins/Mensheviks) followed by extremists (Jacobins/Bolsheviks) and powerful leaders (Robespierre/Lenin) who instituted terror. The endgame in France was 'Thermidor' when the counter-revolution turned on Robespierre and the Jacobins, who were consigned to the guillotine themselves. Thermidor opened the way for the emergence of a counter-revolutionary military dictator in the form of Napoleon Bonaparte. There was frequent speculation among Bolsheviks about the prospects for a Russian Thermidor and the emergence of Bonapartism. As a relatively cultured Bolshevik, Trotsky had talked in these terms himself and he knew that, as head of the armed forces, he most closely fulfilled the requirements for being a Russian Bonaparte. His critics were quick to make such accusations. It was partly to divest himself of this embarrassment that, in January 1925, he resigned as commissar for military and naval affairs, depriving himself of one of his major political assets. This also tended to show another weakness of Trotsky, his political naiveté. He was so convinced that history worked itself out irrespective of individual action that he looked almost fatalistically on the struggle in which he was engaged. History would choose the successor, not a series of squalid political deals and manoeuvres.

At this point, the dispute was conducted in the Politburo. Trotsky, throughout 1925, had no specific responsibilities and was assigned to a variety of tasks by Stalin.[50] His defeat over controlling the army had apparently fatally weakened his position in the succession race, at least insofar as the triumvirate began to fracture. Trotsky was no longer the leading enemy. At some point, and it is not clear exactly when, Kamenev and Zinoviev, who considered themselves to be the senior figures in the party, began to realize they might have backed the wrong horse. Stalin increasingly seemed to be the threat and they even began, bit by bit, to turn towards Trotsky as an ally against Stalin. Interestingly, according to Boris Bazhanov, a senior party secretary of the time who fled and wrote his memoirs, Stalin had had warmer relations with Trotsky than Kamenev. At Bazhanov's first Politburo meeting in 1923 he noted that Trotsky had arrived first. Zinoviev was next to walk in and he ignored Trotsky. Kamenev gave him a brief nod as he arrived but it was Stalin who 'greeted him in a most friendly manner and vigorously shook hands with him across the table'.[51] By 1925, however, the situation was changing. The Politburo, consisting of seven members – Stalin, Trotsky, Kamenev, Zinoviev, Rykov, Tomsky and Bukharin – was splitting along new lines. The factionalism was driven by events. 1925 saw a growing crisis in NEP. The pace of change was slowing down, the scissors crisis was beginning to hit and the Politburo was divided on the response. The 'right' – Bukharin, Rykov and Tomsky – argued for more committed support of NEP. In practice, this meant greater concessions to the 'middle peasant'. Unwisely, Bukharin called on them to 'enrich yourselves', an historic phrase uttered by a French liberal politician, Guizot, in the 1840s. Together with admitting that socialism would evolve at 'snail's pace' or at the speed of a notoriously slow 'peasant pony', Bukharin was cutting deeply into the optimistic and proactive instincts of most militants. Kamenev and Zinoviev now positioned themselves on the left of the party, arguing for less concessions to peasants and a more energetic attitude to industrialization. Stalin said little, at first, and took the role of mediating between rather than joining the factions.

It should be noted that the 'succession dispute' was intrinsically tied up not so much with personalities but with policies. However, as 1925 continued, the personality issue came increasingly into play, driven first by Stalin's opponents. As Kamenev and Zinoviev began to realize their error, so the debate became more heated. Tension increased at meetings of the Politburo. Stalin came out in defence of Bukharin and of NEP. The right also ridiculed the left for excessive reliance on 'world revolution' as saviour of the

Russian Revolution. Instead, Stalin and Bukharin argued that capitalism had stabilized itself after the revolutionary crisis of 1918–1923 and that socialism in one country was still the only way forward.

There were unmistakeable signs of Stalin's growing predominance in late 1925. He had already survived the risky moment of discussion, in the Central Committee (18 May 1924) and Thirteenth Party Congress in late May 1924, of Lenin's 'Letter to the Congress' in which he had pointed out Stalin's *grubost'* (rudeness). As described by Bazhanov, and quoted by Trotsky, 'painful embarrassment paralysed the whole gathering. Stalin . . . felt small and miserable. Despite his self-control and forced calm, one could clearly read in his face that his fate was being decided.'[52] Though he remained silent during the discussion, in which Zinoviev supported Stalin, Trotsky made his feelings known through his body language. The testament was passed, in accordance with Lenin's wishes, to the Thirteenth Party Congress in May 1924 where it was discussed in closed session but no action was taken. Stalin even offered to step down but his gamble paid off and no one challenged him directly.[53] Incidentally, whether from guile or genuine weariness we do not know for sure, he repeated the manoeuvre even more spectacularly on 19 August 1924 when he requested the Central Committee to relieve him of his duties because he could no longer work 'honourably' with Kamenev and Zinoviev. He asked for convalescent leave and a less pressurized posting suggesting an 'unobtrusive' position abroad or to be sent to, of all places, Turukhansk, where he had been in Siberian exile.[54] In another supreme irony, having decided not to publish it, the testament was published in New York and Trotsky, who had leaked it, was forced to write an article denying the document's existence and claiming the American publication was a vicious fabrication.[55]

However, Stalin was not completely rid of the burden of Lenin's criticism. At the Fourteenth Congress (18–31 December 1925), out of desperation as much as anything else, Kamenev and Zinoviev tried to revive it into an attack on Stalin. Kamenev roused his supporters in the Moscow party, which he headed, and Zinoviev rallied support from his Leningrad fiefdom. It was ineffective. Shouts from the floor for Stalin to resign were drowned out by ovations in his support. Seizing the moment, Stalin had the Polit-buro expanded to include his allies Molotov, Voroshilov and Kalinin. This strengthened the 'Stalinist centre' in the face of the left and, increasingly, right oppositions. 1926 was a year of pro-longed decline for the left in the party. Overcoming years of personal hostility and mutual aversion, Kamenev and Zinoviev formed a 'United Opposition' with Trotsky. Stalin sent another close associate and southerner, Sergei Kirov, to Leningrad to replace Zinoviev and winkle out his supporters. In July 1926 Zinoviev was expelled from the Politburo. Despite or perhaps because on 4 October 1926, Trotsky, with Kamenev, Zinoviev and others wrote a dignified admission to being a 'faction' (remem-ber factions had been outlawed at the Tenth Party Congress, with the enthusiastic support of all three) and to criticizing Stalin, Stalin was able to expel Trotsky himself from the Politburo. In any case there had been a severe and dramatic breach between Trotsky and Stalin which was essentially unbridgeable. The decisive dra-matic twist took place on 1 November 1926 at the Fifteenth Party Conference. Stalin's report including some typically savage sarcasm at Trotsky's expense. The infuriated Trotsky pointed his finger at Stalin and burst out that 'the first secretary (Stalin) poses his candidature to the post of gravedigger of the revolution'. Trotsky could hardly have been more foolish. In response, Stalin 'turned pale, rose, first contained himself with difficulty, and then rushed out of the hall slamming the door'.[56] Afterwards, when Trotsky returned home, he found his friends were shocked and remon-strated with him, realizing as one of them put it, that 'we under-stood that the breach was irreparable'.[57] The downward spiral was speeding up for the oppositionists and the final crises occurred in 1927. Trotsky tried to rally support and held public demon-strations but he could only number his followers in the hundreds. He was not being defeated just by Stalin's 'machine', which was how he tended to explain it, but by the overwhelming support for the party 'centre' led by Stalin and for its political position. As a leading biographer argued many years ago, Stalin was neither the 'leader of an anti-revolutionary reaction . . . [A]mong the Bolshevik leaders of the twenties he was primarily the man of the golden mean' who 'abhorred extreme viewpoints'.[58] The *coup de grace* came at a full meeting (plenum) of the Central

Committee on 23 October 1927. Trotsky spoke in defence of himself and Zinoviev, who were facing a resolution expelling them from the Central Committee. He brought up charges from Lenin's testament saying Lenin's premonition about the danger of Stalin's rudeness (*grubost'*) had come true and this was the moment to act. It was Stalin who was risking a split in the party.

Stalin, in his heavy but effective manner, once again turned the accusation on its head. In a *tour de force* Stalin had opened this speech by saying:

> First of all about the personal factor. You have heard here how assiduously the oppositionists hurl abuse at Stalin, abuse him with all their might. That does not surprise me, comrades. The reason why the main attacks were directed against Stalin is because Stalin knows all the opposition's tricks better, perhaps, than some of our comrades do, and it is not so easy, I dare say, to fool him. So they strike their blows primarily at Stalin. Well, let them hurl abuse to their heart's content.
> And what is Stalin? Stalin is only a minor figure.

From this gesture of (mock?) humility, Stalin went on to quote from the large stock of anti-Lenin quotations by Trotsky from the years between 1906 and 1917 when he polemicized against Lenin, who he described in 1913 as 'the professional exploiter of all that is backward in the Russian labour movement'. But the centrepiece of Stalin's response faced the charges from Lenin's testament head on:

> It is said that in that 'will' [testament] Comrade Lenin suggested to the congress that in view of Stalin's 'rudeness' it should consider the question of putting another comrade in Stalin's place as General Secretary. That is quite true. Yes, comrades, I am rude to those who grossly and perfidiously wreck and split the Party. I have never concealed this and do not conceal it now. Perhaps some mildness is needed in the treatment of splitters, but I am a bad hand at that. At the very first meeting of the plenum of the Central Committee after the Thirteenth Congress I asked the plenum of the Central Committee to release me from my duties as General

Secretary. The congress itself discussed this question. It was discussed by each delegation separately, and all the delegations unanimously, including Trotsky, Kamenev and Zinoviev, *obliged* Stalin to remain at his post.

What could I do? Desert my post? That is not in my nature; I have never deserted any post, and I have no right to do so, for that would be desertion. As I have already said before, I am not a free agent, and when the Party imposes an obligation upon me, I must obey.

A year later I again put in a request to the plenum to release me, but I was again obliged to remain at my post. What else could I do?[59]

It was game, set and match to Stalin. Trotsky and Zinoviev were expelled from the Central Committee and then, in November, from the party itself. In January 1928 Trotsky was exiled to Alma Ata, capital of the Central Asian Republic of Kazakhstan. The following year he was forced to leave the USSR itself and settled for a while on the Turkish Black Sea island of Prinkipo.

Stalin in the late 1920s

Had Stalin now become Stalin? Not quite. The bitter succession struggle was, nonetheless, a key phase in his emergence. As Lenin feared, the party leadership – though not the membership – had split utterly. The most talented leaders of world communism and world revolution were at each other's throats more than at those of their imperialist enemies. There was no one big enough and influential enough to maintain unity now that Lenin was gone. Stalin appears to have done what he could to hold the party together, though his critics, on the basis of speculation rather than evidence, would say this was merely an act.

In any case, the issues and differences were irreconcilable. World revolution or socialism in one country. Continue with NEP or revert to 'war communism'. These were dilemmas that needed decisions. It is crucially important to realize that Stalin's rise to power was tied up with these critical issues of policy. Personality differences came to play their part, certainly, but this was not a vanity contest for the prize of power. At this point, all parties, including Stalin, wanted power for the sake of their policies, not themselves. Their tragedy arose from the deep differences between the emerging visions of the future of the revolution. All put the good of the revolution and the good of the party first. They all subscribed to a view of party infallibility. Even in defeat, and it may have contributed to that defeat, Trotsky was not willing to push his views to the extreme in opposition to the party. It was, he said, not possible to be right against the will of the party.

Starting from the importance of the issues themselves gives us a more realistic perspective on Stalin's rise. In the first place, there was little support for Trotsky's policies. His attack on the party in which he believed so deeply, was contradictory. You, the party, he had argued, are degenerating through bureaucratization and careerism; but since one cannot be right against the party, this degenerate party has to reform itself. By comparison, Stalin's constant and heartfelt praise for the achievements of party and revolution was obviously more attractive to party members. Trotsky's calls for new revolutionary upheavals, within the USSR and beyond, fell on deaf ears. The mood of the mid-twenties in the country was one of a desire for stability. Despite the dislike of NEP expressed by many party militants including Stalin himself, there was recognition that a period of consolidation was necessary and, after all, it had the authority of Lenin behind it. It would not go on forever; but, it seemed, NEP was necessary for the time being.

If Trotsky had made a serious tactical error in attacking the party, Stalin's other leading opponents, Kamenev at the head of the Moscow party and Zinoviev with the backing of Leningrad (the new name of St. Petersburg/Petrograd adopted in honour of Lenin on his death in 1924) and the Communist International, undermined their own positions of power. First they allied with Stalin in the triumvirate to have a united front against Trotsky, whom they all resented as a latecomer to Bolshevism with dangerous ideas. Then they realized their 'left wing' position of wanting to move away from NEP to a more rapid industrialization and transition to socialism was closer to Trotsky's views than to Stalin's. At that time Stalin was protecting Bukharin and his allies Rykov and Tomsky, in the name of centrism, NEP and party unity. Stalin asserted at this time, that he would not give the left 'Bukharin's blood'. Having bitterly opposed Trotsky, they then chose to jump on his already sinking ship, a blunder of the first magnitude. Many historians say they had underestimated Stalin though they would have had to be really imperceptive to do that. Everyone was aware of Stalin as an active and energetic force in organizing the party and in his special interest area of nationalities. In this respect, his ideas were integrated into many of the principles on which the constitution of the USSR, proclaimed on 30 December 1922, was established in place of the Russian Socialist Federative Soviet Republic. He had been in every leading party group since 1917. He was idolized at party congresses. How could he be underestimated? More likely, his reluctance to get involved in the left/right polemic of the mid-1920s led them to think he was pliable and could be ignored. One close observer at the time said that what distinguished Stalin at this moment was that he spoke rarely and did not gossip. According to secretary Bazhanov Stalin 'did not confide his innermost thoughts to anybody. Only very rarely did he share his ideas and impressions with his closest associates. He possessed in a high degree the gift for silence, and in this respect he was unique in a country where everyone talked far too much.'[60] What Stalin's opponents failed to see or refused to recognize was that the centrist position was the strong and popular position. Trotsky, above all the others, could not accept this. If he was being defeated it could only be because Stalin controlled the party machine and packed it with his own supporters and excluded Trotsky's, not because Stalin was right and Trotsky was wrong. One more Trotskyist myth became accepted as the norm.

Associated with this was the view that Stalin was a particularly vindictive and bitter person who played a long game and could maintain a grudge silently but forever. One of Trotsky's friends, Piatakov, said, when he was in despair at Trotsky's ill-judged 'gravedigger of the revolution' comment, that 'Stalin will never forgive him until the third or fourth generation'.[61] However, while the personal bitterness reached new levels, there is no evidence to suggest this was beyond the norms that can be found in many power struggles, even in leadership contests in democratic political parties. True, Stalin did have the added dimension of the Georgian code of 'honour', but that had not reached extraordinary or morbid levels. The disputes of the mid-1920s had certainly poisoned inner-party politics; but for the time being, Stalin had not shown himself to have 'monstrous' characteristics. The vision that he was a brooding Ivan the Terrible, skulking secretly in the Kremlin, plotting the downfall of friends and rivals, driven by a massive personal lust for power has no evidence to support it at this stage.

The final emergence of Stalin and his associates was not yet complete but the next political twists and turns are closely tied in with decisions about the future of the revolution and will be discussed early in the next chapter. For the moment we should recall comments by one of the leading historians of these matters, Isaac Deutscher, whose comment on Stalin's coming battle with his former allies on the right applies equally to his battle with the left. Though deeply sympathetic to Trotsky, Deutscher had the clarity of vision to argue that:

> It would be easy for the historian to pass unqualified judgment on Stalin if he could assume that in his fight against Bukharin, Rykov and Tomsky he pursued only his private ambition. This was not the case. His personal ends were not the only or most important stakes in the struggle. In the tense months of 1928 and 1929 the whole fate of Soviet Russia hung in the balance.[62]

Notes

1 Service, R. (2000) *Lenin: A Biography*, London, Macmillan, p158, tells us Lenin was most probably informed of this likelihood by doctors in Switzerland.

2 Lewin, M. (1969) *Lenin's Last Struggle*, London, 1969, has a very full account from the Trotsky perspective. Service (2000) Chapter 19, pp208–218 and Kotkin, S. (2014) *Stalin, Volume 1: Paradoxes of Power 1878–1928*, New York, Penguin, Chapter 11, pp472–529, also have detailed discussion.

3 Fotieva, L. A. quoted in 'Journal of Lenin's Duty Secretaries', *CW*, 42, or MIA, http://www.marxists.org/archive/lenin/works/1923/mar/06.htm#bkV42E618.

4 *CW*, vol 28, p405.

5 Lenin, V.I., 'Letter to the Congress', 23/24 December 1922 in *CW*, vol 36, pp593–611, or MIA, http://www.marxists.org/archive/lenin/works/1922/dec/testamnt/index.htm.

6 Ibid.

7 Tucker, R. (1974) *Stalin as Revolutionary 1879–1929: A Study in History and Personality*, London, Chatto and Windus, pp254–267, is one of the best accounts of the Georgian Affair. Kotkin also has a substantial discussion of it in Kotkin (2014), pp475–481.

8 Lenin, V.I., 'The Question of Nationalities or "autonomisation"', 30 December 1922, *CW*, vol 36, pp603–611, MIA, http://www.marxists.org/archive/lenin/works/1922/dec/testamnt/autonomy.htm.

9 Lenin, V.I., *Sobranie Sochinenii*, vol 54, pp674–675.

10 Ibid, pp329–330.

11 Fischer, L. (1964) *The Life of Lenin*, New York, Harper & Row, p647 and Tucker (1974), pp272, 276–277.

12 Tucker (1974), pp276–277.

13 Ibid, p270.

14 MIA, https://www.marxists.org/archive/lenin/works/1922/dec/testamnt/congress.htm.

15 Sakharov, V. (2003) *"Politicheskaia zaveshchanie" Lenina: real'nost' istorii i mify politiki*, Moscow; Kotkin (2014), pp498–501.

16 Trotsky, L. (1975) *My Life*, Harmondsworth, Penguin, p502.

17 Montefiore's *At the Court of the Red Tsar* is based on material of this kind.

18 Read, C. (2005) *Lenin: A Revolutionary Life*, New York, Routledge, Chapter 3.

19 Ibid, pp223–224.

20 The versions in his autobiography, *My Life*, and in the biography of Stalin do not tally.

21 Thatcher, I.D. (2009) 'Trotskii and Lenin's Funeral, 27 January 1924: A Brief Note', *History*, 94 (314), April, pp194–202. Quotes from pp200, 202 and 202 f 35.

22 Stalin, J.V. (1924) 'On the Death of Lenin', A Speech Delivered at the Second All-Union Congress of Soviets, *Pravda*, 30 January. In *Selected Works*, Tirana, 1979, MIA, http://www.marxists.org/reference/archive/stalin/works/1924/01/30.htm. Capitalization in the original.

23 Stalin, J.V. (1924) 'Lenin: A Speech Delivered at a Memorial Meeting of the Kremlin Military School', 28 January. *CW*, vol 6, MIA, http://www.marxists.org/reference/archive/stalin/works/1924/01/28.htm.

24 This was said, for instance, by Leon Lipson at the L.S.E. Memorial Meeting for Leonard Schapiro on 23 January 1984. The speakers on this sad occasion mostly proved him right.

25 Stalin, J.V. (1924) *Foundations of Leninism*, CW, vol 6, *Moscow*. pp71–196, MIA, http://www.marxists.org/reference/archive/stalin/works/1924/foundations-leninism/index.htm.

26 Trotsky, L. (1966) Statement of 1924 on Stalin's growing powerbase, in *Stalin: An Appraisal of the Man and His Influence*, vol 2, London, Picador (1974).

27 Davies, S. and Harris, J. (eds) (2005) *Stalin: A New History*, Cambridge, Cambridge University Press.

28 Lenin, V.I., *SW*, vol 3, pp758–759.

29 Lenin, V.I., *SW*, vol 3, p764.

30 On key aspects of NEP see Siegelbaum, L. (1992) *Soviet State and Society between Revolutions, 1918–1929*, Cambridge, Cambridge University Press; Suny, R. (2010) *The Soviet Experiment: Russia, the USSR, and the Successor States*, 2nd edition, Oxford, Oxford University Press; and McDonald, T. (2011) *Face to the Village: The Riazan Countryside under Soviet Rule, 1921–1930*, Toronto, Toronto University Press.

31 The process has been chronicled and analysed in Read, C. (1992) *Culture and Power in Revolutionary Russia: The Intelligentsia and the Transition from Tsarism to Communism*, London, Macmillan; and Finkel, S. (2008) *On the Ideological Front: The Russian Intelligentsia and the Formation of the Soviet Public Sphere*, New Haven, CT, Yale University Press.

32 Male, D. (1971) *Russian Peasant Organisation before Collectivisation: A Study of Commune and Gathering 1925–1929*, Cambridge, Cambridge University Press; and Danilov, N. (1988) *Rural Russia under the New Regime*, Bloomington, IN, Indiana University Press.

33 Luxemburg, R. (1961) *The Russian Revolution and Leninism and Marxism*, Ann Arbor, MI, University of Michigan Press, p71.

34 Lenin, V.I., 'Speech at the Opening of the Tenth Party Congress', 8 March 1921 in *SW*, vol 3, p558.

35 This had been the message since spring 1918 and the change of policy associated with the publication of Lenin V.I., 'The Immediate Tasks of the Soviet Government', *Pravda* and *Izvestiia*, 28 April 1918, *CW*, vol 27, pp643–680.

36 Quotations from *The New Course*, Chapters 4, 5 and Appendix I. MIA, http://www.marxists.org/archive/trotsky/1923/newcourse/x01.htm.

37 Ball, A. M. (1986) *Russia's Last Capitalists: The NEPmen, 1921–1929*. Berkeley, CA, University of California Press. For their subsequent fate see Fitzpatrick, S. (1986) 'After Nep: The Fate of Nep Entrepreneurs, Small Traders, and Artisans in the "Socialist Russia" of the 1930S', *Russian History*, 13 (1), pp187–233.

38 Ustrialov, N. (nd) *Belyii Omsk*, unpublished manuscript in Ustrialov Archive, Hoover Institution, Stanford, CA.

39 Read, C. (1990) *Stalin in Power: The Revolution from Above*, London, Macmillan, pp189–199; and Agursky, N. (1980) *Ideologiia National Bolshevizma*, Paris, YMCA Press.

40 See, for example, Pyman, A. (2010) *Pavel Florensky: A Quiet Genius: The Tragic and Extraordinary Life of Russia's Unknown da Vinci*, London, Bloomsbury Academic.

41 There are many guides to Marx's theories. Among the best are McLellan, D. (1971) *The Thought of Karl Marx*, London, Macmillan; and Harvey, D. (2010, 2013) *A Companion to Marx's Capital*, 2 vols, London, Verso.

42 A prime example is provided by Alexandra Kollontai, leader of the Workers' Opposition up to its dissolution in 1921, who was Soviet ambassador to Norway (1923–1925), Mexico (1926–1927) and Sweden (1930–1945). She died peacefully in Moscow in 1952 shortly before her eightieth birthday.

43 Deutscher, I. (1961) *Stalin: A Political Biography*, Oxford, Oxford University Press, p228.

44 Ibid, p297.

45 Tucker (1974), p292.

46 Ibid, p294.

47 Ibid, p296.

48 Cook, L. (forthcoming) *Inside Lenin's Government: Executive Power and Political Culture in the Early Soviet State*.

49 Harris, J. (2005) 'Stalin as General Secretary: The Appointments Process and the Nature of Stalin's Power' in Davies, S. and Harris, J. (eds) *Stalin: A New History*, Cambridge, Cambridge University Press, pp63–82. The quotations are from pp77–78. The source of Stalin's quoted conversation is RGASPI f. 558, op. 11, d. 1122, 11, pp161–165.

50 Deutscher (1961), p297.

51 Bazhanov, B. (nd) *Stalin. Der rote Diktator*, Berlin, quoted in Deutscher (1961), p275.

52 Bazhnov (nd), p32, quoted in Tucker (1974), p289.

53 Service, R. (2004) *Stalin: A Biography*, Basingstoke, Macmillan, p223; and Kotkin (2014), pp546–549.

54 *Rodina*, 7, 1994, p72. Service includes a summary and a short extract in English at Service (2004), pp223–224.

55 Tucker (1974), p291.

56 Deutscher, I. (1959) *The Prophet Unarmed: Trotsky 1921–1929*, London, Macmillan, p296.

57 Ibid, p297.

58 Deutscher (1961), p295.

59 Stalin, J.V., 'The Trotskyist Opposition Before and Now', Speech Delivered at a Meeting of the Joint Plenum of the Central Committee and the Central Control Commission of the C.P.S.U. (B.), 23 October 1927. *CW*, vol 10, MIA, http://www.marxists.org/reference/archive/stalin/works/1927/10/23.htm#I.

60 Bazhanov, B. (nd), p21, quoted in Deutscher (1961), p274.

61 Quoted in Tucker (1974), p446.

62 Deutscher (1961), p317.

4   Storming fortresses

With the expulsion of Trotsky, Kamenev and Zinoviev from the party, Stalin and his associates had considerably more power and, therefore, freedom of action than they had had before. It was not, however, complete. Bukharin, Rykov and Tomsky still represented the party right within the Politburo. Once again, the evolution of power was tied up more with policies than personalities. The end of the New Economic Policy (NEP) and the fall of Bukharin were intimately linked.

At first sight this seems strange. After all, Stalin had defended Bukharin from the attacks of the left throughout the early and mid-1920s. By 1928, however, the situation had altered radically. Stalin and his associates were no longer sharing Bukharin's outlook. Stalin, who had always been uneasy about NEP, started to criticize it more and more. By 1928 he was proposing a complete break with its key provisions. So extensive was the transformation that it has become known as the 'Great Turn', the 'Second Revolution' or the 'Stalin Revolution'. These names are entirely justified as, in a certain sense, the consequences were at least as great as those of 1917–1922. At the heart of the new policies was a renewed drive for socialist transformation and productionism in the form of industrialization. Another great irony was that this was, in broad terms if not in detail, the approach proposed by the recently defeated Trotsky and the Left Opposition. What had brought Stalin – for it was his influence which was, for the first time, paramount in making the change – to apparently adopt the mantle of the left?

The sources of the 'Great Turn'

It is possible to trace three main sources for Stalin and the party leaders' change of heart. First, in 1925 a survey of Russia's defence capability, conducted by Commissar for Defence Mikhail Frunze, concluded that although the Soviet Union had more men under arms than any other major power, its massive frontier and diplomatic isolation created a correspondingly massive operational requirement. The armed services were thought to be underequipped to meet it. They needed up-to-date weapons and, given the hostility of the outside world, they would have to make them for themselves. To do that would require heavy industry.[1]

The defence review had been conducted because there was a spectre of apprehension in Moscow that, in the longer term, some kind of showdown with the capitalist powers was likely and it was necessary to be prepared. There was also a fear that, in the light of the upcoming tenth anniversary of the revolution, the capitalist world might try to complete the task of suppressing communism/bolshevism which it had begun in 1917, but failed to complete. It was in this atmosphere that a war scare in 1927 added to the apprehension. After raiding the Soviet trade delegation in London, operating as ARCOS, the Conservative government broke off diplomatic relations with the USSR. They had only been established two years earlier by the minority Labour government. Such an act is usually a prelude to a declaration of war. Certain military manoeuvres by Britain and France seemed to confirm the threat. We now know there was no specific threat at that time but the fact that the crisis came to nothing was not the point. It had given even greater weight to the issue of the USSR's defensive capabilities. The question of what would have happened in the event of an attack, focused the mind of Soviet war planners. Once again, the strategic need for heavy industry to provide armaments was reinforced.[2] There are also indications that the elite was disturbed by reports from the OGPU (secret police) that much of the population looked forward to an international conflict as a way to ending Bolshevik rule.[3]

The second consideration is that, although the Left Opposition had been unpopular in the party and had been easily routed, it was not directly the ideas it held on the revolution's future which had brought it to its sorry state. Many party militants were sympathetic to its principles and NEP never captured their imagination. It was their refusal to abide by party discipline which had enabled them to be isolated and expelled. One of the consequences of this conjuncture was that although the most forthright spokespeople of the left had been expelled, leftist ideas were still more acceptable to many who remained in the party. There was still recognition of the need for a breathing space, as it had been called by Lenin, but the party, apart from the still-dominant right led by Bukharin, was still committed to resuming a more militant course as soon as possible.

The third and perhaps most immediate and tangible source of change was that NEP was going through yet another crisis.[4] Its basic feature was a failure on the part of the state to procure the food resources it needed. Unprecedentedly for peacetime, food rationing had to be introduced in the cities. It was this crisis which made the leadership focus on exactly where the revolution was going and what its next steps should be. Such questions had resonated throughout the 1920s but the lack of a decisive leadership because of the factional disputes had led to policy drift. No initiatives were able to unite the squabbling party so policies continued piecemeal. By 1928, however, a leadership was emerging that was nothing if not decisive. Tragically, that did not mean it was necessarily correct.

The 'Great Turn': Stalin and the making of the decision

The period from 1928 to the outbreak of war on the Eastern Front in 1941 – a kind of long 1930s – has generated a massive historical literature. While it is necessary to take the broader context into account, the present task is to try to maintain a focus on Stalin rather than produce a general history.[5] The two have often been conflated; but on the basis of an immense amount of important new material released from the archives since 1991, and of a rich historiography of many aspects of the period, it is possible to give a fresher and more convincing and consistent account of Stalin's role and activities in the turmoil of the thirties.

It is less easy, however, to get any greater insight into Stalin's mind and personality at this time.

The defeat of the Left Opposition in late 1927 had apparently resulted in Bukharin, Rykov, Tomsky and other defenders of NEP riding high and unchallenged in the party. They were also on apparently excellent terms with Stalin. This was especially the case with Bukharin. In his testament Lenin had correctly pointed to Bukharin as one of the party's most popular personalities. He was slightly younger than the rest of the leadership and was a sparkling thinker and conversationalist.[6] He was a leading performer on the leadership's weekend *dacha* and dinner party circuit. Stalin, too, was a genial host to his colleagues in those days and his daughter, Svetlana, recalled the times fondly;[7] Molotov also recalls that 'Bukharin would visit Stalin' and that he was 'a very sociable, kind and intellectual person' and 'A very good man, very kind. A decent person, undoubtedly. A man of ideas.'[8] Bukharin, at that time and even after his political defeat was a close friend of Stalin and his troubled second wife Nadezhda Alliluyeva.

However, none of this overrode the growing political difference between him and Stalin. The chief issue at stake was the peasantry. How should the leadership respond to the crisis peaking in late 1927–1928 when insufficient quantities of grain were being supplied to the cities? On the one hand, Bukharin and the supporters of NEP thought there should be a rise in the price that the state paid for grain. This would give the peasants greater incentive to sell more of their surplus produce to the state. The problem with this solution was that it went against the deep-rooted instincts of the party. They were getting fed up with the slow pace of socialist construction under NEP. To make further concessions meant reducing the pace even further since resources allocated to the peasants would reduce the amount available for industry. The point here was that the political will of the party, towards industrialization, conflicted with the economic realities of the situation. It was the drive to industrialization itself and the high level of state resources committed to it which was the problem. Arguably, state spending needed to be scaled back; the Leninist breathing space should be prolonged. State investment could not be increased either towards industry or agriculture.

However, most of the party and Stalin, in particular, thought that it was possible to defy 'bourgeois' economic laws through massive exercise of will. To try to understand Stalinism, at this point, through economics is pointless. Stalinism saw itself as a war on economics and the country was to pay the price.

Many party members had had enough of 'conciliating' peasants and cutting back on industrialization. One of them was Stalin. Within weeks of defeating and expelling Trotsky from the party, Stalin took the first steps towards adopting more radical and leftist policies. In particular, he remembered the party's first 'approach' to the peasantry in the form of coercive armed requisitioning, Indeed, as we have seen, in his Tsaritsyn posting, he was a participant claiming near-miraculous success in his first days of activity. In the longer term, requisitioning had, as we have also seen, proved disastrous and the NEP 'retreat' had been adopted to restore stability. Stalin, however, began to revive elements of the earlier approach in 1928. First of all, he personally went to central Siberia to supervise a sweep of the countryside to seize grain reserves being withheld by peasants, a reprise of his own activities of June 1918 on arriving in Tsaritsyn. As in 1918, he returned with substantial quantities of grain but his *fait accompli* had stirred up opposition in the Politburo and Central Committee. His provincial adventure was not only unauthorized by his colleagues, it had been hidden from them. Not surprisingly, many were outraged, especially Bukharin. Stalin's view, that not only the 'rich', so-called kulaks, but also 'middle-peasants' should be coerced appeared to be a repetition of the Civil War era disaster of forced requisitioning. But Stalin, although he had intervened rarely in the great industrialization debate of the 1920s,[9] was nurturing a radical change of direction even beyond the scope of what the Left Opposition had envisaged. He was planning a massive turn towards industrialization and the collectivization of agriculture. The aim of this was to break what many in the party saw as the peasant stranglehold on socialist transformation, to make an industrial breakthrough and to make the country more defensible. The devil, as usual, was in the details. How could this broad, desirable (from the point of view of party militants) and necessary new orientation possibly be achieved?

Stalin's local 'experiment' in grain requisition showed the way. Military-command methods were seen as the only possibility. The response of Bukharin and the right was to say that such an approach was unsustainable, impossible even. It meant investing resources before they had been accumulated or, in his evocative phrase, building today's factories with tomorrow's bricks. It could not, they argued, be done. Only an economic illiterate could think it could be done. In this situation Stalin was faced with two problems – a political battle for the acceptance of his approach and, astonishingly, the development of some kind of practical strategy to realize the vast dreams which were easy to talk about but so elusive to achieve. 1928 was a crucial year. Not surprisingly, at this moment a purely 'voluntarist' slogan appeared, no one knows where from. 'There is no fortress', it stated, 'that the Bolsheviks cannot storm.' Stalin seems to have used the words for the first time on 13 April 1928 at a meeting of Moscow party activists. 'Nowhere in the world are there fortresses which cannot be taken by the working people, by the Bolsheviks.'[10] Only a gigantic exercise of will and coercion from above would achieve the goal.

The Stalin Revolution begins: collectivization, cultural revolution and industrialization

For 15 months the battle raged. At a local level, food shortages were being tackled by increasingly violent coercion by party and soviet cadres. There would be no resolution until the fight at the top was resolved. Bukharin and the right tried to get what they considered to be some kind of economic realism into the debate. Simply forcing peasants to hand over grain would, in the longer run, be as counter-productive as it had been during 'War Communism'. But Stalin had a new card in his hand. The Fifteenth Party Congress, the one which had expelled the Left Opposition, had also passed a last-minute motion calling for an acceleration in the construction of collective farms. If, so the argument put by Stalin stated, one third of peasants could be attached to collective farms, then the grain supply for the state would be sufficient. There would be no fear of a fall-off in production.

The Bukharinites were not impressed. A full-scale production collective like the proposed state farms (*kolkhozy*) would not work. Instead, peasants should be encouraged to form co-operatives to help them purchase inputs to their farms to obtain group credit for expanding investment and to market their produce. This was not enough for Stalin. At the Central Committee Plenum in July he formulated his approach. It was necessary, he argued, to extract 'tribute' from the peasantry, 'a kind of supertax'.[11]

Leftists could hardly believe their ears. What Stalin was proposing sounded very similar to the ideas of the Left Opposition economist E. A. Preobrazhensky who had talked about accumulating the necessary capital for industry by treating the peasantry as 'internal colonies' which had to be 'exploited' as capitalism had exploited its internal and worldwide colonies. Oddly, the same Plenum approved the quintessentially Bukharinist policy of raising the state grain price. However, this may have been a ploy to show it would not work. It didn't and continued poor grain collection figures gave more momentum to Stalin's campaign. Even so, the confrontation remained indirect in that the issues predominated and accusations of factionalism and deviations in the party only emerged bit by bit.

Clearly, Stalin was not simply using the crisis as an excuse to eliminate his remaining opponents. He was using it to assert his vision of the revolution's future. Nonetheless, more direct assaults began by the end of the year. At the end of January and early February 1929 the Politburo, meeting jointly with Stalin's old fiefdom of the Central Control Commission of the party, passed a resolution condemning the Bukharinites for factionalism. The trap door was opening and in April 1929, at a Central Committee Plenum, also held in conjunction with the Central Control Commission, the earlier resolution was ratified and Bukharin was removed as editor of *Pravda* and Tomsky from his position on the Central Council of Trade Unions. In November Bukharin was expelled from the Politburo and he and Rykov and Tomsky published a grovelling apology and withdrawal of their ideas.

Politically Stalin and his supporters had eliminated all organized opposition. However, they had done so with probably overwhelming support in the party. The Left Opposition had only mustered 4000 votes from 728,000 voting members at the Fifteenth Party Congress in December 1927 and Bukharin and his supporters had lost all influence in the Central Committee of 121 members and the Central Control Commission of a surprising 195 members. While Stalin certainly had a bureaucratic element to his success it would be wrong to attribute it entirely to that. The membership at large had not responded to the left and they shared Stalin's dislike of NEP and of kulaks. As mentioned earlier, Trotsky had been more correct than he realized when he said of Stalin that:

> The dialectics of history have already hooked him and will raise him up. He is needed by all of them; by the tired radicals, by the bureaucrats, by the Nepmen, the upstarts, by all the worms that are crawling out of the upturned soil of the manured revolution. He knows how to meet them on their own ground, he speaks their language and he knows how to lead them. He has the deserved reputation of an old revolutionist, which makes him invaluable to them as a blinder on the eyes of the country. He has will and daring. He will not hesitate to utilize them and to move them against the Party. Right now he is organising himself around the sneaks of the party, the artful dodgers.[12]

It was a theme he returned to several times, though in less fetid language. 'It was as the supreme expression of the mediocrity of the apparatus that Stalin himself rose to his position.'[13] In 1937 he repeated the same notion: 'Stalin is the personification of the bureaucracy. That is the substance of his political personality.'[14]

Trotsky's depiction of the party is all the more piquant in that he had already said in the heat of battle in 1924 that 'we can only be right with and by the Party, for history has provided no other way of being in the right . . . And if the Party adopts a decision which one or other of us thinks unjust, he will say, just or unjust, it is my party, and I shall support the consequences of the decision to the end.'[15] The massive hypocrisy of the final sentence is breathtaking in that Trotsky was not prepared to accept the party majority on major issues. It was precisely his refusal to do so which played into Stalin's hands. In addition, Trotsky did not realize the full implications of what he was saying. Stalin was, indeed, supported by the bureaucracy – in other words, the party – but neither Trotsky nor Lenin was prepared to admit the much-lamented 'bureaucratization' of the party was an intrinsic outcome of their approach to revolution. It was not a 'degenerate' or diseased accident, it was part and parcel of the deepest implications of Leninist revolution. Stalin stole a march on his rivals by not only recognizing but building his power base on it.

However, collectivization was not the only portentous policy initiative which Stalin and his associated were pursuing in 1928 and early 1929. As the influence of the Stalin group rose, so certain signature policies also emerged. In 1928, following a series of disputes and disasters at a coalmine in the town of Shakhty in the Donbas region, some 80 kilometres/50 miles from Rostov, a group of Stalin's old bugbear, *spetsy*, were put on trial. They were mining engineers accused of 'wrecking'. They were subjected to the first economic show trial.[16] The charge of wrecking became a handy way to shrug off failings and disasters but, given the atmosphere of hostility to *spetsy* on the part of many militants, it may have been more than a cynical exercise in scapegoating. In any case, the trial was a clear signal to many that reliance on specialists was no longer the favoured approach. Hundreds of thousands of them had been persuaded to return to Soviet Russia in the 1920s and many had, as we saw in the case of *Vesenkha*, risen to responsible positions. They were now becoming suspect and many who had opposed them began to seize the moment to start blaming them for problems.

Their accusers often came from the ranks of newly educated workers and peasants. A rapid cultural revolution was raising levels of literacy, especially in the rural areas, in the mid to late 1920s. Since the revolution there had been attempts to spread culture, education and advanced skills to men and some women of working-class and peasant origin. An independent organization called *Proletkul't* had tried to nurture a form of class consciousness it called 'proletarian culture'. Its claim to independence had caused it to be brought to heel in 1920 and kept on a tight leash within the Education Ministry.[17] The ministry also supervised other initiatives for rapid transition of adult workers and peasants from the lowest to highest levels of education. Workers' Faculties (*rabfaky*) were attached to universities to give rapid preparation for a new elite who would enter university after only two years or so of education. By a process of positive discrimination (*vydvizhenie*) they were promoted into important party, state and economic managerial positions. The aim was that these rough-hewn daughters and sons of the masses would replace the politically untrustworthy 'bourgeois' specialists. Naturally, Stalin, with his long-term preference for tough, reliable workers over bourgeois remnants, was fully supportive of such people. His lectures on Leninism in 1924 had been delivered at the Sverdlov, formerly Proletarian, University, the party's own school for rapid advancement. Not only were *rabfak* graduates close to his heart, it has been plausibly argued that Stalin was close to theirs.[18] They saw him as a role model closer to their own experience than the café intellectual 'Old Bolsheviks' such as Bukharin, Trotsky and many others.

There were a host of other cultural policies emerging which have been broadly described as a turn to the left – that is, to more rapid transition to socialist values, in the cultural sphere. It should be borne in mind that 'consciousness' – values – was not a luxury for Leninists but a necessity. Only with the emergence of some form of working-class consciousness – based on co-operation, collectivism and the pre-eminence of labour in human life – could the revolution become self-generating.[19] The left turn affected many areas of cultural policy. The 'League of Militant Godless' began a more direct assault on religion compared to the stand-off from 1922 to around 1928.[20] In literature and the arts the mid-1920s era of encouraging 'fellow travellers' to join the socialist enterprise was replaced by the emergence of militant left organizations in all areas. In painting, sculpture, literature and so on across the cultural spectrum into academic disciplines including sciences, history and philosophy, militants with radical manifestos tried to claim a party-backed monopoly to 'manage' their field in the light of ideological principles. The stridency of their claims to ideological supremacy was great but their artistic talents were often very limited. Nadezhda Mandel'stam, the wife of one of Russia's greatest poets of the period, Osip Mandel'stam, pithily described the situation. The country was being overrun with poets, but there was no poetry.[21] Once again, Stalin, himself a former poet of sorts, seemed to be the poster boy, literally, for these developments. It would be too much to argue that Stalin was somehow propelled into power by this wave of militancy from below, but it would also be too much to argue that it was entirely manipulated from above. What it does show is the confluence of ideas of socialist construction developing in the post-1917 generation with those of the party leadership in general and of emerging Stalinism, in particular.

Important though these cultural developments were, the main show in town was the policy of rapid industrialization. Where did this initiative fit within the framework of the 'Great Turn'? As with other areas, Stalin had taken the line of being a fully convinced Bukharinite as late as the Fifteenth Congress (December 1927) when he talked in terms of opposing Preobrazhensky's proposed treatment of peasants as internal colonies. Such relations of 'exploitation' were equivalent to the 'capitalist method of industrialization'. Under socialism, there would be a balance so that growth would come in all sectors and industrialization would be accompanied by improvements in living standards for everyone including the peasants.[22] He did, however, believe a more rapid tempo was possible than that envisaged by his rivals. Even Trotsky had talked of 50 or 100 years being necessary before socialism could out-produce capitalism; but for Stalin, talking to the Comintern Executive on 7 December 1926, it would be possible to take 'giant strides' and outperform capitalism in a much shorter time. Those proposing a long perspective were in thrall to 'the superstitious faith of the petit bourgeois in the almighty power of the capitalist system'.[23] Typically, Stalin was promising the incompatible best of both worlds, fusing left and right programmes – steady, balanced growth over a short, intensive period.

The moment for the new leaders did not come all at once. The idea of some sort of economic plan had emerged in Lenin's ideas during the civil war.[24] A preliminary committee had been set up to draw up an inventory of Russia's resources. It was packed with 'pre-revolutionary' scientists and experts in various necessary skills, very few of them Bolsheviks. Initially, a 'plan' for electrification emerged, generating the slogan from Lenin that 'Communism equals Soviet Power plus the Electrification of the Entire Country'. As we have seen, Trotsky claimed to be setting up and partially implementing a transport 'plan' focused on getting the railways back in shape. However, such initiatives focus our attention on the vital issue of what a 'plan' means. The concept of an all-embracing, centrally directed set of orders for all, affecting all economic actors, was far from anyone's imagination. In reality, the idea of planning was widespread in the industrial world in the 1920s, not least in capitalist-dominated countries. The model for many was the German war economy which had, supposedly, shown that the uncertainties of the market could be stabilized by conscious state intervention.[25] But, for this idea of planning, the operative word was 'intervention' not 'control', which even most Soviet planners did not envisage, at least at the beginning. Instead, the notion of planning was not much different from what today is called 'economic policy' – that is, government action to create positive conditions for economic growth. In this sense, *Vesenkha* and the State Planning Commission (Gosplan) had been working since 1925 to produce a perspective plan. As time went on, even in developing the plan, the stakes rose and it became a more and more ambitious project.

Even after its original implementation it continued to change almost beyond recognition. The initial fruit of Gosplan's labour emerged as the first version of the First Five Year Plan and was officially implemented on 1 October 1928 and ratified officially in spring 1929, a curious reversal of procedure akin to taking action first and deciding what to do second. As such, its illogicality mirrored the whole process. The next step was the abandonment of the 'starting-point' plan and the adoption, in April 1929, of an upgraded version, optimistically described as the 'optimal' version. It envisaged the hitherto unprecedented goal of 20 per cent annual growth in industry. Its other, detailed goals were equally fairy tale. The already unreachable targets of the 'starting-point' variant were increased, even doubled, in the 'optimal' variant. To take one iconic example, tractor production was to reach 55,000 per year in the 'starting-point' variant and 170,000 in the 'optimal' variant. Even further into the level of fantasy, Stalin declared, on 27 June at the Sixteenth Party Congress, that the plan could be fulfilled in many areas 'in three years, or even in two and a half'. To consolidate this position he launched the slogan 'The Five Year Plan in Four Years' and even gave supposed examples where it had been fulfilled in two years.[26]

Economists then and now have been, not surprisingly, bemused by the First Five Year Plan. It had nothing in common with economic reality which demanded that before you could invest in something, you had to accumulate capital to invest. Stalin was, among other things, apparently skipping the investment stage. The process was also ploughing ahead without balancing inputs into a factory enterprise, with outputs. Today's factories needed today's bricks before they could be constructed, didn't they? Bukharin developed his critique and fought tooth and nail through 1929 to defend his ideas, to defend NEP and to defend his political career. He wrote an article entitled 'Notes of an Economist' which outlined his main objections to what was going on. There needed to be an equilibrium between production and consumption, investment and accumulation and so on. The root of progress was to build on the growing prosperity of the village so that industry could expand through meeting the needs of an expanding peasant market. This meant that the process of industrialization should not impoverish the village.[27] In July 1928, in a tragic mini-replication of Trotsky's tactical error, Bukharin tried to form links with Kamenev against Stalin. In a secret meeting, Bukharin was making more emotional statements. Stalin was, he said, 'Genghis Khan'.[28] In a sense Bukharin was correct. Like his medieval Mongolian predecessor Stalin was achieving what he did by commanding vast armies to follow his lead and improvise their support and survival as they went along. Unfortunately for Bukharin, Kamenev reported the remark to Stalin who may not have been impressed!

Perhaps more surprisingly, it was not only his opponents who had trouble with the absence of rational economics in the plan process. Valerian Kuibyshev was head of *Vesenkha* and a Politburo member since 1927. As well as being the co-ordinating body for running state-owned industries, *Vesenkha* was also involved in planning. But even the loyal Kuibyshev was 'struggling vainly to square the statistical circle'.[29] In a letter to his wife he wrote that 'I can't balance it out . . . I have to shoulder a virtually unbearable burden.'[30] Again it was the issue of balances, of equilibrium, that was causing the incomprehension. Comprehensive planning was a complex, some would say impossible, task. Every output needed carefully measured input. To produce a tractor required a vast array of inputs – metal obviously, manufactured components, rubber for tyres, the transport infrastructure to bring them together. There had to be a place for the work to take place, a factory, which needed building materials, electricity supply, machine tools, a production line each of which also needed inputs. On top of all that there was labour, human resources, which needed housing, transport, leisure facilities, food and other shops, and so on which also needed inputs. To decree the production of 170,000 tractors was to decree the need for the inputs and the inputs to the inputs and so on *ad infinitum*. In the conditions of late 1920s Soviet Russia, such a super-refined system was impossible. Kuibyshev, Bukharin and many others were only stating the obvious.

Stalin was, of course, aware of the wave of scepticism surrounding the process. In his Sixteenth Congress speech he revelled in confronting it. 'Some comrades' he said, 'are sceptical about the slogan "the five-year plan in four years." Only very recently one section of comrades regarded our five-year plan . . . as fantastic; not to mention the bourgeois writers whose eyes pop out of their heads at the very words "five-year plan".'[31] In a sense, he agreed with them: 'No five-year plan can take into account all the possibilities latent in the depths of our system and which reveal themselves only in the course of the work, in the course of carrying out the plan in the factory and mill, in the collective farm and state farm, in the district, and so forth.' But, of course, he went on to defend what was happening: 'Only bureaucrats can think that the work of planning *ends* with the drafting of a plan. The drafting of a plan is only the *beginning of planning*. Real guidance in planning develops only after the plan has been drafted, after it has been tested in the localities, in the course of carrying it out, correcting it and making it more precise.'[32]

Stalin's conceptualization of the process was vastly different from the theoretical precision of the economists. It was more akin to a military campaign. Stalin described it as 'the *organization of the offensive of socialism along the whole front* – that is the task that arose before us in developing our work of reconstructing the *entire* national economy.'[33]

Unsurprisingly, Stalin quoted the slogan that there was no fortress the Bolsheviks could not storm. Storming was the essence of the Stalinist approach. Throw people, exhortations and orders at problems and they would be overcome regardless of prerequisites. Stalin occasionally referred back to Lenin's own conclusion in his last articles that, in Napoleon's words '*On s'engage et puis, on voit*' – meaning roughly that one engages the enemy and then sees what happens. There were other continuities with Lenin as well. For Lenin, politics, including violence, had usually taken precedence over economics.[34] There was even a Leninist precedent for attempting to solve economic problems by executing people, at least in theory as there is no clear evidence that it was put into practice as Lenin had ordered.[35] The atmosphere of the Five Year Plan and collectivization was one of 'battles', 'enemies', 'fronts', 'armies', 'brigades' and the like. Class struggle had been heightened into open warfare. Stalin was reverting to the, in his view, glory days of the Civil War when a handful of Bolsheviks took on the world and defeated it. Throughout the power struggle Stalin had exuded confidence and pride in the party, the revolution, the workers and their achievements. Where his opponents talked of errors and shortcomings, Stalin spoke the language of success, never more so than in 1930 in his 'Political Report' to the Sixteenth Party Congress. It was one long list of extraordinary (not to mention greatly exaggerated) successes in grain production, present and future industrial output and revolutionary breakthroughs at home and abroad where he pointed to an ailing capitalism in the wake of the Wall Street crash. The image of capitalist confusion and heroic socialist construction was a compelling story he sold to himself, first of all, and then to colleagues, the party, part of the Soviet population, the Communist International and a worldwide chain of fellow travellers.

The material realities underpinning this heroic epic were, of course, highly questionable. Collectivization had been an immensely costly process. Peasants had slaughtered their own livestock, in many cases, because they lacked the grain to feed themselves and their animals. There had been a concealed war in the countryside through the winter of 1929–1930. The slogan 'Liquidate the *kulaks* as a class' (which did not mean kill them, it meant uproot them from their social position) was launched and what had started as, in theory, a voluntary process, turned into an increasingly violent, coercive, quasi-military campaign. Weak though they were in terms of weapons, peasants resisted with whatever they could find, usually farm implements like scythes and axes and hammers. The battles were often brutal and deadly on both sides. According to Churchill, in conversation with Stalin during the wartime conferences, Stalin compared the intensity of the fight to the one against the Nazis, declaring collectivization to have been 'harder'.[36] The process was, Stalin informed his visitor, 'very bad, but necessary'.[37] According to one of the most thorough studies of the process, so intense was the struggle that the military warned that it was not sustainable. The army of peasant recruits might be pushed too far in supporting the collectivization brigades and change sides to support their fellow peasants. The brigades themselves were largely focused around volunteer workers and, especially, young women and men from the party youth organization, the Komsomol.[38] But they were closely supported by the local militia, plus the *Narodnyi Kommissariat Vnutrennykh Del* (NKVD) or People's Commissariat for Internal Affairs (the Cheka in all but name) and, ultimately, the army. The whole process was on a knife edge.[39]

On 2 March 1930 the front page of *Pravda*, the party newspaper, was occupied by an article over Stalin's signature. It was entitled 'Dizzy with Success'. It began, conventionally enough, with praise for the overwhelming success of collectivization. By 20 February, Stalin boasted, 50 per cent of peasant households had been collectivized. 'That means that . . . we had *over fulfilled* the Five Year Plan of collectivization by more than 100 per cent.' It was 'a tremendous achievement' which showed 'That a *radical turn of the countryside towards socialism may be considered as already achieved.*' Nothing unusual so far. However, after several paragraphs the reader's attention would have been gripped by a change of tone:

> But the successes have their seamy side, especially when they are attained with comparative 'ease' – 'unexpectedly' so to speak. Such successes sometimes induce a spirit of vanity and conceit: 'We can achieve anything!', 'There is nothing we

can't do!' People not infrequently become intoxicated by such successes; they become dizzy with success, lose all sense of proportion and the capacity to understand realities; they show a tendency to overrate their own strength and to underrate the strength of the enemy.

Stalin then went on to say that, while the party as a whole was sound, certain elements had become dizzy with success. They had forgotten that 'Collective farms must not be established by force. That would be foolish and reactionary. The collective-farm movement must rest on the active support of the main mass of the peasantry.' However, 'leftist' impatience had led to distortions:

> I say nothing of those 'revolutionaries' – save the mark! – who *begin* the work of organising artels [work collectives] by removing the bells from the churches. Just imaging removing the church bells – how r-r-revolutionary!
>
> How could there have arisen in our midst such blockheaded exercises in 'socialisation', such ludicrous attempts to overleap oneself, attempts which aim at bypassing classes and the class struggle, and which in fact bring grist to the mill of our class enemies? . . .
>
> They could have arisen only as a result of the blockheaded belief of a section of our Party: 'We can achieve anything!', 'There's nothing we can't do!'

The short article is packed with Stalin themes, not to mention the use of his heavy, repetitive style as a bludgeon to make sure everyone got the point. The claim that the process was voluntary went against all the practices encouraged from above. For someone who had himself proclaimed there was no fortress the Bolsheviks could not storm, to say activists were carried away through believing 'there is nothing we can't do' is breathtakingly hypocritical. The wrapping up of chastisement and blame for failure in a packaging of success was becoming a Stalin hallmark. The ponderous and undefined battle against, as he put it, 'those who lag behind' and 'those who run too far ahead' left Stalin, as usual, at a supposedly moderate centre. But the ploy succeeded in that blame was diverted from the policy-makers to its implementers, another emerging feature of the Stalin approach to failure and correction of, often his own, mistakes. The immediate outcome was a reduction in the tempo of collectivization so that a more realistic figure of 25 per cent of households collectivized emerged in June 1930.

Nonetheless, one of the most controversial aspects of the agrarian transformation lay ahead – the famine of 1932–1933. No one doubts there was a vast famine in which 5 to 7 million people died. The cause of it, however, has become controversial. Since the publication of Robert Conquest's book[40] there has been a bitter controversy about whether the famine was deliberate or 'accidental'. For many, especially Ukrainian nationalists, the famine constitutes a deliberate act of terror by Stalin: an act of genocide against the Ukrainian population, a death-famine, the *holodomor*. The obvious objection to this theory, namely that many other regions were severely affected, including some which were Russian, is more or less ignored. Without doubt the famine was a crime of the first magnitude but there is little evidence for deliberation nor is there a convincing reason for it. Stalin and his associates were not averse to brutal tactics – the harrowing of Georgia was a classic example as we have seen – but there was no cause for such a response in 1932 since, by then, the extreme crisis of collectivization had been weathered. It is more likely that the crime consisted in over-procurement of grain by requisitioning squads similar to those of the Civil War. They were charged with bringing in the 'surplus' from the now collectivized farms. As in the Civil War, there was an assumption that peasants would hide as much grain as they could so the squads often took great quantities of grain from whatever they could find. Wherever they went they left peasants with insufficient grain to grow the crop the following year, or even to tide them over the winter. When climatic conditions also created shortages the crisis hit hard. The number of deaths has been variously calculated but probably amounts to 5 million or even more. As such, it represents the largest loss of life in the 1930s, much beyond the main purge period of 1936–1939.

It was only in early 1932 that the authorities at the centre took on board the depth of the disaster they had created. At this point, say proponents of the *holodomor* concept, they should have released grain reserves to meet the need. The most careful study has shown that reserves were insufficient. A great deal of the extorted grain had already been exported to buy machinery and so on for the developing industries. Much of what was left had to serve as a strategic reserve in case of war. War might seem a remote possibility from the European perspective, but in 1931 the Japanese had invaded the Asian mainland and the old antagonisms of the Russo-Japanese War of 1904–1905 were beginning to re-emerge and it might be necessary to defend the country. The leadership decided to release some reserves but it was far from enough. Like so many Stalinist crimes it arose from criminal negligence rather than criminal intent. What did the regime have to gain from it? They knew very well, and had just gone through it for a second time, that violent coercion of the peasants and, even more, famine, far from securing the position of the leadership posed a great danger to them and to their project.

The crisis ran through to the next harvest. The errors were not repeated in the following years and over-procurement did not raise its ugly head again until the desperate conditions of wartime and recovery.[41]

One final point about collectivization. It is, not only because of the dreadful famine, usually considered to be a complete failure, one which was endemic in the Soviet system. In particular, through keeping food consumption standards, especially of meat, quite low compared to the West, it is also said to have contributed to the final collapse of the system. However, there is one important proviso to be made here. Over the next decades, Russian society was transformed. By the time of Stalin's death the population was about 50/50 rural urban. By the 1980s it was predominantly urban. In other words, where 80 per cent of the population fed the non-peasant 20 per cent in the first third of the century, by the end of the Soviet Union a small rural population was feeding a much vaster urban one. Traditional peasant agriculture is unlikely to have achieved even the modest levels of productivity characteristic of Soviet agriculture. Capitalist agriculture might well have been more successful still but we will never know as, obviously, it was politically off the agenda. However, given the climatic challenges and the environmental fragility of Russian agricultural zones, it is unclear what levels of output could be expected. Collectivization did succeed in providing enough grain and foodstuffs to support mass industrialization, urbanization and, in stark contrast to peasant-based production in 1914–1917, a massive war effort from 1941–1945. While harvests fluctuated, the state procurement of grain was both reliable and much larger than it had been before collectivization.[42] In other words, collectivization led to production that was far from optimal but much greater and more reliable, for the authorities, than traditional peasant agriculture. Henceforth, the burden of low harvests was to fall almost entirely on the peasants. Also, without the rural productivity gains, there would have been no surplus peasant labour to migrate to towns and cities and to form, when needed, an immense army.

While collectivization has been almost universally condemned as a failure, industrialization has evoked a less hostile reaction. It had many faults but, at the time and, for some analysts, since, there have been admirers. The Promethean endeavour of building vast industries from scratch appealed to the romantic streak of many observers, including foreigners. There was a great deal of foreign involvement in industrial development, particularly the purchase of advanced machinery and the use of imported expertise, mainly in engineering.[43]

By and large, the targets of the First Five Year Plan were not met. Precise calculations, as usual, are difficult and all output figures are subject to a significant margin of error. However, roughly speaking, it is possible to get an idea of what was achieved. One of the most solid figures is that the industrial workforce rose from 11 million to 22 million in the plan period. This is a colossal rise and, perhaps surprisingly, was way ahead of the plan figure of 15 million. It also uncovers the secret of the plan. The advances were based on labour-intensive operations, not capital-intensive ones. It was people, not resources, who were thrown at problems. The labour history of the 1930s is fascinating. Wherever and however one looks at the great industrial construction sites the overwhelming presence of the workforce imposes itself. The super-projects of the late 1920s led the way. Photographs of the Dnepr dam being built to supply hydro-electricity show massive numbers of underequipped workers crawling up and down perilously erected scaffolding and hauling materials up and down in buckets attached to ropes. Hardly any construction machinery can be seen. Muscle power and spades predominated over mechanical diggers and bulldozers. Even cranes were relatively few and far between. A brilliant account of the development of the Magnitogorsk complex portrays a young, unskilled, drifting worker contingent initially living in army field tents, having nothing on which to spend their not very substantial pay apart from vast quantities of vodka (including lethal, home-made *samogon*). The scene depicted as a whole is one of chaos and this was typical of the period.[44]

It is also counter-intuitive that, in the supposedly rigid and centralized bureaucratic system of the party, state and planners, there was a highly mobile workforce. Many attempts were made to increase labour discipline; but though they resulted in random 'offenders' being arrested and sent to the growing number of labour camps, they did not cow the workers as a whole into compliance. If conditions were too tough or if better wages seemed to be on offer elsewhere, they would move on. It was a paradox that ran through all Soviet (and post-Soviet) society that the population of this over-rigid and over-centralized system was highly mobile.

Other plan targets were mostly under-fulfilled. According to recalculated post-Soviet era figures the main results of the economic tempest of 1928–1932 was that agriculture declined from output valued at 58 billion roubles in 1928 to 41.9 billion roubles in 1932. Industry, on the other hand, grew from 24.2 billion roubles to 37.6 billion. Other sectors, including services, grew from 41.5 billion roubles to 56.2 billion roubles.[45]

What do these figures mean? What did the experience of the First Five Year Plan mean? First of all, they mean the economy, at this stage, was not planned in any rational sense. In a pioneering study, Naum Jasny, himself a food resource planner in Soviet Russia for a time, described what was going on as 'Bacchanalian planning'.[46] Bacchus was a Roman god not only associated with delirium and moral collapse but also of intoxication as the cause. As such it fits the process very well. Millions of commands flew around. Harassed managers tried to implement them. If they failed they risked exposure as 'wreckers' or 'saboteurs'. The culture of blame became deadly. Scapegoats had to be found for everything from output failures to railway crashes. Following on from the Shakhty trial of 1928, a second show trial of Russian *spetsy*, the so-called *Prompartiia*, the Industrial Party, was held at the end of 1930 and a third trial, this time of foreign engineers from Britain, was held in 1933, the Metro-Vickers Trial. All were accompanied by denunciation and counter-denunciation between the defendants and by confessions made, sometimes withdrawn and then reinstated. Some foreign observers accepted the legality of the proceedings.[47] The reality of these trials was spoken by Allen Monkhouse, a defendant in 1933, who said from the dock 'this trial is a frame-up against Metropolitan-Vickers engineers based on evidence of terrorized prisoners'. There was much more of this to come. For the time being, sentences in most cases were light, though there were a small number of executions of people implicated, such as Peter Palchinsky, who was executed in 1929 before the trial even began. However, as was the case later on in the decade, show trials were only the tip of the iceberg. Some Menshevik émigré estimates suggest that 7000 engineers were arrested at this time.[48]

By 1933/1934 the maelstrom of transformation was losing much of its initial, chaotic force. In a quintessentially Stalinist term, the tempo was falling. What had been achieved? In real terms the increases in output had been less than the plan called for but were still impressive, especially against the backdrop of continuing crisis and economic depression in the United States and much of the capitalist world. Despite falling short in terms of detail, on the large-scale the plan had succeeded. It had been a game-changer. The great lumbering supertanker of the Russian economy had, at great cost, been hauled round onto a new course. The process was only beginning but Russia was being dragged out of its perennial dependence on the peasant economy. The ties of tradition and of an agrarian economy had been broken and the promise of a turn towards industry, engineering, education and science was under way. In less than five years the foundations of an industrial society had been created. However, one might agree, and worse was to come, that, in the words of an historian who has spent 50 years delving into the murkiest aspects of Stalin's rule, Stalinism was one way to achieve industrialization in the same way that cannibalism was one way to achieve a high protein diet.[49]

Stalin, the cult of personality and the Congress of Victors

In 1933, nevertheless, Stalin stood victorious. The cult of his personality was taking off. It had begun by stages but the first major step had been his (false) fiftieth birthday celebrations in December 1929. Like the British monarch, he had adopted an 'official birthday' but in his case, the real one was over a year earlier. The propaganda apparatus and court flatterers in the Kremlin began to crank out the superlatives. Particularly pleasing must have been the slogan 'Stalin is the Lenin of Today'. It was always what he had aspired to and it was from Lenin that he had derived his inspiration. One might argue that he had torn through Lenin's testament, not only in personal terms of retaining his post as general secretary of the party, but in political terms in smashing into the *smychka* (alliance) between peasant and worker which Lenin said should not be violated. Setting aside official pseudo-arguments that collectivization fulfilled the terms of the *smychka* because it brought town and country into ever-closer union of production, consumption and exchange, it should be remembered why Lenin had come to believe in it. His early efforts had all been geared to coercing the peasants through forced requisition and attempting to develop class struggle in the countryside. He had only slowed down because the peasants had defeated the best efforts of party and state and the result had been the NEP. In the hearts of party militants, the model of transition in effect from 1918 until the adoption of the NEP, conventionally but misleadingly called 'war communism' even though it was adopted before the Civil War flared up again in June 1918, was not an aberration brought about by the civil war but a deeply considered method of constructing socialism. The militants, including Stalin, liked it because it was driven by a sense of urgency completely absent in the NEP. It was not only National Bolsheviks like Ustrialov who had dreamed that the NEP was a step towards reversion to liberal capitalist 'normality' and away from revolution rather than towards socialism. Party militants feared that was the case as much as Ustrialov had hoped it might be so. In essence, Stalin was reverting to his, and much of the party's, preferred option of rapid transition. Lenin had been forced to abandon that approach because the peasants were stronger than the government. Stalin had picked up the initiative and broken the peasantry. Would Lenin have approved? We will never know but it is at least arguable to think that he might have done.

But it was not only the issue of transition that caused the urgency. In one of his most famous speeches, given to an audience of factory managers in 1931, Stalin had made his pitch for what he was doing:

> It is sometimes asked whether it is not possible to slow down the tempo somewhat, to put a check on the movement. No, comrades, it is not possible! The tempo must not be reduced! On the contrary, we must increase it as much as is within our powers and possibilities. This is dictated to us by our obligations to the workers and peasants of the USSR This is dictated to us by our obligations to the working class of the whole world.
>
> To slacken the tempo would mean falling behind. And those who fall behind get beaten. . . . All beat [old Russia] – because of her backwardness, because of her military backwardness, cultural backwardness, political backwardness, industrial backwardness, agricultural backwardness. They beat her because it was profitable and could be done with impunity. . . . It is the jungle law of capitalism. You are backward, you are weak – therefore you are wrong; hence you can be beaten and enslaved. You are mighty – therefore you are right; hence we must be wary of you.
>
> That is why we must no longer lag behind.

The assault on backwardness was framed, however, not in traditional terms of Russian nationalism, which was often mistakenly attributed to Stalin, but rather in wholly new revolutionary terms. Russia was important not because it was Russia but because it was the homeland of socialism and, as such, a beacon of hope for the poor and exploited around the globe:

> In the past we had no fatherland, nor could we have had one. But now that we have overthrown capitalism and power is in our hands, in the hands of the people, we have a fatherland, and we will uphold its independence. . . .

We are fifty or a hundred years behind the advanced countries. We must make good this distance in ten years. Either we do it, or we shall go under.

That is what our obligations to the workers and peasants of the USSR dictate to us.

But we have yet other, more serious and more important, obligations. They are our obligations to the world proletariat. They coincide with our obligations to the workers and peasants of the USSR But we place them higher.[50]

The passage has attracted many commentators, not only for its ringing rhetoric and quintessentially Stalinist content but also because it was, indeed, ten years later, in 1941, that the German invaders crossed the border into the USSR. Stalin, of course, did not know this but apart from the conviction that they had ten years to break Russian backwardness there are several other important elements. Stalin explains his new brand of patriotism. Under tsarist rule the worker had no country, but after the overthrow of capitalism there is a socialist fatherland to be defended. Perhaps even more surprisingly the fusion of 'socialism in one country' and 'world revolution' leads the man supposedly indifferent to the non-Soviet world to say that their duty to the world proletariat is even higher than that to the Soviet proletariat.

Just over a year after that speech the process of industrialization was put on a slower but more sustainable footing. In the bogus guise of fulfilment the plan was wound up and declared to have been an enormous success. The period from the second half of 1932 to 1934 is sometimes referred to as one of 'thaw' or even, in the eyes of some observers, a time of the 'great retreat'.[51] This last description has been challenged in terms of pointing out that there was no retreat from the broader goal of socialist construction.[52] That is certainly the case but there was undoubtedly a significant reversal of some important policies not least in the field of culture. The 'leftist' dominance in terms of proletarianization of the arts and ideology which had generated the frenzied atmosphere of rapid transformation in 1928 to 1931, was brought under control. Many of the poets without poetry, like Leopold Averbakh, the main figure in the so-called Russian Association of Proletarian Writers (RAPP from its Russian initials) had denounced many writers much more talented than he was. It was now his turn to be arrested. The eminent historian E. V. Tarlé, who had been implicated in the fake *Prompartiia* (Industrial Party) trial, was released and returned to his professorial chair in Leningrad. Theatre and cinema reverted to the norms of the 1920s and audiences were no longer subject to interminable harangues about revolutionary duty written by committed but sadly untalented militants. In fact, a genuinely popular cinema began to emerge, even including dance and glamour spectaculars derivative of the Busby Berkeley movies in Hollywood. Of course, ideological messages were not abandoned but they were wrapped in softer and more subtle packaging. They were probably all the more effective for that. The first great popular propaganda success, the film *Chapaev*, was made in 1934. Earlier silent movies, such as Eisenstein's masterpiece *The Battleship Potemkin* (1925), had been acclaimed in Europe and North America. The footage of his film *October* (1927) is so realistic that images from it are often shamefully used as though they had been shot during the actual days of revolution. The image of the non-existent heroic 'Storming of the Winter Palace' came from his film, not history. Eisenstein has even been credited with inventing the basic language of modern film through *montage*. Simply put, the meaning of the film was created through editing and juxtaposing images with one another. Dziga Vertov more or less invented the documentary film. But despite the great intellectual achievements, the films of the 1920s lacked a crucial ingredient: popularity. There was no point in making a film no one wanted to see. But *Chapaev* was a rip-roaring success. It was based on the education of a partisan leader, Chapaev, in the Civil War. Along with his comic sidekick Petka he is distinguished by revolutionary commitment and reckless bravery. However, under the tutelage of a quiet, moustachioed, pipe-smoking political commissar (who did he remind the audience of?) the undisciplined band is formed into an organized and effective fighting unit. As such, it was a metaphor for the relationship between the party and the population but especially between Stalin and his people.

Clearly, ideological aims had not been abandoned in the moment of victory. Instead, like the economy, it entered a calmer and more sustainable phase. The doctrine of socialist realism, whose roots go back to the previous decade, was codified and decreed for all artistic endeavours. Its principles were threefold. Any work of art should be based on the party point of view (*partiinost'*), the principles of class (*klassovost'*) and be easily understood by ordinary people (*narodnost'*). This opened the way to generations of dull but worthy depictions of Soviet life, showing, in the words of one cultural administrator, not life as it is but life as it will be.[53] In place of the deadly domination of RAPP a Union of Soviet Writers was set up which created comfortable conditions for approved writers but shut all routes to publication to anyone else.

A final general point about culture. Although socialist culture was intrinsically collectivist, praising group achievements over the individual, Stalin, Stalinism and Stalinist culture had a curious Nietzschean element of the hero, the superman or woman who led the way. Not only did the cult of personality portray Stalin in this way it was also a time of individual, Soviet-style 'celebrity culture' of heroes and heroines. The difference from contemporary capitalist celebrity was that Soviet celebrities had actually done something. Pioneer aviators were among the most popular figures of the cult, the predecessors of post-war cosmonauts. Explorers and scientists were also lauded. Even workers. The figure of the norm-busting Stakhanov was held up, in 1935, as a national hero and exemplar. He had, supposedly, produced a massive amount of coal in a single shift. In a world of labour-intensive and voluntaristic, exhortative economic 'planning' this is not surprising. Collective achievements were not ignored but Stalinism also promoted the super-achieving individual in an almost capitalist and individualist fashion.

In this way, film and the arts maintained a surprisingly full life in the 1930s despite the threats and shadows which fell on many exponents. They were not extinguished by the darkness of the mid-1930s despite growing problems. Leading individuals such as the poet Osip Mandelstam and the theatre director Vsevolod Meyerhold died in the camps and world-renowned figures like the brilliant young composer Dmitrii Shostakovitch faced serious criticism of their works. In the face of tighter censorship, the doctrine of socialist realism and a stifling bureaucratic control of the process the number of feature films made every year was severely reduced in the 1930s compared to the 1920s. Sergei Eisenstein, only managed to complete one major film project in the 1930s. However, at another level, Soviet cinema led a relatively charmed life and grew in popularity in terms of items like *Chapaev* which were big hits with the Soviet audience. Within similar doctrinal controls, literature also flourished to the extent that a few Soviet writers became best-sellers in the country. Although many of Russia's most creative and original writers were censored and their works remained unpublished or came out in restricted editions, for the first time officially approved film makers, writers and artists were making big connections with the mainstream audiences.

There were achievements in science and technology which attracted worldwide attention. The young physicist Peter Kapitsa worked with Rutherford at Cambridge. Despite being forced to stay in Russia in 1934 his career flourished and, in his later years after the war, he even stood up to Beria in a dispute in which he gained Stalin's personal support. Explorers and aviators opened up new lands, mapped barely known territories like Severnaya Zemlya, the last piece of the earth's surface to be discovered, and made record breaking flights to inhospitable regions. The rescue of the polymath academician Otto Shmidt's ice-bound Arctic research team in 1938 was followed by the international media. Sports opportunities also expanded. From 1924, with a break during the cultural revolution of 1928–1932, the Soviet Union was one of the only countries in the world to have a daily sports newspaper, *Krasnyi sport* (*Red Sport*),[54] with a mass circulation of millions. It covered national and international sport.

Throughout the upheavals of the 1930s, Stalin had maintained a curious relationship with intellectuals. As for any pope, ayatollah, moralizer or mobilizer there were those who were on Stalin's side, whom he courted almost affectionately at times. On the other hand, there were those who were against the socialist project whom he ruthlessly opposed unless they were thought to be capable of being won over or, especially in the case of foreign intellectuals, useful to the cause in which case a few ideological imperfections could be overlooked. While at some level Stalin's dalliance with intellectuals appears odd, it does, in fact, arise from sometimes underestimated aspects of the communist project. Economic, political and social engineering were all subject to the same goal, as far as Stalin was concerned – the liberation of working people from the yoke of class domination. The ultimate aim of Marxism was the transformation of human nature or, to put it another way, freeing human nature from the characteristics in which it was trapped as a consequence of class. Briefly, the idea goes back to Marx himself who said the hitherto existing history of humanity was only its prehistory.[55] Many Russian Marxists had taken up the theme. While Stalin had not been in the forefront of those who emphasized cultural revolution, in the 1930s he made his own baleful contribution. The idea of the New Soviet Person emerged in official propaganda. Such a person would cast aside market and capitalist values of competition, individualism (that is, selfishness) and material greed and replace them with collective and co-operative values, denial of self to the point of martyrdom in extreme cases and service of the community as a duty for all. There was also an assumption that scientific and rational values would replace the religious superstition of the past.

It is not our current task to explore this fascinating debate in general but only to pick out Stalin's place in the process. Although it is not an area which is given much priority in analysis of Stalin's personality and politics, it is extremely revealing of his ideas, values and personality. Perhaps the key phrase in understanding his approach is one he used in addressing the founding congress of the Soviet Writers' Union where he described writers, and implicitly the creative intelligentsia as a whole, as 'engineers of the soul'. In Cold War times the phrase was often derided and linked to his comment that everyone was a cog (*vintik*) in the machine of society. But both of them had multiple layers of meaning. In calling intellectuals 'engineers of the soul' Stalin was doing no more than express a concept which had been embedded in party consciousness since the revolution. The role of the intellectual was to assist the party in creating the new culture and consciousness, carrying out the sweeping cultural reformation without which communism would fail. Communism sought a revaluation of all values and this Nietzschean phrase reminds us that of all the branches of Bolshevism, Stalinism, consciously or unconsciously, absorbed or paralleled key Nietzschean values. The idea of the strictly rational, atheist New Person itself had Nietzschean echoes. But there was also the lauding of heroes of science, exploration, aviation, sport and, highly prominent in the mid-1930s, the cult of super-workers like the legendary Stakhanovites.[56] Then there was the rising cult of all cults, the cult of the leader. If values were to be revalued who would be in the forefront of the process if not the intellectuals? They would fashion the culture which would inhabit and guide the new social machine. They would have a key role in socialist construction.

For that reason the rewards available to supportive intellectuals were very considerable. The Soviet intelligentsia was reorganized in Stalin's day into a series of professional associations of which the Writers' Union is best known. However, they also existed for visual artists, musicians, cinematographers, scientists and even lawyers. Those enjoying membership of such associations could lead comfortable lives with secure incomes, highly subsidized lodgings in some of the Soviet Union's most desirable apartments, access to imported goods and often access to foreign cultural goods (films, music, scholarly journals) unavailable to the masses. The workload expected of these officially approved intellectuals was fairly light. Needless to say, the process also gave rise to a layer of cultural administrators who rarely shared the talents of those whom they administered. Some were protective and helpful but many intervened officiously and obstructively in cultural life. Outside of the official organizations, cultural production was all but impossible. All access to distribution of cultural products – print media, galleries, concert halls and so on – was controlled by the authorities. Many intellectuals produced for the public but also kept works which would not pass the censor in their desk drawer.

Stalin was clearly proud of officially approved intellectuals of whom Maxim Gorky was the most illustrious up until his death in 1936. Relationships between Stalin and the intellectuals, not to mention between officialdom and intellectuals, were unlikely to be anything other than variable, even volatile. There was little common ground to be found between the inconstant nature of intellectuals who were always seeking something new and original and the heavy, grinding, utilitarian mechanisms of the mobilizing party-state. It is also an area full of rumours and personal tales of narrow escape and unnecessary tragedy. For example, as late as 1931 the writer Evgeny Zamiatin, who had written an early satire on the utopian future entitled *We* in 1921, which was a forerunner of Aldous Huxley's *Brave New World* (1932) and George Orwell's *1984* (1948), was able to write to Stalin requesting permission to leave the USSR. Even though Zamiatin had smuggled his book abroad to be published by Russian émigrés in Prague in 1929, permission to emigrate was granted through the mediation of Gorky, who had been providing such a service for dissident intellectuals since the early days of the revolution. On the other hand, no one was able ultimately to save Osip Mandelstam, who had written a poem which was derogatory of Stalin personally; though even here, his first arrest in 1934 resulted in a much lighter sentence of exile rather than imprisonment thanks to a plea for clemency by Bukharin. Tragically, the choice of protector may have been the cause of a second arrest in 1938, after Bukharin's own execution, and a sentence Mandelstam did not survive. Mandelstam himself expressed the situation with tragic brilliance and irony: 'Only in Russia is poetry respected, it gets people killed. Is there anywhere else where poetry is so common a motive for murder?', a thought which applied to Russia's great nineteenth-century national poet Pushkin as well as himself.

However, it was not only Soviet intellectuals who were important to Stalin. From early soviet times intellectuals from overseas had mediated the Russian Revolution for international audiences. John Reed had brilliantly mythologized the October Revolution. Other visitors were harsher, like Bertrand Russell.[57] In addition to the growing number of communists worldwide, many of whom, especially among the leaders, were intellectuals, the 1930s was the high point for what became known as 'fellow-travellers' or, more literally, 'travelling companions' (*sputniki*). The term had emerged in the 1920s and was applied to intellectuals within the USSR who were, in some significant sense, sympathetic to the revolution but unprepared to be fully committed to the extent of joining the party. During the 1930s, driven, above all, by a common hostility to fascism and Nazism, many left and left-leaning liberal intellectuals from the West visited the USSR and, in most cases, sang its praises. Those who did not, like André

Gide, who wrote a deeply critical account of his visit,[58] were ostracized by the equivalent of the politically correct centre-left as being virtually Nazi sympathizers in the binary vision of mid-1930s Europe. The Manichean good/evil outlook was heightened after the Spanish Civil War broke out and the USSR was the only active defender of the Spanish government and state against internal right-wing rebellion supported by troops supplied by Hitler and Mussolini. Unlike Gide, however, many others were happy to provide glowing accounts of Stalin's rapidly growing, anti-fascist Soviet Union. One of them, the French communist Henri Barbusse, even produced the first substantial, not to say sycophantic, biography of Stalin.[59] At the time of his death in 1935 Barbusse's views had brought him into conflict with one of the great truth-tellers about Stalin's rule, Victor Serge. However, anti-Stalinist views were not welcome in Europe as the ravages of fascism and Nazism increased. Serge and others were seen as Trotskyist apologists rather than genuine prophets. Ironically, Serge himself was only released from the gulag by the skin of his teeth thanks to a campaign by Western, especially French, intellectuals to have him released in 1936 after two years of harsh exile. Once again Stalin relented in the face of left intellectual pressure. Ironically, the French authorities refused to admit him but he was allowed to return to his native Belgium. The years 1933 and 1934 were a moment when tempos of change reduced and consolidation appeared to be the order of the day. It was a period of triumph and confidence for Stalin. It had been a complicated time for him personally. In late 1932 he suffered personal tragedy. His wife Nadezhda committed suicide after a public row with him. Through the 1920s she had been his staunch Bolshevik comrade and companion. They had a daughter, Svetlana, and a son, Vassili. In the Cold War her death was portrayed in the West as a political act of protest against her husband. However, the evidence suggests she had a recurring mental illness, a kind of bipolar disorder which finally overwhelmed her. As at the time of the death of his first wife, Ekaterina Svanidze, mother of his other son, Yakob, Stalin was heartbroken and even, according to some eyewitnesses, reduced to tears at the funeral.

Memoirs of the period, including those of his daughter Svetlana, depict, in these years, a somewhat claustrophobic but by no means sombre life of the party leaders in the Kremlin 'village' where most of them lived and worked during the week and in their extra-urban *dachas* (grander than a cottage, less imposing than a country house) at the weekend. In the midst of the crisis Stalin maintained a number of idiosyncrasies. He took considerable pride in his *dacha* garden and would point out the flowers and shrubs to Svetlana when she was a child. After the war he was, according to Molotov and Svetlana, inordinately proud of a lemon tree he had managed to raise in his *dacha*. Molotov was mystified by Stalin's sense of achievement. Perhaps the secret is that it was, for Stalin, both evocative of Georgia and the south as well as symbolizing in miniature the Promethean promise of the socialist revolution which would enable lemons to be grown even in Moscow.[60]

During this period, counter-intuitively, Stalin and the other leaders would periodically walk around the streets of Moscow with minimal security. There are photos from the early 1930s which show this and memoirs, especially of one of Stalin's last such trips, discussed in the next chapter, on Svetlana's birthday in November 1935 when, at Svetlana's request, they made an informal visit to the newly opened Moscow Metro. It was not unusual, on these occasions, for Stalin to receive an ovation from the ordinary citizens whom he met. Stalin took them as instinctive approval of his leadership but cold warriors would point to the supposed consequences of not applauding – a visit from the secret police. Oddly, it may well be that the more likely interpretation was Stalin's, until 1936 at least, because, although it is hard to judge with any accuracy, there was considerable support for the leadership and the ongoing revolution. In the countryside, this was, of course, not the case, by and large, but the issue of popular involvement in and support for the leadership is a very lively and contentious issue.[61]

Within the party there is little doubt that Stalin and his allies reigned supreme. Nonetheless, there were many critics. One of the most prominent was Martemyan Ryutin, a party member from Moscow. He produced what was one of the last significant protests in the party against Stalin. In an unpublished (*samizdat*) pamphlet-type document of some 200 pages entitled 'Stalin and the Crisis of the Proletarian Dictatorship' he called for reinstitution of all expelled Old Bolsheviks, including Trotsky and Bukharin; for a slowing down of the rate of industrialization and collectivization; and described Stalin as the revolution's 'evil genius' and 'gravedigger of the revolution'. The document circulated at the height of the chaos in 1932 through a group of friends who called themselves the Union of Marxist-Leninists. It circulated widely and a number of prominent former oppositionists, including Kamenev and Zinoviev, are thought to have read it. On 23 September 1932 Ryutin and his associates were arrested. A specially convened meeting of the Central Control Commission Presidium took place on 27 September. Their report called for those involved to be banished from Moscow. According to what one historian calls a 'persistent myth' derived from Boris Nicolaevsky and popularized by Robert Conquest, Stalin is supposed to have called for the death penalty for Ryutin, a demand eloquently opposed by Stalin's close associate Sergei Kirov. There is no evidence to support this and, as has been pointed out, Stalin had supported lenient rather than vindictive sentences in similar cases before.[62] Ryutin was, nonetheless, eventually executed in the Great Purge in 1937.

Ryutin's ideas did not penetrate deeply into the party. For every dissident there seemed to be ten willing volunteers who would do the party's will in town or country. Stalin stood at the head of these militants and no matter what the country as a whole believed, he was idolized by them. Stalin also bewitched many foreign observers and leftists. In a mixture of genuine admiration for the actual industrial achievements of the time together with a leaven of naiveté, wishful thinking, deliberate suspension of critical faculties, falling for Soviet propaganda and deception and a desire to have 'no enemies on the left' when fascism and Nazism were on the rise, a generation of European and American admirers of Stalin sang his praises. Not only committed intellectuals such as Henri Barbusse, but journalists like Walter Duranty, diplomats like the US ambassador, Joseph Davies and the ranks of communists around the globe bought into the Stalin myth. Dissenters such as André Gide, Victor Serge and British journalist Malcolm Muggeridge were not listened to or dismissed as dupes of the right.

For all the terrible mistakes he had made alongside the achievements, Stalin's popularity in 1933/1934 was at an all-time high within and beyond the USSR. The 1934 Seventeenth Party Congress acclaimed him. It became known as the Congress of Victors since a crucial and irreversible victory in the struggle for socialism seemed to have been won. The delegates were not to know that, by the time of the next party congress in 1939, over 1000 of them would have been arrested. For the moment, however, Stalin appeared to have won the fight and the leadership was full of confidence. Stalin appeared to have, finally, become Stalin. However, there were three more immense events to come: the purges, World War II and the Cold War. From Stalin's point of view these were all intimately linked. They were different aspects of a single struggle against the barely distinguishable phenomena of imperialism and fascism. There were other Stalins yet to emerge.

Notes

1 See the account by Sokolov in M. Harrison (ed) (2008) *Guns and Rubles: The Defense Industry in the Stalinist State*, New Haven, CT, Yale University Press, pp31–49.
2 Samuelson, L. (2000) *Plans for Stalin's War Machine: Tukhachevsky and Military-economic Planning (1925–1941)*, London, Routledge; and Hudson, H. (2012) 'The 1927 Soviet War Scare: The Foreign Affairs-Domestic Policy Nexus Revisited', *The Soviet and Post-Soviet Review*, 39, p1.
3 See Simonov, N. S. (2000), 'The "War Scare" of 1927 and the Birth of the Defence-industry Complex', in Barber, J. and Harrison, M. (eds) *The Soviet Defence Industry Complex from Stalin to Khrushchev*, London, Routledge, pp33–46.
4 It is far beyond our scope to give a full explanation of the complexities of the economy at this time. The most accessible introduction to the issues can be found in Davies, R. W. (1998) *The Soviet Economy from Lenin to Khrushchev*, Cambridge, Cambridge University Press.
5 There are many books which have a helpful broad overview. To name but two: Suny, R. (2011) *The Great Experiment: Russia, the USSR and the Successor States*, 2nd edition, Oxford, Oxford University Press; and, much briefer, Read, C. (2001) *The Making and the Breaking of the Soviet System*, London, Macmillan, Chapters 4 and 5.
6 There is an excellent biography of Bukharin which has stood the test of time: Cohen, S. (1980), *Bukharin and the Bolshevik Revolution: A Political Biography 1888–1938*, Oxford, Oxford University Press.
7 Alliluyeva, S. (1967) *Twenty Letters to a Friend*, New York and London, Harper & Row.

8 Chuev, F. (1993) *Molotov Remembers: Inside Kremlin Politics*, Chicago, IL, Chicago University Press, pp174 and 118.

9 The classic account is Erlich, A. (1960) *The Soviet Industrialisation Debate*, Cambridge, MA, Cambridge University Press. More recent accounts are led by Nove, A. (1992) *An Economic History of the USSR 1917–1991*, Harmondsworth, Penguin; Davies (1998); and, the most detailed account, Davies, R.W. (1989) *The Industrialisation of Soviet Russia: The Soviet Economy in Turmoil 1929–1930*, Harmondsworth, Penguin.

10 My thanks to Mark Harrison for this reference. It can be found at: https://www.marxists.org/reference/archive/stalin/works/1928/04/13.htm.

11 He used the term several times including in a speech of 9 July 1928, *CW*, vol 11, MIA, https://www.marxists.org/reference/archive/stalin/works/1928/07/04.htm.

12 Trotsky, L. (1968) *Stalin*, London, Oxford University Press, p215. Quoted above p112.

13 Trotsky, L. (1975) *My Life*, Harmondsworth, Penguin, p522.

14 Trotsky, L. (1937) *The Revolution Betrayed*, London, Routledge, p11, or MIA, https://www.marxists.org/archive/trotsky/1936/revbet/index.htm; http://www.marxists.org/archive/trotsky/1936/revbet/ch11.htm.

15 Trotsky, L. Speech at the Thirteenth Party Congress, May 1924.

16 As we have seen, the first major political show trial of SRs was in 1922, and there were a number of forerunners in the revolutionary tribunals and elsewhere in the early Bolshevik years. See Rendle, M., 'Revolutionary Tribunals and the Origins of Terror in Early Soviet Russia,' *Historical Research*, http://onlinelibrary.wiley.com/doi/10.1111; and the same author's forthcoming book. See also the article by Aaron Retish in *Home Front*, Book 4 of the RGWR project (forthcoming).

17 Mally, L. (1990) *Culture of the Future: The Proletkul't Movement in Revolutionary Russia*, Berkeley, CA, and Oxford, Oxford University Press; various articles by John Biggart; and Read, Christopher (1990) *Culture and Power in Revolutionary Russia*, London, Macmillan, pp11–132, 145–155.

18 Fitzpatrick, S. (1979) *Education and Social Mobility in the Soviet Union 1921–1934*, London, Cambridge University Press.

19 The theme is discussed in Read, C. (1990), pp189–199; especially Chapters 3 and 4; and throughout Tucker, R. (2005) *Lenin: A Revolutionary Life*, New York, Routledge, especially pp223–224.

20 See Daniel Peris on the League of Militant Godless in Read, C. (2003) *The Stalin Years: A Reader*, Basingstoke, Macmillan; Pospielovsky, D.V. (1987) *A History of Marxist-Leninist Atheism and Soviet Anti-Religious Policies*, London, Macmillan; and Luukkanen, A. (1994) *The Party of Unbelief*, Helsinki, Suomen Historiallinen Seura SHS.

21 Fitzpatrick, S. (1994) *The Cultural Front*, Ithaca, NY, and London, Cornell University Press; and Fitzpatrick, S. (1978) *Cultural Revolution in Russia*, Bloomington, IN, Indiana University Press.

22 Stalin, J., Speech at the Fifteenth Congress of the CPSU.

23 Tucker, R. (1974) *Stalin as Revolutionary 1879–1929: A Study in History and Personality*, London, Chatto & Windus, p398; and MIA, https://www.marxists.org/reference/archive/stalin/works/1926/11/22.htm.

24 Lenin V.I., 'Integrated Economic Plan', *Pravda*, 22 February 1921, *CW*, vol 32, pp137–145, or MIA, https://www.marxists.org/archive/lenin/works/1921/feb/21.htm.

25 Feldman, G. (1966) *Army, Industry and Labour in Germany 1914–18*, Princeton, NJ, Princeton University Press, argues that the German war economy was actually highly inefficient.

26 Stalin, J., 'Political Report of the Central Committee to the Sixteenth Congress of the C.P.S.U. (B.) June 27, 1930', II.3; *CW*, vol 12, MIA, http://www.marxists.org/reference/archive/stalin/works/1930/aug/27.htm#I. See Tucker, R. (1990) *Stalin in Power: The Revolution from Above 1928–1941*, New York and London, W.W. Norton & Co, p96. For more detailed accounts of the plan see Davies (1989, 1998); and Nove (1992).

27 Bukharin, N.I. (1993) 'Notes of an Economist'. Extracts available in Daniels, R. V. (1993) *A Documentary History of Communism from Lenin to Gorbachev*, Lebanon, NH, University Press of New Hampshire, pp166–169. Regrettably, it is not (as of September 2016) among the extensive works of Bukharin in MIA; but an online version derived from a translation by Bertram Wolfe for *Khrushchev and Stalin's Ghost*, New York, Praeger, (1957), can be found in the Radio Liberty archive at: http://www.osaarchivum.org/greenfield/repository/osa:872fbbdf-156e-412d-8898-74a1ed978fe4#1.

28 Deutscher, I. (1961) *Stalin: A Political Biography*, Oxford, Oxford University Press, p314, quoting Souvarine, Boris, *Staline*, Paris, Plon (1935) p483.

29 Tucker (1990), p95.

30 Quoted in ibid.

31 Stalin, 29 June 1930, *CW*, vol 12, MIA, http://www.marxists.org/reference/archive/stalin/works/1930/aug/27.htm#I.

32 Ibid.

33 Ibid.

34 Lenin, *SW*, vol 3, p527.

35 Pipes, R. (1997) *The Unknown Lenin*, Princeton, NJ, Princeton University Press.

36 Rees, L. (2009) *World War II Behind Closed Doors: Stalin, the Nazis and the West*, London, BBC Books, p161.

37 Churchill, W., *The Second World War*, vol 2, New York, Houghton Mifflin, p272.

38 See Viola, L. (1999) *Peasant Rebels under Stalin*, Oxford, Oxford University Press; and Viola, L. (2002) *Contending with Stalinism*, Ithaca, NY, Cornell University Press.

39 Erickson, J. (2001) *The Soviet High Command: A Military-Political History 1918–1941*, 3rd edition, London, Routledge, 2001, pp315–316, discusses the frenzied efforts of the army Political Administration to retain the loyalty of the largely peasant army. Unsurprisingly, the army was kept out of the collectivization campaign almost entirely.

40 Conquest, R. (1986) *Harvest of Sorrow: Soviet Collectivisation and the Terror-Famine*, New York and Oxford, Oxford University Press.

41 The debate is enormous: Ellman, M. (2008) 'The Political Economy of Stalinism in the Light of Archival Revelation', *Journal of Institutional Economics*, 4 (1), April 2008, pp99–125; and Davies, R.W., Wheatcroft, S. and Tauge M. 'Stalin, Grain Stocks and the Famine of 1932–33' in Read, C. (ed) (2003) *The Stalin Years: A Reader*, Basingstoke, Macmillan.

42 Ellman, M. (1975) 'Did the Agricultural Surplus Provide the Resources for the Increase in Investment in the USSR during the First Five Year Plan?', *The Economic Journal*, 85, December, pp844–863.

43 See, for example, Schulz, K.S. (2003) 'Building the "Soviet Detroit"' in Read (2003); Scott, J. (1942) *Behind the Urals: A Russian Worker in Stalin's City of Steel*, London, 1942; and Chamberlin, W.H. (1934) *Russia's Iron Age*, Boston, MA, Harvard University Press.

44 Kotkin, S. (1995) *Magnetic Mountain: Stalinism as a Civilization* Berkeley, LA, and London, University of California Press.

45 Davies, R. (1998) *Soviet Economic Development from Lenin to Khrushchev*, London, Macmillan, p82, based on Moorsteen, R. and Powell, R.P. (1966) *The Soviet Capital Stock 1928–1962*, Homewood, IL, R.D. Irwin, pp620–638. Figures based on 1937 prices.

46 Jasny, N. (1961) *Soviet Industrialization 1928–1952*, Chicago, IL, Chicago University Press, p73. Having left Russia for Germany, Jasny left in 1933 as Hitler came to power and worked thereafter in the United States. During the Cold War his expertise was used by the US government and military to estimate the actual harvest in the USSR in order to gauge its military potential. This confirms the importance attached to grain reserves, not only in connection with the famine of 1932–1933 but also well into the post-war era. 'His estimates of grain harvests in the U.S.S.R. served for many years as the basis for the investigations into the Soviet military potential', Ronall, J.O. (2013) *Jewish Virtual Library*, http://www.jewishvirtuallibrary.org/jsource/judaica/ejud_0002_0011_0_10008.html.

47 There is an excellent discussion and set of sources on the Metro-Vickers Trial useful for teaching at http://spartacus-educational.com/RUSmetro.htm.

48 Abramovitch, R. (1962), *The Soviet Revolution 1917–1939*, New York, International Universities Press, p382.

49 Conquest R. (2008) *The Great Terror: A Reassessment*, London, Oxford University Press, p461.

50 Stalin, J.V., 'The Tasks of Business Executives', Speech Delivered at the First All-Union Conference of Leading Personnel of Socialist Industry, 4 February 1931, *Pravda*, 5 February 1931; *CW, vol 13*,

MIA, http://www.marxists.org/reference/archive/stalin/works/1931/02/04.htm.

51 Timasheff, N. (1946) *The Great Retreat: The Growth and Decline of Communism in Russia*, New York, E.P. Dutton.

52 Hoffman, D.L. (2004) 'Was there a "Great Retreat" from Soviet Socialism? Stalinist Culture Reconsidered', *Kritika*, 5 (4), pp651–674. Timasheff is defended in Lenoe, M. (2004) 'In Defense of Timasheff's *Great Retreat*', *Kritika*, 5 (4), pp721–730.

53 Lunacharsky, A. V., 'Sotsialisticheskii realizm', *Sobranie sochinenii*, 8, p615, quoted in, for example, Rosenthal, B. G. (2010) *New Myth, New World: From Nietzsche to Stalinism*, Philadelphia, PA, Pennsylvania State University Press, p303. Russian version available at: http://lunacharsky.newgod.su/lib/ss-tom-8/o-socialisticheskom-realizme.

54 After 1946, it changed its name to *Sovetsky sport* (*Soviet Sport*). It continues to be published to the present day.

55 Marx, K. (1859) *Preface to a Contribution to the Critique of Political Economy*, MIA, https://www.marxists.org/archive/marx/works/1859/critique-pol-economy/preface.htm.

56 Rosenthal (2010) discusses this question.

57 Reed, J., *Ten Days that Shook the World* was first published in 1919 and has been reprinted many times since, including an electronic version from Digi-Medi-Apps, 2012; and Russell, B., *The Practice and Theory of Bolshevism*, was first published in 1920 (as *Bolshevism: Practice and Theory*) and many times since, most recently as an eBook by The Floating Press, Auckland, 2014.

58 Gide, A. (1936) *Retour de l'URSS*, Paris, Gallimard, available as an eBook via Project Gutenberg.

59 Barbusse, H. (1935) *Stalin a New World Seen Through One Man*, London and New York, Macmillan.

60 Medvedev R. and Medvedev, Z. (2003) *The Unknown Stalin*, London, I. B. Tauris, p194.

61 A seminal work in this discussion is Hellbeck, J. (2006) *Revolution in My Mind: Writing a Diary under Stalin*, Cambridge, MA, Cambridge University Press. There are multiple excellent works by David Hoffman and notable contributions by Siegelbaum, L. and Sokolov, A. (2000) *Stalinism as a Way of Life: A Narrative in Documents*, New Haven, CT, and London, Yale University Press; and Fitzpatrick, S. (1999) *Everyday Stalinism: Extraordinary Life in Extraordinary Times*, Oxford and New York, Oxford University Press.

62 Getty, J. A. and Naumov, O. (2010) *The Road to Terror: Stalin and the Self Destruction of the Bolsheviks, 1932–1939*, London, Yale University Press, p34; Nikolaevsky B. (1965) 'Letter of an Old Bolshevik', in *Power and the Soviet Elite*, New York, Praeger; and Conquest. R. (1990) *The Great Terror: A Reassessment*, Oxford, Oxford University Press, p24.

5 Nine circles of hell

During the moment of 'victory' in 1933 and early 1934 there was no indication that the relatively relaxed atmosphere, or, in Stalin's own language, the 'reduced tempo' of change, would not be the norm for the indefinite future. The First Five Year Plan had been a chaotic scramble with ambiguous results. Institutionally and physically, the foundations of industry had been laid. It had even succeeded beyond expectation in producing, within the aims and objectives of productionism, its most desired commodity – workers, because building up the number of workers in Russia and reducing the number of peasants was essential if socialism was to be built. Those foundations appeared to be the basis for steady and sustained growth. In the words of the leading expert on the Soviet economy, 1934–1936 was 'a period of spectacular economic development'. How so? 'Many of the factories started during the First Five Year Plan were brought into operation' and agriculture began to recover. National wealth, according to an American estimate, increased by a massive 55 per cent between 1932 and 1937. In town and country labour productivity improved and 'the standard of living improved greatly' compared to 1933 with the result that 'In 1935 all consumer rationing was abolished.'[1]

In his *Report to the Seventeenth Party Congress on the Work of the Central Committee* (29 January 1934), one of the most important speeches of his career, Stalin had a twofold message to get across. There were miraculous achievements and victories to be celebrated but there was still work to be done and there was no room for complacency and arrogance. First, the achievements:

the socialist form of social and economic structure – now holds undivided sway and is the sole commanding force in the whole national economy . . .

During this period, the U.S.S.R. has become radically transformed and has cast off the aspect of backwardness and medievalism. From an agrarian country it has become an industrial country. From a country of small individual agriculture it has become a country of collective, large-scale mechanized agriculture. From an ignorant, illiterate and uncultured country it has become – or rather it is becoming – a literate and cultured country covered by a vast network of higher, secondary and elementary schools functioning in the languages of the nationalities of the U.S.S.R.

New industries have been created: the production of machine tools, automobiles, tractors, chemicals, motors, aircraft, harvester combines, powerful turbines and generators, high-grade steel, ferro-alloys, synthetic rubber, nitrates, artificial fibre, etc., etc.[2]

Villages, too, had been transformed:

The appearance of the countryside has changed even more. The old type of village, with the church in the most prominent place, with the best houses – those of the police officer, the priest, and the kulaks – in the foreground, and the dilapidated huts of the peasants in the background, is beginning to disappear. Its place is being taken by the new type of village, with its public farm buildings, with its clubs, radio, cinemas, schools, libraries and creches; with its tractors, harvester combines, threshing machines and automobiles. The former important personages of the village, the kulak-exploiter, the bloodsucking usurer, the merchant-speculator, the "little father" police officer, have disappeared. Now, the prominent personages are the leading people of the collective farms and state farms, of the schools and clubs, the senior tractor and combine drivers, the brigade leaders in field work and livestock raising, and the best men and women shock brigaders on the collective-farm fields.

Stalin was especially proud of the cultural transformation that had been wrought:

> As regards the cultural development of the country, we have the following to record for the period under review:
>
> (a) The introduction of universal compulsory elementary education throughout the U.S.S.R., and an increase in literacy among the population from 67 per cent at the end of 1930 to 90 per cent at the end of 1933.
>
> (b) An increase in the number of pupils and students at schools of all grades from 14,358,000 in 1929 to 26,419,000 in 1933, including an increase from 11,697,000 to 19,163,000 in the number receiving elementary education, from 2,453,000 to 6,674,000 in the number receiving secondary education, and from 207,000 to 491,000 in the number receiving higher education.
>
> (c) An increase in the number of children receiving pre-school education from 838,000 in 1929 to 5,917,000 in 1933.
>
> (d) An increase in the number of higher educational institutions, general and special, from 91 in 1914 to 600 in 1933.
>
> (e) An increase in the number of scientific research institutes from 400 in 1929 to 840 in 1933.
>
> (f) An increase in the number of clubs and similar institutions from 32,000 in 1929 to 54,000 in 1933.
>
> (g) An increase in the number of cinemas, cinema installations in clubs, and mobile cinemas, from 9,800 in 1929 to 29,200 in 1933.
>
> (h) An increase in the circulation of newspapers from 12,500,000 in 1929 to 36,500,000 in 1933.

In particular, Stalin emphasized the widening participation of workers and of women in the new order of things:

> Perhaps it will not be amiss to point out that the proportion of workers among the students in our higher educational institutions is 51.4 per cent of the total, and that of labouring

peasants 16.5 per cent; whereas in Germany, for instance, the proportion of workers among the students in higher educational institutions in 1932–33 was only 3.2 per cent of the total, and that of small peasants only 2.4 per cent.

We must note as a gratifying fact and as an indication of the progress of culture in the countryside, the increased activity of the women collective farmers in social and organisational work. We know, for example, that about 6,000 women collective farmers are chairmen of collective farms, more than 60,000 are members of management boards of collective farms, 28,000 are brigade leaders, 100,000 are team organisers, 9,000 are managers of collective-farm marketable livestock sectors, and 7,000 are tractor drivers.

While the actual figures in the above boasts need to be taken with a pinch of salt there is no doubt the fundamental transformation he describes was in the process of taking place. Remnants of the old Russia had been uprooted and a new, modern, science-based Soviet Union was emerging. However, there was a second, potentially more sinister, aspect to Stalin's message. Successes were all very well but that did not mean the task of building socialism was completed:

It is evident that all these successes, and primarily the victory of the five-year plan, have utterly demoralised and smashed all the various anti-Leninist groups. It must be admitted that the Party today is united as it has never been before. *(Stormy and prolonged applause.)*

Does this mean, however, that the fight is ended, and that the offensive of socialism is to be discontinued as superfluous? No, it does not. Does it mean that all is well in our Party, that there will be no more deviations in the Party, and that, therefore, we may now rest on our laurels? No, it does not. We have smashed the enemies of the Party, the opportunists of all shades, the nationalist deviators of all kinds. But remnants of their ideology still live in the minds of individual members of the Party, and not infrequently they find expression.

This was not the moment to end the 'socialist offensive':

> That is why we cannot say that the fight is ended and that there is no longer any need for the policy of the socialist offensive . . . Take, for example, the question of building a *classless socialist society*. The Seventeenth Party Conference declared that we are advancing towards the formation of a classless socialist society. Naturally, a classless society cannot come of its own accord, as it were. It has to be achieved and built by the efforts of all the working people, by strengthening the organs of the dictatorship of the proletariat, by intensifying the class struggle, by abolishing classes, by eliminating the remnants of the capitalist classes, and in battles with enemies, both internal and external. The point is clear, one would think.
>
> And yet, who does not know that the enunciation of this clear and elementary thesis of Leninism has given rise to not a little confusion in the minds of a section of Party members and to unhealthy sentiments among them? The thesis that we are advancing towards a classless society – put forward as a slogan – was interpreted by them to mean a spontaneous process. And they began to reason in this way: if it is a classless society, then we can relax the class struggle, we can relax the dictatorship of the proletariat, and get rid of the state altogether, since it is fated to wither away soon in any case. And they fell into a state of foolish rapture, in the expectation that soon there would be no classes, and therefore no class struggle, and therefore no cares and worries, and therefore it is possible to lay down one's arms and go to bed—to sleep in expectation of the advent of a classless society. *(General laughter.)*

In other words, state vigilance had to be maintained and it was no time for permanent relaxation. There were enemies within and without to be confronted and when that moment came it was unlikely to provoke 'general laughter'. There was still an agenda of social transformation to be completed: 'we must not lull the Party, but sharpen its vigilance; we must not lull it to sleep, but keep it ready for action; not disarm it, but arm it; not demobilize it, but keep it in a state of mobilization for the fulfilment of the Second Five Year Plan. Hence, the first conclusion: *We must not become infatuated with the successes achieved, and must not become conceited.*'

As it turned out, the situation was made all the more critical by the growing realization of the dangers flowing from the ascendancy of Hitler and also by the thunder flash of the assassination of Kirov in December 1934 discussed below. For the time being, however, the regime, in general, and Stalin, in particular, far from being paranoid, as is so often suggested, were brimming with confidence. Internal opposition had been dealt with. The Stalin leadership was unchallenged, not only because of coercion but also because of elements of popularity within and beyond the party. In these years, Stalin and his allies would occasionally walk the streets of Moscow with minimal security to measure the public mood. They were met with idolization more common for film stars. Even as late as November 1935 such excursions took place. Stalin's sister-in-law, Maria Svanidze, in her diary which was published after the collapse of communism, tells us about Stalin's daughter Svetlana asking her father to visit the newly opened metro. Touchingly, Stalin's close associate Lazar Kaganovich, who had supervised the construction of the metro, actually acquired ten tickets for Svetlana, her aunts and her bodyguard. At the last minute, Stalin decided he would join in. While his security advisers were understandably apoplectic at the suggestion, Stalin was determined. The little group descended to the platform. In the words of one account, when they stepped out of the train to admire the Okhotnyi riad station 'Stalin was mobbed by fans'.[3] According to Maria, Stalin remained jovial throughout though his associates, handlers and Vasilii, his son, were sick with anxiety.[4]

Despite the optimism, the confidence and the apparent beginnings of economic success, the USSR was teetering on the brink of hell. From 1935 to the German invasion in 1941, the ever-present element of repression was ratcheted up to now well-known but still unbelievable levels. Precise calculation of victims is all but impossible given the complexity of the repressive system itself, which involved executions, labour camps, conventional prison and the looser confinements of exile and labour colonies. The number of conventional criminals in the system – thieves, murderers, rapists and robbers – confuses the overall numbers. In the Cold War, Western estimates of the numbers in the camps varied greatly. Timasheff, the author of *The Great Retreat*, proposed a figure of 2.4 million in the system at the end of 1937. Robert Conquest, probably the best known and most widely read but not the most accurate, historian of *The Great Terror* (1968), as he entitled his main book, claimed a total number of 9 million camp residents (excluding criminals but including political prisoners in prisons) at the end of 1938. Post-Soviet calculations, based on much sounder sources, suggest the number of forced labourers altogether in all categories of places of confinement came to 2.5 million in 1933; 2.6 million in 1937; 3.3 million in 1941 and 5.5 million in 1953.[5] These figures look odd for 1937 when there was a wave of arrests which one would expect to cause a spike in the figures. However, two elements may help to explain this. First, the figures do not include those who were simply exiled – that is, who were free, except they were not allowed to live in certain areas, notably the major cities. Conventionally, 1 million 'kulak' families, so about, 4 to 6 million people, were uprooted during collectivization. Two million were officially exiled. In addition, there were direct executions. From 1927 to 1941 no less than 792,000 were executed for 'counter-revolutionary and other particularly dangerous state crimes', of whom 682,000 were executed in 1937 and 1938, the peak purge years. Calculations of 'excess deaths'[6] suggests a total of 7 to 14 million from 1926 to 1939. 'On all estimates, most of these deaths occurred during the 1932–3 famine.'[7]

The quantum of human misery encapsulated in these bare statistics is incalculable. There have been many studies of the era and of the camps. Alexander Solzhenitsyn's pioneering monumental three-volume transcription of stories, eye-witness accounts and some documents gave the widest insight into the unimaginable experiences of the time.[8] There have been a multitude of memoirs of former inmates and scholarly studies of widely varying quality.[9] Important though it undoubtedly is to know what we can about one of the lowest points of human experience, it has been focused on almost to the point of obsession. The present study, focused on Stalin's life and his personal role in such events, is not the place for a general evaluation. However, we do need to investigate the nature of this unprecedented turn in Soviet history, not least asking where it came from and what impact it had. To achieve this let us look at some examples of life in the gulag, examine its origins and concentrate on Stalin's role.

The gulag in the 1930s

The detention system of the Soviet state, known as the gulag from the Russian acronym of the 'Main Camp Administration' (*Glavnoe upravlenie lagerei*)[10] was a vast and, like most of its siblings, highly inefficient bureaucratic apparatus. It had in its charge millions of prisoners and exiles of various kinds, not to mention hundreds of thousands of prison guards whose lives could be almost as harsh as that of the prisoners. It is hard to make meaningful observations that apply to this vast and variable system, which reached out from the People's Commissariat for Internal Affairs (NKVD)-controlled Lubianka in central Moscow to the frozen extremities of Kamchatka on the Pacific, to the mountains of Alma-Ata (now Alma-Aty) and the deserts of Kazakhstan. In pursuit of two objectives – the security of the camp and the need for labour in inhospitable areas – many of the camps were in some of the harshest conditions on the planet. In the Siberian tundra and the arctic north, where prisoner-dependent nickel smelters polluted the pristine white of the permafrost, temperatures could fall to −50 degrees Celsius. In the deserts they could rise to the 40s. In ideal circumstances survival would be difficult for those not born to the conditions. In the terrible conditions of oppression, forced labour, minimal equipment and totally inadequate food supplies it is hardly surprising that the death rate in the camps ran at about 7 per cent per year from 1936 to 1941.[11] Clearly, surviving a harsh 10- or 20-year sentence was unlikely.

One man who did so was Karlo Stajner, a Yugoslav communist of Austrian origin imprisoned and exiled from 1936 to 1956, a period commemorated in the title of his supremely illuminating and comprehensive memoirs *Seven Thousand Days in Siberia*. Many of his stories reflect the many sides of this appalling process.

One of them, told to him by the Palestinian communist Joseph Berger who lived through it, illustrates a key component of the horror which is often forgotten. A detachment of 400 prisoners and guards was sent to set up from scratch a new camp settlement in Gornaya Shoriya. From the remote railhead in Stalinsk (Novokuznetsk) they were marched for three weeks into the virgin forest and taiga. Forty tough Siberian horses carried supplies and equipment. Twenty prisoners died on the march, their bodies eaten by wolves. The survivors set up tents and were allowed to rest. 'There was enough to eat and the prisoners regained their strength quickly. The work wasn't hard because no quotas had been set yet.'[12] More prisoners trickled in until there were 1200 but problems only really began to arise when winter set in and 2 metres of snow cut the settlement off; in Stajner's words 'the NKVD had forgotten one minor detail, people and horses have to be fed. They had brought enough provisions for two months.'[13] Rations were cut and the occasional airdrop plus some hunting success eked out a living mainly for the guards. Nonetheless, typhus took hold and the medical staff (most camps had them) were helpless because they lacked medicines. By spring only 300 prisoners were left alive with barely the strength to bury their dead comrades. The only response of the NKVD was to bring in thousands of new convicts. The whole experience shows that one of the most deadly aspects was simply the inefficiency of the bureaucracy which sent people into the middle of nowhere and forgot about them. One of the key differences between the gulag and the Holocaust is that the latter was built on clear criminal intent while the terrible toll of mortality in the former came in part from criminal neglect. Not that that made much difference to the victims.

An even more horrific example of inefficiency and neglect leading to unimaginable horror has been focused on in recent years. In 2002 the Russian-based society *Memorial* (Memorial), devoted to gathering material on the camp system, placed a set of documents on its website related to one of the most remote camps based on Nazino Island in the West Siberian Nazina River near its confluence with the Ob. In May 1933, a period of relative 'thaw' in the process of repression, 6114 people were sent to this island as a place of exile. A total of 27 died on the barge taking them from Tomsk to Nazino, a journey which, ironically, took them past Stalin's brief 1912 place of exile, Narym. The barge contained about 4 kilograms of flour per person and little or nothing by way of tools and equipment. There were two commanders and 50 newly recruited guards who lacked proper footwear and uniforms. On the first day of arrival there were 295 burials. Although it was early May and the river ice had melted, the harsh winter did not relent and there was significant snowfall. Only days after arrival there were reports that, out of 70 more deaths, five corpses showed signs of cannibalism. The situation went from bad to worse. Unsurprisingly, typhus set in. By the end of summer, only three months after their arrival, only 2200 out of 6700 deportees were still alive. Only 200 to 300 of them were deemed fit enough to work.[14]

The events described by Stajner and the Nazino catastrophe illustrate some of the less widely understood but crucial aspects of the repression of the 1930s, especially its murderous inefficiency. The victims in these and many other cases were not meant to die; but the ramshackle nature of the state administration in many of its aspects and the camp administration, in particular, condemned them to do so by omission more than intent. In these cases, and many others, victims were caught up in a maelstrom of jumbled planning, mass indifference and murderous neglect. Ironically, official report after official report denounced this state of affairs. The only reason we know so much about the Nazino affair is because of reports of state and party officials who were horrified by it. One of them, Vassilii Arsenevich Velichko, summarized the situation in a letter to Stalin which was circulated to Politburo members.[15] It was rare for any corrective action to be taken. In a climate of headlong industrialization, rural famine and approaching war the vast network of imprisoned criminals and 'enemies' were the lowest priority for investment and the allocation of scarce supplies. Unsurprisingly, the years of greatest difficulty nationally – 1941 and 1942 – saw the highest death tolls in the camps.[16]

Local action could also be responsible for some of the worst aspects of the purges. In another story told to Karlo Stajner, in 1935, 300 nuns and associated religious women were being held in a camp on Muksulma in the former monastery complex in the

Solovetsky Islands in the White Sea in the far north. The nuns refused to work on the grounds that the Soviet authorities were Antichrist. Their offer to work in the hospital was refused. They were confined to punishment cells where they received 300 grams of bread and a pot of hot water each day and some camp soup once every five days. Every ten days they were ordered to work and refused. Eventually, they were led out of the cells and made to stand in a long line. The other prisoners were brought out to watch. The nuns were ordered to work and made the customary refusal to work for Antichrist. The camp commander shot the first nun with his revolver. The second gave the same answer and she was shot. He continued till he ran out of bullets, ordering the assembled guards to shoot the rest in salvos of rifle fire. When all were dead he proclaimed to the camp inmates that 'there was no room for parasites in the Soviet Union. Anyone who refused to work would be treated exactly as these women were.'[17] Even a hardened prisoner said that after the story was told 'we weren't able to sleep for a long time'.[18]

Although local 'initiatives' like this and local chaos contributed to the scale and horror of the repression there can be no doubt that the chief responsibility lay with the central authorities, including Stalin. Indeed, no one has ever put forward the ludicrous allegation that the centre did not know what was happening. If anything, the general sense of the repression has gone in the opposite direction, often assuming that it was all directly attributable to Stalin. Like Tsar Ivan IV in Eisenstein's wonderful film, Ivan/Stalin is seen as a paranoid and cruel ruler sacrificing self, family and country to the national cause.[19] There may be some truth in this but the portrait of the tsar rising above even the terrified courtiers (boyars) who skulk behind pillars in the Kremlin and a cowed and frightened population who awaited royal decrees as they would devastating storms, does caricature Stalin's rule at this time. Of course, he knew what was happening in general, but he did not set it up, run it and carry it through on his own. Contributory factors like the local arbitrariness of the commander who executed the nuns without even a legal fig leaf to cover his atrocious act or the complete lack of effective planning which condemned the thousands of Nazino, Gorniya Shora and many other prisoners to death were not simply willed by Stalin or the centre. However, the responsibility does lie with the centre though contemporary understanding suggests it is more diverse than the paranoia of Stalin alone.

Areas where the personal responsibility of Stalin and his associates is unequivocal start with the vast list of 682,000 executions of 1937 and 1938. In most cases these sentences were imposed by NKVD troikas – that is, three officer/judges without a jury. A brief, secret trial usually resulted in a guilty verdict, in many cases accompanied by a 'confession' extorted by torture or threat to family. Where the death penalty was invoked it was carried out swiftly, often immediately after the trial, to ensure no appeals could be made to complicate the process. Where significant figures in the party and state were concerned the list of proposed executions was presented to Stalin personally who signed them off. Even though this veneer of pseudo-legality was extraordinarily thin it does seem to have worked to shield those involved in the process from feeling excessive guilt. Camp guards, for example, mostly seem to have believed their prisoners were guilty as charged. So did a wide spectrum of Soviet society, though things might have been different had the falsity of the confessions and the vast scale of repression been known at the time. The quasi-legal forms may also have salved the conscience of the executioners. The man who is thought to have executed more fellow humans than any other (possibly excluding perpetrators of massacre in Rwanda and elsewhere) is Vassilii Blokhin. He was an NKVD major general who maintained a career as a state executioner and dirty work operative, supposedly with the personal approval of Stalin,[20] from 1926 until Stalin's death in 1953, a change of circumstances to which he was unable to adapt and he committed suicide in 1955. In addition to having, it is said, personally executed 7000 Polish prisoners of war at Katyn in 1941, he is also deemed responsible for a multitude of deaths in the basements of the NKVD's Lubianka headquarters in central Moscow, including his own bosses Iagoda and Yezhov, the high-ranking defendants in the show trials and the victims of the secret trial of military leaders. Apparently, only when his rank was taken from him and his work denigrated instead of praised did his self-belief collapse.[21]

The main driving force of the repression certainly came from the centre. In late Soviet times the key decrees on arrest and executions were published in their original format for the first time. A series of waves of repression were prepared and carried out by the NKVD. The main ones included several orders for the arrest of members of minority nationalities including Order No 00447 aimed at former enemies such as white guards and kulaks who, supposedly, had not made their peace with the Soviet system and others directed at Germans (00439), Koreans (1428–326CC), Poles (00485), Greeks and others. They were all issued over Yezhov's signature in summer 1937. The decrees had a preamble defining the categories subject to repression followed by *'limity'* – that is maximum numbers who could be imprisoned and arrested broken down by 64 NKVD administrative units covering the whole USSR. Every major branch of the NKVD received numbers like the sample for seven of those districts given here:

Table 5.1 Selected figures for execution and arrest from NKVD Order No 00447

Territory	Category 1 (Death Sentence)	Category 2 (Imprisonment)	Total
Belorussian Republic	2000	10,000	12,000
Georgian Republic	2000	3000	5000
Crimea	300	1200	1500
West Siberia	5000	12,000	17,000
Leningrad oblast' (province)	4000	10,000	14,000
Moscow oblast'	5000	30,000	35,000
Odessa oblast'	1000	3500	4500

Source: Acton, E. and Stableford, T., *The Soviet Union: A Documentary History. Volume One 1917–1940*, Exeter, University of Exeter Press, 2005, pp376–378

What do the decrees tell us? First, the repressions were targeted against broad categories of 'enemies of the people' – that is, people deemed to be actively opposed to the socialist project. Second, the numbers were not simply proportional to local population but were obviously negotiated by central and local NKVD according to their perceptions of how active 'oppositionists' and 'enemies' were in each circumscription. Third, the total numbers in the documents were way below the actual figures of victims.

No 00447, for example, includes a maximum of 268,950 arrests divided into 193,000 to face prison, exile and forced labour and 75,950 to face the death penalty. These larger totals are partly explained by the 'snowball effect' of the local NKVD feeling it necessary to show their zeal in the pursuit of arrests by requesting ever-larger targets from the centre, not to mention the fact that there were several other, similar decrees.[22] Fourth, the whole approach of setting '*limity*' suggests the centre was aware of the potential for local chaos in carrying out the process.

Finally, before returning to our main focus of Stalin's role in this chaotic and murderous process, there are the show trials to be considered. In many ways these are the most personal and intimate to Stalin, since he knew all the leading victims, and personally observed part of the proceedings. There were three major show trials and one parallel secret trial of military leaders. The trials were as follows. The first trial was in August 1936 and the principals among the 16 defendants were Kamenev and Zinoviev, the second and third most important figures in the party before the October Revolution. The chief defendant at the second trial, held in January 1937, was Karl Radek, a leading figure in the Communist International and a former friend and political associate of Trotsky. In return for damning testimony against his fellow defendants – though he refused to implicate Bukharin – he was spared the death penalty and given a ten-year sentence. Nonetheless, on the orders of Beria, he was killed in a labour camp by an NKVD agent in 1939. At the third trial, in March 1938, which had 21 defendants, another once-mighty Bolshevik leader, Bukharin, was forced into confession and convicted. In a parallel but secret trial a number of leading generals, including Marshal Tukhachevsky, one of the century's leading military geniuses, were convicted of plotting with foreign enemies, including Nazi Germany. The eight defendants were executed immediately after the trial on the night of 11/12 June, supposedly by Blokhin.

Stalin and the waves of repression

Trying to fathom the mind and motivation of Stalin with respect to these waves of repression is immensely challenging and, arguably, an exercise which has never been satisfactorily accomplished. Trying to penetrate Stalin's role and contribution takes the researcher into dark places way beyond the experience of most people. Not infrequently, the very nature of the repressions is taken as the key evidence. Only a paranoid, a monster, a maniac, a psychopath, an evil genius, the argument goes, could have accomplished such acts, therefore such descriptions must apply to Stalin. Vacuous clichés of this kind abound in biographies of Stalin, in histories of the period, in popular representations in film and literature, in journalism and last, but by no means least, in swarms of student essays. In many respects, simplistic characterizations of this kind indicate that the author has given up on trying to achieve a better or deeper understanding. However, is it possible to go beyond the clichés?

Certainly, there are dark, barely explicable and arbitrary and inconsistent acts in what Stalin does in these years – 1934–1941 – and beyond. The intimacy of some of the killings is hard to explain. Sadly, Stalin is far from alone among emperors, empresses, kings, queens, dictators and gangsters through the ages who have been able to rid themselves of close associates, lovers, friends and even close relatives including parents, children and brothers and sisters who have become rivals for power or otherwise inconvenient. Of course, Stalin's victims far exceed those of, say, Henry VIII killing inconvenient wives; but the evil core and the arguments of expediency rise up in both cases. The complexities and contradictions are hard to fathom. Stalin was not an unfeeling person. He grieved deeply over the loss of his first wife, Ekaterina Svanidze, in 1907 and wept over the tragic suicide of the mentally unbalanced Nadezhda Alliluyeva. He was a devoted and loving father to their daughter Svetlana, but very contemptuous towards his elder son Iakob, (Ekaterina's son) who was supposedly cruelly mocked by Stalin for being unable to shoot straight after a failed suicide attempt.[23] The complexities of Stalin's mind are also encapsulated in the story that, when Iakob was in a German prisoner-of-war camp, the Nazis tried to take advantage of their illustrious captive by offering to exchange him for a number of high-ranking German prisoners in Soviet camps, including von Paulus who had been captured at Stalingrad. Stalin's reply was truly Spartan – the millions of Soviet prisoners in German hands were all, he claimed, like sons to him so the Germans should release them all.[24] He refused to grant himself special indulgence even where his own son was concerned. In the end, Iakob was said to have thrown himself on an electric fence in the Sachsenhausen camp. His other son, Vassili (Nadezhda Alliluyeva's son), spent the war as a flyer in the Soviet air force and lived until 1962. His solid career in the air force may, in itself, have been a veiled criticism of his father who only flew once in his life, in 1943 when he went to Tehran for the wartime conference. All of Stalin's major journeys were by train. But the arbitrariness extended beyond his immediate family. There were occasions when he removed the names of old comrades from earlier struggles, like those in Georgia, from lists of arrests and even executions. However, his devoted sister-in-law, Anna, as we have already seen, was imprisoned in 1948 apparently for publishing a positive but unapproved memoir of Stalin and the Alliluyev family in 1917.[25] Around the same time, in a truly bizarre exercise, Stalin had Polina Zhemchuzhina, the wife of his closest political associate Viacheslav Molotov, arrested. Molotov, knowing that among other things his loyalty to Stalin and the party was being tested, did not even lift a little finger in defence of his wife, who, on release after Stalin's death, went back to her husband and accepted he could have acted no differently. Any personal reaction would have brought greater disaster for them both. Bolshevik hardness penetrated perpetrator and victim in this strange cameo. Molotov's description of his wife as 'a real Bolshevik' was undoubtedly justified. Of course, these acts occurred at different phases of Stalin's life some of them after great events like the war had made its mark on him and weariness and old age were beginning to take their toll, but, even so, the contrasts in his personal behaviour during the peak years of his power are striking.

The peculiarities of Stalin's outlook may well have been, to an incalculable degree, affected by the fact that the first shot of the purges was not fired *by* one of Stalin's men but *at* one, his close associate Sergei Kirov who had been appointed to the important post of party chief in Leningrad in 1926. He replaced the disgraced Zinoviev and his brief was to clean up the presumed nest of oppositionists left behind. The fact that Kirov was shot in his office and the assassin, a mentally disturbed man who admired the populist terrorists of the nineteenth century, would have had to pass several layers of security to reach him, has been an important element in an argument which blamed Stalin for supervising the murder. Recent detailed and balanced work by Matthew Lenoe has shown this to be very unlikely.[26] The evidence that there was a split between Stalin and Kirov is practically non-existent and, as so often, the argument has gone in the familiar circular fashion – it was a despicable act; Stalin was all-powerful and prone to despicable acts, therefore he did it. The fact that, uniquely of all his victims, the name of Kirov was honoured throughout the Soviet years – a main thoroughfare in Leningrad; the city's world famous ballet; a town; a class of Soviet destroyers all bore his name – is taken as confirmatory evidence of Stalin's duplicity and malevolent genius. However, even circumstantial evidence suggests a different reading of the event. Stalin appears to have been shaken by it and went immediately to Leningrad by train to personally interrogate the assassin, Nikolaev, in his cell. On the way he drafted a three-point decree setting up courts of three appointed judges (troikas) from the NKVD who would investigate and try cases of treason rapidly, limit the trial to one day where possible, exclude the possibility of appeal and carry out the sentence, usually the death penalty, immediately after the trial. Some who argued for Stalin's guilt[27] have insisted that this vicious piece of legislation was pre-drafted and brought in when the planned murder of Kirov provided the pretext. However, the decree is very brief and crudely conceived and shows every sign of an ill-thought-out instinctive reaction to an unexpected event.[28] The fact that it was not immediately followed up also suggests improvisation in the face of an unexpected emergency. If one looks at the Kirov murder from the point of view of it being an anti-party and anti-Stalin act then what follows looks more logical. If a close associate and personal friend of Stalin, a member of the brotherhood of Georgian and South Russian revolutionaries, could be reached by the opposition, then so could anyone, including Stalin. Given the rise of Hitler and the destruction of the second largest Communist Party in the world, the German KPD, not to mention constant boasting by Trotsky that he had tens of thousands of followers in the USSR waiting for the word to rise and overthrow the Stalin leadership, it is scarcely surprising that security went to the top of Stalin's agenda. In his camp in Siberia, Joseph Berger picked up a story from a close associate of a former friend of Stalin, Beso Lominadze, that Stalin had remarked that he had been insufficiently vigilant over protecting Kirov but that now 'the chips would fly'.[29] Whether that is true or not it does seem that the murder sparked off a new direction in Stalin himself.

Many decades letter, in his conversations with Chuev, Molotov, who was as close to Stalin as almost anyone at this time, said little about the purge years but he did say that, yes, mistakes were made; but he remained unbending that it was necessary to eliminate the guilty at all costs, even if innocent people were destroyed as well.[30] There is no reason to think that this does not apply to Stalin and other purge leaders at that time. It was a warfighting mentality. In conventional war a just objective can often only be achieved by the death of the innocent. Generals on the Somme, bomber commanders in World War II and those behind the firebombings of Hamburg, Dresden and Tokyo plus the atomic destruction of Hiroshima and Nagasaki thought the same. For the Stalinists, class war claimed the same utilitarian, realpolitik morality. This, of course, does not justify Stalin's actions but reminds us that despicable atrocities come in many forms and evoke a variety of reactions.

The whole purge process looks more like panic than planning. Within a few weeks, trainloads of 'Kirov's murderers' were being deported from Leningrad. Tens of thousands, some say 100,000,[31] were expelled from the city to the east. There was a party purge from May to 1 December 1935 in which 190,000 members were expelled.[32] A new vocabulary and a new tone appeared in official discourse. The term *dvurushnik* (double-dealer, double-faced) began to be heard. Stalin was particularly fond of this term and he also used another favourite, that his opponents were being Jesuitical – that is cleverly hypocritical. A *Pravda* editorial of 13 August 1936 was entitled 'Despicable Double-Dealers' and in it Stalin denounced Kamenev, Zinoviev, Trotsky and their followers for 'acting like Jesuits'. Such terms suited the situation in that those about to feel the murderous hand of the Stalin state were not just its longstanding class enemies but included many who seemed to be its apparently most loyal servants. The first into the dock, in January 1936, were Kamenev and Zinoviev. Eventually they cracked and admitted links to the Kirov murder. In this opening salvo Kamenev was given a five-year sentence, Zinoviev ten. This was an excuse for nearly 700 more of their alleged supporters and fellow plotters to be arrested and exiled. Another ominous signal had come in April 1935 when the law was altered to allow the full range of its punishments, including death, to be applied to children of 12 and above. However, the full process was far from having hit top gear. That took another year. After the first Kamenev-Zinoviev trial yet another exchange of party cards, aimed at rooting out more oppositionists, was instigated and thousands more members were excluded. Kamenev and Zinoviev were put on trial again, alongside 16 other defendants, from 19–24 August and executed on the 24/25 August.

If a crisis such as this could have arisen and reaction to it have dragged out so long and in such a way that the chief defendants had to be tried twice, obviously the security services would have to bear the brunt of the blame. In the wake of the trial, Stalin decided it was time for changes. On 25 September 1936, at his vacation home in Sochi, he wrote to Kaganovich and Molotov that the head of the NKVD, Yagoda, 'was clearly . . . not up to his task' of unmasking the traitors and he should be replaced by Yezhov. The secret police were, said Stalin, 'four years late in this matter'.[33] The appointment of Yezhov was followed by a great increase in the pace of the terror. In 1937, there was no Sochi vacation. Instead, the documents and policies establishing mass purges were being developed. On 3 July 1937 Stalin had signed an instruction to the NKVD that enemies should be dealt with. In response, the NKVD leadership had asked the local branches to report on the numbers of potential enemies of the people in their area and had used the information sent back to control the process. The centre feared that the local branches might get out of control and arrest far too many people, thereby disrupting the economy and society so much the whole campaign would be counter-productive. This is, in fact, what happened. As we have seen, the most important decree arising from this process, operational order No 00447 of 30 July 1937, was aimed at a wide category of former White Guards and class enemies such as kulaks, who 'continued to engage in disruptive, anti-soviet activities'. The aim, in the words of 00447's author, Yezhov, was to get rid 'once and for all of the entire gang of anti-Soviet elements who undermine the foundations of the Soviet State'. It was followed by further decrees targeting suspect nationalities (notably those with focal centres outside the USSR such as Poles, Germans and Koreans) and, in a third wave, further categories of wreckers, saboteurs and double-dealers.[34] According to Werth, a dozen such processes have been identified,[35] though none was on the scale of 00447, which accounted for almost half of the victims of the period.[36]

Once the operational orders were issued from above the police, party and state bureaucracies ground out their uneven and crude responses noted above. In reality, despite multiple interventions from the highest authorities, the process had deep elements of chaos and anarchy within it. Over some 18 months it ravaged Soviet society. Although, at heart, it might be seen as a desperate exercise in social engineering, or, at least, as a means of eliminating 'enemies of the people', as we have seen it caught up innocent bystanders as well as the ill-thought-out 'target' groups. While it reached into a wide range of social groups and ethnicities it did hit harder in the centres of power – major cities and among the managerial bureaucracy of party, state and economy. It took a heavy toll of senior civil servants, party members and enterprise managers. Promotions, into the shoes of the executed and arrested, grew rapidly in number.[37] Many brought the unwanted bonus of a heightened risk of arrest.

It seems to have been the chaos which was being generated which was instrumental in causing it to be reined in. In this respect it followed the familiar cycle of a Stalinist project – a central launch; inefficiencies being met by ratcheting up the stakes; a greater degree of chaos ensuing leading to emergency abandonment and partial reversion to the status quo. By late 1937 economic production was being threatened by the removal of so many key administrators and the fear and uncertainty of many of their replacements. Yezhov himself was arrested as a scapegoat for many of the supposed 'excesses' of the process. After his arrest the process wound down rapidly. His place as head of the NKVD/OGPU (secret police) was taken by Lavrentii Beria, another Georgian of long acquaintance with Stalin. He held the post until Stalin's death, shortly after which he was himself arrested and executed in December 1953, giving him the distinction of under-going one of the USSR's last major political executions.

What can be said to summarize such a tragic set of events as the purge? Certainly, in the 'minimal definition' of Nicolas Werth:

> The extreme diversity of the victims makes difficult any legal qualification of this crime, which appears to be in a class of its own: 800,000 people executed in secret (over half of them under Order no 00447) by means of a bullet in the back of the head after a pretence of justice; this over a period of sixteen months, at a rate of 50,000 executions per month or 1,700 per day for nearly 500 days. Let us therefore content ourselves with a "minimalist" classification: the Great Terror was one of the worst and largest mass crimes carried out by the Stalinist State against one per cent of its adult population.[38]

However, there is one consideration that makes the whole terrible process even more poignant, even tragic. While we cannot know for certain what might have happened in history, it is hard to avoid the conclusion that the terror was not only 'one of the worst mass crimes carried out by the Stalinist state', even worse it was an unnecessary, even counter-productive, mistake. It under-mined the security of the USSR not only internally by pointlessly killing and exiling productive and creative people, turning them in to a burden who had to be guarded and, minimally, fed and transported and so on, but also externally. The purge of the military leadership seems especially damaging. The chief victim, Tukhachevsky, was surely destined to have been a rock of Soviet resistance to the *Wehrmacht* had he lived. The Gestapo could hardly believe their luck that their cunning interventions and self-serving contacts with the Soviet security services, which helped to incriminate Tukhachevsky and others,[39] had reaped such rich dividends. The purge spread throughout the Soviet officer corps. Traditionally, about one third were thought to have been arrested but revisionists, calculating a much larger officer corps than was once assumed, put the figure at 4–7 per cent arrested.[40] In foreign eyes the war-fighting ability of the Soviet Army was vastly reduced. Hitler was encouraged to attack while the USSR remained weak. It would only be necessary, Hitler said, to kick in the door and the whole structure would collapse. Britain dismissed the USSR as a crucial ally in the critical years of 1937–1939, estimating the Polish Army was stronger. These mistaken calculations played a vital part in the terrible international errors of Britain and Germany which led to war, as we shall see in the next chapter. For the moment we have not only the horrible knowledge of the death and misery caused by the purges, but also the likelihood it was not only a total waste of valuable life and resources, it led directly to even worse horrors of invasion and occupation. As the USSR pulled back from the ninth circle of Dante's hell in late 1938 and 1939, it was not to know that a hitherto unplumbed depth of hell, a tenth circle, was about to open up.

Notes

1 Davies, R. W. (1998) *Soviet Economic Development from Lenin to Khrushchev*, Cambridge, Cambridge University Press, p54.
2 See MIA, https://www.marxists.org/reference/archive/stalin/works/1934/01/26.htm. All quotations from this speech come from this source.
3 Montefiore, S. S. (2004) *Stalin: The Court of the Red Tsar*, London, Phoenix.
4 Murin, I. G. and Denisov, V. N. (eds) (1993) 'Diary of Maria Svanidze', *Iosif Stalin ob ob"iatiakh semi. Iz lichnogo arkhiva*, Moscow, Rodina.
5 Davies (1998), p49.
6 'Excess deaths' is a calculation of the numbers who died over and above the natural death rate for a given period. The attempt here is to give the most accurate possible figure for total 'unnatural' deaths in these years, to calculate the total number of victims of the processes of the time. Needless to say, it is an exercise fraught with complexities and uncertainties but is the best we have.
7 Davies (1998), p50. The figures quoted in this paragraph are from pp48–51.
8 Solzhenitsyn, A. (1973) *The Gulag Archipelago*, 3 vols, London and New York, Harper & Row.
9 There are many extraordinary memoirs by former *zeks* (prisoners), including Ginsburg, E. (1967) *Into the Whirlwind*, London, Collins; and, especially notable for the authors' 20-year survival in the camps and their unflinching commitment to Marxism, are Berger, J. (1972) *Shipwreck of a Generation* (US title *Nothing but the Truth: Stalin's Prison Camps*), London, Harvill; and Stajner, E. (2008) *Seven Thousand Days in Siberia*, London and New York, International Publishers. A multitude of scholarly studies include Khlevniuk, O. and Staklo, V. (2004) *The History of the Gulag: From Collectivization*

to the Great Terror *(Annals of Communism Series)*, New Haven, CT and London, Yale University Press; Baron, N. (2007) *Soviet Karelia: Politics, Planning and Terror in Stalin's Russia, 1920–1939*, London, Routledge; Applebaum, A. (2004) *Gulag: A History*, London and New York, Anchor Books. The controversial Courtois, S. (ed) (1999) *Black Book of Communism*, Cambridge, MA, Harvard University Press, has been criticized for exaggeration even by some of its contributors such as Nicholas Werth whose much better grounded accounts are used below.

10 This is a commonly used shortened version of its full name – *Glavnoe upravlenie ispravitelno-trudovykh lagerei i kolonii* (The Main Administration for Corrective Labour Camps and Colonies).

11 Bacon, E. (1994) *The Gulag at War: Stalin's Forced Labour System in the Light of the Archives*, London and New York, Macmillan.

12 Stajner (2008), p82.

13 Stajner (2008), p83.

14 Details from Werth, N. (2007) *Cannibal Island: Death in a Siberian Gulag*, Princeton, NJ, and Woodstock, NY, Princeton University Press, pp121–170.

15 Khlevniuk and Staklo (2004), pp64–70, includes extracts from Velichko's letter to Stalin and from official reports.

16 Figures from Bacon (1994).

17 Stajner (2008), pp58–59.

18 Stajner (2008), p59.

19 Perrie, M. (2001) *The Cult of Ivan the Terrible in Stalin's Russia*, London and New York, Macmillan.

20 Montefiore (2004), pp200, 340–341.

21 For a gruesome tour of the dark world of Blokhin and associates see Rayfield, D. (2005) *Stalin and His Hangmen: The Tyrant and Those Who Killed for Him*, New York, Random House.

22 The word *limit* is rather ambiguous. It can mean a ceiling on numbers, which suggests a maximum, or it can mean a quota – that is, a target to be achieved. In the administrative-command system of the 1930s the latter meaning seems to have been uppermost in the minds of the local police authorities and over-fulfilment assumed to be the desired response. The universal requests for extra numbers seems to have unsettled the centre and encouraged them to think there were far more 'enemies' out there than they had originally expected.

23 Montefiore (2004), p10.

24 *Time*, 1 March 1968.

25 Alliluyev, S. and Alliluyev, A. (1968) *The Alliluyev Memoirs*, New York and London, Putnam.

26 Lenoe, M. (2010) *The Kirov Murder and Soviet History*, New Haven, CT, and London, Yale University Press, and 'Fear, Loathing, Conspiracy: The Kirov Murder as Impetus for Terror', in Harris, J. (ed) (2013) *Anatomy of Terror: Political Violence under Stalin*, Oxford and New York, Oxford University Press, 2013, pp195–215.

27 For example, Conquest, R. (1989) *Stalin and the Kirov Murder*, London, Hutchinson.

28 See text in Acton, E. and Stableford, T. (2005) *The Soviet Union: A Documentary History, Vol 1, 1917–1939*, Exeter, University of Exeter Press, pp366–371.

29 Berger (1972), pp167–168.

30 Chuev, F. (1993) *Molotov Remembers*, Chicago, IL, Chicago University Press, p274 and pp272–283; 285–297.

31 Tucker (1992), p305.

32 Ibid, p311.

33 Davies, R. W, Khlevniuk, Oleg V., Rees E. A., Kosheleva, Liudmila P. and Rogovaya, Larisa A. (eds) (2003) *The Stalin-Kaganovich Correspondence 1931–1936*, New Haven, CT, and London, Yale University Press, pp359–360.

34 There is a superb summary of the purge process in Werth, N. (2010) 'The NKVD Mass Secret Operation No 00447 (August 1937– November 1938)', *Online Encyclopedia of Mass Violence*, 24 May 2010, http://www.massviolence.org/The-NKVD-Mass-Secret-Operation-no-00447-August-1937, ISSN 1961–9898.

35 Werth (2010), p1.

36 Werth (2010), p6.

37 Hough, J. and Fainsod, M. (1979) *How the Soviet Union Is Governed*, Cambridge, MA, Harvard University Press, p175.

38 Werth (2010), p6.

39 Khrushchev, N., *Speech to the Twenty Second Congress of the CPSU*, April 1961, alleges forged documents framing Tukhachevsky and others were passed by the Gestapo to Moscow via President Benes of Czechoslovakia. If true it does not explain whether Stalin had, as it were, 'commissioned' the forgeries in the first place, as is frequently alleged, or simply been duped by them.

40 There is an excellent account of the military purge, which suggests that Molotov and Kaganovich, at least, believed a military coup was being planned though no serious evidence has ever been uncovered, in Taylor, B.D. (2003) *Politics and the Russian Army: Civil Military Relations 1689–2000*, Cambridge, Cambridge University Press, pp154–164.

6 Stalin, the Soviet Union and the world in the 1930s

The terror was not the only item on Stalin's agenda in the 1930s. It was not even the one on which he spent the most time. There were many other issues. The perennial problem of economic growth was at the top, closely associated with the ever-more pressing issues of international relations and defence. As we have seen, many other things were also happening. There was a continuing cultural revolution and expansion of education. Internal political stability began to revolve around the growing cult of Stalin. As the 1930s progressed, the Soviet Union was drawn deeper into international relations. The overwhelming force behind many of these developments was the need to prepare for war.

While the clouds of war certainly influenced ideological struggles, it was in the fields of economy, diplomacy and politics that war preparation can be seen most clearly. As we have already mentioned, the Great Purge was curtailed by Stalin and the other leaders because it was threatening serious disruption to the Soviet economy. Growth rates were poised to fall. By reining in the terror, economic progress was able to return to planned levels. The contingency of war had played an important part in the planning process since its inception in the 1920s. Certain key decisions were taken for strategic rather than economic reasons and they were to pay off in the war years. For example, the great vehicle construction plant at Cheliabinsk in the Urals could prioritize production of agricultural machinery or military equipment, notably tanks, according to necessity. A second important element was the dispersal of industry and the necessary infrastructural construction to areas beyond the Urals. To set up factories, towns, roads, railway lines, power supplies, including vast hydroelectric schemes, was expensive and flouted market principles but they proved their worth as war approached.

Although the main clash between Germany and the USSR did not begin until June 1941, it is often overlooked that Soviet military forces were engaging the Axis enemy much earlier. In the long perspective the first manoeuvres of World War II were undertaken by Japan in 1931. In pursuit of its longstanding ambition to establish a permanent colonial presence on the Asian mainland, Japan sent forces to Manchuria in 1931 and attacked China in 1937, hoping to take advantage of China's Nationalist/Communist civil war. Once the Nationalists had come to a temporary agreement with the Chinese Communist Party to fight jointly against the invader, the USSR became an important supporter of the beleaguered government. But in separate incidents Soviet and Japanese troops fought one another, first at Lake Khasan in July and August 1938 and, more importantly, at Khalkin Gol in 1939.[1] As a result of their experiences the Japanese declined to attack the USSR again and the two countries maintained an uneasy neutrality which relieved the Soviet Union of the danger of fighting on two fronts against the Axis powers. Economic and military statistics underline the USSR's turn towards a war footing at this time. The armed forces expanded from 1.5 million in 1937 to 5 million by the time of the German invasion. In 1940, Soviet military output was 2.5 times what it had been in 1937.[2]

However, it was not in the Far East that the main drama was to be played out. The heart of Europe became the primary focus of events with the Far East in second place. From 1936, a surrogate European war for and against Fascism was being fought in Spain by regular troops from Spain, Nazi Germany, Fascist Italy and the Soviet Union and international volunteers, mostly but not exclusively on the anti-fascist side, from the United States, Britain, France, Ireland and from among left-wing exiles from Germany and Italy. Tragically, the anti-fascist side was riven with conflict between liberals, democratic socialists, Stalinists, Trotskyists and anarchists, a factor contributing massively to its eventual defeat in 1939.[3]

The events in the Far East did, however, open up one other crucial development. It is yet another irony of Soviet history that, at the darkest moments of internal turmoil and the bacchanalia of repression, Stalin and the USSR were becoming central figures in the Great Power diplomacy of the 1930s. In 1933, as terrible famine trapped large swathes of the south from the western border to the Caucasus, Volga and Urals, the United States officially recognized the country for the first time. The main motivation was the United States' need for strong allies against Japan. The young Stalin can have had no inkling that, at the peak of his career, he would not only be drawn into the great game of international diplomacy but would become one of the most powerful arbiters of international history the world has seen before or since. How did these developments affect Stalin? How did Stalin affect these developments?

To some extent, Stalin's growing involvement in international diplomacy reflects the wider evolution of the party in this area. In the heady days of the October Revolution, the arch-prophet of world revolution, Trotsky, became the first Soviet Commissar for Foreign Affairs, a post he did not expect to hold for long. His task as commissar was, he said, to publish the secret treaties on war aims and then 'shut up shop'. In other words, given the party's perspective on world revolution, diplomacy would have no place. If the aim of Bolshevism was to overthrow capitalism then there was no scope to negotiate with capitalist states in a diplomatic fashion. Like many naive Bolshevik battle plans this one barely survived the first encounter with the enemy. Trotsky himself got sucked into playing an almost disastrous diplomatic game with the Central Powers in the first six months of the revolution. The outcome, the Treaty of Brest-Litovsk, was perhaps unavoidable but it was truly a disaster. As the civil war flared up, diplomacy appeared to fade as world revolution took the centre of the agenda. The waning civil war, however, reversed the process. Diplomacy with neighbouring states, many of them breakaways from the Russian Empire, established borders and set up trade agreements. The Russo-Polish War of 1920 ended in a flurry of diplomatic activity. In March 1921, as Soviet Russia turned away from the immediate prospect of world revolution, it even made its first agreement with a major capitalist 'enemy',

Great Britain, in the form of a trade treaty. In 1922, the victors of Versailles – Britain, France and the United States – were stunned by a treaty between the two main losers, Germany and Russia, signed at Rapallo. For the remainder of the 1920s and even more so in the 1930s, the importance of diplomacy increased in the eyes of the Soviet leaders.

However, the objective of world revolution was never abandoned. The result was an uneasy compromise between two completely contradictory ways of relating to the outside world – conventional diplomacy and the aim to destroy capitalist states through world revolution. It was of no help in resolving the contradiction to claim that the state engaged in diplomacy and the party in subversion through its international wing, the Third Communist International (Comintern), since state and party were led by the same people with ever-decreasing differences between the two. In reality, the aims of the capitalist states were not much different. They were ideologically just as much opposed to the USSR as it was to them. However, like rival gangs with malevolent intent towards each other, agreements were reached in the absence of the ultimate apocalyptic conflict between them. The contradiction was felt deeply on both sides and was never fully resolved even as the USSR collapsed late in the century. It created a complex, cynical and insincere basis for international relations. Before turning to the detail, one further myth, as usual largely of Trotskyite origin, needs to be laid to rest. Stalin never turned his back on world revolution. As we will see, it remained a permanent part of his mental map.

Before 1930 Stalin had had little involvement with international relations. However, as an activity, he took to it like a duck to water. This is not to say he was an expert but he appeared engaged in the process and to be enthusiastic about it, even, perhaps, amused in the early days, that little Soso from Gori should be figuring out how to outwit the wily imperialists of Britain and the naive upstarts from the United States as they, too, took an ever-greater role on the international scene. Stalin had long 'loved gazing at maps, surveying his country like a sovereign. This way . . . he could get some idea of how millions were labouring to bring his decrees to life.'[4] He even took steps to ensure the Soviet Army was trained to read maps. When the time came Stalin also pored over international maps with equal interest and absorption. Looking behind the scenes in the early 1930s we can see that Stalin exuded confidence in the face of imperialist threats. Stalin expressed himself clearly, if crudely, to Molotov on 9 September 1929 when Britain was attempting to restore diplomatic relations with the USSR. Stalin assessed that the British needed the restoration more than the Soviet Union did and that, therefore, the Soviet Union should make no concessions. In Stalin's words: 'We really would be worthless if we couldn't manage to reply to these arrogant bastards briefly and to the point: "*You won't get a fucking thing from us!*"'.[5] Even as the rise of Hitler began to cast its shadow the tone prevailed. In a letter of January 1933 Stalin congratulated Molotov on a speech, praising its 'confident, contemptuous tone with respect to the "great" powers' and Molotov's 'delicate but plain spitting into the pot of the swaggering "great powers" – very good. Let them eat it.'[6]

In his public persona, too, Stalin was full of confidence and optimism. As we have already seen, such optimism filled one of his most famous speeches, the one about lagging behind given in 1931.[7] In it, he brought together themes of revolution, industrial construction, the threat of invasion and the superiority of socialism.[8] But it also contained, again as we saw, important elements relating to the Stalinist understanding of the concept of 'socialism in one country'. This consisted of a new Soviet patriotism having nothing to do with past chauvinism: 'In the past we had no fatherland, nor could we have had one. But now that we have overthrown capitalism and power is in our hands, in the hands of the people, we have a fatherland, and we will uphold its independence.' But Stalin did not stop there. International obligations were even more important: 'We have yet other, more serious and more important, obligations. They are our obligations to the world proletariat. They coincide with our obligations to the workers and peasants of the U.S.S.R. But we place them higher.'[9] The revolutionary process was seamless and global. The time had come where international problems were rising to the top of the agenda.

Stalin had not been especially involved in international relations before 1930. By and large, foreign policy was conducted by the suave and untypical Bolshevik Maxim Litvinov, so Westernized he even had an English wife, Ivy, who outlived him and retired to Lyme Regis to live out her last years. Comintern had been run by Zinoviev until his fall. Later, and not inappropriately, foreign communists such as Georgii Dimitrov (from Bulgaria), Palmiro Togliatti (Italy), Wilhelm Pieck (Germany) and some Soviet politicians like Dmitrii Manuilsky came to the fore. However, Stalin's apprenticeship in world politics was rapid, driven by the initial storms preceding the great cyclone of World War II. We have already noted the Japanese invasion of Manchuria in 1931 which, through a series of skirmishes, turned what had been a civil war in China between communists and nationalists into a full scale Sino-Japanese war by 1937. Italy invaded Abyssinia (Ethiopia today) in 1935. In 1936 the Spanish Civil War broke out, drawing in Soviet arms and advisers for the government and German and Italian troops and aircraft in support of the fascist rebels led by Franco. Thus, by 1936, the battle lines of world war were already nearly fully developed. Unilateral German expansion 'revising' the Versailles Treaty began in 1936 when troops were sent in to reoccupy the Rhineland which had been a designated demilitarized zone, a prelude to the later fate of the Sudetenland, Czechoslovakia and Austria in 1938 and the Polish Corridor, Danzig and Poland itself in 1939. There was, then, plenty of international action on which Stalin could cut his teeth.

The overwhelming themes of Stalin's world view were confidence and hope. Capitalism was in turmoil following the Wall Street Crash in 1929 and the long drawn-out depression which followed, especially in the United States. By comparison, the Soviet Union was forging ahead into a, for many, inspirational people's industrialization.[10] In ideological terms there were those who even talked of 1929–1930 as the final crisis of capitalism though Stalin himself did not subscribe to this super-optimistic position. By and large, however, Marxists did view the crisis as 'normal' for capitalism, something which may have reduced their sensitivity to the special characteristics of fascism which, in their view, was no more than the logical next step for a racist, imperialist, monopolist, militaristic, undemocratic pre-1914 capitalism passed through the brutalizing meat grinder of global war. Nonetheless, Soviet international policy had been largely marginal in the 1920s apart from its unexpected treaty with Weimar Germany in 1923. Comintern had turned away from the great powers to concentrate on trying to subvert their colonies and dependencies, a policy which had undergone a major setback in China in 1927 when the communists were massacred by their supposed allies, the Chinese Nationalists. The 'Great Turn' in Moscow leading to the Stalin Revolution of 1928–1932 was paralleled in foreign relations with a similarly militant stance of class struggle in which no alliances were to be made with any non-communist forces. The Great Retreat of 1933 was also reflected by a change in international direction towards, once again, allying with non-communists, especially those considered to be 'antifascist'. Adopted earlier such a policy might have blocked the rise of Hitler but by 1933 it was too late. Be that as it may, as the situation changed rapidly after the 1931 Japanese invasion of Manchuria, Stalin kept a close eye on what amounted to a revolution in Soviet international orientation.

The centrepiece of the new approach was the assumption that the best way to stop Hitler and Nazism was to form an alliance between all those who were threatened by it. The initiative was called 'collective security' and it became the foundation of Soviet strategy towards the outside world. The preliminary steps actually preceded Nazi victory in Germany (January to March 1933) and had arisen in response to Japanese imperialism which threatened the interests of the United States as much as those of the USSR. Through 1932 and 1933 the two countries put out feelers towards one another which culminated in formal recognition on 16 November 1933. Relations were cordial. Shortly after recognition US Ambassador Bullitt hosted a banquet for the generals of the Red Army captured in the memoirs of one of the embassy's staff, Charlie Thayer. Guests included:

> Voroshilov who was nattily dressed in a white summer tunic glittering with medals and ribbons. . . . On the Ambassador's left sat General Budyonnyi, father of the Russian Cavalry, his enormous black moustache sprouting like outriggers from his upper lip. Around the table were all the leading Soviet military men of the thirties: Yegorov, Tukhachevski, Khmelnitskii, and a dozen others. . . . The table was heaped with caviar and foie gras, pheasant and duck. A squad of fast

waiters ran around behind the guests, filling glasses with half a dozen kinds of vodka, champagne and whisky.[11]

As a result of a chance vodka-fuelled remark picked up by Budyonnyi – a great horse enthusiast – and Voroshilov, Thayer became Senior Polo Instructor to the Red Army and, after rounding up suitable horses from all over the Soviet Union and mallets, balls and other kit from London, polo diplomacy softened hostilities. The first game, at the Moscow River resort of Serebriannyi Bor (Silver Forest), attracted a small but select group of spectators including Litvinov, Voroshilov (Commissar for Defence at the time), several members of the Politburo and Ambassador Bullitt. Regular games were played through the summer (1935) followed by indoor practice in the winter, until players went, in increasingly large numbers, 'on manoeuvres' from which they never returned.[12] The cordiality, interrupted by the purges rather than the fictional manoeuvres, was hardly foreseeable but closer relations with the arch-capitalists did make sense. Germany was becoming the pariah state and was expelled out of one door of the League of Nations as the USSR entered through another in 1934.

Collective security appeared to be making headway. Unfortunately, bringing it to fruition was harder than teaching polo to the Red Army elite. France and Czechoslovakia responded most positively and mutual alliances were set up by which the parties agreed to come to each other's defence in case of attack. However, international realities did not throw up neat solutions and the first big test of collective security was the outbreak of right-wing rebellion in Spain against the Republic. Hitler and Mussolini were quick to send substantial assistance, including troops and aircraft, when General Mola raised his army against the newly elected centre-left Popular Front government. Mola's death in a plane crash in 1937 left Franco in sole leadership of the rebellion.[13] The Spanish generals, not to mention the rest of the world, can hardly have expected Stalin would respond by direct intervention in the Civil War. Why did the USSR intervene unilaterally in this crisis? Doing so jeopardized the wider aim of collective security since Britain and the United States had an unenforced policy of non-intervention which the USSR was violating, thereby making agreement with Britain less likely. Thus, intervention appeared to be a threat to Soviet foreign policy aims. Despite assumptions rooted in Trotsky's interpretation that Stalin cared little for the international revolution, the most influential motive for Soviet intervention was the international working-class solidarity Stalin had praised so highly in 1931. True, the main focus of Soviet policy was, as ever in these years, the threat from Germany and to sit idly by and do nothing as Germany and her allies tore up an independent, left-leaning democracy would signal Soviet weakness to Berlin. However, active intervention would upset Britain. Stalin decided the solution would be 'cautious intervention',[14] initially via back channels but, increasingly out in the open. Certainly, the solidarity angle was the professed reason. In a telegram to the Spanish Communist Party, Stalin, in the name of the Soviet Central Committee, stated that:

> The workers of the Soviet Union are merely carrying out their duty in giving help within their power to the revolutionary masses of Spain. They are aware that the liberation of Spain from the yoke of fascist reactionaries is not a private affair of the Spanish people but the common cause of the whole of advanced and progressive mankind. Fraternal greetings, J. Stalin.[15]

Indeed, it is hard to see any other powerful motive. Some have argued that it was a hard-nosed economic transaction since 'like an accomplished "barrow boy" Stalin systematically swindled the Spanish of several hundred million dollars by rescuing their gold reserves'[16] and keeping them in payment for arms. However, the prospect of returning the funds to a fascist government siding with Hitler after the war was completely unrealistic. The view that Stalin's aim was 'to keep the war going as long as possible by embroiling Hitler without offending the western powers'[17] is also improbable since it was impossible. Intervention clearly alienated Britain and the United States though it did encourage France, threatened with near-encirclement by fascist powers in the event of Francoite victory.

The Spanish Civil War was clearly a point under which a line could be drawn. On one side was a coalition stretching from liberal conservatives to anarchists; on the other, fascist national-ists. France, itself governed by a left of centre Popular Front including communists, was desperate to intervene to ensure republican victory, but could only do so with British support. From 1936 to 1939, Britain was the crucial player in the international arena. It was torn between severely conflicting pressures. Ideologically, Britain supported democracy and therefore should have sided with the Spanish Republic. However, the same impulse also made it want to keep its distance from the dictatorial USSR which was helping the Republic. However, interests usually trump ideologies in international relations and here, too, there were conflicting pressures. It was traditional British policy to ensure no one power dominated the European continent and this could have led it into an anti-German alliance. However, it did not want to be anti-fascist as that would mean alienating Mussolini's Italy and Britain harboured an illusion that it could split Mussolini from Hitler and come to a naval agreement with it. This would, Britain hoped, mediate Italy's aim of turning the Mediterranean into what Mussolini called 'Our Sea' ('*mare nostrum*'), a development threatening Britain's Suez route to India. Britain thought Hitler's threat to Austria might alienate him from Mussolini, making an Anglo-Italian alliance possible. Also high on Britain's priorities was a desire to do a deal with Japan to prevent an attack on Hong Kong, Singapore and, eventually, India itself. While such interests might dictate a joint Soviet, American and British alliance against Japanese expansionism, Britain, as a former ally of Japan, had not given up on the possibility of an agreement with her. Thus, Britain appeared to prioritize agreements with Italy and Japan rather than the USSR.

The complexity reached its peak in 1938 with the first Czechoslovak crisis. In pursuit of his avowed goal of bringing all Germans under his rule, Hitler had re-entered the Rhineland in March 1936. His next target was the ribbon of Germans who lived along the hilly border of western Czechoslovakia, in the Sudetenland. To negotiate his demands Mussolini mediated with Britain and France and helped set up the fateful Munich Conference. The USSR, Czechoslovakia's main ally, was not invited. The shameful story of how British Prime Minister Neville Chamberlain appeased Hitler and agreed to the German takeover of the Sudetenland in exchange for a promise from Hitler that it was his 'last territorial claim in Europe' has been told many times. What has been less commented on is that, according to the first mainstream Soviet-era biographer of Stalin, Dmitrii Volkogonov, himself a general enjoying excellent and unprecedented access to military archives and current and former military personnel, Stalin was prepared to go to war over the issue. Foreign Minister Litvinov was instructed to make this plain on several occasions, starting in March 1938. Partial mobilization was introduced and the Soviet Union reassured Czechoslovakia on 20 September that it was prepared to fight to defend the country. Seventy divisions were put on combat readiness. But, as Volkogonov, himself no apologist for Stalin, wrote, on 30 September 1938 'the Munich Agreement was signed and Stalin realized that fear of the "Communist contagion" was greater than the voice of reason. And he was right.'[18] France's abandonment of its treaty obligations to Czechoslovakia was particularly worrying to Stalin. It meant there was a risk of the USSR being isolated in the face of a Nazi onslaught if the Western democracies were prepared to stand by and watch the destruction of democratic Czechoslovakia. Even so, efforts to come to an agreement with Britain to contain Hitler continued, but a harder line was emerging in Moscow. On 3 May 1939, the suave 'Westerner', Maxim Litvinov, was replaced as foreign minister by the tougher and more 'Stalinist' Vyacheslav Molotov, known to his colleagues as 'iron arse' from his ability to sit unflinchingly through interminably tedious meetings and negotiations.[19] Molotov reassured the French *chargé d'affaires* in Moscow that the change of personnel did not signify a change of line;[20] but Litvinov made one last, unofficial, appeal to the West to deal before it was too late.[21]

Stalin was busy reading books by Western writers who pointed to the fundamental untrustworthiness of Hitler, notably Conrad Heyden's *History of German Fascism*, and about the ideological fanaticism with which the German people and army were being imprinted by Goebbels propaganda machine (Dorothy Woodman, *Germany Arms*) which also made them unstable alliance partners. He also had an analysis of German military strength drawn up showing, amongst other things, an army numbering 3.7 million, over 3195 tanks, 4000 aircraft and 107 warships.[22] But the

British were negotiating with the USSR with glacial slowness, a feature which also contributed to the German ambassador in London, Dirksen, informing Berlin that, in his opinion, Britain would not fight alone if Germany were to attack Poland. Continuing talks between Dirksen and influential British diplomats such as Sir Horace Wilson, in summer 1939 in an attempt to 'build bridges' at the last moment between Berlin and London, did little to reduce Stalin's concern at being left isolated. His preferred option of an agreement with Britain and France seemed as far off as ever in summer 1939 and, without such an agreement, the USSR was in danger of facing Hitler alone, an outcome Stalin was not yet prepared to entertain. Sensationally, and under extreme pressure from Hitler, between 13 and 23 August a diplomatic revolution was conducted which produced a series of rapidly drafted treaties between Germany and the USSR on trade, and, ultimately, a ten-year non-aggression agreement signed on 23 August. There were also secret protocols to partition Poland and to allow the Baltic States to pass into Soviet hands. Voroshilov as defence minister, announced that it was not the non-aggression agreement which ended talks with Britain and France, but the impasse reached in those talks, by a continuing failure on Poland's part to agree to allowing passage of Soviet troops through Poland in the event of war, which gave the USSR no option but to sign the treaty.[23] Britain and France were stunned by the turn of events. On 1 September, the fateful invasion of Poland by Germany took place. On 3 September, Britain declared war on Germany. On 17 September, in accordance with the secret protocols, Soviet troops moved into eastern Poland to 'protect' it from Hitler. They also invaded the Baltic States. The war had begun but, as yet, the main protagonists maintained a cynical 'peace' in which neither side believed.

Despite the agreement and despite the conventional view that the USSR joined the world war in 1941 when it was invaded by Hitler, the years preceding that invasion were actually characterized by intense, closely linked military and diplomatic action. The advance into eastern Poland and the Baltic States, though meeting little opposition, was one of the USSR's largest military operations. The ensuing Soviet occupations of Estonia, Latvia and Lithuania were yet another ugly mark on the Soviet Union's reputation.

Impelled by the frenetic preparations for the coming major clash, no quarter was shown to these newly absorbed 'bourgeois' states. From Stalin's point of view, they were dominated by all the classes and groups the revolution had broken up in the USSR – fierce nationalists, property owners, churches, independent political parties, former White Guards, small but hostile armies and police – and pitifully weak 'pro-Soviet' communists and sympathetic leftists. The harrowing of the Baltic States – repeated in 1944 when Soviet power returned after having been driven back in 1941 – was an unprecedented crime leaving scars down to the present. The gulag was filled with a whole new generation of victims.

However, in Stalin's mind this was simply an inevitable process driven by the sacred cause of defending the socialist motherland. Similarly, Finland was targeted. Though officially neutral, many of its leaders were already sympathetic to Hitler in his guise of anti-bolshevik crusader. Should war break out, Finland might well join with that crusade. Its border was only some 20 kilometres (12 miles) from the outskirts of Leningrad, making the Soviet Union's second city and one of its industrial powerhouses, highly vulnerable. Initial attempts by the USSR to exchange territories near Leningrad for parts of Karelia in the north were rejected by the Finnish government. Stalin saw no alternative and ordered an invasion of Finland which began on 30 November 1939. Initial difficulties led to a longer campaign than expected and it was only in March 1940 that a peace treaty was signed in Moscow. Most Finnish writers argue that, through gallant defence, the Finnish armed forces had prevented the Red Army from achieving a total takeover of the country.

Be that as it may, the treaty gave the USSR more territory than it had demanded before the war and 30 per cent of Finland's economic resources. With respect to defending Leningrad, the gains were crucial but guaranteed that Finland would join with Hitler, which was likely anyway, in the assault on the USSR. After the launching of the German invasion, Finnish forces were deployed to hold the line north of Leningrad, between the Baltic and Lake Ladoga, thereby completing the blockade of the city which cost 1 million Soviet lives.

The Winter War with Finland has attracted much attention but even more significant developments in the east are often underestimated. The Battles of Lake Khasan (1938) and Khalkin Gol (1939; Nomonhan in Japanese) were substantial conflicts which stood out from a lengthy series of skirmishes. At Khalkin Gol the Japanese Sixth Army was defeated by a Soviet force led by its new commander Georgii Zhukov. Some 60,000 troops are thought to have been killed or wounded, largely on the Japanese side. So great was the impact of the battle it appeared to have significant consequences for Japanese strategy. Seeking raw materials to fuel its industrial and imperial ambitions Tokyo had a choice – encroach on eastern Siberia and Russia's maritime provinces on the Pacific or turn south towards the Philippines and a clash with the United States.

The matter was still in the balance in 1941. On his way to and from Berlin, the Japanese Foreign Minister, Matsuoka, stopped off in Moscow. On his first visit he offered to buy the northern half of the bleak island of Sakhalin from the USSR. 'Are you joking?' was Stalin's response.[24] On his way back a week or so later on 8 April Matsuoka received a last-minute change of plan from Tokyo. A treaty of neutrality was signed at once and the Japanese government undertook to respect the Soviet and Mongolian status quo. Stalin had pulled off a crucial gamble. There would be no second front for him to worry about, a great relief only three months before the eventual assault from the West. However, the treaty caused unease in China which feared it would face renewed pressure from Japanese expansion to replace influence and resources lost in Siberia and Mongolia. Ironically, it was the United States which was destined to bear the consequences of the change of direction at Pearl Harbor and beyond. This seemed a poor recompense for the United States' efforts since 1932 to enlist Soviet support against Japan, though, in another frequently unnoticed consequence, in August 1945, the USSR did, under agreement with the United States and Britain, invade Manchuria, an event which, it has been argued, was at least as effective as the nuclear bombs dropped on Hiroshima and Nagasaki in bringing about unconditional Japanese surrender.[25]

Though precise casualty figures are controversial, it is likely that in this period of 'peace' the USSR had lost 126,875 dead and 188,671 injured in the Finnish conflict[26] and 7974 killed and 15,251 injured on the Khalka River.[27] The time purchased through the agreement with Germany in August 1939 had not only been costly in this way, it was also running out. However, there was still time for one of Stalin's most disastrous mistakes which almost brought him down.

When it came, in the early hours of 22 June 1941, the German attack gained immediate momentum and, within weeks, had made advances beyond all expectations. Stalin has frequently been blamed for this, including most likely by himself. The story of German–Soviet relations and Stalin's assumptions about what might happen is twisted and complex. As late as May 1941, talking to his inner circle, Stalin said the 'conflict was inevitable, perhaps in May next year'.[28] At least two of the main strands of the controversy are embedded in this short statement. First, it demonstrates that Stalin had no illusions about the treaty with Germany. It was only a device to buy time, not a permanent reorientation of Soviet policy. This was supported by his crucial speech of 5 May 1941[29] in which he told military graduates war was, indeed, inevitable and they must prepare for the ultimate struggle to destroy fascism. Interestingly, Stalin said it would be an offensive war.[30] Second, it shows that Stalin was unprepared for the attack shortly before it came.

Why this was so is very hard to explain. For months, intelligence from a multitude of sources had been pouring in suggesting Hitler was concentrating forces in the east and preparing his attack. Captured German aviators who had crossed the frontier, defectors from the German Army and Air Force, his own spy in Tokyo, Richard Sorge, and Western intelligence from Churchill, in particular, all warned of the same thing – an imminent German attack in spring 1941. Stalin had convinced himself this was wrong and came from two sources which were trying to catch him out. On the one hand there was Britain, desperate to embroil the USSR in the war as soon as possible to help its (by then) solitary fight against Germany before it was too late. The other was Germany itself. Stalin had noted that Germany had the habit of faking 'provocation' as a cause for it to attack. The invasion of Poland was preceded by a faked 'Polish' attack across the border on a German radio station. Stalin was obsessed with ensuring no Soviet action might take place that could constitute a 'provocation'. Even the attack itself elicited this reflex and there was a brief delay before all-out defence was ordered. Even the eastern disposition of German forces did not persuade him of Hitler's intentions. Did he swallow the official lie fed to him by Hitler that they were being moved east to get out of range of increasingly intensive British bombing? We do not know for certain. We do know that some of Stalin's military advisers, notably Zhukov in a note ironically dated 15 May 1941, the initial target date for Barbarossa to begin, even suggested the Soviet Union should take advantage of this mass assembling of German forces by actually engaging in a surprise attack which would fall on the *Wehrmacht* while it was in a confused state and not yet combat ready.[31]

Of course, it is easy for us to say Stalin should have been more expectant of an attack because we have the precious gift of hindsight. Stalin had other intelligence pointing in other directions. There were reports of rumbling dissatisfaction in Germany and potential refusal of German workers to join a struggle against the USSR.[32] Stalin also believed that Hitler would fully settle matters in the west before an eastern attack to avoid being caught in a two-front war. As it was, the Balkans remained the only unconquered target on the European mainland apart from the USSR itself, but the campaign there might have been crucial. First, Hitler, as Stalin surmised, did want it concluded before attacking the USSR. However, the subjugation of Yugoslavia and Greece took longer than expected as Germany faced some of the most bitter and savage fighting of the war in the mountainous terrain. The assault on the USSR, known as 'Operation Barbarossa', was postponed for six vital weeks. It had been initially scheduled for 15 May. As we have seen, Stalin expected an attack in May but a year hence. While any assault on Russia might be considered foolhardy, if it was to have any chance of success it needed to start as early in the year as possible as the weather window between the spring thaw and the onset of winter was very narrow and the winter day lengths were very short. Hitler appeared to have missed the window for 1941 and this may well have been part of Stalin's calculation. The latter part of June, it seemed, was too late for a serious assault.

Stalin had made many mistakes but there had been some significant strengthening of defences, particularly in the south-west where Stalin expected the main blow to fall since Ukrainian grain, Donbas coal and Caspian oil were key targets for the German economy. The Soviet generals expected Moscow to be the main thrust but Hitler himself had ordered his priorities as Leningrad first, Donbas second, Moscow third. However, Hitler, in his overconfidence of victory arising from success in the west plus the apparent self-destruction of the Red Army in the purges, supposedly demonstrated in the Winter War, attacked all three more or less equally, expecting, as he said, only to have to kick in the door for the whole rotten structure to fall. When the blow fell, so rapid was the German advance that it seemed that Hitler's prediction might come true.

The initial catastrophe has opened up one final controversy. In his 'secret' speech of February 1956 which criticized many aspects of Stalin's rule, Khrushchev claimed Stalin had disappeared for several days suffering a nervous breakdown of some kind and was unable to face the unexpected catastrophe. Less credence is given to this idea today. It has been shown, from entries in Stalin's Kremlin appointment book and memoirs of Zhukov and others, that Stalin worked strenuously in these early days of the war.[33] His 'breakdown' appears to be much less significant than Khrushchev implied. Although Molotov was chosen to announce the outbreak of war to the Soviet population in a broadcast speech over the radio, Stalin appears to have been active in restructuring the key central elements of government, on lines similar in some ways to those of his beloved civil war. Nonetheless, he does appear to have spent a day or maybe two (28 to 30 June) on which he was listless, depressed and unsure of what to do, none of them very 'Stalinist' features. One of the leaders close to Khrushchev, Anastas Mikoyan, does give an interesting anecdote about Stalin's state of mind at this moment. A high-powered delegation from the Politburo decided to approach Stalin about forming a State Defence Committee to centralize the necessary military and economic initiatives to conduct the war. They were worried to hear from Molotov that Stalin 'was in such a state of prostration that he wasn't interested in anything, he had lost all initiative and was in a bad way'. By contrast, Mikoyan continued, the delegation 'were sure that we could organize the defence and put up a proper fight. None of us was in a downcast mood.' When they arrived at his *dacha* Stalin was surprised to see them: 'What have you come for?' was his immediate response. Molotov explained the plan and that Stalin would head the committee. Stalin's response was simply to say 'Fine.' It seems very likely that at first Stalin thought they might have come to replace him, even arrest him. This was not impossible, after all it is what Stalin himself might well have done to someone else. Amazingly, the delegation had itself considered that 'if Stalin were to continue to behave in this way, then Molotov ought to lead us and we would follow him'.[34] Stalin's career was within a whisker of ending in disgrace and even arrest. One other significant moment. On 29 June he even shocked Molotov and others around him by responding to the ever-increasing military reverses by saying 'Lenin left us a great inheritance and we, his heirs, have fucked it all up!'[35]

These cameos may be brief but they tell us a great deal about Stalin. In the first place, one of his key characteristics, his exuberant confidence in the revolution and the future deserted him in this darkest hour. Perhaps he had a better sense of the dangers ahead than his more confident colleagues, but even so it was a remarkable moment in his life. Second, the myth of him being all-powerful is definitively burst by these stories. What stopped the delegation from arresting or sacking Stalin was not his power or his ability to summon guards or whatever, it was the delegates' support for him. Had they seriously wished to replace him with Molotov, there was absolutely nothing to stop them, but what they really wanted was to have the real Stalin back. Stalin certainly ruled by fear, but his followers felt lost without him and saved his career at this vital moment. Finally, the most enduring characteristic of the young Koba and the adult Stalin remained the identification with Lenin and his cause. It was not Russia that was lost, it was the danger of losing Lenin's revolutionary inheritance that weighed on Stalin's mind. His confidence had deserted him and, for once, he was lost for a response, but the devotion to Lenin and his revolution still burned within him. Within a few days he was back in full command and the greatest test of his, and the revolution's and the country's life was about to begin.

Notes

1 Varner, D. (2008) *To the Banks of the Halha: The Nomohan Incident and the Northern Limits of the Japanese Empire*, Philadelphia, PA, Pennsylvania State University Press.

2 Davies, R. W. (1998) *The Soviet Economy from Lenin to Khrushchev*, Cambridge, Cambridge University Press, p55.

3 There is an extensive literature on the Spanish Civil War. The beginner might well start with George Orwell's ant-Stalinist account of his own experiences and thoughts, *Homage to Catalonia*, of which there are many editions.

4 Volkogonov, D. (1991) *Stalin: Triumph and Tragedy*, London, Weidenfeld & Nicholson, p190.

5 Lih, L., Naumov, O. and Khlevniuk, O. (1995) *Stalin's Letters to Molotov 1925–1936*, New Haven, CT, Yale University Press, p178.

6 Ibid, p232; Read, C. (2008) 'The View from the Kremlin: Soviet Assumptions about the Capitalist World in the 1920s and 1930s' in Casey, S. and Wright, J. (eds) *Mental Maps in the Era of Two World Wars*, London and New York, Oxford University Press, p53, discusses these quotes.

7 Mentioned in Chapter 4.

8 Stalin, J. V. 'The Tasks of Business Executives: Speech Delivered at the First All-Union Conference of Leading Personnel of Socialist Industry', 4 February 1931, in *CW*, vol 13, MIA https://www.marxists.org/reference/archive/stalin/works/1931/02/04.htm.

9 Ibid.

10 Scott, J. (1942) *Behind the Urals: An American Worker in Russia's City of Steel*, London, Houghton Mifflin. There is an excellent account of foreigners' views in David-Fox, M. (2012) *Showcasing the Great Experiment: Cultural Diplomacy and Western Visitors to the Soviet Union 1921–1941*, Oxford, Oxford University Press.

11 Thayer, C. (1950) *Bears in the Caviar*, Philadelphia, PA, and New York, Lippincott, pp116–117.

12 Ibid, pp118–129.

13 Mola may, inadvertently, have paralleled or even encouraged Stalin in two ways. In 1936, he used words that could have been Stalin's: 'we must extend the terror; we must impose the impression of dominion while eliminating without scruples everyone who does not think as we do'. He also coined the phrase 'fifth column' to designate the enemy within. The phrase has been adopted by scholars of the purges, notably Oleg Khlevniuk, to explain Stalin's motivation for the purges. We do not know if Stalin was aware of these comments of Mola but he would certainly not have allowed himself to be outdone in toughness by his fascist enemies.

14 Tucker, R. (1992) *Stalin in Power: The Revolution from Above 1928–1941*, New York and London, W. W. Norton & Co, p351.

15 *Pravda*, 16 October 1936.

16 Montefiore, S.S. (2004) *Stalin: the Court of the Red Tsar*, London, Phoenix, p204. The actual amount was $518 million carried in 7800 boxes. Tucker (1992), p351.

17 Montefiore (2004), p204.

18 Volkogonov (1991), p348.

19 Watson, D. (1996) *Molotov and the Soviet Government: Sovnarkom 1930–1941*, London and New York, Macmillan; Watson, D. (2005) *Molotov: A Biography*, London and New York, Macmillan; and Roberts, G. (2012) *Molotov: Stalin's Cold Warrior*, Washington, DC, Potomac Books.

20 Volkogonov (1991), p349.

21 Mastny, V. (1976) 'The Cassandra in the Foreign Commissariat: Maxim Litvinov and the Cold War', *Foreign Affairs*, 54 (2), pp366–376.

22 Volkogonov (1991), pp352–353.

23 *Pravda*, 27 August 1939.

24 Volkogonov (1991), p388.

25 Stephen Ambrose, for one, expressed this idea in footage edited out of the television series *The World at War*. Channel 4, 1973–1974. The omitted footage was shown by the series producers at a conference at Warwick University in 1977.

26 Krivosheyev, G. (1997) *Soviet Casualties and Combat Losses in the Twentieth Century*, 1st edition London, Greenhill Books, pp77–78.

27 Krivosheyev, G. (1993) *'Grif sekretnosti sniat': poteri Vooruzhennykh Sil SSSR v voynakh, boevykh deystviyakh i voennykh konfliktakh*, Moscow, Voenizdat pp77–85.

28 Volkogonov (1991), p393.

29 Stalin, J., 'Speech to Military Graduates of the Frunze Academy 5 May 1941'. The speech was not published at the time for obvious reasons. Wind of its contents and its references to an offensive war first surfaced from German interrogations of captive Russian officers who had been present. See Broekmayer, M.G. (2004) *Stalin, the Russians and Their War: 1941–1945*, Madison, WI, University of Wisconsin Press, pp21–23. The original Dutch edition was published in Amsterdam in 1999.

30 Nevezhin, V.A., 'Stalin's 5 May 1941 Address: The Experience of Interpretation', *Journal of Slavic Military Studies*, 11 (1), pp116–146.

31 Volkogonov (1991), p398.

32 Volkogonov (1991), p399.

33 Medvedev, R. and Medvedev, Z. (2003) *The Unknown Stalin*, London, I.B. Tauris, pp230–234.

34 Mikoyan quoted in Volkogonov (1991), p411.

35 Kumanev, V. (1998), 'Iz vospominanii o voennykh godakh', *Politicheskoe Obrazovanie*, 9, p75, quoted by Volkogonov (1991), p410.

7 The tenth circle of hell: invasion, occupation, victory – war without limits

Operation Barbarossa (22 June 1941 to 7 January 1942)

The German invasion opened up the most savage war in human history. Over 30 million people were to die on the Eastern Front. Stalin and the Soviet Union reeled from the opening blows. Whether he had a fit of depression or not Stalin quickly recovered and on 3 July broadcast a rousing call to arms over the radio. The list of places already lost to the German advance – named by Stalin as 'Lithuania, a considerable part of Latvia, the western part of Byelorussia and part of Western Ukraine' – plus the warning that 'fascist aircraft are extending the range of their operations, bombing Murmansk, Orsha, Moghilev, Smolensk, Kiev, Odessa, Sevastopol' must have alarmed rather than reassured his audience. Nonetheless, Stalin claimed, completely falsely, that Hitler's finest armies had been destroyed because 'this army had not yet met with serious resistance on the continent of Europe. Only on our territory has it met with serious resistance. And if as a result of this resistance the finest divisions of Hitler's German-fascist army have been defeated by our Red Army, this means that it too can be smashed and will be smashed, as were the armies of Napoleon and Wilhelm.' Significantly, Stalin stated that even the finest German people would join the struggle which would become universal embracing 'the whole of our valiant Red Army, the whole of our valiant Navy, all the falcons of our Air Force, all the peoples of our country, all the finest men and women of Europe, America and Asia, and, finally, all the finest men and women of Germany' who will 'denounce the treacherous acts of the German-fascists, sympathize with the Soviet Government, approve its conduct, and see that ours is a just cause, that the enemy will be defeated, and that we are bound to win'. Stalin painted a picture, which must have terrified his audience, of a 'cruel and implacable enemy' intent not just on defeating the Red Army but enslaving the population and destroying their economy and culture. To face the threat the whole country had to go on to a war footing. No resources would be left behind for the advancing enemy 'not a single locomotive, a single railway car, not a single pound of grain or gallon of fuel. The collective farmers must drive off all their cattle and turn over their grain to the safe keeping of the state authorities . . . All valuable property . . . grain and fuel that cannot be withdrawn must be destroyed without fail.' Populations in occupied areas were called upon to 'blow up bridges and roads, damage telephone and telegraph lines, set fire to forests, stores and transports . . . conditions must be made unbearable for the enemy and all his accomplices. They must be hounded and annihilated at every step.' Characteristically, Stalin did not forget the need to 'wage a ruthless fight against all disorganizers of the rear, deserters, panic-mongers and rumour-mongers; we must exterminate spies, sabotage agents and enemy parachutists, rendering rapid aid in all this to our extermination battalions . . . All who by their panic-mongering and cowardice hinder the work of defence, no matter who they may be, must be immediately hailed before a military tribunal.' The heart of the message was that 'The Red Army, Red Navy and all citizens of the Soviet Union must defend every inch of Soviet soil, must fight to the last drop of blood for our towns and villages, must display the daring, initiative and mental alertness that are inherent in our people.' The final words of the frightening but stirring speech were 'Forward to victory.'[1]

Although the speech was the work of many hands in the Central Committee and the Soviet 'Cabinet', Sovnarkom,[2] the defining imprint came from Stalin. Like the speech to administrators almost exactly ten years before (in which he had predicted that the Soviet Union had ten years to catch up in preparation for just such an invasion) Stalin edited the final version. It included many of his key themes. Once again he exuded exuberant optimism in ultimate victory. The prediction of a savage total war was sadly borne out by future events. The invocation of the party of Lenin was present but muted. The appeal to 'the finest men and women' around the globe cut class out of the immediate picture. The lies about destroying enemy forces was the kind of distortion that all combatants used to build morale. The assertion that Kaiser Wilhelm's army had been destroyed in World War I was also fanciful but acknowledgement that the defeat of Germany was the work of the 'Anglo-French armies' was rare and foreshadowed the new political alignment, as did his expressions of gratitude to Churchill and the US government for promised aid and support. The emphasis on enemies within was foreboding but very Stalinesque. The speech hit home, ironically for some analysts. According to the first and still the most intimate 'inside' biography of Stalin which is especially rich on his links with the military to which the writer himself belonged, Dmitrii Volkogonov argued that 'The speech had a powerful effect, giving, as it did, simple answers to many questions which were tormenting the people. Paradoxically, the chief cause of the catastrophic beginning of the war, namely Stalin's personal rule, now came to embody the hopes of the people. The faith was working.'[3]

A week later, on 10 July, Stalin was prevailed upon by his generals to become supreme commander, but the appointment was not announced for many weeks. It was another month (8 August) before he agreed to chair meetings of the General Staff. This uncharacteristic slowness may be connected to the dreadful reverses the Red Army was suffering. In the first weeks of the war it was a retreating rabble, its air cover having been largely destroyed. In the first three weeks of war it had retreated more than 500 kilometres (300 miles). Some 30 divisions had been overrun and a further 70 had lost some 50 per cent of their personnel. A total of 3500 aircraft had been destroyed, many of them on the ground. Half of the available fuel and ammunition at the front had been lost. The truth was too awful to tell Stalin who was fed false figures showing German losses outweighed Soviet losses.[4]

A mini-purge of generals deemed responsible was the near-inevitable consequence in the Stalin sphere. Despite having tried to alert Stalin in the weeks before the war began and requesting permission to take up more effective battle stations for his troops, the commander of the Western Front, General Dmitrii Grigorevich Pavlov, was tried for treachery. Several other generals were also accused. The pattern was similar for all of them. They were committed Soviet patriots who had fought hard for their country. Several of them, including Pavlov, offered to fight on as privates in what had been their armies as their punishment – all to no avail since they were mostly sentenced to death and immediately executed. One defendant already killed in action was tried in absentia and sentenced to a death he had already undergone. A particularly harrowing case was that of Major General Ponedelin, also tried in absentia since he had been wounded and captured in August by the Germans while unconscious. He was accused of voluntarily working for the Germans and he, too, was sentenced to death; but, surprisingly, when he returned to the USSR after a hideous four years in German prisoner-of-war (POW) camps, he was not executed but given five years in the gulag. For unknown reasons, perhaps the threat of renewal of his sentence, in 1950 he appealed to Stalin for release. On reviewing his case the original death sentence was re-instated, probably because he had been a prominent example of a 'coward and deserter' in Stalin's Order no 270 (1941), and Ponedelin was shot.[5]

No amount of scapegoating and recrimination was going to stop the German advance. It took several weeks before the Red Army was even able to put up a fight as it retreated; but gradually the army did pull itself back into some sort of shape. In these weeks and throughout the war Stalin became the hands-on arbiter of all major and many less important decisions. Economic issues, the priorities for production and distribution, the disposition of troops, the production targets for rifles, aircraft and so on all passed across his desk. A multitude of decisions were made and plans put into practice. One of the most extraordinary was the successful transfer of factories from the western borderlands to safer locations in the Urals and beyond. According to the most recent Russian research at least 2593 enterprises were moved east together with an estimated 25 million workers with their families. Many of the destination sites were completely undeveloped and, in one case, 8000 women in a tank factory were living in holes dug in the ground. By 1942, substantial armaments were beginning to flow from these evacuated factories, of which only 55 were not yet productive.[6] Many mistakes were made. Stalin's own whims risked being turned into policy as when his old friend Budennyi, civil war cavalry leader and former polo aficionado as we have seen, argued for a positive role for cavalry in the forests of Bielorussia (Belarus). Newsreel of the time shows large cavalry units charging with sabres drawn towards German gun positions.[7] Nonetheless, after a short time this outdated suggestion was, in fact, rejected. Later in the war, more important decisions of this kind also turned out to be wrong, as we shall see.

However, in the first weeks of war, nothing could stop the German advance. In a poorly documented story, Beria is said to have told his interrogators after his own arrest that he, Stalin and Molotov tried to contact Berlin via the Bulgarian ambassador with a view to making a Brest-Litovsk-style separate peace. According to Beria it was the ambassador who persuaded them they would win in the end 'even if they were to retreat to the Urals',[8] words almost identical to those of Lenin himself in 1918 around the time of the actual Brest-Litovsk Treaty. The story came to Volkogonov in conversation with Beria's prosecutor, Marshal Kiril Moskalenko, who also claimed the former ambassador had verified it 'in conversation with us'.[9] The ambassador's confidence seemed over-optimistic for some time yet. On 19 September, Kiev, the founding city of Russia, was lost. It was one of the greatest military defeats of all time. General Kirponos, in charge of the defence, was refused all requests to redeploy and extract his troops from the approaching encirclement. Instead he was expected to fight to the last. On 11 September Stalin told him over the telephone 'Kiev must not be abandoned . . . That is all. Goodbye.' To this the beleaguered commander replied: 'Your orders are clear. That is all. Goodbye.' On 17 September, despite Stalin's orders, the War Council finally sanctioned a break-out from the encirclement, but it was much too late. The defence forces had been broken apart and lost contact with their superiors and each other. The city fell with the loss of almost half a million men. Clearly the catastrophe added to the risk to Moscow to such an extent that, on 15 October, Stalin ordered the evacuation from the capital of governmental and party bodies and foreign embassies to Kuibyshev (Samara) on the Volga. The result was panic among civilians many of whom tried to flee, only to come up against deadly blocking detachments manned by determined police who turned them back or shot them. At considerable personal risk Stalin remained in the city. On the chief Soviet holiday, 7 November, he took the salute on the Lenin Mausoleum as troops filed past and headed straight for the front.

Despite the traumatic losses, in slow, painful steps all the frenzy of reorganization in the first months of the war began to pay off. In a small but prophetic encounter in November at Aleksino a brigade of newly designed T-34 tanks was concealed in a wood as the 4th Panzer Division hurtled past them unaware of their presence. At the right moment the T-34s were launched into the flanks of the Panzers inflicting a defeat which shocked the German military. As the Panzer commander, General Heinrich Guderian, noted in his memoirs, 'the Russians had already learned a few things'.[10] Bigger defeats were to come as the Germans battled mud and then historically low temperatures and extended lines of communications in addition to gradually more effective Soviet defence. Nonetheless, the advance continued. Relying on his superspy Richard Sorge in Tokyo, who assured Stalin that Japan was too preoccupied planning and carrying out what turned out to be the attack on Pearl Harbor, Stalin felt it was safe to gamble on withdrawing troops from the Far East and throw them into a counter-offensive in front of Moscow, which began on 5 December and ended a month later on 7 January. To Hitler's great disgust, despite German reconnaissance forces having come within 5 miles of the city and actually reaching a city tram terminus at Khimki on 27 November, Moscow had been secured from the German assault. The costs of the battle were biblical. Figures for dead and wounded are hard to specify with certainty. One reliable, but not necessarily definitive, source says there were 658,000 casualties during the retreat and a further 370,000 in the month-long counter-offensive in the Battle of Moscow alone.[11] According to official Soviet figures, casualties on the German side numbered 400,000. Losses of material and equipment were proportionately massive. One key statistic illustrates the German dilemma. Up to the end of January 1942 the German Army lost 4241 tanks. Only 873 replacements had been delivered out of a total of 2842 tanks produced in total in Germany between June 1941 and the end of January 1942. In terms of trucks, motorcycles and motor vehicles, 25 per cent were lost, 'a bloodletting from which the most mobile forces never recovered'.[12]

However, one thing was certain. The Germans had suffered a massive reverse. Not so much a defeat as a failure to reach key objectives. Kiev had fallen but Leningrad, beginning to suffer the cruellest siege in history, and Moscow had held out. German strategy for a short, sharp war had failed. Predictions that the system would simply collapse under pressure, shared by Nazi and Allied intelligence, had proved to be false. In fact, apart from his listless, depressive state just after the attack had begun, fear of collapse was not something entertained seriously, even for a moment, by Stalin and his associates. In 1939, the paragraphs added personally by Stalin to his report to the Eighteenth Party Congress had dismissed the possibility and ended on a confident note: 'Some people in the western media are claiming that the purge . . . has "shaken" the Soviet system and brought disintegration. Such cheap gossip merits only our contempt.' He even added that in 1937 the government got 98.6 per cent of the votes in the elections to the Supreme Soviet of the USSR. After the purge of Bukharin and others in 1938, the figure rose to 99.4 per cent in the elections to the Supreme Soviets of the Union Republics. 'So,' Stalin thundered, 'where are the signs of this disintegration and why did they not show in the election results?'[13] One might state the obvious – that the purges had created a false unity by scaring people into voting for the party – but for Stalin, it seems, the election results had some importance as did the recruitment of a million new party members on the eve of the war to replace the 330,000 or so who had been purged. For Stalin, the purges had strengthened the system not undermined it and 1941 had shown he was more correct than Hitler and the rest in their assessment of the USSR's stability. At no point in the war did the system appear to be following its tsarist predecessor into war-induced collapse. Even dissident minority nationalities, notably Bielorussia (Belarus) and Ukraine which were soon under occupation, and where significant numbers joined the invaders, did not go over wholesale to the Nazis. However, the Nazis themselves, through, as we shall see, their own sense of superiority and invincibility (which survived the Battle of Moscow but not the disasters further down the road in 1943), contributed to this outcome by implementing occupation policies which, hard though it is to believe, were even more devastating than the worst of collectivization or the purges and cost more lives. The invader's first gamble had failed and the prospect of a rapid victory had disappeared. There was a great deal of fighting and suffering still to come but in a long, drawn-out war of attrition the advantage was likely to swing in Stalin's direction. He had escaped the worst consequences of some bad mistakes. Would his luck hold in the next phase of battle?

Losses in the south (January–November 1942)

The leaders of both Germany and the USSR had plenty of issues on which to reflect as the Moscow counter-offensive reached its objectives and both sides paused to regroup in the radically new situation. In preparatory planning before 22 June Stalin had been convinced the main German thrust would be in the south, drawn that way by Germany's ever-desperate need for grain and oil.[14] He was wrong. Germany's leading generals, Halder and von Brauchitsch, had wanted to concentrate on capturing Moscow. Hitler, however, had overruled his planners in favour of splitting Operation Barbarossa into the three targets of Leningrad, Moscow and Kiev. The odd outcome was that, despite Stalin's movement of troops to Ukraine, it was Kiev that fell and Moscow and Leningrad that held on by the skin of their teeth. But what would the German Army do next? The strategy for 1942 began to develop as full-scale fighting re-emerged after the spring thaw. Germany, at last, decided to prioritize the Southern Front and plunged ahead towards the Black Sea, southern Russia and the Caucasus. By contrast, the siege of Leningrad was neither lifted nor significantly intensified. The city was left to rot away in a process of ghastly attrition. Similarly, the Moscow Front remained relatively stable. However, in the south, success piled on success for the advancing *Wehrmacht*. They broke out of their Orel, Belgorod, Taganrog line in late June and quickly took Rostov on Don, which fell on 27 July with hardly a fight compared to the inch-by-inch urban conflicts of 1941. In August the German forces stormed on to Krasnodar, Maikop and Stavropol and, though Soviet forces held the eastern coast of the Black Sea, Germany was poised to attack Ordzhonikidze (Vladikavkaz) and even threaten Groznyi. So confident was Hitler that he split his assault forces into two, ordering a northern splinter to advance on Stalingrad (Tsaritsyn) with a view to making a breakthrough, crossing the Volga and eventually rolling up the Soviet Moscow Front from the east.

By the end of 1942 and into the first half of 1943 something like one third of the European territories of the USSR plus the Baltic States were exposed to the most ferocious occupation policies in history. Where there was some initial expectation that the Germans might be liberators among part of the occupied populations, the proportion of which is almost impossible to determine with precision, the true nature of the invasion soon became obvious to all. In the east, Japan had at least pretended its vast plans for racist colonization were based on ridding Asia of white imperialists and presenting its own new order as liberationist. In Europe the Nazis were so certain of their success and so contemptuous of the forces ranged against them they did not even conceal their objectives. The war was based on Aryan racial values and, in the words of *Mein Kampf*, Hitler's personal manifesto, the role of Slavs in the Third Reich was to be 'hewers of wood and drawers of water' – slaves in other words. The German Governor of Ukraine, Erich Koch, described himself in his inauguration speech as a 'brutal dog' whose task was 'to suck all the goods we can get hold of from Ukraine'. He warned his enforcers they would be expected to show 'the utmost severity towards the native population'. Even more simply he described the task to a questioning subordinate as 'annihilation of Ukrainians'.[15] The front line in executing such Nazi policies were the *Einsatzgruppen* (extermination squads) whose numbers were expanded to 11,000 personnel to meet the growing demand for annihilation. They came in behind the front-line troops to seek out Jews and communists. Behind them came a range of police units who, among other things, enforced the segregation all young men of fighting age, the deportation of labourers (of 2.8 million deportees, 2.3 million are believed to have come from Ukraine) and the selection of half a million young women aged 18 to 35 for assignment to German households for 'domestic purposes' and eventual 'Germanization',[16] which is only explicable in terms of them being expected to be used as Aryan breeding stock. In addition, girls as young as 13 were snatched from the streets and forced into military brothels.[17] Some 2 million prisoners of war died in Nazi custody and at least 2 million Soviet Jews died at the hands of the *Einsatzgruppen*, mobile gas van detachments, ghetto-firing and lynching squads and extermination camps. Even without including civilian siege deaths of at least 80,000 in Kharkov and around 100,000 or more in Kiev, it is clear that the Nazi forces had done the impossible. In only two and a half years they had at least matched and probably exceeded Stalin's death totals for more than a decade from collectivization in 1929 to the outbreak of war. Only defeat and retreat brought an end to the viciousness.

To face up to such a ruthless and unconstrained enemy whose war aims were racial subjugation and selective annihilation, only the toughest methods would hold up. As we have seen, from the outset the whole of the USSR and the military, in particular, were subjected to even more stringent discipline than before the war. The Soldier's Oath, drafted by Stalin in 1939, committed the soldier to defend the USSR 'courageously, skilfully, creditably and honourably, without sparing my blood and my very life to achieve complete victory over the enemy. And if through evil intent I break this solemn oath, then let the stern punishment of the Soviet law, and the universal hatred and contempt of the working people, fall upon me.'[18] Soldiers and officers were arrested and executed for surrendering. Stalin did not claim special favours for himself. When informed his son by Ekaterina Svanidze, Iakob, had been captured by the Germans he refused to negotiate for his release in exchange for a leading German general, believed to be Field Marshal Friedrich von Paulus who had been captured at Stalingrad. According to one version, reflecting on the incident after the war, he said he could not show favour because all the Soviet military were his sons. The Bolshevik mentality was especially suited to war. Duty was paramount. Personal life and feelings were secondary. It was not that the true Bolshevik did not have feelings, but she or he ruthlessly suppressed them as have many military commanders and politicians before and since. The correct thing was to fulfil one's duty with gusto and regardless of cost to self, to family, friends or strangers. It was a classical case of ends justifying means. Toughness was the highest virtue when dealing with jobs that had to be done. The scorched earth policy advocated in Stalin's radio broadcast at the beginning of the German invasion and the speech on the 7 November holiday in 1941, when Stalin insisted there should be a military parade despite the dire circumstances, all emphasized the message. However, it was taken a step further in Order No 270 (August 1941) which threatened to arrest the families of soldiers who surrendered and to deprive families of 'all state benefits and assistance' if they were captured. The theme continued. On 28 June 1942 Order No 227 included the ringing, unambiguous phrase 'not one step back' (*ni shagu nazad'*). The forceful words were backed up by forceful actions. Blocking detachments surrounded threatened cities, notably Moscow, to prevent unauthorized departures. Similar detachments followed some army units into action. Punishment battalions put those who had committed crimes in harm's way as an alternative to imprisonment and execution. Some 442,000 men served in them. A further 158,000 were sentenced to be shot and 436,000 arrested and imprisoned.[19] Terror was returning to the centre of Soviet life but it would not be true to say that it had a decisive impact. All the evidence from memoirs, reminiscences, literature and later accounts shows that most of the Soviet citizens who fought did so from 'positive' reasons of support to liberate the country from the invaders rather than the 'negative' element of fear.

Hatred of the enemy, harsh discipline plus growing industrial and armaments production, boosted in certain critical areas, including trucks and radios imported under the American Lend-Lease scheme, were the drivers propelling the Soviet fightback The losses of 1942 were only halted, albeit in spectacular fashion, at the end of the year and in early 1943 in the form of the legendary Battle of Stalingrad, followed four months later by the less well known but even more decisive Battle of Kursk.

In late summer 1942 the German forces were buoyant. On 19 August they began what looked like a final assault on the city of Stalingrad. By 25 August they had reached the Volga and established a salient on the far side. The central group also reached the outskirts. Over 600 bomber raids killed some 40,000 civilians trapped in the city. The expectation of the German commander von Paulus that the city would be taken in days seemed highly likely and even the Soviet commanders appeared to agree.[20]

Stalingrad (September 1942–2 February 1943)

There is an argument about exactly who thought up the plan for the Battle of Stalingrad. One thing is certain. For once it was not Stalin. His senior commanders Vatutin, Vasilievsky and Boiko all have some claim to the bold plan to conduct a massive operation of encirclement. However, Stalin did inject a crucial ingredient. Although, for once, he left the precise details to his commanders he had already defined the significance of the developing battle. Stalin had been sleeping only two hours a night through the summer as what appeared to be a new catastrophe was developing. Despite having seen the importance of the southern sector for Germany in 1941, in 1942 he had neglected it for the central and northern sectors. However, in August he was steadfastly focused on the south and on 27 August he recalled Zhukov from his post as commander of the Western Front defending Moscow and two days later ordered him to Stalingrad to investigate. On 3 September Vasilievsky, the chief of staff, reported to Stalin that German tanks had broken through to the suburbs of the city. Stalin was enraged and bellowed down the phone: 'What's the matter with them? Don't they understand that if we surrender Stalingrad, the south of the country will be cut off from the centre and we probably will not be able to defend it? Don't they realize this is not only a catastrophe for Stalingrad? We would lose our main waterway and soon our oil, too!' Vasilievsky's tense reply was hardly reassuring: 'There is still a chance that we won't lose the city.' Stalin called him back a few minutes later but, wisely, Vasilievsky was elsewhere and could not be found. So Stalin dictated a message and sent it to Zhukov who was still in Stalingrad: 'The situation in Stalingrad has got worse. The enemy is six miles from the city. Stalingrad could be captured today or tomorrow if the northern group does not give immediate assistance . . . Delay is tantamount to a crime.'[21] Back in Moscow together with Vasilievsky, Zhukov's initial response, on 12 September, was unhelpful. Stalingrad, he argued, could not be defended with its current supplies, personnel and equipment. Reserves were essential. 'Another solution', as he and Vasilevsky called it, was needed. At first Stalin was more interested in the short-term defence of the city but he gave them 24 hours to outline such a solution. On 13 September they presented a colossal three front (Stalingrad; South-Western; Don) plan for a counter-offensive encirclement that was code named Operation Uranus. Stalin accepted his commanders' suggestions. The weak point was that Zhukov said it would take 45 days to prepare the implementation of the counter-offensive, 45 days the city did not seem to have.

The battle for the city had two crucial phases left to play out. The first was ferocious defence to buy those essential days. The second was the actual operation to counter-attack. The optimistic expectations of Paulus were slowly turning, literally, to ash. Advances measured in tens of kilometres gave way to those measured in kilometres. Then it was hundreds of metres. Key points such as the small hill, the Mamaev Kurgan, changed hands several times. The railway station changed hands 15 times.[22] There was a 58-day siege of a massive Soviet-held grain silo. The local Soviet commanders, Chuikov and Yeremenko, put up a ferocious defence of suicidal intensity. To maintain their fanaticism they were not even told of the counter-offensive until it was about to begin. One can only agree with the judgement of one of the leading historians of Russia's war effort that 'how the Red Army survived in Stalingrad defies military explanation'.[23]

But survive they did. The preparatory period enabled the Red Army to build up a force of over 1 million men, 14,000 heavy guns, 1000 tanks and, crucially, 1350 aircraft.[24] Increasingly aware of the decline in air superiority, which he initially attributed to the impact of attrition upon his own forces rather than the totally undetected Soviet build-up, Paulus, under pressure from Hitler, opened up a desperate attempt to finally seize the city on 9 November. A 500 metre wide corridor to the river was punched through, once again dividing the Soviet forces in the north and south of the city from each other. However, within three days the offensive was halted through exhaustion. Paulus was calling on Berlin to allow him to abandon the campaign and break out to save the remnants of his army. When the German Chief of Staff, Zeitzler, supported the request, Hitler screamed his refusal: 'I will not leave the Volga!'

By contrast, Stalin had at least learned there were times to leave operational decisions to the military and that the timing of the counter-offensive was one such occasion. Zhukov ordered it to begin on 19 November. Only hours before was Chuikov indirectly informed to expect a 'special order'. The second phase of the battle had begun. Rokossovsky's army from the Don Front to the north and Vatutin's force from the South-Western Front were unleashed. Yeremenko's reinforced Stalingrad Front army increased pressure in the centre of the now vastly extended battlefield. After the one and only attempt to relieve the city through a last-ditch attack by Manstein from the German Don Front which, despite gaining some 60 kilometres, had failed by 24 December, Paulus's troops in the city were abandoned to their fate. The same day Paulus circulated an order of the day to his troops which rejected any offers of a truce and claimed 'deliverance was already on its way'. In words reminiscent of Stalin himself, not to mention Hitler, Paulus proclaimed that 'we all know what threatens us if the army ceases to resist: certain death awaits most of us, either from the enemy bullet or starvation and suffering in Siberian captivity. One thing is sure: whoever surrenders will never see his nearest and dearest again. We have only one way out: to fight to the last bullet, despite growing cold and hunger.'[25] Paulus was able to talk the talk but he was not able to walk the walk. The pocket of entrapment diminished day-by-day and eventually Paulus was found by a junior Soviet officer and arrested on 31 January. Hitler was enraged that he had been so cowardly as to not commit suicide. No doubt he would have been ten times more apoplectic had he known Paulus would live out his days in post-war East Germany as a pliant instrument of communist propaganda. On 2 February the last German resistance in the main pocket was silenced. A German force of 330,000 had been reduced to a remnant of less than 80,000 in the pocket. Some 10,000 who evaded initial capture continued a sporadic resistance for up to a month but the battle was lost. The Soviets had taken well over 1 million casualties including nearly half a million dead. The well-known words of

Chuikov were all too true: 'Approaching [Stalingrad] soldiers used to say: "We are entering hell." And after spending one or two days here, they say: "No, this isn't hell, this is ten times worse than hell."' Perhaps for that very reason the reaction to the victory in the USSR was subdued. There were no euphoric outbursts. One source said people walked with a prouder step but, despite the profusion of military and diplomatic memoirs we do not have a 'reaction shot' of a delighted Stalin. He was, of course, massively pleased and relieved but not euphoric. His terse congratulatory telegram is also rather enigmatic. It was dated 25 January, before the end of the battle, and was addressed equally to the Stalingrad, Leningrad and Grozny sectors. There had been significant fighting in the latter two but nowhere near the importance of Stalingrad:

> As a result of two months of offensive engagements, the Red Army has broken through the defences of the German-fascist troops on a wide front, routed 102 enemy divisions, captured over 200,000 prisoners, 13,000 guns and a large quantity of their war material, and advanced about 400 kilometres (250 miles). Our troops have won an important victory. The offensive of our troops continues.
>
> I congratulate the Red Army men, commanders and political workers of the South-Western, Southern, Don, North Caucasian, Voronezh, Kalinin, Volkhov and Leningrad fronts on their victory over the German-fascist invaders and their allies – the Rumanians, Italians and Hungarians – at Stalingrad, on the Don, in the North Caucasus, at Voronezh, in the Velikie Luki area and south of Lake Ladoga.[26]

The low-key celebration and the equating of Stalingrad with events on the North Caucasus is hard to explain, especially since in Britain and, to a lesser extent the United States, the victory was greeted with massive relief and enthusiasm as the turning point of the war. In the USSR the celebratory instinct was probably muted because of several factors. The immense casualties did nothing to arouse joy nor did the awareness that there were equally great sacrifices to come. Congratulating all the fronts together also recognized that heroism did not depend solely on the significance of the battle. It was also the case that, according to Bolshevik values, the dead and the survivors had done no more than fulfil their Bolshevik duty and that should be expected, not elevated to a super-status. It might also mitigate jealousies among the generals but it could also prevent any of them outshining the supreme commander himself. Stalin did, however, ensure that the heroes were generously rewarded with the highest military medals of honour. Generals Zhukov, Vasilievsky, Chuikov, Rokossovsky and Yeremenko were the worthy first recipients of the newly instituted highest military honour, the Order of Suvorov, 1st Class. Stalin promoted himself to Marshal of the Soviet Union and, thereafter, mostly wore military uniform in public. However, there was no grand public celebration. There was still a war to be won. Churchill had perhaps best captured the significance of the moment in his Mansion House speech of 10 November, a speech which celebrates British victory at El Alamein but fails to refer to the Soviet Union even once. Nonetheless, the characterization of the moment fits early February, 1943. 'Now this is not the end. It is not even the beginning of the end. But it is, perhaps, the end of the beginning.'

Spring and summer 1943: The Battle of Kursk and after

Commanders on both sides of the Eastern Front had plenty to reflect on for the rest of winter. Who would go on the offensive and where and when? Perhaps the dominant feeling of the period was Hitler's deep desire for revenge for Stalingrad. He was determined to reverse its effects and throw everything into what he expected to be a massively successful drive against the USSR which would, after so much delay and cost, deliver Moscow into his hands. In his early thinking about the battle, three months before it happened, Hitler proclaimed 'the victory at Kursk must have the effect of a beacon seen around the world'.[27] This was in stark contrast to the reality of early 1943 which saw a massive retreat of German and Allied forces in the south of the Soviet Union, not to mention growing difficulties in North Africa and the threat of an Allied attack across the Mediterranean which actually began on 10 July with the invasion of Sicily. Rostov was recovered by the Red Army, as was Belgorod; and Soviet forces were poised near Orel, Kharkov and Smolensk, which remained under occupation. Although Stalingrad had swung the balance much more towards the USSR, the next moves could still be fatal for either party.

The obvious target for a German attack was the 200 kilometre wide and 100 kilometre deep salient punched into the German front line around Kursk. Hitler's plan was to attack on the two flanks, cut through behind the salient and role the front up northwards and break through to threaten Moscow from the east. Both Hitler and Stalin knew that the next steps would probably be decisive and it may have been this which seems to have induced an uncustomary caution in Hitler. Everything had to be just right. The initial date for the attack, 3 May, was postponed to 3 June. That date came and went. More days and then weeks crept by. Only on 6 July did the attack begin.

For Stalin and the Soviet commanders the delay was unnerving. Kursk was one of the most complex and meticulously planned battles of all time involving a wide range of military arts. In addition to 'normal' preparation the Soviet defensive lines had been multiplied many times so they were six deep in key locations and there were a further two lines in front of the reserves some 250 kilometres to the rear. Over 400,000 mines were laid in the forward areas. In addition, partisans and intelligence were to play a key role. The scope of partisan warfare in the occupied areas has not been fully researched. It is believed there were some 300,000 partisans in the forests and marshes of Belarus and the western borderlands of the Soviet Union. Most of them were either remnants of broken Soviet armies or refugees, many of them Jewish, who had fled from the *Einsatzgruppen* and the Gestapo. Some 30,000 were thought to be reinforcements parachuted behind or infiltrated through German lines. Their relationship with local populations were variable mainly because of the risk of savage reprisals by the occupiers against villages thought to be harbouring partisans. In an extreme case the German 707th Infantry Division executed 10,000 'partisans' in a month in reprisal for the death of two men from their own ranks. Further west there were also Ukrainian nationalist partisans in the occupied areas who fought alongside the Nazis for a while but at other points against both sides. Stepan Bandera, an inmate of Sachsen-hausen camp at this time, an ironic situation for an anti-Semite, later emerged as their best-known leader, still commemorated today as a national hero despite his collaboration with the Nazis.

By the time of the Battle of Kursk, the Soviet partisans had been integrated into the broader strategic plan and had instructions to conduct sabotage in co-ordination with the opening of the battle. Some 10,000 of them are thought to have carried out hundreds, even thousands, of acts of sabotage in the first few days of the battle. However, although of some value, especially in blowing up dumps of aviation fuel, their contribution was not decisive and German lines of communication were not severely damaged. Soviet aircraft preparation was also unprecedented. 2900 aircraft had been assembled on 150 genuine airfields in the battle zone, not to mention 50 decoys. 1.3 million troops, around 3500 tanks and 19,000 artillery pieces were in place. Forty per cent of Red Army personnel and 75 per cent of its heavy equipment were concentrated in the battle zone. On the German side were just under 1 million German and Allied soldiers, 2700 tanks, 2000 aircraft and 11,000 artillery pieces. 'They were about to fight the largest setpiece battle in history.'[28] The stakes could not have been higher.

Unsurprisingly, the defenders were very unsettled as weeks of inaction passed by. Could the blow fall elsewhere? Was there an elaborate bluff being played? Another unprecedented contribution to the battle came from intelligence. In his memoirs Marshal Vasilevskii claimed 'Our intelligence was able to determine not only the general intention of the enemy . . . the direction of his attacks, the composition of the striking groups and of the reserves, but also to establish the time of the beginning of the fascist offensive.'[29]

The main source was from Ultra intercepts provided by British Enigma code-solvers in Bletchley Park. As well as the official sources, John Cairncross, who worked there, was passing material directly to his Soviet handler in London. Much of it was channelled through the 'Lucy' spy ring based in Switzerland to conceal its original source from the Germans as much as from the Soviets. Enigma is said to have provided the complete German order of battle, an enormous asset. It also gave the date of the invasion and the postponements, but as they lengthened the credibility of the incoming intel was questioned. Another prime spy source, Richard Sorge at the German embassy in Tokyo, sent confirmatory information. More regular sources – defectors across the front line, soldiers taken by snatch squads, crashed airmen – also provided up-to-date information. However, the intelligence harvest was not as straightforwardly useful as it looked. German intelligence was, of course, aware of some of this and used the more conventional channels to spread disinformation, the most important of which was strong information that the whole campaign had been abandoned. Stalin, in particular, was very irritated. He was also totally unreceptive to the communiqué which reached him from Churchill and the Western Allies on 2 June that the expected invasion of France and the opening of a second front was being postponed to 1944. Not without justification he replied that the decision would create 'exceptional difficulties for the Soviet Union and leaves the Soviet Army, which is fighting not only for its country but also for its allies, to do the job alone, almost single-handed'. As we shall see in the next chapter, this incident and others, convinced Stalin that, as in the 1930s, Britain was prepared to let the USSR and Germany fight to the death while it watched from the side lines.

Whether or not he was aware of Bismarck's famous quip that you could do anything with bayonets except sit on them we do not know but that was Stalin's situation. As a man of action who relished taking the initiative the delays were interminable. On several occasions he urged a pre-emptive attack on all that German armour within 160 kilometres (100 miles) of the front. His generals fortunately held him back. Their battle plan, the classic Soviet 'deep battle' with 150 miles of defensive lines, would have been ruined. It required the German forces to move forward into their own destruction. To somewhat ease the tension Stalin did sanction raids on German airfields whose co-ordinates were supplied by Cairncross's smuggled intel. The Germans sustained significant losses of 500 aircraft in three waves of attack, not quite as disabling as the German raids on Soviet airfields in June 1941, but a form of payback all the same.[30] In May and June rumours of Hitler deciding to abandon the Kursk operation increased as German disinformation tried to make the most of the delay and play further on the enemy's frayed nerves. Then the front went quiet. And then, all hell broke loose. At 2:00 am on 5 July a captured German soldier confirmed 3:00 am as the starting time. Zhukov immediately ordered artillery and air strikes which caught the German forces cold, even to the extent of thinking they were facing an unexpected full-scale Soviet offensive. They delayed their attack for 90 minutes but at 4:30 am it went ahead. In his memoirs Zhukov recalled that Stalin's voice was strained with nerves when he reported the attack and that in the background, as Overy recounts, Zhukov 'heard "a terrible rumbling". The noise of guns, rockets and bombs all merged together, to Zhukov's ears, into a "symphony from hell".'[31]

The symphony went on for 11 days. The elite of the German armed forces, units which were still undefeated, crashed into the Soviet defence lines. The Waffen SS and the three toughest SS Panzer units – Das Reich, the Leibstandarte Adolf Hitler Guards and the Totenkopf (Death's Head) divisions and the Panzer Grenadier Grossdeutschland division – spearheaded the attack. A key encounter at Prokhorovka pitted 850 Soviet tanks against 600 German ones. The crack Soviet 5th Guards Tank Army was ordered up to face the assault on Stalin's personal order, which arrived on the birthday of Divisional Commander General Pavel Rotmistrov. The Germans had the edge in tank quality but Rotmistrov made the most of the quantity and manoeuvrability of the T-34, the Soviet main but not best battle tank. The KV range and the giant Stalin tank were better gunned and better armoured but the testimony to the advantage of the weaker but swifter T-34 came from a German participant in the battle: 'We found ourselves taking on a seemingly inexhaustible mass of enemy armour – never have I received such an overwhelming impression of Russian strength and numbers as on that day. The clouds of dust made it difficult to get help from the Luftwaffe, and soon many of the T-34s had broken past our screen and were streaming like rats all over the battlefield.'[32]

Other snapshots can give a sense of this immense battle. The Fourth Panzer Army's advance towards Prokhorovka was preceded by a softening up artillery barrage around Belgorod 'which, in fifty minutes, expended more shells . . . than the combined total fired by German guns in the French and Polish campaigns'.[33]

The confusion of the battlefield at micro-level is caught by the story of one adventurous German major named Franz Bäke who volunteered to make a bridgehead by means of a daring ruse. He took a captured T-34 and some German tanks and armoured personnel carriers which were made to look as though they had surrendered, and, under instructions of complete personal and radio silence, advanced into Russian territory. Bäke and his men sat on top of their tanks smoking but not talking. They moved through Soviet lines, passing infantry and armoured units as they went. Close to their goal they were rumbled but the Russian forces hesitated. Bäke and his men reached their objective, a bridge across the Donets at Rzhavets, shortly after it had been blown up. Even so they found a footbridge still intact, crossed the river and established the vital bridgehead in the confusion. By dawn they had a secure position and larger forces had followed up to establish German control. However, they were bombed by a 'friendly' formation of Heinkel's who were unaware of Bäke's success. The bridgehead held but in a severely weakened state so that the advantage of the operation was lost.[34]

If confusion was the order of the day at the micro level the macro extent of the battle was unprecedented and has never been repeated in a single battle. The battle zone was too large to fit into southern Britain. To get an idea of its scope, if the southern limit, south of Kharkov is imagined to be Portsmouth, the northern limit, near Sukhinichi between Briansk and Kaluga, would be somewhere near Newcastle. Kursk, itself would be north-east of Birmingham. The battle zone would extend west to Aberystwyth and east to Norwich. The key conflict, at Prokhorovka, would, ironically, be somewhere near Bletchley Park. Reserves who entered the battle were initially held in areas as far away as the equivalent of Limerick on the west coast of Ireland and across the North Sea as far as Amsterdam.

On 12 July, the German High Command aborted Operation Zitadelle, as they called it. On 15 July the raging rockets, bombs and guns fell silent. The symphony from hell was finished, leaving 70,000 Soviet dead. The battle had shifted the tectonic plates. Kursk was the beginning of the end. The full weight of the elite Nazi armed forces had been flung against the defensive wall of Soviet steel and had been annihilated. Soviet losses had also been colossal but German generals were quick to realize that they were vulnerable because of the greater recuperative power of the Soviet Union. In the face of Soviet attack, they would be hard put to gather sufficient forces to defend their positions. Soviet generals knew the same thing and were not slow to capitalize. Already, on 12 July, a counter-offensive from the Bryansk Front at the northern limit of the battle zone was launched. It was called Operation Kutuzov in honour of the general who is usually credited with having the greatest responsibility for the defeat of Napoleon and his army in 1812. It encountered heavy resistance but after bitter fighting a breakthrough was achieved. Orel was liberated on 5 August and Bryansk on 18 August. On 3 August a similar offensive was launched from the southern limit of battle and Belgorod was recovered on 5 August but, on account of stiff German resistance round their strongpoint in the area, it was only on 28 August that the objective of the operation, the re-conquest of Kharkov, was finally achieved. This southern counter-attack was codenamed Operation Commander Rumyantsev after one of Catherine II's generals whose defeat of the Germans at the fortress of Kolberg had opened the road to Berlin in 1761 during the Seven Years' War. Another 183,000 were added to the pile of Soviet dead in these operations. In two months, as Richard Overy points out, the Soviets had lost almost as many men as the British Empire and US forces combined throughout the war.[35] In a thoughtful and balanced discussion Overy also modifies the widely argued notion that the Soviets under Stalin were especially careless with human life. Instead, Overy attributes it to a longer tradition of Russian and Soviet military culture in which any sacrifice which had to be made would be made. In any case, he also points out a number of overlooked facts. First, as equipment and military skill and experience accumulated, the Soviet casualty rate fell by half between the Battles of Moscow and Kursk and by another half in 1944 to 25 per cent of the original rate. In addition, 'one awkward fact that makes it difficult to accept that the Soviet system as such squandered its manpower in war: the Tsarist armies between 1914 and 1917 averaged 7000 casualties a day, compared with 7950 a day between 1941 and 1945. The figures are not entirely reliable but they give a sense of proportion.'[36]

Unsurprisingly, Stalin was in 'a joyously jubilant mood' when visited by Generals Antonov and Shtemenko to sign the victory communiqué on 24 July, according to Shtemenko's memoirs.[37] Unlike Stalingrad, when Stalin was not especially celebratory, the overwhelming victories of Kursk and the follow-up counter-attacks brought him to the realization that the victories were not being sufficiently noted. 'Do you read history?' he enquired of his bemused generals. 'If you had read', he went on, 'you would know that in the old days, when troops won victories, all the bells would be rung . . . We're thinking of giving artillery salutes and arranging some kind of fireworks in honour of the troops who distinguished themselves and the commanders who led them.'[38] On 5 August the liberation of Orel and Belgorod was the first victory celebrated in this way with carefully worked-out gun salvoes according to the importance of the victory.[39] For whatever reason, perhaps to underline his supposed military credentials, or to impress the Allied leaders or maybe just growing curiosity as much as anything, Stalin also decided, to the dismay of his security detachment, that he wanted to visit the front for himself. He left on 1 August by a heavily camouflaged and heavily armoured train supplied with special Kremlin provisions, which headed for a point north-west of Moscow. He spent the following night in the hut of an elderly peasant woman in a village which, apparently without his knowledge, had been emptied of its real inhabitants, filled with soldiers from the NKVD and made to look more like the front than it actually did. Stalin was horrified to learn an entire NKVD division had been deployed to guard him. Nonetheless he received his generals in the village hut and slept on a simple rustic bed. The visit was rounded off by two moments of farce. Stalin decided to pay the elderly lady for her hospitality but had no money on him, as usual. Nor did any of the top brass present whom he denounced as scroungers. Second, according to a story heard by Anastas Mikoyan, later to be deputy prime minister under Khrushchev, on the way back to the train in a convoy of vehicles, Stalin needed to defecate and stopped the convoy. Since no one could assure him the roadside had not been mined, he pulled down his trousers and by doing his business on the road itself, in full view of his assembled entourage, 'shamed himself', in Mikoyan's words – though it is hard to see what his alternative might have been! In any case, as one source mentions, it was something of 'a metaphorical commentary on his treatment of the Soviet people'.[40]

Payback: to Berlin (Autumn 1943–May 1945)

If Kursk was history's greatest battle, history's greatest military campaign still lay ahead. As Guderian and others had feared, the Soviet Union would renew its military personnel and equipment much more rapidly than Germany, which had lost at least half of its armour and heavy guns at and after Kursk. It was also beginning to scrape the barrel for conscripts. By the end of the war Hitler's forces were packed with teenagers down to the age of 16 and middle-aged men normally considered too old to serve. Germany was still not defenceless in the face of the developing Russian steamroller but it was close to needing a miracle to survive. The loss of its best soldiers, armour and guns would need time to replace, time the Soviets were not going to give them. The initiative was firmly with the Red Army. One often meets the opinion that, in military terms, the Battle of Kursk was a draw, neither side conceding its ground. This is a mystifying judgement. The Kutuzov and Rumiantsev counter-attacks had been massively successful. The rest of the history of the war was one of explosive Russian advances and German retreat, crumbling and collapse.

Correctly, German military planners especially feared Russia's capacity to re-equip itself rapidly. Not only did the Soviet Union have its own ever-expanding resources, it was also benefiting more from Lend-Lease. Stalin had been dismissive of the niggardliness of British aid earlier in the war but by 1943 onwards the supplies, which, of course, had to be paid for, were beginning to be of significant help in certain areas. According to some calculations 50 per cent of Soviet aviation fuel came from the United States. A large component of its truck and jeep pool was also supplied, especially valuable commodities when the Red Army was making rapid advances. Lend-lease radios were also invaluable to improve communications. In the early phases of the war only the lead tanks in armoured columns had radio contact with the battle commanders. If that was knocked out the unit became instructionless. By the time of Kursk, most tanks had their own radios. Finally, canned meat, the legendary spam, and canned fruit were added to the military and civilian diet. Nonetheless, there is no doubt the bulk of Soviet equipment and many crucial innovations, like the multiple Katiusha rocket-launchers which saturated the battlefield at Kursk, were of purely Soviet invention and construction. Food supply also held up, a consequence of the harsh collectivization of 1929–1936 which put the onus of shortages on the village and developed an efficient and sufficient, if sparse, supply of key foodstuffs to city, industry and military.

With exceptions about to be noted, in dramatic contrast to 1914–1918 the country not only remained solid behind the army, the party and Stalin, it was arguably the time when state, party and people were tied in a tighter unity than ever before. Party membership soared. In 1938 there were 1.9 million members and 3 million in 1942. By 1944 the figure had risen to just under 5 million.[41] Membership of the Komsomol (the Young Communists – that is, the organization for young adults) rose even faster. To be in the party was to buy into an ideology of being in the forefront of battle – whether on the military or home front – and inspiring others by virtues of courage, self-sacrifice and heroism. By comparison with peace time, party membership was not a ticket to privilege. Three million party members gave their lives in the war, 12 per cent of the deaths for some 5 per cent of the population. As we have seen, terror played a part but there is no question that, after Kursk, the Soviet war effort was on a roll. Morale was recovering fast, industry was working flat-out on weapons. Harsh lessons of early mistakes in the war had been learned. Stalin's commanders had grown in confidence and expertise and Stalin had learned to trust them and realized his own limitations as a war commander. According to Volkogonov he had shown himself to be a mediocre tactician but more competent and imaginative as a strategist.[42] By 1943, although he was still deeply involved in all aspects of the war, he had learned to leave the final decisions to his generals.

One aspect of military art which the Soviets had perfected was decoy – the use of diversion and disguise to fool the enemy. In the next military campaign these features were used *par excellence.* As the Red Army drove deeper into Ukraine in late summer and autumn, heading for Kiev, it encountered the marshy terrain of the region. The Germans dismissed the areas as impassable; the Soviets used them to advantage. They waterproofed their T-34s and plunged in and concealed themselves completely in the forests. Two entire tank armies were concealed in this way. The Germans had no idea they were there. A feint to the south drew German forces towards it and then, on 3 November, Vatutin unleashed his hidden armies in the north achieving complete tactical surprise. On 6 November Kiev was liberated.

The annual 7 November celebrations had a special buoyancy about them. As a result of the massive campaigns from Crimea to the northern Carpathians, the line Hitler demanded should be held at all costs, the Dnepr River, had been severely breached in the south and the north. By the end of 1943 it had been completely lost to Germany. Once again, German forces were in headlong retreat. There was nothing that could turn their fortunes around. As a coda to the symphony from hell, another place associated with a Great War symphony of a very different kind, Leningrad, was liberated on 26 February 1944. In the savage siege maintained by German and Finnish forces for almost 900 days, up to a million inhabitants had died of starvation, illness and enemy action.

The military history of the final phase of the war is spectacular in terms of unimaginable scale. The centrepiece operation of 1944, Operation Bagration, named after another defender of Russia against Napoleon, smashed the final remnants of Hitler's Army Group Centre. The campaign was the largest in military history. On the German side were 3.1 million troops, 3000 aircraft and 2300 tanks; on the Soviet side: 6.4 million men, 13,400 aircraft and 5800 tanks.[43] It was a dread-inspiring force infused with a deep desire for victory and vengeance.

The Germans also had two complicating factors they had not faced earlier. Regular and ever-increasing Allied bombing raids from Britain by American and British air forces were tying up two-thirds of their fighter aircraft, one third of their artillery and one fifth of their ammunition. On D-Day, 6 June, Allied forces finally opened the second front and established a small beachhead in Normandy. Up to the last, Stalin had remained sceptical – 'What if they meet up with some Germans! Maybe there won't be a landing then, just promises as usual.' The German forces were barely distracted by the landings. There were 228 divisions on the Eastern Front leaving 58 divisions in the west of which only 15 were initially in the vicinity of the landings. Over 75 per cent of German forces remained facing the 'mighty avalanche' as Shtemenko called it.[44]

It began to hit on 23 June 1944, three massive years and one day after the launch of Operation Barbarossa. In the judgement of a fine historian of Russia's war effort 'In little over a week Bagration had proved to be an astonishing success.'[45] A roll call of liberations resulting shows that early promise continued: 3 July, Minsk; 13 July, Vilnius (capital of Lithuania); 23 July, Lublin in eastern Poland; 26 July, Brest-Litovsk; 27 July, L'viv. On 25 July they reached the Vistula, establishing small, fiercely contested bridgeheads in the following days. Some Soviet units had been advancing at 25 miles (40 kilometres) per day at the height of the conflict. In a month and a day the front across a vast area from the Romanian border to the Baltic had been pushed back from 100 to 250 miles (160–400 kilometres). By comparison, the Allies in the west had only just broken out of their Normandy beachhead, though having done so they, too, advanced swiftly against disorganized and retreating German armies.

Another roll call of cities captured by the Red Army's southern thrust shows the dramatic speed of success but also a key and growing complication. Most of them, after Odessa (10 April 1944) were in foreign countries. The entanglements arising from this will be discussed in the next chapter.

Apart from its size the final phase of the war has thrown up numerous controversies. This is not surprising as every advance came with political costs and responsibilities. The straightforward though colossally demanding need to liberate core cities of the Soviet Union was giving way to advances into complex, non-Russian, non-Slav and non-Soviet regions. Liberated areas were also, in the ever-suspicious mind of Stalin, full of collaborators who had to be punished. In other words, a predominantly military war from 1941 to early 1943 was turning increasingly, as Clausewitz taught, into one where the aspect of 'politics by other means' began to dominate. Stalin, always a wily politician ahead of any other aspects of his personality, was going to have to chart a path through a more complex world. Needless to say, historians have been divided on many of the great issues thrown up.

In one of the most widely acclaimed accounts of Stalin's wartime diplomacy (to which we will shortly turn our attention) the author states that, having promised to embark on an offensive to coincide with D-Day Stalin sent his troops on a minor campaign in Finland. Indeed, he did do that and, such was the learning curve of the Soviet armed forces, that it flattened Finnish resistance much more quickly than in the disastrous Winter War of 1939–1940. However, it was only a prelude to divert Germany from the central thrust of Operation Bagration which did achieve complete surprise. In the chorus of acclaim around the book hardly any reviewers noticed or commented upon this extraordinary omission which reflects the lack of awareness of the war in the east of Europe.[46] Mastny's omission is all the more surprising since, without mentioning Bagration, the author finds the Red Army pausing malevolently at the gates of Warsaw as spectators to the heroic anti-fascist uprising of the anti-Russian, nationalist Polish Home Army which it had supposedly encouraged and could and should have helped. How they got there via Finland is not explained. But the author is far from alone in blaming Stalin for standing viciously by as the uprising was crushed by SS units. In 'the single biggest atrocity of the war' 250,000 civilians were slaughtered in reprisal for the pathetically under-equipped and premature uprising of the heroic but doomed force of 20,000 Home Army partisans. Churchill in his memoirs 'berated his former ally for lack of considerations of honour, humanity, decent commonplace good faith' in not coming to the city's assistance. Once again, Overy gives a better balanced and more judicious view based on the evidence.[47] While he agrees with Churchill that 'Stalin was, indeed, poorly supplied' with such characteristics; nonetheless, 'the truth is far more complicated'. The Soviets, he argues, simply did not have the strength to go straight in to Warsaw and, in any case, since the uprising was 'instigated not to help out the Soviet advance but to forestall it', it would have been against their political interest to pull the chestnuts out of the fire for their opponents. But chiefly Overy argues that, in evidence supported by new German sources as well, German resistance stiffened at this moment and made it hard for the Red Army to hang on to the small bridgeheads it had established over the Vistula. Stalin personally had been dismissive of the whole adventure, telling its political leader Stanislaw Mikolajczyk, head of the London Polish government in exile, to his face that the so-called Home Army was no army. 'Without artillery, tanks, aircraft . . . in modern war it is nothing.' Stalin's much-vaunted opposition to parachute drops was based on the likelihood that, given the small area of the uprising, any supplies dropped would more likely be a gift to the Germans rather than the beleaguered Poles. When he did agree to make a few drops it was purely as a political gesture to his allies. Overy's conclusion is that 'Could the Red Army have captured Warsaw in August 1944 and saved its population from further German barbarities? The answer now seems unambiguously negative. Soviet forces did not sit and play while Warsaw burned. The city was beyond their grasp.'[48]

However, reference to this harsh treatment of a potential enemy reminds us that, as the Soviet Army advanced westwards, so fierce reprisals were inflicted on those left behind by the retreating Nazis who were deemed to have been collaborators and traitors to the motherland. Admissions to the gulag camps and labour colonies peaked in 1941 at 854,000 and fell to 331,000 in 1944, including criminals who were the majority rather than politicals.[49] Blocking detachments and the like accounted for 158,000 death sentences in the war years.[50] But far worse than the regular operation of the terror apparatus was Stalin's vindictive pursuit of small nationalities who were deemed to have been collaborationist. Volga Germans, Chechens, Crimean Tatars were deported *en masse*. Entire families, entire villages were scooped up. Loyally serving officers and men were arrested on the front line for having the wrong nationality. It was another idiotic operation rooted in collective suspicion and the concept of collective guilt, mixed with the Stalinist principle that all the guilty have to be dealt with even at the cost of innocents getting caught up in the process which was implemented by a ruthless and cruel but still ramshackle state bureaucracy. About 1.5 million people are thought to have been arrested of whom 231,000 died in the process, though the figures are highly disputed.

Despite this wartime reckoning with internal 'enemies' the external foe still had to be beaten. It was only on 11 January that the full weight of the Red Army was able to force a passage across the Vistula and enter and rapidly take Warsaw. This was the first move in the advance to Berlin which was a campaign of deep advance into the homeland of the enemy. It was marked by revelation of the worst German atrocities – a pile of burned bodies of women and children had greeted them in Minsk in 1944 but now they were reaching the remnants of Nazi death camps. The barely living skeletons of those too close to death to bother evacuating greeted the Red Army in Majdanek. Red Army troops filed through to observe the survivors and the warehouses full of clothes and trinkets taken from the innumerable inmates. According to the commander of troops in that sector, Vassili Chuikov, 'hate raged in the heart of our soldiers'.[51] And that was before they reached Auschwitz on 27 January.

These were unimaginable times in the areas through which the two great armies passed. The Nazis settled scores brutally as they left, massacring prisoners, slaves and suspected enemies. Villages were burned to the ground, towns demolished. Evidence of these horrors wound up the incoming Soviet troops even further and put them in an even more vengeful mood to make the collectively responsible perpetrators pay. Everything they saw and had been told about the bestial enemy appeared to be true. Tragically, though unsurprisingly, they thought only to take revenge on the enemy. The Soviet Army descended on Germany as bitter avengers who drank, raped and looted.[52] In some cases the army authorities disciplined the more disgraceful outbreaks but, by and large, blind eyes were turned in the spirit of Stalin himself, who shocked the young Yugoslav communist, Milovan Djilas, by saying that the soldiers should be permitted to 'amuse' themselves after all they had been through. More pertinently, perhaps, he also invoked Dostoevsky and the 'complicated thing that is man's soul, his psyche . . . Imagine a man who has fought from Stalingrad to Belgrade – over thousands of kilometres of his own devastated land, across the dead bodies of his comrades and dearest ones! How can such a man react normally? . . . You have imagined the Red Army to be ideal. And it is not ideal nor can it be . . . The important thing is it fights Germans – and it is fighting them well. Nothing else matters.' Oddly, Stalin went on to the case of a soldier who did act normally and defended a woman from the forced attentions of a major who shot him and was arrested and tried and sentenced to death. Stalin, however, released the major and sent him to the front where 'he is now one of our heroes'.[53]

The offensive rolled on to the final military controversy of the war. Chuikov claimed Berlin could have been taken in February. Not many agree with him. In fact, as the Soviet Army neared the vast city with its last holdouts of fanatical Nazis including Hitler himself, a cautious pause was called to enable the forces to regroup. Conquering Berlin was no turkey shoot. As the man in charge of the operation pointed out 'During the course of the entire war we had never had to take such a strongly fortified city as Berlin. Its total area was equal to about 900 square kilometres (350 square miles). The subways and the extensive underground network afforded enemy troops flexibility of movement. The city itself and its environs had been carefully prepared for stubborn defence. Each street, square, crossroad, house, canal, and bridge was a component part of the overall defences of the city.'[54] Stalin showed more caution than his generals who were in an unacknowledged race to have the honour of taking the city. He even had to restrain Zhukov, the one Stalin had chosen to lead the final assault, when he asked to be able to head for the River Oder. Stalin pointed out to him that 'When you reach the Oder you will have separated yourself by 150k from the 2nd Bielorussian Army Group's flank. This cannot be permitted now.' He was instructed to wait 15 days or so while the 2nd Bielorussian Army completed its operations and regrouped across the Vistula. Zhukov's insistence was met only by a promise from Stalin to consider his request and get back to him, but, Zhukov informs us, he did not receive any answer that day.[55]

Stalin's caution was well judged. Flanking attacks from remaining pockets of German resistance were being considered. The final battle when it came was immense and among the bloodiest of the war. Stalin was himself musing on the costs as the war reached its conclusion. Zhukov reported that when Stalin finally summoned him to finalize the details of the assault on Berlin Stalin was in an unusually sombre mood and said 'What a terrible war. How many lives of our people it has carried away. There are probably very few families of us left who haven't lost someone near to them.'[56] He was thinking of his own son Iakob who had, bravely and in a manly fashion in his father's view, committed suicide in his German camp: 'A real man! A noble man right to the end!'[57] A sharp contrast to his drunken, womanizing playboy half-brother Vassili, Nadya's son, who played on his connection to his father but whom Stalin had to rein in on many occasions. There was still much more grief to come before the final surrender. The assault force came to 2 million men and 7500 aircraft. Zhukov's army alone had 3155 tanks and self-propelled guns. On 15 April the attack began. It was a messy affair that moved in fits and starts. On 20 April the Red Army reached the eastern suburbs and advanced street-by-street in the face of fierce but increasingly sporadic and under-equipped resistance. On 30 April there was a ten hour, floor-by-floor battle inside the Reichstag, ending with two Soviet sergeants hoisting the Red Flag from the roof, a scene immortalized in an aerial photo. Even so, Berlin did not surrender until dawn on 2 May. On 25 April, Soviet and American armies had met at Torgau. On 9 May the Soviets declared the war to be officially over (a day later than the Western armies) and on 11 May the final fighting subsided. The offensive in East Prussia had cost 319,000 more Soviet dead from October 1944 to April 1945. The last days in Berlin cost thousands more.[58] The war was, however, over and for the moment celebration was the order of the day. Stalin proposed a victory toast 'To the Soviet people!' but uniquely added a toast to the Russian people, the 'outstanding nation' in the Soviet Union.[59] Why only them? From war the situation was turning back to politics.

Notes

1 Stalin J. V., 'Radio Broadcast 3 July 1941', MIA, https://www.marxists.org/reference/archive/stalin/works/1941/07/03.htm.
2 Volkogonov, D. (1991) *Stalin: Triumph and Tragedy*, London, Weidenfeld & Nicholson, p413.
3 Ibid, p414.
4 Ibid, p417.
5 Ibid, p423.

6 Kagan, F. (1995) 'The Evacuation of Soviet Industry in the Wake of "Barbarossa": A Key to Soviet Victory', *Journal of Slavic Military Studies*, 8, pp389–396, quoted in Overy, R. (1998) *Russia's War: A History of the Soviet War Effort 1941–1945*, London, Penguin, pp170–171.

7 Kopalin, I. and Varlamov, L. (directors) (1941) *Moscow Strikes Back*, Moscow, Tsentralnaia studiia dokumental'nykh fil'mov. The 55-minute film won an Oscar that year.

8 Volkogonov (1991), pp412–413.

9 Ibid, p413.

10 Glantz, D. (1995) *When Titans Clashed: How the Red Army Stopped Hitler*, Lexington, KY, University Press of Kentucky, pp80–81.

11 Glantz (1995), Appendix, Table B.

12 Fritz, Stephen G. (2011) *Ostkrieg: Hitler's War of Extermination in the East*, Lexington, KY, University Press of Kentucky, pp214–215.

13 Volkogonov (1991), p344.

14 Roberts, G. (2006) *Stalin's Wars: From World War to Cold War 1939–53*, New Haven, CT, and London, Yale University Press, p74.

15 Overy, (1998), p133.

16 Ibid.

17 Gertjejanssen, W.J. (2004) Victims, Heroes, Survivors: Sexual Violence on the Eastern Front During World War II, PhD thesis, University of Minnesota, 2004. The references to 13-year-old victims occur at pp181, 301, 306. Abstract available at: http://www.victimsheroes survivors.info/VHS%20abstract.html.

18 See https://www.marxists.org/reference/archive/stalin/works/1939/02/23.htm.

19 Overy (1998), p160.

20 Ibid, pp165–166.

21 Volkogonov (1991), pp461–462, quoting TsAMO, 3.11 556. 10.9.

22 Overy (1998), p173.

23 Ibid, p175.

24 Ibid, p177.

25 Volkogonov (1991), p463.

26 See https://www.marxists.org/reference/archive/stalin/works/1943/01/25.html.

27 Mawdsley, E. (2005) *Thunder in the East: The Nazi-Soviet War 1941–1945*, London, Hodder Education, p263.

28 Overy (1998), p201, for quotation and figures.

29 Mawdsley (2005), p265.

30 Overy (1998), p202.

31 Ibid, p203, including quotes from Zhukov.

32 Cross, R. (1993) *Citadelle: The Battle of Kursk*, London, Michael O'Mara Books, 1993, p215.

33 Ibid, p171.

34 Ibid, pp207–210.

35 Overy (1993), p212.
36 Ibid, pp214–215.
37 Bialer, S. (ed) (1969) *Stalin and His Generals: Soviet Military Memoirs of World War II*, New York and London, Pegasus, p361. See also Shtemenko, S. M. (1981) *Generalnyi shtab v gody voiny*, Moscow, Voenizdat.
38 Bialer (1969), pp362–363. Stalin was not using the royal 'we'; he was referring to other generals present.
39 Ibid, p363.
40 Montefiore, S. S. (2004) *Stalin: The Court of the Red Tsar*, Harmondsworth, Weidenfeld & Nicholson, pp465–466 for the details of Stalin's visit and the final comment.
41 Rigby, T. H. (1968) *Communist Party Membership in the USSR 1917–1967*, Princeton, NJ, Princeton University Press, pp52–53.
42 Volkogonov (1991), pp464 and 474.
43 Overy (1998), p236.
44 Ibid, p240.
45 Ibid, p243.
46 Mastny, V. (1979) *Russia's Road to the Cold War*, New York and London, Columbia University Press.
47 Overy (1998), pp246–249.
48 Ibid, p248.
49 Bacon, E. (1994) *The Gulag at War: Stalin's Forced Labour System in the Light of the Archives*, London, Macmillan, p167.
50 Overy (1998), p160.
51 Chuikov, V. (1967) *The End of the Third Reich*, London, MacGibbon and Kee, p41.
52 See Overy (1998), pp260–262.
53 Djilas, M. (1963) *Conversations with Stalin*, London, Penguin, pp87–88.
54 Extract from Zhukov's memoirs in Bialer (1969), p512.
55 Ibid, p506.
56 Overy (1998), p264.
57 Montefiore (2004), p455.
58 Overy (1998), p262.
59 See https://www.marxists.org/reference/archive/stalin/works/1945/05/24.htm.

8 World stage, final act

The post-war agenda

The final military actions of the Red Army in Europe had brought about a revolution on the international scene. The army's northern drive had taken it back into the Baltic States and deep into Finland. In the centre, Soviet troops had smashed their way through Poland and Germany. Perhaps the most complicating front, however, was in the south. The advance took in Romania, Bulgaria, the edge of Yugoslavia (north-east Serbia), Hungary and Czechoslovakia. In addition, Soviet troops had invaded northern Iran. There was a civil war in Greece where Britain was attempting to reassert Western control by, incredibly, bombing Athens in support of former Nazi collaborators who were fighting the anti-Nazi resistance movement. Why? Because the resistance was predominantly communist in composition. In Yugoslavia the communist revolution led by Tito (and also, unexpectedly, supported by Britain during the war) had fought its own way into power without the Red Army. In Austria, although its military operations in the area had been minimal, the USSR was allocated an occupation zone in the country and its capital Vienna which were divided in the same way as Germany and Berlin. Politically, communism was an increasingly potent force in France and Italy and left-leaning Popular Front governments were spreading in Central and South America. Finally, in accordance with obligations to the United States and the Allies which it took on at Yalta, on 8 August the USSR invaded Japan as part of the growing assault on the Japanese home islands. In all these situations taken separately there were vast political complications and a wide range of future possibilities.

However, there were a whole range of other problems facing Stalin of even more crucial importance and of equal complexity. In the forefront was the most pressing issue of all – the recovery of the devastated economy of the USSR and the restoration of its obliterated infrastructure. The official figures are eloquent enough about the scale of the problem. Over 27 million people had died; 1700 towns had been destroyed; the railway system was in ruins; 25 million people were without homes. Finally, internal political changes had occurred. The cult of Stalin's personality had broadened for sure and, as we have seen, party and *komsomol* membership had soared. However, the hero generals, especially Zhukov, had become increasingly popular. Did they constitute a political threat as the war wound down? Internally, Molotov, Beria and more technical leaders like the chief party economic planner, Nikolai Voznesensky, had been Stalinist stalwarts but would they remain loyal? Some ideological concessions had been made in the war. For example, the Orthodox Church had been allowed to reopen many churches and its head, the Patriarch of Moscow, attended some official state celebrations. Links with overseas diplomats, cultural attachés and military liaison officers had created a 'mini-thaw' in East-West relations allowing some greater intellectual and cultural interchange between the two. What was to be done about these developments? Obviously, the view from Stalin's 'little corner' (*ugol'ok*), his modest study and office in the Kremlin, was very like a pre-storm sky – complex cloud formations, full of contrasting light and dark shades with distant flashes and rumbles. What would happen when the full force of the storm hit? For sure, Stalin and his fellow leaders had a great deal to think about. In order to discuss these complexities we will look first at the international scene and the emergence of the Cold War, then the task of economic reconstruction and finally the political and ideological outlook of Stalin's final years.

From Grand Alliance to Cold War: 1941–1953

As the Moscow counter-offensive was getting under way in late 1941 the war had taken a radical turn on the other side of the planet. On 7 December 1941 Japan attacked the US fleet in Hawaii. The attack was supposed to so weaken the Pacific Fleet that the United States would have no means with which to conduct a war against Japan. Once again, a supposedly knockout blow had failed and instead of making it impossible for the United States to fight Japan it made the war global. At last, the Soviet policy of collective security had come into effect. The unlikely alliance of the USSR, United States and Great Britain had finally emerged; though, of course, key members of the alliance such as France, Czechoslovakia and Poland had been wiped from the map and Germany bestrode Europe from Norway to Greece. For the time being, at least, historical necessity, realpolitik if you like, had broken the Soviet Union's isolation. An awkward relationship between the cynical, dictatorial anti-imperialists of the USSR and the hypocritical, liberal, democratic/oligarchic imperialists of the North Atlantic had to be quickly worked out. Stalin, now thrust to the very centre of world politics, was in his element. From the point of view of the historian the emergence of Stalin into the full light of the international political stage brought him into contact with a very wide range of people over whom he had no control or significant influence leading to a profusion of memoirs and the like constituting a priceless source.

Barbarossa had created an instant entente between Britain and the USSR which was increasingly expressed in the warmest terms on both sides. At the same time it contained the germs of many themes that later dominated their relationship. On 8 July 1942 Stalin received the first 'Personal Message' from Churchill. 'We are all very glad here', Churchill began, 'that the Russian armies are making such strong and spirited resistance to the utterly unprovoked and merciless invasion of the Nazis . . . We shall do everything to help you that time, geography and our growing resources allow.' The first concrete agreement had two elements: '(1) mutual help without any precision as to quantity or quality, and (2) neither country to conclude a separate peace'. On 18 July Stalin sent his first 'Personal Message' to Churchill. He, too, reflected the official warmth of the occasion: 'The Soviet Union and Great Britain have become fighting Allies in the struggle against Hitler Germany. I have no doubt that our two countries are strong enough to defeat our common enemy in the face of all difficulties.' However, signs of future tensions were already emerging. With supreme, almost British, understatement Stalin continued: 'It may not be out of place to inform you that the position of the Soviet troops at the front remains strained.' Stalin already knew what he wanted as first priority: 'It seems to me, furthermore, that the military position of the Soviet Union, and by the same token that of Great Britain, would improve substantially if a front were established against Hitler in the West (Northern France) and the North (the Arctic).' Three days later Churchill's reply arrived, the first of many pointing out, with perfect reasonableness at first, that nothing could yet be done: 'I beg you to realize the limitations imposed upon us by our resources and geographical position . . . We have examined the possibilities of attacking occupied France and the Low Countries. The Chiefs of Staff do not see any way of doing anything on a scale likely to be of the slightest use to you.' This bucket of cold water did not fundamentally change the tone but the next exchanges began to focus on what could rather than could not be done. That meant mainly supplies, but here, too, there were differences. Stalin wanted fighter aircraft but they were currently the main defence keeping the Nazis at bay in the English Channel. Perhaps surprisingly, as early as 28 July, Churchill was smoothing the way for President Roosevelt's personal representative, Harry Hopkins, to visit Moscow and set up what became Lend-Lease supplies. Even though the United States was noncombatant at this point, Churchill enthusiastically underlined Hopkins's impeccable anti-fascist credentials: 'I must tell you that there is a flame in this man for democracy and to beat Hitler . . . You can trust him absolutely. He is your friend and our friend.' No doubt having been glad to find something positive for Stalin he also ended the message on a militant note, aware that Stalin would have taken a dim view of excuses for inactivity in terms of a second front. 'A terrible winter of bombing lies before Germany. No one has yet had what they are going to get.'[1]

Stalin was far from satisfied and, as the situation of his armies became even more perilous, he sent a very stark message to Churchill on 3 September 1942. It began with customary but brief cordiality: 'Please accept my thanks for the promise to sell to the Soviet Union another 200 fighter aeroplanes in addition to the 200 fighters promised earlier. I have no doubt that Soviet pilots will succeed in mastering them and putting them to use.' However, Stalin soon took up a darker tone, emphasizing the possibility of defeat:

> I must say, however, that these aircraft . . . cannot seriously change the situation on the Eastern Front . . . because during the last three weeks the position of the Soviet troops has considerably deteriorated in such vital areas as the Ukraine and Leningrad . . . The Germans look on the threat in the West as a bluff, so they are moving all their forces from the West to the East with impunity, knowing that there is no second front in the West nor is there likely to be one. They think it perfectly possible that they will be able to beat their enemies one at a time – first the Russians and then the British . . . What is the way out of this more than unfavourable situation? I think the only way is to open a second front this year somewhere in the Balkans or in France, one that would divert 30–40 German divisions from the Eastern Front, and simultaneously to supply the Soviet Union with 30,000 tons of aluminium by the beginning of October and a minimum monthly aid of 400 aeroplanes and 500 tanks (of small or medium size).

Stalin realized he had been talking very frankly: 'I realize that this message will cause Your Excellency some vexation. But that cannot be helped. Experience has taught me to face up to reality, no matter how unpleasant it may be, and not to shrink from telling the truth, no matter how unpleasant.' Churchill sent an evasive reply on 4 September.

Concluding this initial exchange of personal messages on 13 September, Stalin was trying very hard to get some military contribution out of Britain even making an astonishing proposal that British troops should travel via the Arctic or Iran and fight alongside the Red Army in the USSR. Incidentally, the note ended with an early appearance of yet another issue that was later to loom large in East-West relations. Britain had offered to soften the financial blow of destroying the Soviet Navy vessels in Leningrad and Kronstadt by sharing the cost of replacing them later.

However, Stalin already knew who was going to pay. 'Responsibility for the damage would be borne, not by Britain but by Germany. I think, therefore, that Germany will have to make good the damage after the war.'[2]

It is worth dwelling on these early exchanges because they highlight so much of the complexity of the sudden relationship between two states devoted to each other's destruction. The cordiality was not entirely empty and, from the beginning, the talk was very frank. The fundamental difference between the two was also clear. Britain prioritized the dispatch of supplies and equipment but showed great caution about military operations. On the other hand, Stalin prioritized boots on the ground and was less happy about being, as he saw it, fobbed off with minimal supplies, especially since Britain was itself short of key items like fighter aircraft. Stalin soon formed the impression that lasted through the war that Churchill and the British government were more interested in buying and selling than in fighting and that they were quite possibly still pursuing their policy of the 1930s to set up a cataclysmic conflict between Germany and the USSR which would leave both of them weakened and allow Britain to step in and rule over the remains. Only a firm commitment of military forces could persuade Stalin that Britain was fully serious about the war. Finally, the exchange also showed that even at this early stage, Stalin was already thinking about reparations from the invaders once the war was over.

The initial exchange of brave messages between London and Moscow led to a flurry of visits. Harry Hopkins's visit helped ease the way toward the USSR signing the Atlantic Charter – the Anglo-American joint declaration of peace aims of which the most important were that the signatories would not seek to expand their territories as a result of war, that self-determination should apply in liberated areas and that trade and natural resources should be available to all – and also the first Lend-Lease credit of an immense, for the time, US$1 billion dollars. Stalin also met foreign diplomats such as Sir Stafford Cripps, the British ambassador, on a more frequent basis. What impression did Stalin make on his visitors?

In August 1942 Churchill, who had a great appetite for adventurous travelling during the war went to Moscow to visit, as his wife Clementine quipped, 'the ogre in his den'.[3] Indeed, Churchill was treated to unprecedented access to Stalin and his private surroundings, even falling asleep on Stalin's own modest divan in his Kremlin rooms, visiting Stalin's *dacha* (country house) outside Moscow and being guest of honour at a glittering official dinner in one of the spectacular halls in the Kremlin. The visit itself was a game of two halves. In the early stages Stalin was mocking the British war effort and making sarcastic comments about British soldiers being afraid of engaging with Nazis. The atmosphere became so bad that Churchill was preparing for a premature return home.

Inhospitable Stalin's attitude may have been, but it was not all that surprising. The big news Churchill had brought with him to Moscow was the Anglo-American decision that no major second front could be opened for the foreseeable future, even though as recently as 12 June, Molotov had been assured on his visit to Washington and London that the second front would be opened in 1942. There were other complexities in the background. The British supply route to northern Russia had been suspended after convoy PQ17 was destroyed following an order of 4 July recalling the naval escort and ordering the merchant ships to disperse, a situation Stalin found 'in the view of our experts, puzzling and inexplicable'. Stalin objected to Churchill that the arguments for suspending the route, also 'according to our naval experts . . . are untenable'.[4] On the positive side, however, a somewhat forgotten treaty had been signed on 26 May by Molotov in London committing Britain and the USSR to 20 years of mutual aid and assistance. They also agreed not to interfere in the affairs of other states and not to form alliances aimed against the other side.

In other words, even in 1941 and 1942, there was a hot and a cold dimension to the relationship. On Churchill's first day in Moscow the cold blast dominated. Churchill went to bed in a foul mood. The next day was hardly better though things began to improve when Churchill, with the aid of maps and a globe, always a favourite of Stalin, explained the nature of British operations in North Africa. Churchill remarked that Stalin was very quick on the strategic uptake and showed 'swift and complete mastery' of military strategy. Stalin also surprised the British by saying 'Let God help the success of this enterprise!'[5] Nonetheless, criticism of the reluctance of the British to fight and not-so-veiled insults at the expense of the British Army and Navy continued to rankle deeply with Churchill. Stalin perhaps realized he had gone too far and later in the day a better mood was constructed. A reluctant Churchill was prevailed upon by his advisers to attend the evening's gala banquet. Slowly, the mood lightened. Recently released documents about Operation Bracelet, the British code name for Churchill's visit, have confirmed our knowledge and expanded our sense of the atmosphere of the moment.[6] According to his aid Cadogan: 'Nothing can be imagined more awful than a Kremlin banquet, but it has to be endured.' There was no little upper-class British snobbery in this remark reflected in the observation of a British officer present who said of Stalin that 'it was extraordinary to see this little peasant, who would not look out of place in a country lane with a pickaxe over his shoulder, calmly sitting down to a banquet in these magnificent halls'.[7] However, 'Unfortunately, Winston didn't suffer [the banquet] gladly.' According to his personal physician, Lord Moran, he returned to his *dacha* in a very bad mood. 'Did Stalin not realize who he was speaking to? The representative of the most powerful empire the world has ever seen?' he complained.[8] However, next morning, it was British snobbery to the rescue as the British ambassador, Sir Archibald Clark Kerr, persuaded Churchill not to be 'offended by a peasant who does not know any better'.[9] Churchill was persuaded to resume discussion. 'He was determined to fire his last bolt, and asked for a private talk, alone, with Stalin.' Most reports, however, say it was Stalin who invited Churchill to intimate and informal talks in Stalin's Kremlin rooms. Whatever the truth, at around 1:00 am Cadogan was summoned to Stalin's private rooms in the Kremlin:

> There I found Winston and Stalin, and Molotov who has joined them, sitting with a heavily-laden board between them: food of all kinds crowned by a sucking pig, and innumerable bottles. What Stalin made me drink seemed pretty savage: Winston, who by that time was complaining of a slight headache, seemed wisely to be confining himself to a comparatively innocuous effervescent Caucasian red wine. Everyone seemed to be as merry as a marriage bell.

The evening eventually broke up some time after 3:00 am, leaving Cadogan just enough time to get back to his hotel, pack his bags and leave for the aerodrome at 4:15 am. Despite his slightly irreverent tone, Cadogan knew that the talks had had important results: 'I think the two great men really made contact and got on terms. Certainly, Winston was impressed and I think that feeling was reciprocated . . . Anyhow, conditions have been established in which messages exchanged between the two will mean twice as much, or more, than they did before.'[10] The atmosphere could hardly have been different compared to the earlier frostiness. As Churchill returned to *his dacha*, primarily to prepare for his departure, he was in a buoyant mood compared to the previous night. Clark Kerr records that he was in a 'triumphant mood' and had 'cemented a friendship' and that it was a 'pleasure' to work with that 'great man'.[11] In the end the meeting had been a brilliant success and, in the intimacy of Stalin's private rooms the relationship had been dramatically turned around. Little Soso had charmed the great imperialist out of his tree.

Many other Western visitors encountered Stalin in the next few years. Recently released British Intelligence archives have a story of a visit by the American politician, Wendell Willkie in October 1942. The information reached 'C', the chief of the Secret Intelligence Service, Sir Stewart Menzies, from a 'trustworthy channel':[12]

Willkie . . . made a great impression on Stalin, and the reverse is certainly the case . . . Willkie showed great interest in the new Russian sub-machine gun . . . At Willkie's request Stalin sent somebody to bring in a specimen, and within five minutes, one was brought in. Barnes [an accompanying journalist] was very nervous, because by this time everybody was in a high state of intoxication. He gives full marks to Sir Archibald Clark-Kerr who gracefully took the gun out of Voroshilov's hands and span the drum to make certain it was quite empty before handing it to Willkie. A banal and drunken incident followed when Cowles placed an apple on top of his head, Willkie aimed the gun and pressed the trigger, and Cowles jiggled the apple off his head. At this everyone laughed, and Stalin said: 'You know you ought to be careful carrying a machine gun in the Kremlin'. Willkie replied: 'Why should I care? It isn't my apple.' Stalin laughed so much, he almost rolled off his chair.[13]

People like Willkie, a Republican who had opposed Roosevelt but later became his roving ambassador, and Churchill were unlikely soulmates for Stalin but they did find a great deal in common. Willkie, despite his apparent right-wing credentials, had spoken out in favour of civil rights for Black Americans and addressed a 1942 Convention of the National Association for the Advancement of Colored People. In 1943 he defended race rioters in Detroit, blaming both Republicans and Democrats for ignoring the issue of race. He also chimed in with the developing idea of world government which was appealing to Roosevelt, Churchill and Stalin as the war progressed and wrote a powerful book in favour of it entitled *One World*. From very diverse points of view a coalition in favour of collaborative international co-operation seemed to be building in the dark days of the war as the desire to avoid any future repetition of the great disaster trumped, for the time being at least, deep ideological differences.

The spirit strengthened in 1943 and 1944 as the problems of victory began to attract attention. In 1943 Roosevelt, the great embodiment of future world government and the idea of the United Nations, met Stalin for the first time at the Tehran Conference. The venue was not entirely to Stalin's liking since it would necessarily involve his one and only flight. He was always queasy about aircraft. However, to get to Tehran he took the train from Moscow to the end of the line in Baku, from where he flew, uneasily, to Tehran. The meeting was hosted in the Soviet Embassy. Under the pretence of strengthening their security, Stalin successfully persuaded Roosevelt and Churchill to move into the embassy compound rather than risk possible attack in the crowded streets and souks of the city every morning and evening as they commuted to the conference. This gave him the inestimable advantage of being able to bug their every conversation. In fact, Roosevelt and Churchill were fully aware that they were likely to be bugged and Roosevelt cleverly turned it to his advantage. He proposed to Churchill that they talk frankly anyway and that, by exposing themselves in this way, Stalin would see they were not planning to trick him on the issues. It seems to have worked because Stalin expressed surprise at the openness of their 'private' conversations. According to the memoirs of Beria's son, Sergo, who was co-ordinating the bugging and reporting its contents to Stalin, 'He even went so far as to ask us for details of the tone of the conversations: did he say that with conviction? . . . did he say that resolutely?'[14]

The purpose of the conference was to co-ordinate the military endgame for the war in Europe and to bring the Pacific War into the picture. The conference confirmed the Anglo-American decision taken at Casablanca in January, that only unconditional surrender of Germany would be accepted. This reassured the Western Allies that the USSR would not stop fighting once it had liberated its own territories and make a separate peace with the enemy. Though it was not the only motivation, it is ironic that it was in conformity with this deeply held desire of the Western Allies that, in 1944–1945, Stalin's armies continued their drive into the heart of the Reich and occupied territories they were later accused of grabbing. In a side conference in Cairo with Chiang Kai Shek representing China, Churchill and Roosevelt agreed they would also demand unconditional Japanese surrender.

Almost all accounts of Roosevelt's relationship with Stalin say more or less the same thing. Roosevelt, naively for some, realistically for others, was sure he could get on well with Stalin and that they could build a world together in collaboration rather than conflict in the post-war world. Roosevelt even cosied up to Stalin at Churchill's expense, implying that he and Stalin, the United States and the USSR, were the future, Churchill and the British Empire, the past. The archetypal example of this was the next, and most important, of all the wartime conferences, held between 7 and 12 February 1945 at Yalta in Stalin's Black Sea residence in the Crimea. There were two main areas of discussion. What was to be done in Europe once the final defeat of Hitler, only a few weeks away, was confirmed? Second, what was to be done about Japan where the situation was very different? Far from winding down, the conflict there was building to a potentially difficult and costly (in human lives as well as materials) invasion of the Japanese home islands. By this time, relations between the

'Big Three' were cordial but intractable problems were looming that no amount of bonhomie could wipe away.

In the forefront of the difficulties was Poland. There was general agreement that all the powers had an interest in keeping Germany under supervision and, in addition as we have seen, Stalin had wanted Germany to pay compensation for wrecking the western Soviet Union. A key difficulty was that, to have influence in Germany, the Soviet Union would have to have influence in Poland. At Yalta the Polish eastern border was shifted westwards approximately to the so-called Curzon Line of 1919 and its western borders were established on the line of the Oder and Neisse rivers. A further point of conflict with the London Poles was emerging as the advancing Soviet forces pushed the Polish population out of the easternmost ethnic areas back into the new state borders. There was no solution to the Polish problem at Yalta and it became the litmus test for East-West relations and the trigger of the Cold War. Vital Soviet interests and Polish self-determination were at odds with each other. In the spirit of Tehran-Yalta co-operation a compromise might have been possible. Had there been Poles who were genuinely representative of their country *and* prepared to talk to Stalin the outcome might have been different but there were two groups vying to be the government – one, in London, which was derived from the pre-war government and totally distrusted Stalin and a second set up initially in Lublin in eastern Poland, composed of communists who supported Stalin but had little support in Poland. If a compromise solution was ever possible for Poland, one of the key elements that might have brought it about changed drastically on 12 April 1944 when Roosevelt suddenly died and Vice-President Harry Truman, who lacked FDR's diplomatic knowledge, experience and skills and subtlety, not to mention his close, positive relationship with Stalin, was sworn in as president and began to institute a much more intransigent line in dealing with the USSR.

Nonetheless, there is no clear evidence of Stalin preparing a big land grab and Sovietization of other countries in the period more or less up to Yalta. The vision of world government through the United Nations was still a passion of FDR and Stalin, to all intents and purposes, went along with it. But the issue of spheres of influence was also apparent. On a second visit to Moscow in August 1944, nearly six months before Yalta, Churchill had proposed what he called 'the naughty agreement' to Stalin. Apparently on the spur of the moment, in one of his direct conversations with Stalin, Churchill took a piece of paper and wrote down the percentage influence to be exerted over several eastern European countries. Romania would have 90 per cent Soviet and 10 per cent Western influence. Greece would be the opposite – 90 per cent British/American and 10 per cent Soviet. Yugoslavia and Hungary would each be 50:50 with Bulgaria 75 per cent Soviet and 25 per cent Western. Stalin drew a broad tick over the page. The following day Stalin upped Soviet influence to 80 per cent in Hungary and Bulgaria and Churchill agreed. Significantly, Poland was not on the list. This 'percentages' agreement can be read in a number of ways but it does appear to show that the concept of totally exclusive spheres had not yet emerged as Stalin's preferred option. However, after Yalta and especially after Roosevelt's death, the atmosphere of compromise was fading. Later in the year, following the British general election of 1945, Churchill was voted out of office and, with new Prime Minister Clement Attlee focusing on domestic reconstruction, the lead in British foreign policy was taken by the new foreign minister, Ernest Bevin, a deep-dyed anti-communist, like Truman. Bevin had been schooled in the hard knocks conflict between the Labour and Communist Parties in the British trade union movement and was not inclined to believe compromise was possible. Stalin, always a shrewd observer, saw the way the wind was blowing. In April 1944 in a famous and much-quoted comment from a conversation with Milovan Djilas, a young and idealistic Yugoslav communist at that time, Stalin said: 'This war is not as in the past. Everyone imposes his own system as far as his army can reach. It cannot be otherwise.'[15]

The reason why these words have become so well-known is largely because they have been used to justify the view that Stalin had a deeply concealed but firm policy to grab and Sovietize as much territory beyond the USSR's borders as possible. As usual, reality is more complex. First of all, the Yugoslav context of Stalin's words is usually ignored. It was advice to the Yugoslavs that they should liberate their own territory, such as Trieste/Rijeka from Western occupation.[16] More important, the nature of Stalin's vision for the post-war world was much less cut-and-dried than any interpretation based on this sole quotation. First, there is no reason to doubt that Stalin believed that some sort of co-operation with the United States and Great Britain would continue. The energy and attention the Soviets put into getting an acceptable structure for the emerging United Nations organization suggests it had a part to play in their thinking. The location of power in the Permanent Council and the veto for all, not to mention the setting up of separate representation for Ukraine and Bielorussia (Belarus), to provide some re-balancing of numbers in the face of Western domination, all tell the same story.

In March 1946, Stalin replied to questions put by an American correspondent for Associated Press named Eddie Gilmore. One of the questions was 'What importance do you ascribe to the United Nations Organisation as a means of safeguarding world peace?' Stalin answered:

> I ascribe great importance to the United Nations Organisation inasmuch as it is a serious instrument for maintaining peace and international security. The strength of this international organisation lies in the fact that it is based on the principle of the equality of States and not on the principle of the domination of some over others. If the United Nations Organisation succeeds in the future, too, in maintaining the principle of equality, then it will undoubtedly play a great positive role in guaranteeing universal peace and security.[17]

While official statements are not the strongest evidence it is worth recalling that Stalin and Soviet policy almost always supported collaborative action where possible. When asked by the left-leaning correspondent of *The Sunday Times*, Alexander Werth, in September 1946, 'Do you believe in the possibility of friendly and lasting co-operation between the Soviet Union and the Western democracies despite the existence of ideological differences, and in "friendly competition" between the two systems?' Stalin replied unequivocally: 'I believe in it absolutely.' He also rejected the possibility of a new war and the notion that the West was engaging in a 'capitalist encirclement' of the USSR: 'I do not think that the ruling circles of Great Britain and of the United States of America could create a "capitalist encirclement" of the Soviet Union even if they so desired, which, however, I do not assert.'

Finally, two related questions were put to him: 'Do you believe that with the further progress of the Soviet Union towards Communism the possibilities of peaceful co-operation with the outside world will not decrease as far as the Soviet Union is concerned? Is "Communism in one country" possible?' Again his response was unequivocal: 'I do not doubt that the possibilities of peaceful co-operation, far from decreasing, may even grow. "Communism in one country" is perfectly possible, especially in a country like the Soviet Union.'[18]

Such were the key messages which Stalin wanted to put across to the Western audience at a time of increasing tension, racked up not least by Churchill's speech at Fulton, Missouri which popularized the notion of an 'iron curtain' falling across Europe 'from Sczeczyn to Trieste'. Like Stalin's own statements Churchill's speech itself was complex and supported conciliation and collaboration through the United Nations – 'I have a strong admiration and regard for the valiant Russian people and for my wartime comrade, Marshal Stalin', he asserted – and even proposed an international UN police force. Like Stalin, too, there were blatant untruths, not least talking of 'the liberties enjoyed by individual citizens throughout the British Empire' which would have been news to millions of Indians, Black South Africans, Hong Kong Chinese and so on. Nonetheless, the interaction of a rhetoric of peace and of blaming the other side for disturbing it was already taking root. Obviously, to get a better idea of Stalin's actual intentions and policies, we will be on firmer ground if we look at what was being done.

One of the interesting and apparently anomalous features of the growing Soviet influence in its occupied territories was that, at least before 1948, they were far from fully Sovietized and, indeed, were eventually Sovietized to different degrees and according to a variety of models, none of which exactly replicated the situation in the USSR itself. In East Germany, the emerging ruling party was not a pure communist party but the so-called 'Socialist Unity Party' based on an early alliance of Communists and Social

Democrats which was followed by a forced amalgamation of the two into a single party. In Poland, there was a government of 'National Unity', headed by a London Pole, Mikolajczyk, though largely composed of pro-Soviet Lublin Poles. Despite extensive vote-rigging and manipulation, Mikolajczyk's Peasant Party did participate in the 1947 election, winning a small number of seats in the parliament (*Sejm*). In Czechoslovakia, the president was a Social Democrat, the veteran statesman Eduard Benes and the London-based Zdenek Fierlinger, also a Social Democrat, was prime minister until, in the first and relatively free election of May 1946, the Communists became the largest party with 2.7 million out of 7.1 million votes and 114 out of 300 seats in the Constituent Assembly. It was a similar picture in Hungary, Bulgaria and Romania where nominally anti-fascist fronts took power. It was only in 1947–1948 that real hardening into 'Soviet-type' systems took place and single, essentially communist, parties took power and economies were, to varying degrees, nationalized and subjected to forms of central planning, usually in less rigorous forms than in the USSR itself. For example, collectivization was enforced in Hungary and elsewhere, but in Poland individual peasant farming survived.

In Cold War interpretations this was often seen as the pre-planned, Machiavellian unfolding of a secret blueprint. No clear evidence has been produced to support this. Instead, the hardening of the Cold War seems to have been a somewhat improvised and, from Stalin's point of view, reactive as much as proactive process.

A comprehensive account of these momentous years and processes would require a vast study of its own. There are, however, some key elements in Stalin's approach which we need to look at. He had more pressing problems on his plate than the propagation of communism. These were the reconstruction of a vast country and the need for future security from a repeat of the invasion. In both of these areas Germany was the key and, if that was so, Poland was also a critical problem. We can also add that, as a result of the wartime triumph, Stalin approached these problems not only with his customary confidence but also with a cruder, more repulsive, swagger and boorishness. He was also increasingly affected by ill health and it was widely noted that he became more prone than ever to mood swings which were threatening to his entourage and to consistent and reliable policy-making. In war he had impressed not only Churchill, who, as we have seen still referred to him as a comrade in his iron curtain speech of 1946, but also Roosevelt and many others with his grasp of what was going on. There was no discourse among his visitors and allies that he was the psychopathic monster of Cold War rhetoric and a million student essays but the war had produced another and, ultimately, an ailing and final Stalin. That final Stalin had, as usual, a massive agenda. In the wider world, collaboration with the United States soon turned into confrontation and the challenge of nuclear weapons had to be met. However, unlike the near-isolation of the pre-war years, a small flock of communist states nestled under the Soviet wing. The massive, unexpected and ambiguous bonus of China joining this select company in 1949 opened up new horizons. At home, the unimaginable costs of the war had to be met and the plight of millions of homeless and jobless people had to be addressed. In politics, Stalin had to face his own mortality and the issues of succession and legacy raised their heads. In particular, the Cold War focused the cultural conflict between East and West and socialist values had to be secured against the siren call of an increasingly consumerist capitalism. One might have thought this was no country for an old man, but, as Stalin approached his seventieth birthday (December 1948) he was as engaged as ever with guiding the revolution in the direction to which he was committed.

Exactly what that direction was, when one comes to Eastern Europe, is still a matter of impassioned debate. In the absence of any clear evidence – Stalin's statement to Djilas about systems and armies often has pride of place – there is a persistent argument that Stalin was intent on a power grab. There was no 'blueprint' or anything like it ever found. The notion that Stalin wanted to institute communism in Eastern Europe can be 'refuted' by another isolated statement of Stalin's which, in a way, cancels out the Djilas comment. In wartime discussion with Eduard Benes Stalin said communism would fit Germany like a saddle fits a cow.[19] It is possible to piece together a more likely, but still not proven, case that there was much more improvisation and chance in the emergence of post-war communist regimes. There are a number of factors which point in this direction.

Official discussion of war aims and settlement in the USSR have been largely ignored but more recent studies have made interesting discoveries.[20] In authoritative journals and newspapers the line being put was that there would be a series of popular fronts on the pre-war French and Spanish models across Europe. There were certain key factors leading in this direction. The established elites of most continental European countries had thrown in their lot with the Nazis and were now about to reap the hurricane. In Italy, France and Germany the future of capitalism teetered on the brink of political collapse. Even in Britain, which had not had to make any deals with Nazis apart from the shameful one at Munich, a left-leaning Labour government was re-elected by a landslide of seats (though not so much in votes) and proceeded with the most radical programme of any British government, nationalizing key but bankrupt industries like steel, coal, road and rail transport and setting up an extensive welfare state and the National Health Service as the people's 'reward' for fighting the war. In continental Europe, former resistance movements, dominated by the left, had immense prestige and were on the edge of government. Communists were included in General de Gaulle's French government of unity. Communists were the largest party in Italy. The same was true in Czechoslovakia and in Germany and elsewhere Communist Party membership increased to record levels, buoyed largely by the great prestige of the Red Army and its hard-won victory. In Greece, the left appeared to be on the verge of victory in civil war. In Yugoslavia a communist government led by Tito and the partisans had fought their way into power more or less independently but with assistance almost as much from Britain as from the USSR. The continent lay exposed to a democratic transition to the left of unprecedented proportions.

These processes had been keenly observed in Moscow which, in any case, was convinced the tide of history was, as always, on its side so hasty action was not needed. It is also clear that the hybrid parties and governments which gradually emerged in the Soviet-occupied areas reflect the view that a direct transition to communism was not on the cards but a series of popular fronts was. Needless to say, the same scenario, heightened by the fact that leftist governments and popular fronts were spreading like mushrooms in Latin America and the fate of China and Indochina were still in the balance, was being viewed with increasing anxiety in Washington. Not just Europe but the world seemed to be on the edge of a democratic and leftist revolution.

This is not the place to fully analyse the outcome of this process and the United States' use of the immense wealth and military power it had accumulated through the war. Its dominant position was all the greater given that the resources of its rivals – Britain, France, Germany, Japan, the USSR – were severely depleted. This left the United States with a world economic monopoly and a political monopoly breached only by the remaining military power of an otherwise devastated USSR. An array of economic institutions was inspired by the liberal economist J. M. Keynes who stressed the importance of government regulation to keep markets in balance. The most important – the World Bank and the International Monetary Fund – were the guardians of capitalist recovery. A full study of the Marshall Plan and its equivalent in Japan; the alliance with the mafia to bring 'democracy' to Italy;[21] the largely successful restoration of the old elites, even those contaminated by Nazi collaboration, is way beyond our scope here. Our focus remains on Stalin and his take on these developing possibilities and counter-tendencies which were the political arena of the early Cold War.

To simplify a complex situation, it is reasonable to say that there were two models, with a multitude of variants, about what might happen after the war. They were a settlement based on spheres of influence or one based on so-called universalism. Spheres of influence implied each of the victors had its own area of control. Universalism meant all the victors had access, though not necessarily equal, to all liberated and former enemy territories. The 'percentages agreement' could be interpreted in either way but was predominantly universalist. US policy-makers had an intense argument about which model to follow. On the one hand there were the proponents of the so-called 'Yalta axioms' who suggested the possibility and desirability of a continued policy of co-operation and agreement with the USSR in the style of Yalta and the rival position of the 'Riga axioms'[22] which emphasized a Soviet Union determined to achieve world domination.[23] The Riga axioms became the basis of the Cold War and of US global foreign policy. Did Stalin contribute to their success by playing into their hands?

As has been noted many times, Germany was the key to everything and, for the USSR, Poland was the key to Germany since it lay in between the Soviet Union and Germany. Stalin's much-desired access to Germany for security and reparations reasons could only be achieved with the consent of Poland. The great tragedy of the moment was that no such consent was likely to be given by an independent Poland. During the war Stalin complained to Eduard Benes, 'Are there no Poles who will talk to us?'[24] He would not have had to look far to find out why such partners in dialogue were in short supply. In the early stages of the war some 400,000 Poles had been imprisoned by the Soviets. Most were released by October 1941 and many had left the USSR. However, some 20,000 officers and government officials were unaccounted for. When, in 1940, the Polish ambassador, Kot asked what had happened to them Stalin, in a piece of political theatre since he knew, called Beria to find out. On receiving the reply, Stalin did not answer but moved the discussion to a new topic. The 20,000 in question had been separated out into re-education camps at Kozelsk and elsewhere along the western borderlands with the aim of turning them, under Beria's supervision, into a sympathetic elite to run the 'new' Poland once Germany was driven out.[25] The failure of the project to persuade the recalcitrant Poles of the virtues of Soviet Communism, plus the threat of war and the overrunning of the camps led to the brutal decision to shoot them all on Politburo orders of 5 March 1940. In March and April the sentence was carried out. Seven thousand Kozelsk prisoners were shot single-handedly in 28 nights by Blokhin, who used a series of German Walther pistols to make it look like a German atrocity. The rest were shot at a number of locations. The Kozelsk bodies, buried in the nearby forest of Katyn, were soon discovered by the Germans as they advanced and the Soviets played a grim play-acting game of denying their own responsibility and diverting blame to the Germans. Only in the Gorbachev era did the Soviet government admit the truth. The issue has poisoned Russo-Polish relations even down to the present. There were many more irritants and obstacles such as Russian colonialism, which had not lain very hard on Poland but had repressed nationalist revolts, and, later, the controversy over lack of Soviet help for the Home Army uprising in Warsaw in 1944. So intransigent were the London Poles that, as we have seen, Stalin set up a communist-based government-in-exile in Moscow and then in Lublin in eastern Poland once it had been liberated. Interestingly, this was the only such 'puppet' government Stalin set up at this time, in itself indicating greater complexity in Stalin's intentions than simple installation of communists all over the Soviet-occupied areas.[26] The net result was that the likelihood of a genuine rapprochement with a 'strong and independent Poland' as Stalin claimed to expect to emerge after the war, was highly unlikely.

Was any alternative possible? Theoretically, there was 'Finlandization'. The term has often been used with a sneer by Western diplomats and analysts out of contempt for a failure to stand up to the 'aggressor'. It is seen as a kind of 'appeasement'. However, one could argue that Finland emerged much more successfully from the war than it might have. Both Finland and Poland had been key provinces of the Russian Empire under the tsars. Both had crucial strategic significance to Russia. However, unlike Poland, Finland had been a very active ally of Hitler and was a collaborator in the ghastly siege of Leningrad and, as such, might have expected the harsher treatment meted out to the defeated enemy states, like Germany itself. However, in exchange for Finland's recognition of the 1940 border, the establishment of several small mainly naval bases and a commitment to neutrality, Finland maintained complete independence and reverted to a greater democracy than it had been before 1939. It benefited considerably from being a staging post for Soviet trade with the rest of Europe and the United States. It cannot be ultimately proven one way or the other because the Poles would not play the conciliatory game of the Finns but the possibility of Finlandization may well have been on the table for Poland. Such a solution would have been all that the Soviet Union wanted – a commitment not to join an anti-Soviet alliance system, a series of transit bases to Germany and a non-hostile, if not actually friendly, government. One may well understand the Poles, distaste for Stalin, especially in connection with Katyn, but nations have swallowed worse in order to get better deals. Japan, for example, had to ignore the infinitely more terrible atrocities of Hiroshima and Nagasaki to get a very benevolent deal out of the United States. Had they been as intransigent as Poland they would most likely have fared worse. However, all this remains speculative. Soviet policy in Poland escalated from a modified government of mainly Lublin Poles (only Mikolajczyk was prepared to join in from London – was boycott by the rest a wise move or did it help Stalin gain more control in Poland?) to a single-party communist state and Sovietized society and even show trials by 1948/1949.

So Poland slid into Sovietization and history does not recognize 'what if?'. There are no counterfactuals. The example of Poland was, in some ways, even more significant and crucial to the development of the Cold War than the fate of Germany. Poland had been an ally while Germany was the chief perpetrator of atrocities and the instigator of the most ferocious war ever seen on earth, so there was little sympathy for it. Demilitarization and compensation were the minimum on the minds of Stalin, Churchill and de Gaulle, if not so much for Roosevelt. But, it was ultimately on the settlement for Germany that the fate of Europe as a whole would depend. It was here that the Riga and Yalta axioms came into their ultimate conflict.

The last Allied conference of the war took place in the dramatic surroundings of the Berlin suburbs, at Potsdam in July 1945. Churchill was still Britain's representative though he was now accompanied by the Labour Party leader and deputy prime minister, Clement Attlee. On the last day of the conference they learned that, in the British general election, Attlee's party had been elected by an overwhelming majority and Churchill's leadership of Britain had come to an end. The leader of the American delegation was the new president, Harry Truman.

Stalin and Molotov travelled to Berlin by train. Stalin was still a reluctant flier, even claiming doctor's orders for not travelling by plane,[27] though his troublesome son Vassili by Nadezhda Alliluyeva had been a daring if reckless, not to say drunken and ill-disciplined, air force officer throughout the war. As usual Stalin was accompanied by a massive security presence. While in Berlin most of the participants, including Stalin's entourage, could not resist the urge to visit the ruins of the central city and the iconic buildings, including the bunker, from which Hitler had ruled, but Stalin himself did not do so.[28]

The agenda was vast. Stalin wanted to confirm the westward movement of Poland's borders; claimed former Russian Imperial territory from Turkey; claimed a part of the German and Italian fleets and a new base for them at Königsberg in east Prussia (eventually renamed Kaliningrad) and called for strong measures to weaken the position of Franco in Spain. Clearly Stalin had scores to settle from the Spanish Civil War. On the key issues of Germany and the continuing war against Japan, Soviet success was mixed. While there was wide agreement about demilitarization and sympathy for Stalin's claim for around US$10 billion in reparations, to be paid in cash, in products and in removed factories, the Western Allies were reluctant to enforce payment from their rich Ruhr and tried to divert as much as possible onto the Soviets own zone in the east. For its part, the USSR agreed to honour exactly the Yalta provisions about it joining the war against Japan. By and large the outcome of Potsdam was to agree to draw up treaties rather than to finalize decisions. It was the last of Churchill's encounters with Stalin and they had one of their characteristic wide-ranging trips through the politics of the world. Churchill was magnanimously granting Stalin the right to warm water ports, some control of the Straits (as essential to USSR as Gibraltar to Great Britain, Stalin argued) at other people's expense. Stalin affirmed he would not Sovietize eastern Europe and when upbraided by Churchill that the 50:50 percentages agreement on Yugoslavia was not being observed Stalin replied it was 10 per cent Britain, 90 per cent Tito and 0 per cent USSR when it came to influence, a figure that was closer to the mark than it seemed.[29] By and large, the spirit of co-operation and even some cordiality had continued at Potsdam.

However, events thousands of miles to the west of Potsdam, in Whitesands, New Mexico and, three weeks later in Hiroshima (6 August) and Nagasaki (9 August) thousands of miles to the east, overshadowed the conference. The nuclear age was beginning. Its complexities are still with us and its birth is still shrouded in controversy. The first American-British A-bomb test, held while the conference was in session on 17 July, was no surprise to

Stalin. Leftist sympathizers among the scientists had been passing on crucial information. Truman was bursting with excitement about the devastating new weapon when he told Stalin about it. Truman was disconcerted by Stalin's apparent indifference to the news, which has frequently been put down to Stalin not immediately grasping its significance. However, this was far from the case. Within his own delegation he responded energetically and with some characteristic shrewdness. Essentially, he had three reactions. First, the bomb's main 'target' was the USSR. For Stalin, it was unnecessary to use it against Japan since it was 'doomed' anyway. Second, the weapon was so devastating it would have to be banned. Third, until that happy time every effort needed to be made to end the capitalist monopoly of atomic weapons. In a rare direct comment, in the already-noted interview with Alexander Werth of September 1946, Stalin maintained:

> I do not believe the atom bomb to be as serious a force as certain politicians are inclined to think. Atomic bombs are intended for intimidating the weak-nerved, but they cannot decide the outcome of war, since atom bombs are by no means sufficient for this purpose. Certainly, monopolistic possession of the secret of the atom bomb does create a threat, but at least two remedies exist against it: (a) Monopolist possession of the atom bomb cannot last long; (b) Use of the atom bomb will be prohibited.[30]

At Potsdam, Stalin had, rather offhandedly, asked Truman how much developing the bomb had cost. The reply was US$2 billion.[31] Shortly after, realizing what was required, Stalin put Beria in charge of nuclear weapon development. When Beria, some time into the process, claimed the work was being held up by a shortage of electric power, Stalin ordered a severe cut for a whole region and diverted its power to the A-bomb developers. Before pursuing this story it is necessary to look at how Potsdam, the bomb and Soviet entry into the war in the east began to affect inter-Allied relations and how the German question evolved and Cold War began.

A key reason for concessions to the USSR at Yalta had been the need to encourage it to join in what was expected to be a tough and bloody endgame to the Pacific war as the moment came to carry the conflict into the Japanese home islands. Once again, the West wanted to enlist the endless manpower and might of the Red Army to do a large portion of its fighting. Stalin was not unwilling since the USSR had issues with Japan over Sakhalin, the Kurile Islands and Manchuria. There was also an incipient Chinese Communist versus Nationalist civil war emerging as the common enemy, Japan, was expelled from China and other footholds it had taken during the war.

The USSR agreed at Yalta to join the Pacific war within three months of the defeat of Germany. Bang on schedule on 8 August, three months to the day after the end of hostilities in Europe, the Red Army invaded Manchuria. On 14 August, Japan surrendered unconditionally to the United States. Serious fighting continued in the Soviet-Japanese conflict zone for some two weeks after this. The Soviet campaign had been devastating. In the words of one leading authority who has given it the attention it deserves 'the Manchurian campaign in many ways represented the peak of Soviet operational art'.[32] In a couple of weeks over a 5000-kilometre (3000 mile) front, the Red Army had penetrated up to 800 kilometres (500 miles) and split the Japanese Army into fragments. Its forces had advanced over deserts, great rivers, mountains and by air drop. 'For once, Soviet casualties were relatively light . . . 12,000 dead.' Japan lost 80,000 dead and 500,000 prisoners.[33] If the facts are relatively clear, the political and international consequences flowing from this intensive month are much less so. It is not our brief to untangle them all but rather to look at the position of Stalin as he faced the growing heap of problems.

Officially, the United States dropped the bombs to shorten the war and save American lives. No one would deny the importance of that argument. However, a number of Western historians have also pointed out that the growing power of Stalin and the USSR was a major consideration in the decision-makers' minds. A number have agreed with Stalin that the main aim was to warn the USSR of the truly awesome power of the new weapon. Some have argued that, now they had the weapon, the United States did not need Soviet help in the war as Japan would soon surrender. On this view the point was to end the war quickly and keep Stalin out of the Japanese settlement as much as possible. Whether it was an intention or not, once Japanese surrender was happening the United States did all it could to keep the USSR at bay. Among other things it refused to officially invite the USSR to join the war even though it had been agreed at Yalta, refused to allow the USSR to receive the Japanese surrender and refused it an occupation zone on Hokkaido, one of the northerly major islands of the Japanese archipelago.[34]

It was over issues of this kind that the spirit of Yalta began to weaken and the elements of mutual suspicion and competition began to rear their heads. The USSR recovered southern Sakhalin and the Kurile Islands, the last being a sore point in Russo-Japanese relations down to the present. In a move which still resonates today, the Korean peninsula was divided into occupation zones to fill the vacuum after the Japanese surrender. The USSR occupied North Korea, the United States occupied South Korea.

Stalin had, at least on the surface, continued to cling to the discourse of collaboration and the importance of joint action through the fledgling United Nations while Truman was taking an increasingly unilateral line. At first it was little more than a change of emphasis, but it soon hardened and deepened over the bitterly contested question of a settlement of the German problem.

Officially, Soviet policy towards Germany remained orientated to the same objectives from 1945 to 1990. Germany should be united but neutral, that is it should not belong to a military bloc. In other words, Germany, too, would undergo a version of 'Finlandization'. The maintaining of a unified Germany was important to the USSR as it would facilitate 'universal' access of all occupying powers to all areas enabling it to take reparations from the richer Rhineland industrial zone. At the same time, Stalin increasingly recognized the determination of the United States to take steps to limit Soviet influence, especially given the immense prestige of communism and the left compared to the compromised, pro-Nazi elites across the continent and beyond. The outcome was a tit for tat game of escalating, conflicting policies. Both sides increasingly pursued a policy of control in their own zone.

Arguably, the United States was proactive in this process while Stalin's responses remained cautious and reactive. With even victorious Britain bankrupted by the war and on the verge of losing the engine-room of its power and influence, India and the British Empire, and although, in essence, the United States and the USSR were the only two left standing after the war, their power was asymmetric. The United States had military bases from East Anglia to Okinawa and was immeasurably wealthier. In an unverifiable statement it is often said to have produced 50 per cent of the world's manufactured products in 1945.[35] It also enjoyed a nuclear monopoly for the time being. The USSR had an infrastructure in ruins. It still had a vast army but it was expensive to keep together and the troops were sorely needed for the civilian task of economic reconstruction.

Not surprisingly, the United States was prepared to use its great advantages to pursue its own policies. In February and March 1946, the United States began to produce an 'intellectual' rationale for a new set of policies. In a 'Long Telegram' the leading US diplomatic observer of the USSR, George Kennan, argued that the USSR would use every means at its disposal to spread its influence and, in a 1947 article, that it should be 'contained'. For much of the remainder of his long life, Kennan argued that he had been misunderstood. Truman took up the term as a basis for militarizing international relations and producing what the next president, Eisenhower, called a 'military-industrial complex'. Kennan, an old-fashioned liberal who distrusted large standing armies, was horrified. A few days after the Long Telegram, Churchill gave his complex speech in Fulton, Missouri, in which he popularized the phrase 'iron curtain' which, he said, was coming down across Europe. He also called for joint East-West action to stop it and for a UN 'police' force, seconded from national armies, to act as peacekeepers. The caveats of Kennan and Churchill were soon forgotten but the ideas of 'containment' and the 'iron curtain' took on vigorous life. This is not the place for a full analysis but the next few years saw a series of actions by the United States which not only consolidated the US position but also raised the question of 'rollback' – that is, pushing the USSR out of areas under its influence or control.

In the forefront was the Marshall Plan which was opened for discussion in June 1947 and finally approved in April 1948. Its precociations included clauses unacceptable to the USSR which withdrew from the negotiations and pressured its satellites to do the same. Whether the aid would ever have gone to the USSR anyway is a moot point.[36] Also in early 1947, without consultation with the USSR, Britain and the United States amalgamated their German occupation areas into a single 'Bizonia', the first step towards a separate West German state. Nearly three weeks later, rigged elections produced a communist majority in Poland. In December 1947 a communist takeover in Romania dismissed the king and in February 1948 all non-communist ministers resigned under pressure in Prague, leaving a communist government in power. But Germany was still the key and on 21 June a separate currency, the Deutschmark, was introduced across Bizonia and the French zone, taking a further huge step towards a separate West Germany as only the Soviet zone was left with the original currency. Stalin responded immediately by ordering a partial blockade of Berlin which lasted until 11 May 1949. Land routes were cut off but Soviet air traffic controllers continued to guide planes in to Berlin during what became an epic airlift which loomed large in Western propaganda.

This was also a decisive period in that NATO was officially set up on 4 April 1949 and a separate West German state, consisting of Bizonia and the French zone, was set up as the Federal Republic of Germany. Moscow was horrified but not entirely surprised. Only on 7 October was the German Democratic Republic declared in the Russian zone, with East Berlin as its capital, the city remaining an open city with relatively free travel continuing between sectors until 1961 when the wall between East and West Berlin was constructed overnight on 13 August. Only in May 1955, after Stalin's death, was a Soviet equivalent of NATO set up – the Warsaw Pact – in response to the rejection of the post-Stalin Soviet leadership's own application to join NATO and the acceptance of West Germany as a member.

How did these developments look to Stalin?

In a Soviet equivalent of the Long Telegram, the Soviet ambassador in Washington, N. V. Novikov, sent a telegram to Moscow on 27 September 1946, in which he identified the underlying aim of US foreign policy to be 'world domination'. Seen from the Kremlin that was a plausible explanation. Containment and rollback meant an iron curtain was being constructed by the West to keep as much Soviet influence as possible out of Europe. Stalin was much taken with the events of World War I and the Russian Civil War and was acutely aware of the peace settlement. At Versailles in 1919 the question of combating the influence of the fledgling Bolshevik revolution had grown in significance and, especially in the years after 1919, the issue of punishing Germany had become secondary and even counter-productive. Instead, the construction of a *cordon sanitaire* (a perimeter around a zone quarantined to contain disease) and the reconstruction of Germany took over. In the United States a weak Germany was thought to be vulnerable to communism, so the United States led the process of propping it up. The year 1945 and after saw a similar sequence of events and the disease to be contained was still communism. The metaphor changed from *cordon sanitaire* to iron curtain but the underlying processes were very similar. The United States, unsurprisingly since it held most of the cards, pursued its own interests and did not feel it had to be beholden to Stalin for anything very much. From Moscow, American policy seemed at least as increasingly hostile as Soviet policy did when viewed from the State Department and the White House.

Even so Stalin and Soviet policy remained cautious, confused and defensive.[37] Stalin had few cards to play. As we have seen in his answers to Eddie Gilmore of March 1946 he held on to the idea of joint decision-making over international issues. This appears to have continued into 1947.[38] The occasion of the interview was to enable Stalin to reply to Churchill's 'Iron Curtain' speech which had raised the temperature with respect to a preemptive Western strike against the USSR. Stalin was asked where the war scare came from. He replied in his usual conciliatory tones: 'I am convinced that neither nations nor their armies seek a new war. They want peace, and seek to secure the peace. That means that the present war scare does not come from that direction. I think that the present war scare is aroused by the actions of certain political groups who are engaged in propaganda for a new war and thus sowing the seeds of dissension and uncertainty.' The correct response was to engage in redoubled efforts at refuting the warmongers by every means of free speech available.[39]

Each reader will decide how much these (and all other) statements by Stalin were pure propaganda but they were quickly followed by the more solid evidence of actions. Two weeks later on 5 April, Soviet troops withdrew from northern Iran, thereby removing a serious irritant in East-West relations and confirming the notion of spheres of influence. A year later, when the Marshall Plan negotiations began in Paris, Stalin sent a high-powered delegation, led by Molotov which seemed to be ready for serious negotiations. In fact, serious preparation for the Marshall Plan negotiations had included personal meetings between Stalin and leading American policy-makers including General Marshall himself. The theme of these meetings was Stalin's desire to co-operate and the possibility of removing all barriers to such co-operation through frank and sincere negotiation. Presumably, Stalin had the wartime precedent in mind.

However, before the detailed negotiations began, a new and more menacing message began to emerge from Washington in March 1947 when the president, in a speech, enunciated what quickly became known as the Truman Doctrine. It was the duty of America to fight on behalf of 'free people' all around the globe. Truman argued that:

> At the present moment in world history nearly every nation must choose between alternative ways of life. The choice is too often not a free one. One way of life is based upon the will of the majority, and is distinguished by free institutions, representative government, free elections, guarantees of individual liberty, freedom of speech and religion, and freedom from political oppression. The second way of life is based upon the will of a minority forcibly imposed upon the majority. It relies upon terror and oppression, a controlled press and radio, fixed elections, and the suppression of personal freedoms. I believe that it must be the policy of the United States to support free peoples who are resisting attempted subjugation by armed minorities or by outside pressures. I believe that we must assist free peoples to work out their own destinies in their own way. I believe that our help should be primarily through economic stability and orderly political process.[40]

The speech did not officially implicate the USSR but made it perfectly clear who it had in mind by mentioning that 'Poland, Bulgaria and Romania' had had 'totalitarian regimes forced upon them against their will' and 'in violation of the Yalta agreements'. The immediate occasion of the speech was the inability of Britain to sustain its role in fighting for the right in the Greek Civil War against communists who, ironically, were receiving very little support from Moscow.

However, the new orientation went a lot further than a single crisis. It laid down an underlying foundation of future US foreign policy still influential today. In the first place, it completely replaced America's interwar policy with a policy of global intervention, although note that the speech refers to support in economic terms. However, it was accompanied by a reorganization of the state organizations dealing with the outside world, laying the foundations of the 'National Security State' based on the National Security Act, introduced into the Senate on 3 March 1947. This momentous act set up the giants of American foreign policy including the CIA, with a role to spy and engage in covert action to support US policy; a unified Department of Defense, bringing the army, navy and air force commands under joint supervision, housed in the newly constructed Pentagon building and the National Security Council, a largely secret body which discussed and approved policy on America's security anywhere around the globe. In other words, Truman was putting down a formidable challenge to the USSR.[41]

Though the implications of these developments were not yet apparent – indeed the National Security Act itself had not been drafted – Stalin was quick to react by re-emphasizing that confrontation was unnecessary. In April 1947 he met Senator Harold Stassen, a Republican of some standing. 'I want to bear testimony to the fact that Russia (sic) wants to co-operate' was Stalin's key point. He denied having said it was impossible for states with different systems to co-operate and called in his guardian angel, Lenin, as testimony to Soviet preparedness to work with capitalists. He engaged in some sparring with Stassen on the pre-war situation, the difference between Nazism and the United States which had gone to war despite 'the systems' being 'the same' whereas the United States and the USSR had not gone to war with each other despite having 'different systems' as Stalin put it. Stung by Stalin linking the United States and Nazi Germany, Stassen pointed out the differences, but Stalin maintained they were differences of government and politics, not of underlying structures, the point being 'there was a difference in government, no difference in the economic systems. The government was a temporary factor.' This was hardly designed to win over his guest but was testimony to not covering over the cracks and discussing issues frankly. The exchanges were very interesting as the following extract from the official printed version agreed by the two men indicates. Stalin argued that:

> we should adhere to mutual respect of people. Some people call the Soviet system totalitarian. Our people call the American system monopoly capitalism. If we start calling each other names with the words monopolist and totalitarian, it will lead to no co-operation.
>
> We must start from the historical fact that there are two systems approved by the people. Only on that basis is co-operation possible. If we distract each other with criticism, that is propaganda.
>
> As to propaganda, I am not a propagandist but a business-like man. We should not be sectarian. When the people wish to change the systems they will do so. When we met with Roosevelt to discuss the questions of war, we did not call each other names. We established co-operation and succeeded in defeating the enemy.

Stassen: That sort of criticism has been a cause of misunderstanding after the war. Do you look forward in the future to a greater exchange of ideas and news, of students and teachers, of artists, of tourists, if there is co-operation?

Stalin: This will happen inevitably if co-operation is established. For an exchange of goods will lead to an exchange of people . . .

Stassen: As I see it, then, you think it is possible that there will be co-operation provided there is a will and desire to co-operate.

Stalin: That is correct.

Stassen: In the development of the standards of living of the people, mechanization and electrification have been of major significance. The new development of atomic energy is of very great importance to all peoples of the world. I feel that the matter of international inspection, effective controls and outlawing the use for war of atomic energy is of supreme importance to all peoples of the world. Do you feel that there is a reasonable prospect of working out agreements for the long-term future for the peaceful development of atomic energy?

Stalin: I hope for this. There are big differences of views among us, but in the long run I hope we shall come to an understanding. International control and inspection will be established, in any view, and it will be of great importance. The peaceful use of atomic energy will bring great technological changes. It is a very great matter. As for the use of atomic energy for war purposes, this in all probability will be prohibited. It will be a problem in the long run that will be met by the consciences of the people and it will be prohibited.[42]

Here was a reasonable and co-operative Stalin who believed the USSR had a case and a government reflecting the wishes of its people, who looked for collaboration, the outlawing of nuclear weapons, the possibility of inspection to verify the peaceful use of atomic power and a flourishing exchange of key members of each other's populations. Was this really a 'business-like' Stalin or an ultimate deceiver? He could certainly talk the talk but could he walk the walk? He was equally conciliatory in his conversation with George Marshall, saying that, although it might not come about at once 'don't despair . . . On all the main questions – democratization, political organization, economic unity and reparations – it is possible to achieve compromise. Only have patience and don't despair.'[43]

The opening of those negotiations took place in Paris in July 1947. Molotov headed a serious Soviet delegation. However, since the Marshall Plan was the first and major step in the Truman Doctrine of economic support to those subjugated to the USSR it is clear the USSR was not an intended recipient.

Preconditions required passing on the most sensitive economic information. In the USSR's case it would expose the weakness of her economy, the extent of wartime destruction (the official figures were a secret at this time) and the focus and success or otherwise of her efforts at reconstruction. This was all of great strategic importance and would have weighed in any scale measuring the possibility of an attack on the USSR. Molotov was not going to hand it over for nothing. In a fit of mutual recrimination Stalin ordered the Soviet delegation back to Moscow. In a last lingering moment of hope for co-operation even at this late stage, Stalin initially permitted Soviet-occupied countries to continue with their applications. However, only two days later the permission was revoked and they were more or less ordered to withdraw from the negotiation.[44]

The Cold War was fully under way and, while never abandoning the overt policy of peace and co-operation, Stalin faced up to the realities and moved on to the view that there were now 'two camps' in world affairs. Even before the negotiations began, Stalin's most acute observer of American behaviour, Novikov, had written from his Washington Embassy on 9 June that 'in this proposal are the clear contours of a western European bloc aimed at us' and on 24 June that 'a careful analysis of the Marshall Plan shows that in the end it amounts to the creation of a west European bloc as an instrument' of US policy'.[45] In September Stalin set up a body known as Cominform, the Communist Information Bureau, to co-ordinate policies in the Soviet 'bloc', as the terminology put it, but even here there was still caution. It was not a revival of Comintern and was much watered-down and remained fairly ineffective.

More to the point, it became clear that the imperative of ending America's nuclear monopoly as quickly as possible was even more crucial to Soviet security. Talk of nuclear disarmament and peace continued, notably in Stalin's article supporting the radical peace policy of Henry Wallace in the 1948 US presidential election,[46] but it was finding no echo in the new world and was dismissed as empty propaganda which it may well have been but, indefensibly, no effort was made to test it out. Stalin knew the cost of nuclear development would be heavy and hundreds of thousands were deployed on the project overseen by Beria. In typical Stalinist manner they ranged from prisoners working in uranium mines to top scientists such as the brilliant academician and physicist Igor Kurchatov, not to mention imprisoned scientists working in the gulag 'first circle' – relatively privileged (by gulag standards) special centres of imprisonment for working intellectuals known as *sharashki*.[47] Even a serious accident in January 1949, which may have been more deadly than Chernobyl in 1986,[48] was unable to stop the juggernaut and on 29 August the first successful test broke the US monopoly.

Domestic problems: reconstruction of economy and society

It was a fantastic achievement for the team but it was, in particular, a feather in the cap of Beria whose star was rising fast. He also had a leading role in the restoration of Soviet industry and the wider economy after the war. This was another extraordinary achievement. The outcome of the war in economic terms was that a quarter of national wealth had been destroyed.[49] The pattern of destruction was unusual and very different from the 1914 war when industry had been devastated but population less so. In 1945–1946 the human costs of the war were colossal. One third of young males had been killed and even in the 1959 census there were still 20 million more women than men in the country, 15 million of them had been in the 16–45 age range in 1945. At least 25 million people were homeless.[50] Tragically, the human toll continued after the war ended. Again unlike World War I, agriculture had been very badly hit, production falling by one third. The 1945 harvest was 47 million tons, lower per head of population than the famine year of 1921. In 1946, as a result largely of climate, the harvest *fell* even further to 40 million tons. At least a million people died of starvation and disease related to malnutrition in 1947.[51] By comparison, because arms production had been the top priority, industry had held up better than in the previous world war, but it was still in a parlous state and had to face the complex issues of transition back to peacetime priorities. Not surprisingly, here, too, the initial trend was downwards and, as arms production wound down rapidly, overall industrial production fell in 1946 as civilian production had not yet got going sufficiently to take up the slack.[52]

Stalin was faced with multiple problems (not forgetting the international challenges as well). His response was in, some ways, tentative and conciliatory. On 24 May 1945 at a glittering occasion in one of the halls in the Kremlin to honour the leaders of the armed forces Stalin proposed an unusual toast:

> COMRADES! . . .
>
> I should like to propose a toast to the health of our Soviet people, and in the first place, the Russian people.
>
> I drink in the first place to the health of the Russian people because it is the most outstanding nation of all the nations forming the Soviet Union . . .
>
> I propose a toast to the health of the Russian people not only because it is the leading people, but also because it possesses a clear mind, a staunch character, and patience.
>
> Our Government made not a few errors, we experienced at moments a desperate situation . . . A different people could have said to the Government: 'You have failed to justify our expectations. Go away. We shall install another government which will conclude peace with Germany and assure us a quiet life.' The Russian people, however, did not take this path because it trusted the correctness of the policy of its Government, and it made sacrifices to ensure the rout of Germany.[53]

Not only did it single out the Russian people as a superior group among the Soviet population as a whole, a judgement linked, no doubt, to the mistrust shown to so many of the minority nationalities, the deportation of 'traitor' nations and the ongoing guerrilla resistance in Ukraine, funded by the US special ops of the time, but it also acknowledged errors. The belief that the Soviet, and especially the Russian, people were at one with their government was a fundamental assumption of Stalin and, to some extent, the war effort had shown it had some basis in reality. As in external policy towards eastern Europe there were also hints at relaxation of the dictatorship which even extended to apparently reducing censorship of outgoing foreign press reports.[54]

However, the deepening Cold War squeezed out such moments and they were soon replaced by the restoration of a rigid, controlled orthodoxy imposed by Andrei Zhdanov and encapsulated in a speech in Leningrad in August 1946 in which he denounced numerous writers, artists and other intellectuals who were deemed to have drifted too far beyond approved margins. Leningrad was the source of much of this diversity and the journals *Zvezda* and *Leningrad* were also criticized in a Central Committee resolution of August 1946. In particular, Zhdanov in his speech denounced the great poet Anna Akhmatova, whom he described as 'a whore and a nun, in whom licentiousness is combined with prayer' and the short story writer Mikhail Zoshchenko whose works exuded, according to Zhdanov, 'the venom of a brutish hostility to the Soviet system'.[55] Despite the uncompromising words, neither was arrested, though Akhmatova had lost two husbands to repression and her son had spent many years in the gulag.

In the economic sphere the old methods soon returned. At an election meeting on 9 February 1946 Stalin called for old-style production targets of 500 million tons of coal, 60 million tons of steel, 60 million tons of oil and so on. While according to Khlevniuk, economists such as Eugene Zaleski criticized such a 'simplistic understanding of economic development'[56] the results were impressive. 'By the end of the fourth Five-Year Plan (1946–1950) industrial production considerably exceeded and agricultural production slightly exceeded prewar levels.'[57] Perhaps unsurprisingly the figure for capital goods – that is, heavy equipment, machine tools and the like – was at least 82 per cent higher than pre-war, while consumer goods were only some 8 per cent above 1940 levels. Within that range consumer durables – iron bedsteads, radios, clocks, watches for example – fared reasonably well reaching 250 per cent of pre-war levels because they were produced in former armaments factories. Production of armaments themselves fell massively from 1944–1947 but, again as the Cold War began to bite, increased by 40 per cent from 1947–1950. The chief economic weakness was grain production which was not only significantly below its 1940 level in 1950 (81 million tons of grain as opposed to 96 million in 1940) but, on a per capita basis, it was even substantially below 1913 levels in Stalin's last years. In the words of the leading authority 'this had a profound effect on the general standard of living of the population'.[58]

The population was also badly hit by one more severe economic adjustment. As in World War I the simple option of paying for war goods in printed money had prevailed. The result was a massive amount of unusable (because there was nothing to buy) money floating round in the system. Since prices were controlled it did not lead directly to full-scale inflation but it did exacerbate the shortage of goods. Recent research has shown that reversing the effects of this policy had been planned for as early as 1943. The policy was delayed through 1946 for fear of worsening the famine but the night of 14–15 December new roubles were introduced at a rate of one for ten old roubles (with a slightly better rate for bank savings), rationing was ended and prices were raised. Massive vigilance was ordered to accompany the reform. While ending rationing was a plus for the population the other two elements were deeply unpopular and added to the severity of the period. The exchange was presented as a way of depriving war profiteers of their ill-gotten gains and, in his own hand, Stalin added to the decree the words that this was the population's 'final sacrifice' to the war, which somewhat ameliorated the negative effects.[59] Nonetheless, a whole host of offences against state property and in favour of harsh work discipline were introduced and strictly enforced. Rates of imprisonment soared. Over 7 million sentences were issued between 1946 and 1952, an average of 1 million per year. On 1 January 1953, there were 2.5 million people in camps and prisons and 2.8 million in 'special settlements' for deported nationalities and others. This amounted to about 3 per cent of the total population.[60] The figures were inflated by the inclusion of a tragically dwindling band of war prisoners and an abnormal flow of Soviet citizens accused of various degrees of disloyalty in the war, including returned fighters who had sided with the Nazis. Many were summarily executed but many others lived and died in the gulag.

Communist revolution in China and North Korea

Successes in building nuclear weapons and in achieving basic economic recovery were matched by an extraordinary success in international affairs. In the summer of 1949, after a series of attempted coalitions with the nationalist forces of Chiang Kai-shek had collapsed into civil war, the Communist People's Liberation Army swept into Beijing and proclaimed the People's Republic of China with Chairman Mao Tse-tung and Chou En-lai as premier and foreign minister. This was a massive victory for communism. It left the United States reeling, reinforced the anti-communism of the McCarthy era and launched a pursuit of State Department 'traitors' and others who had 'lost' China, though it is unclear who had said it was America's to lose. More pragmatically, mindful of the delicacy of Hong Kong's position, Britain was one of the first non-commmunist major powers to recognize the new government, which it did on 6 January 1950.

American hostility reached fever pitch when the Korean crisis peaked later that year. In a re-run of the German question, Soviet and American forces occupied North and South Korea, respectively, in 1945, as Japanese forces collapsed leaving a power vacuum. Attempts to maintain a condominium, comparable to the 'universalist' approach to Germany, and Soviet proposals for the withdrawal of both occupying armies were replaced by an American policy of setting up, as in Germany, a separate South Korean government, proclaimed on 15 August 1948 to replace the US military government. On 9 September a People's Democratic Republic of Korea under Kim Il-sung was proclaimed. It also claimed sovereignty over the South. On 25 December 1948 Soviet troops withdrew from the North and by 29 June 1949 US troops had withdrawn from the South. While it is beyond our scope to follow the situation which lead to the North attacking the South on 25 June 1950, almost controlling the whole peninsula by September before themselves being pushed back by a returning American force which also came to control most of the country. However, they, in turn, were pushed back in late November and December by a massive Chinese invasion force which led to the original North–South boundary, the 38th parallel of latitude, becoming the border once again. Millions of deaths later both sides were back where they started. For reasons still not fully clarified, the USSR, which had been boycotting the UN at the time, failed to realize the significance of the UN's approach to the Korean problem. It stood aside as the UN passed a resolution, which the USSR would surely have vetoed had its ambassador been present, supporting the use of force to repel the initial invasion by the North. This permitted the legal fiction of the US forces masquerading as a UN army to which 14 other Allied nations contributed.

What was Stalin's role? It seems that he had opposed Kim Il-sung's enthusiasm to invade once the United States had left saying 'we should not meddle too deeply in Korean affairs'.[61] Stalin's natural caution was, however, outweighed by an assessment that the United States had abandoned the peninsula and, after the fall of China, no longer considered it to be part of its sphere of influence. Although he refused to commit Soviet troops at any stage, Stalin gave the green light to Kim in early 1950, significantly after the emergence of Communist China and under the false impression the United States would not react seriously. When they did Stalin still refused to get directly involved and as the North's army was defeated he ordered Kim to prepare to leave the country sending this bleak message on 12 October:

> We feel that continuing resistance is pointless. The Chinese comrades are refusing to take part militarily. Under these circumstances you must prepare to evacuate completely to China and/or the USSR . . . The potential for fighting the enemy in the future must be preserved.[62]

Strangely, only one day later this was rescinded and replaced by the following message from Stalin to Kim:

> I have just received a telegram from Mao Zedong in which he reports that the CC CPC [Central Committee of the Communist Party of China] discussed the situation [in Korea] again and decided after all to render military assistance to the Korean comrades, regardless of the insufficient armament of the Chinese troops. I am awaiting detailed reports about this matter from Mao Zedong. In connection with this new decision of the Chinese comrades, I ask you to postpone temporarily the implementation of the telegram sent to you yesterday about the evacuation of North Korea and the retreat of the Korean troops to the north.[63]

Had Stalin succeeded in bluffing Mao into taking responsibility? Mao expressed it laconically: 'The old man [Stalin] writes to us that we must step up',[64] which they did, to considerable effect, preserving communist power in North Korea. Of course, like Enver Xoxha's Albania, North Korea turned itself into a strange mutation of Stalinism, isolated not only from the wider world but also, increasingly, from the communist bloc itself. Curiously, it was eventually the only place in the world to retain the features of a hardline Stalinism *pur et dur*, pure and tough.

However, Stalin was aware the emergence of another mighty communist power – the physically largest (USSR) and most highly populated (China) countries in the world were now both communist – was not an unalloyed joy. Moscow had long been suspicious of Mao's unorthodox, peasant-oriented communism which, seen through Russian eyes, resembled *narodism* (populism) as much as Marxism-Leninism. Support for the Chinese revolution had been limited by Stalin having one eye on conciliating the United States and encouraging Mao to do deals with his Guomindang Nationalist opponents. The collapse of the later, catapulting the Chinese Communist Party into power, was a surprise to all concerned and could be seen as a possible source of future problems. For the moment, however, the establishment of communism in China, Korea and Indochina (Vietnam and Laos) seemed to be tilting the world balance very heavily in Stalin's direction.

The dictatorship in the final years

Contrary to many widespread assumptions, including those of David Levine's cartoon referred to earlier, Stalin did not control his entourage by means of pure fear. We have already noted the curious incident, as the war began, when Stalin may well have expected he was about to be arrested by his close associates. In fact, once he had established his team – Molotov, Kaganovich, Ordzhonokidze, Voroshilov, Budyonnyi, Kirov, Beria, Malenkov, Mikoyan, Khrushchev and others – he tended to stick with them and they with him. Many of them had been close to him in the civil war and remained so until the end. It has to be recognized that, yes, he was feared, but they also had an admiration for Stalin bordering on adoration at times. He was the smartest, strongest, most confident and toughest of them all. While the flattery it included went well beyond any reality, even at the heart of the cult of personality there was a grain of genuine veneration. Stalin himself did not subscribe to the cult but was prepared to use it to his advantage. While it would be fanciful to suggest the cult was fully genuine it does appear to have reflected views held in the wider population as a series of studies have confirmed in recent decades.[65] In an almost masochistic way his very toughness was one of the reasons he was admired. Even some of his victims, notably Bukharin, refused, at least overtly, to break with him and there were numerous reports that prisoners believed Stalin was unaware of the monstrous extent of gulag injustice. Fear was certainly a key weapon, but it was not the sole foundation of the dictatorship within and beyond his entourage. He was not just a version of Lewis Carroll's Queen of Hearts who could simply and continually order 'off with their heads!'.[66] If his type of authority has any fictional equivalent it is more that of *The Godfather*,[67] someone who was ruthless and prepared to kill those who fell short in terms of duty and honour and to make those close to him suffer if they failed him, but who ruled also through admiration, love and respect of his 'family'. In the words of one of two leading dissidents of the late-Soviet era: 'Unlimited power may have been grounded in fear and supported by an apparatus of terror, but it was enhanced by the existence of genuine mass devotion, encouraged and nourished by an all-embracing and extremely effective network of propaganda and censorship, capable of stifling any criticism.'[68]

In these later phases of his rule, when his wartime status seemed to have catapulted him to an even higher esteem in his entourage, in the country and on the global scale from London to Hanoi, he still believed he had to manoeuvre to keep control of his immediate flock. In classic *Godfather* fashion, Don Stalin took a run at his most trusted adviser, his *consiglieri*, Molotov. In 1945, the Western press was full of feverish speculation about a power struggle between Molotov and Zhukov for Stalin's succession. The resumption by Stalin of his pre-Great Terror practice of taking lengthy vacations – the Politburo granted him six weeks off on 9 October 1945 – was read as an indication that he was in poor health. In fact, a great deal of what was happening in these final years is shrouded in mystery, speculation and Cold War misdirection from both sides making rational, grounded analysis difficult.[69] It is likely that Western speculation had aroused Stalin's suspicions of Molotov who, in Stalin's eyes if no one else's, was taking initiatives in his negotiations with the Allies of which Stalin did not approve. The first step making Stalin furious were reports in the London *Daily Herald* and the *New York Times* that he was about to be replaced as chair of *sovnarkom*, the Soviet cabinet. Instead of dismissing it as one of the first in what became a woefully inaccurate chain of reports by Western Kremlin-watchers, Stalin dispatched a series of irate telegrams to Molotov, Beria, Malenkov and Mikoyan from his vacation residence. The issue was also tied in with the brief relaxation of censorship of press dispatches from Moscow, mentioned briefly above, which Stalin had ordered to be reversed on 2 December. The four recipients stood together and the question was, eventually, sorted out when it was explained the reports had been passed by Russian censors before Stalin ordered the reversal of policy. Nonetheless, Molotov was still blamed by him 'for the appearance of "libels against the Soviet government" in the foreign press'.[70] Worse accusations were to come. Molotov was said to care only about promoting himself through the foreign press and Stalin expressed 'doubts about some of those close to him'. Molotov endured several other humiliations in the crisis which ended with him admitting mistakes, but not crimes, and promising that he would earn not only Stalin's trust but also 'the trust of the party which is dearer to me than my life'.[71]

The affair could have turned out much worse for Molotov but what was it about? It is possible Stalin was worried that his position was being eroded. On the other hand it might simply have been an excuse for a massive retaliation planned, successfully, to warn all four not to step out of line. This is borne out by the return, later in the month, of the Leningrad party leaders, Zhdanov and Voznesensky, into the inner circle. The reshuffle continued into the New Year. Malenkov lost his position as Central Committee secretary, amid accusations of 'covering up irregularities in the aviation industry' during the war.[72] Beria, too, was disciplined in that his protégé, Vsevolod Merkulov, was removed in disgrace from his position as Minister of State Security and replaced by Viktor Abakumov, whom Beria disliked.[73] Coincidentally or not, popular generals like Zhukov were also being manoeuvred into the background at this time.

Perhaps Stalin had simply smelled conspiracy in the solidarity of the four he had left in charge while he was away and was taking steps to break up that solidarity and regain his preeminence, though objectively there is no sign any of them intended to undermine him. Maybe he was simply reminding everyone who was boss. Maybe the issue of succession was beginning to play on Stalin's mind as he passed his 67th (officially 66th) birthday on 6 December. In this respect the odious Beria may have been the main target. As we have already noted he had risen very high. He had been appointed in 1939 to replace Yezhov and sort out the economic, social and political crises left by the blundering purges. His successful leadership of the nuclear weapons project[74] and his role in the reconstruction of industry were increasingly impressive achievements. All of this, however, was outweighed by his loathsome lust and possible paedophilia. Khrushchev claims he cruised the Moscow streets and had his aides persuade young women into his limousine and 'rewarded' them with flowers and presents when they were released. In an extremely curious anecdote, Stalin's own daughter Svetlana records her father warning her not to be alone with him. What does this tell us about power relationships in Stalin's inner circle? The truth about Beria's sexual predations has been, unsurprisingly, confused by conflicting rumours and political exigencies as Khrushchev and others went about justifying arresting and executing him in 1953 after Stalin's death. According to one report, he kept a list of his mistresses. One version says there were 39 names on it. Another says 79. The majority, in this case surprisingly perhaps, seem to have been consensual but others claimed to have been raped. Beria's wife Nina remained loyal, dismissing his activities in this sphere as part of Georgian masculinity and as exaggerated in terms of numbers and violence. 'When', she asked, 'would Lavrentii have had time to make these hordes of women his mistresses? He spent all day and night at work.'[75] Didn't she know that was the oldest excuse in the book?

Stalin's next manoeuvres, the motives for which are also open to broad speculation, were more deadly. This episode has become known as 'The Leningrad Affair' and the most authoritative accounts[76] suggest the following scenario. Stalin's inner circle was divided by rivalry between two factions, each suspicious the other was trying to steal a march with respect to ultimately succeeding Stalin. On one side were the old guard: Molotov, Malenkov, Beria in the forefront; on the other were the returned Leningraders: Zhdanov, Voznesensky and Kuznetsov. In the summer of 1948, Zhdanov fell ill and died in August, thereby depriving the Leningraders of their leader and unbalancing the see-saw of power. Seeing an advantage, Malenkov and Beria brought charges against them which were mostly fairly trivial. They were accused of setting up an international trade fair in Leningrad without permission, misplacing documents and abuse of the patronage system. Probably intended as a minor blow to their rivals, Malenkov and Beria had, in fact, called up a storm. There were numerous advances and retreats in the case indicating some indecision but, in the end, Stalin decided that decisive and murderous action was necessary. More serious fictitious charges were added, including espionage. In September 1950, after lengthy interrogation and torture, Voznesensky, Kuznetsov and the 'ringleaders' were sentenced to death and shot. Sentences of imprisonment, exile and death were passed on hundreds of supposed associates. Why? It is assumed Stalin acted in bad faith, as usual, on this issue but it still does not bear much rational analysis. Voznesensky was the USSR's most effective planner and economic manager. He was young (44 at the time of death). It is suggested his weakness was that he was a pragmatist who was not deeply immersed in ideology and this was anathema to the ideologically correct Stalin. It does not, however, explain why so many innocent lives had to be taken as well.

The final set of manoeuvres were equally ambiguous and ultimately inexplicable. They were also fatally tied up with the USSR's tangled relations with the newly established state of Israel. When it perceived Israel as a thorn in the side of British imperialism its founding was warmly welcomed in Moscow and Israel's formidable ambassador, Golda Meir who went on to lead her country, was a significant presence in Moscow diplomatic circles. However, increasing US involvement in the issue and the hardening Cold War led to a rethink. Israel, far from being anti-imperialist, seemed more like a stalking-horse for American interests in the Middle

East. The USSR began to side with the Arab nations and fiercely criticized Israel, developing a rhetoric of anti-Zionism. The border between anti-Zionism and anti-Semitism is fuzzy at best. In the intensity of Cold War politics the terms became supposedly interchangeable, blurring distinction between racial hatred of Jews in the form of anti-Semitism, and legitimate criticism of the state and politics of Israel, anti-Zionism. What was happening?

Initially, Stalin's moves were a continuation of his threats to Molotov, though in this case it was his Jewish wife, Polina Zhemchuzhina, who was targeted. On 29 December 1949 she was expelled from the party, arrested and imprisoned. Her offence was a too enthusiastic embrace of Golda Meir and of the idea of a Jewish homeland in the Crimea. Molotov initially abstained in the Politburo vote to arrest her but, after being upbraided by Stalin, he 'admitted' this was a mistake.[77] In reality, he recognized the noose was closing around his neck, too, and quickly acceded to Stalin's 'suggestion' that the time had come to divorce her.[78]

The new purge went much further. Anyone who had been overenthusiastic about Israel was suspect. The vibrant Moscow State Jewish Theatre in Moscow was closed down in 1948 and its director, Solomon Mikhoels, died in what is widely considered to be a state-sponsored murder disguised as a traffic accident. The Jewish Anti-Fascist Committee was also closed down and 13 of its leading members were shot in 1952 after being imprisoned for more than three years. At the time of their execution the purge had extended to a group of nine doctors from the Kremlin medical service who were accused of expediting the deaths of numerous leading officials. Six of them were Jewish, although hundreds more, most of whom were not Jewish, were arrested. The complexity is also indicated by the fact that Beria's rival and head of the Ministry of State Security, Viktor Abakumov, was arrested and tortured, presumably as a result of plotting by Beria, and probably Malenkov, with a view to gaining a decisive power advantage by taking over Abakumov's ministry. Abakumov was not released on Stalin's death but remained under arrest and was executed in July 1954 by Stalin's successors on a charge of having prosecuted the Leningrad Affair.

In recent years, evidence published by Zhores Medvedev should make observers hesitate to argue, as is widely done, that a general anti-Semitic campaign was under way. A minority of the accused in the Doctors' Plot were non-Jewish for a start and many prominent Jews remained undisturbed in their positions. Medvedev has also argued that the suspension of the investigation into the plot was ordered by Stalin as one of his last acts before his fatal stroke. In addition, two versions of a letter signed by prominent Jews had been edited to define the difference between loyal Soviet Jewish citizens and the 'Zionists' and 'cosmopolitans' subject to denunciation and arrest. Stalin's death, Medvedev argues, may have prevented the publication of one or other of these letters.[79] In his magisterial biography Robert Service weighs the considerations about Stalin's supposed anti-Semitism very carefully. Stalin criticized many nationalities including Jews but the campaign against 'cosmopolitans' was wider than simply an anti-Jewish manoeuvre. It emerged when relations with the United States were turning very bad. It also became confused with popularity shown towards Israel in general and Golda Meir in particular once Soviet policy towards Israel turned negative. In Service's words, Stalin's 'campaign against "rootless cosmopolitanism" cannot be automatically attributed to hatred of Jews as Jews . . . [Stalin] started to regard Jewish people as subversive elements. Yet his motives were of Realpolitik rather than visceral prejudice.'[80]

Two other 'affairs' also clouded Stalin's last years. Despite taking a two-month vacation in the south in the summer of 1951, vastly improved communications enabled him to keep a much closer eye on the shop while he was away. Warned that of the tribal groupings in Georgia, the Megrels (Mingrelians) were dominating others in the political hierarchy, Stalin quickly noted that Beria was a Mingrelian. When bribery allegations against powerful Mingrelian figures could not be substantiated, Stalin had other charges fabricated. The Georgian party was raked through with arrests. Eleven thousand people were exiled though death sentences do not appear to have been on the order of the day. Beria survived. If he was the target it was no more than a warning, once again, of who was boss.

The other affair was also complex and seems to have been built around an attack on, as was becoming usual, Molotov but also Mikoyan. In a complex series of moves Stalin abolished the leading governing body, the 9-member party Politburo, and replaced it with a 25-member Presidium which, oddly, was to have a 9-member executive, the Presidium Bureau which looked like the Politburo by another name. Molotov and Mikoyan were not nominated for membership and were subjected to open criticism by Stalin. No doubt weakened, even fearful, they were not arrested nor deprived of most of their powers. In other words, like Beria, they survived an attack of which, it is assumed, they were the indirect subjects.[81]

The Leningrad Affair had been direct and deadly. The Mingrelian and Presidium manoeuvres looked like a macabre dance with limited consequences. It is hard to know why Stalin performed them. Even at this stage of his rule was he not aware of how much power he actually had? Was he weakening the Old Guard to open the way for the new when he retired or died? If so, why murder Voznesensky, the most capable of the young pretenders? Was Stalin, at 72, suffering from old age, illness, weariness or simply losing his touch? Certainly he was no longer the robust, confident figure of the war and immediate post-war years. He was now more brooding, spent more time alone in the nearby *dacha* and was no longer surrounded on a daily basis by admiring sycophants. He was alienating his former allies and taunting them with his power without taking decisive steps. The years from about 1949/1950 until the end were dark, unpredictable and dangerous for all concerned. In Molotov's words 'In his last years Stalin suffered from a persecution mania. He was so overwrought, self-seekers had so irritated and worn him down, had incited him against this person and that – he had broken down . . . Consequently able leaders such as Voznesensky and Kuznetsov perished.'[82]

All the more startling, then, that Stalin should reveal one last, highly unexpected, surprise. Having written hardly anything other than a multitude of speeches and reports since he dabbled in the *Short Course* in 1938 and 1939, Stalin returned to ideological reflection in two final pamphlets entitled *Marxism and Problems of Linguistics* (1950) and *Economic Problems of Socialism* (1952). What was in Stalin's mind?

That he should stumble into the field of linguistics, which had dominated Western philosophy since Wittgenstein, was extraordinary. Molotov himself attributed it to Stalin's confidence in the

Russian and socialist future. 'He believed that once the world-wide communist system was established – and he did everything possible to bring this about – the world's main language . . . would be the language of Pushkin and Lenin.'[83] He also added that 'Stalin understood the great historical destiny of the Russian people, the destiny about which Dostoevsky wrote: the heart of Russia, more than any other nation, is predestined to be the universal, all-embracing humanitarian union of nations',[84] In the most careful study of Stalin's ideas Erik van Ree describes Stalin's thought as 'revolutionary patriotism' and the message Stalin incorporated in his writing in linguistics bears this out. Language does not simply follow class or similar criteria. Van Ree compares it, in Stalin's eyes, to society itself and argues that what is distinctive about this pamphlet is that Stalin supports the integrative force of 'society' over 'class' in that class struggle, or any other struggle, should not be pursued to the point of destroying society itself. Language is a symbol of that and emerges through 'social' rather than 'class' factors.[85] He attacked the postulates of Academician N. Y. Marr that languages changed under the pressure of social change. Stalin refuted this by arguing, unexceptionably, that the revolution in Russia had made no fundamental inroads into the nature of the Russian or any other Soviet language. Language stood above immediate class pressures as did, implicitly, culture itself. In van Ree's words 'That this reformulation closely expressed the shift in Stalin's polices from "proletarian" to "popular" to "patriotic" is clear enough.'[86] It should, of course, be borne in mind that this 'patriotism' was not for traditional Russia but for the revolutionary, proletarian-led Russia/USSR Stalin believed he saw when he looked out of the Kremlin windows.

The second intellectual incursion, *Economic Problems of Socialism*, was his political testament. What did Stalin want to impress on his successors? First of all, he stated that the basic structures of Soviet society were sound and did not need to be fundamentally reconstructed. This was a blow to those looking to reform the collective farm system, amongst others. He also, astonishingly, affirmed that the laws of society could not be circumvented by efforts of pure will. How did that fit with a leader who had once sponsored the slogan that 'There is no fortress the Bolsheviks cannot storm'? In the words of one his most eminent biographers this represented 'stupendous hypocrisy' given that 'if ever there had been an attempt to transform an economy through sheer will and violence, it had been at the end of the 1920s under Stalin's leadership'.[87] Or was he renouncing the methods of his first years in power in favour of more measured, Bukharinist, development? In the international sphere all hope of regulating relations with the capitalist world in a peaceful fashion had vanished. Instead, he argued that World War III was inevitable unless imperialism could be overthrown. Koba, the resolute fighter against Western oil companies' cruel exploitation of workers in the Caucasus, had re-emerged in his last writings. Imperialism had to be destroyed. What is more, as this sprawling, evil, global system was cornered like a wild beast by advancing socialism, its resistance would become more violent and desperate than ever. Such were Stain's thoughts and conclusions at the end of his life.

Stalin's last days

The story of Stalin's death has been told many times and embellished in many ways. His oldest associate Molotov, who had, as we have seen, fallen out of favour, was suspicious of the circumstances. For him, the scene was set by the fact that by the end 'Stalin shouldered a burden so heavy that it naturally left him burned out . . . he was utterly drained in every way.'[88] Molotov also was of the, somewhat inconsistent, opinion that 'Stalin did not die a natural death. He wasn't seriously ill. He was working steadily . . . And he remained very spry.'[89] Everyone's favourite candidate as assassin was Beria. Again, Molotov's words: 'Of course this possibility cannot be ruled out. Beria was treacherous and unreliable. He could have done the deed just to save his own skin.'[90] However, no evidence exists to support such a theory nor was it part of the case against Beria when he was arrested later in the year. It is in the nature of strokes to come out of the blue and there is little doubt that it was a stroke that killed Stalin. Slowness to get medical help may have compounded the problem but the basic facts are clear. On 28 February Stalin spent the evening at his favourite *blizhnaia* (nearby) *dacha* with his current four closest comrades – Beria, Malenkov, Khrushchev and Bulganin. They left and Stalin retired to bed. On 1 March his guards were alarmed by his slowness to appear and follow his inflexible routines. There was no sign of him throughout the day and no one was prepared to risk disturbing him. In the evening they were reassured by seeing a light come on in his room but Stalin still did not emerge. Only at 10:00 pm, on the pretext of delivering a parcel from the Kremlin, did anyone pluck up the courage to enter his room. The most powerful man in the world was lying on the floor, barely conscious and unable to speak. Before calling for medical help the guard informed Beria who hurried out to the *dacha*. The four comrades of the last supper made their way to the *dacha* and only then was medical help summoned. Doctors arrived on the morning of 2 March and soon proclaimed the obvious. Stalin had endured a major stroke and his recovery was in question. His daughter Svetlana was summoned. Fighting to the last but without regaining consciousness Stalin lingered on until, at 9:50 pm on 5 March, he became one with his millions of victims.

His successors had a great deal to handle. In Molotov's words once more: 'Although I might not have remained in one piece had he lived on, I have regarded him and still [in 1972] regard him as a great man who fulfilled such immense and arduous tasks as none of us, none of those in the party back then, could have fulfilled.'[91] Within half an hour of his death a high-level meeting soon convened to deal with the gigantic absence at the heart of the system. As one participant, Dmitrii Shepilov, the chief editor of *Pravda*, noted: 'The chair Stalin had occupied as chairman for thirty years was empty; nobody sat in it.'[92] Nor would they.

Notes

1 All quotations are from MIA, http://www.marxists.org/reference/archive/stalin/works/correspondence/01/41.htm.
2 Ibid.
3 Clementine Churchill, letter 4 August 1942, cited in Gilbert, M. (1986) *Road to Victory: Winston S. Churchill 1941–1945*, London, Heinemann, p161. For an excellent fuller account of this historic visit, see Folly, M., 'Seeking Comradeship in the "Ogre's Den": Winston Churchill's Quest for a Warrior Alliance and His Mission to Stalin, August 1942', Brunel University Research Archive, MIA, http://bura.brunel.ac.uk/handle/2438/5738.

4 Message from Stalin to Churchill, 23 July 1942: MIA, https://www.marxists.org/reference/archive/stalin/works/correspondence/01/42.htm.

5 Montefiore, S.S. (2004) *Stalin: The Court of the Red Tsar*, Harmondsworth, Weidenfeld & Nicholson, p427.

6 See http://discovery.nationalarchives.gov.uk/details/r/C557410.

7 See http://ww2history.com/key_moments/Eastern/Churchill_meets_Stalin_in_Moscow. From Richardson, C. (1991) *From Churchill's Secret Circle to the BBC: Biography of Lieutenant-General Sir Ian Bishop*, London, BBC, p136.

8 Moran, Lord Charles W. (1966) *Winston Churchill: The Struggle for Survival: 1940–1965*, London, Constable, p62, quoted in http://ww2history.com/key_moments/Eastern/Churchill_meets_Stalin_in_Moscow.

9 Diary of Archibald Clark Kerr FO 800/300 National Archives Kew, quoted in http://ww2history.com/key_moments/Eastern/Churchill_meets_Stalin_in_Moscow.

10 Cadogan's account derived from http://blog.nationalarchives.gov.uk/blog/winston-was-complaining-of-a-slight-headache/.

11 Diary of Archibald Clark Kerr FO 800/300 National Archives Kew, quoted in http://ww2history.com/key_moments/Eastern/Churchill_meets_Stalin_in_Moscow.

12 FO 1093/238.

13 See http://blog.nationalarchives.gov.uk/blog/winston-was-complaining-of-a-slight-headache/. There are press accounts of Willkie's visit – for example, 'Willkie and the Bear', *Time Magazine*, 5 October 1942, at http://content.time.com/time/magazine/article/0,9171,773729,00.html.

14 Quoted in Service, R. (2004) *Stalin: A Biography*, Basingstoke, Macmillan, p464.

15 Djilas, M. (1962) *Conversations with Stalin*, New York, Harcourt, Brace and World, p114; and Harmondsworth, Penguin, 1963, p90.

16 Roberts, G. (2006) *Stalin's Wars: From World War to Cold War 1939–53*, New Haven, CT, and London, Yale University Press, p405, f62.

17 Stalin J.V. (1946) 'Replies to Questions Put by Mr. Eddie Gilmore, Associated Press Correspondent', 22 March: MIA, https://www.marxists.org/reference/archive/stalin/works/1946/03/22.htm.

18 Stalin J.V. (1946) 'Replies to Questions Put by Mr. Alexander Werth, Moscow, Correspondent of the "Sunday Times",' 24 September: MIA, https://www.marxists.org/reference/archive/stalin/works/1946/09/24.htm.

19 Davies, N. (2004) *God's Playground: A History of Poland, Volume 2: 1795 to the Present*, Oxford, Oxford University Press, p492.

20 For example, Roberts (2006), pp245–253.

21 Mistry, K. (2014) *The United States, Italy and the Origins of the Cold War: Waging Political Warfare 1945–1950*, Cambridge, Cambridge University Press.

22 So called because they were developed by US diplomats in Riga, the capital of Latvia, before the war when it was the United States' chief post for observing the USSR before it had an embassy in Moscow. The Yalta axioms obviously are named after the Yalta conference in honour of its spirit of co-operation and compromise.

23 The best account of this and, indeed, of the origins of the Cold War remains Yergin, D. (1977) *Shattered Peace: The Origins of the Cold War and the National Security State*, New York, Houghton Mifflin. Gaddis Smith correctly notes in his review of Yergin (*Foreign Affairs*, July 1977) that Yergin stresses the caution, confusion and defensive nature of Soviet policy. See https://www.foreignaffairs.com/reviews/capsule-review/1977–07–01/shattered-peace-origins-cold-war-and-national-security-state.

24 Mastny has argued that Stalin was looking for a Polish Benes – that is, someone who would come to an agreement with the USSR. The quote is referred to in many places such as Wettig, G. (2008) *Stalin and the Cold War in Europe: The Emergence and Development of East–West Conflict 1939–53*, Lanham, MD, Rowman & Littlefield, p45.

25 Incidentally, the very fact they were doing this is powerful evidence that Moscow expected to roll Germany back at some point, not remain in alliance with the Nazis.

26 There were, of course, many communist exiles from Germany and eastern Europe enjoying 'protection' in the Soviet Union, though the German and Polish parties, in particular, were subjected to horrendous purges leading some commentators to claim Stalin executed more communists from those countries than Hitler.

27 Roberts (2006), p273.

28 Some fascinating film footage of Berlin in 1945 has come to light and been excellently restored. The title is *Spirit of Berlin: Juli 1945* and can be found at https://vimeo.com/126617484. Its provenance is unclear but it appears to be a colourized film from an American source, possibly even connected to the conference.

29 Roberts (2006), p274.

30 Stalin J. V. (1946) 'Replies to Questions Put by Mr. Alexander Werth, Moscow, Correspondent of the "Sunday Times"', 24 September: MIA, https://www.marxists.org/reference/archive/stalin/works/1946/09/24.htm.

31 Roberts (2006), p292.

32 Ibid, p293.

33 Ibid.

34 See Ambrose, S. (1971) *Rise to Globalism*, London, Penguin, Chapters 3 and 4; and Roberts (2006), pp279–295.

35 Argued by Appleman Williams, W. (1962) *The Tragedy of American Diplomacy*, New York, Dell.

36 Geoffrey Roberts on Stalin and the Marshall Plan in Read, C. (ed) (2003) *The Stalin Years: A Reader*, London, Macmillan.

37 As we have already noted (note 23), these are the terms used by Yergin's reviewer, Gaddis Smith, to summarize Yergin's conclusions. See https://www.foreignaffairs.com/reviews/capsule-review/1977–07–01/ shattered-peace-origins-cold-war-and-national-security-state.

38 Stalin J. V. (1946) 'Replies to Questions Put by Mr. Eddie Gilmore, Associated Press Correspondent', 22 March: MIA, https://www.marxists.org/reference/archive/stalin/works/1946/03/22.htm.

39 Ibid.

40 See http://www.trumanlibrary.org/teacher/doctrine.htm#speech.

41 The consolidation of these processes came in 1950, after the Korean War had begun and China had become communist. NSC 68, a 58-page report from the National Security Council, made containment, understood as 'a policy of calculated and gradual coercion', the official basis of US foreign policy towards the USSR. It rejected the alternatives of 'detente' – that is, collaboration – and 'rollback' – aggressive action to regain countries.

42 It was published under the title 'Coexistence, American–Soviet Cooperation, Atomic Energy, Europe', MIA, https://www.marxists.org/reference/archive/stalin/works/1947/04/09.htm.

43 Roberts (2006), p314.

44 Ibid, pp314–317.

45 Ibid, p315.

46 Stalin J. V. (1948) 'Answer to the Open Letter of Henry Wallace', 17 May. Wallace's proposal, like that of Gorbachev's 'New Thinking' in 1986, included withdrawal of all foreign military bases by all powers and steps towards banning nuclear weapons. See MIA, https://www.marxists.org/reference/archive/stalin/works/1948/05/17.htm.

47 One was memorably depicted by Solzhenitsyn in his novel entitled *The First Circle*, London and New York, Collins/Fontana, 1968.

48 Medvedev, Z. A. and Medvedev, R. A. (2003) *The Unknown Stalin*, London and New York, I. B. Tauris, p163.

49 Harrison, M. (1996) *Accounting for War: Soviet Production, Employment, and the Defence Burden, 1940–1945*, Cambridge: Cambridge University Press, pp157–159.

50 Davies, R. W. (1998) *Soviet Economic Development from Lenin to Khrushchev*, Cambridge, Cambridge University Press, p64.

51 Ibid.

52 Ibid.

53 See MIA, https://www.marxists.org/reference/archive/stalin/works/1945/05/24.htm.

54 Khlevniuk, O. (2015) *Stalin: New Biography of a Dictator*, New Haven, CT, and London, Yale University Press, p271.

55 *Pravda*, 23 September 1946.

56 Khlevniuk (2015), p267.

57 Davies (1998), p65.

58 Ibid, pp65–66. Figures also from here.

59 Khlevniuk (2015), pp274–275. There is an excellent account of the reform in ibid, pp274–280.
60 Source Vert, N. and Mironenko, S. (eds) (2004) *Istoriia Stalinskogo gulaga. Konets 1920-kh-pervaia polovina 1950-kh godov, Volume 1: Massovoye repressii v SSSR*, Moscow, p610. Quoted in Khlevniuk (2015), p268. By comparison in the United States about 68,000 were in prison at any one time from 1946–1950. Langan, P. A. (1991) *Race of Prisoners Admitted to State and Federal Institutions, 1926–86*, May, NCJ-125618 US Bureau of Justice Statistics Department. See https://www.ncjrs.gov/pdffiles1/nij/125618.pdf. Even today, after a massive increase in the last 40 years, the US figure is around 1 per cent of the population in jail. According to the US Bureau of Justice Statistics (BJS), 2,266,800 adults were incarcerated in US federal and state prisons, and county jails at year-end 2011 – about 0.94 per cent of adults in the US resident population. See http://www.bjs.gov/content/pub/pdf/cpus13.pdf.
61 Khlevniuk (2015), p294.
62 Ibid, p296. For a compilation of fascinating documents on the situation see 'New Russian Documents on the Korean War', *Cold War International History Project Bulletin*, 6–7 (Winter 1995–1996) (*CWIHP*). Most of the documents can be found online at http://digitalarchive.wilsoncenter.org/browse.
63 *CWIHP*, http://digitalarchive.wilsoncenter.org/document/113744.
64 Khlevniuk (2015), p296.
65 There is an immense literature on Soviet society in the Stalin era including: Hellbeck, J. (2006) *Revolution on My Mind: Writing a Diary under Stalin*, Boston, MA, Harvard University Press; Neumann, M. (2011) *The Communist Youth League and the Transformation of the Soviet Union 1917–1932*, London and New York, Routledge; Kotkin, S. (1995) *Magnetic Mountain : Stalinism as a Civilization*, Berkeley, Los Angeles and London, University of California Press; Fürst, J. (ed) (2006) *Late Stalinist Russia: Society between Reconstruction and Invention*, London and New York, Routledge; and Tromly, B. (2013) *Making the Soviet Intelligentsia: Universities and Intellectual Life under Stalin and Khrushchev*, Cambridge, Cambridge University Press.
66 Carroll, L. (1865) *Alice's Adventures in Wonderland*, London, Macmillan.
67 Puzo, M. (1969) *The Godfather*, New York, G.P. Putnam's Sons.
68 Medvedev and Medvedev (2003), p50.
69 The best guides are Khlevniuk (2015), pp268–309; and Gorlitskii, Y. and Khlevniuk, O. (2004) *Cold Peace: Stalin and the Soviet Ruling Circle 1945–1953*, Oxford, Oxford University Press. I am deeply indebted to both for their insights and knowledge.
70 Ibid, p271.
71 Ibid, p272.

72 Khlevniuk (2015), p273.
73 Ibid.
74 Holloway, D. (1994) *Stalin and the Bomb: The Soviet Union and Atomic Energy 1945–1956*, Princeton, NJ, Princeton University Press.
75 See Montefiore (2004), Chapter 45, pp513–523 for a colourful and thoroughly researched account. Quotations and information here from pp517–519.
76 Khlevniuk (2015), pp281–283; Gorlizkii and Khlevniuk (2004), Chapter 3; and Medvedev and Medvedev (2003), pp45–8.
77 Khlevniuk (2015), p284. On the Zhemchuzhina affair see a very sympathetic portrait by Montefiore (2004), pp53, 599–605.
78 Released from the camps by Beria after Stalin's death, Zhemchuzhina never complained about her husband's behaviour and the two of them lived out their lives together as unrepentant Stalinists.
79 Medvedev, Z. (2003) *Stalin i evreiskaia problema: novyi analiz*, Moscow, Izdatel'stvo Prava Cheloveka.
80 Service (2004), p568.
81 Khlevniuk (2015) has the most recent account of these events, pp304–307. Gorlizki and Khlevniuk (2004) have the most detailed. Derek Watson (2005) tells the story from Molotov's perspective in *Molotov: A Biography*, London, Palgrave Macmillan, pp234–238.
82 Chuev, F. (1993) *Molotov Remembers*, Chicago, IL, Chicago University Press, p324.
83 Ibid, p188.
84 Ibid.
85 van Ree, E. (2002) *Stalin's Political Thought: A Study in Revolutionary Patriotism*, London and New York, Macmillan, pp269–272.
86 van Ree (2002), p271.
87 Service (2004), p566.
88 Chuev (1993), pp326–327.
89 Ibid, p326.
90 Ibid.
91 Ibid, p327.
92 Khlevniuk (2015), p314.

9   Stalin's afterlife: an inconclusive conclusion

The official communiqué reporting Stalin's death on 5 March caused a shock wave to travel round the globe. From Paris to Beijing and from Berlin to Hanoi repercussions were feared. Nowhere was the shock greater than in the Soviet Union itself. The emerging emotions were complicated and confused. Grief, fear, pessimistic expectations appear to have outweighed hope and even relief that the tyrant was dead. There was no rejoicing officially or unofficially. It was somewhat akin to the death of a stern, cruel patriarch. How would the family fare without his ferocious protection?

In his great novel *Cancer Ward* set in the immediate post-Stalin years, Alexander Solzhenitsyn depicts an ardent Stalin admirer, Rusanov, being shocked to find that, on 5 March 1955, the second anniversary of Stalin's death was not marked by *Pravda* having a black-banded portrait of the dead leader on its front page, or indeed anywhere in the issue. It was an early, small but eloquent indicator of what was to come. What Rusanov would have made of the Twentieth Party Congress in February 1956, we can only speculate. Taking the initiative, and the risk that came with it, the new party first secretary, Nikita Khrushchev, launched into an extreme attack on Stalin's rule. In particular, for tactical reasons as much as anything, Khrushchev highlighted Stalin's mistreatment of the party. Almost taking a move out of Stalin's own playbook, Khrushchev portrayed himself as the new defender of the party against the abuse of Stalin and of Khrushchev's political opponents whom, in classic Stalin fashion, he labelled the 'anti-party' group. He launched, almost for the first time as few others had suggested it, the accusation that Kirov, the symbol of party rectitude in the 1930s, had been assassinated at Stalin's command. Several minor figures were rehabilitated, a trickle which turned into a flood over the following three decades. Nonetheless, Khrushchev's critique of Stalin was limited. The fundamental policies of collectivization and industrialization were not criticized. Most purge victims were not rehabilitated, notably the party leaders such as Trotsky, Bukharin, Zinoviev, Kamenev, Radek, Rykov and so on, whose conviction and sentences were upheld.[1] Even Khrushchev could not destroy Stalin's prestige and legacy in one stroke. The quotation chosen as the epigraph for this book is an example of the limited nature of Khrushchev's critique. In particular, Stalin's symbolic leadership of the anti-Nazi war was something the whole country was proud of and Khrushchev was only able to attack obliquely by raising another hare, notably that Stalin's nerve broke in the early days of Operation Barbarossa. While these two new stories – about Kirov and Stalin's funk – were gifts to anti-Soviet cold warriors, subsequent, more detailed and better grounded investigations have not, as we have already discussed, been able to fully substantiate Khrushchev's claims. Be that as it may, and limited though the critique was, the impact of Khrushchev's speech could hardly have been greater.

The communist world had grown massively after the war. The takeovers in eastern Europe were dwarfed by the emergence of Mao and the Communist Party as rulers of China in 1949. The world's largest countries, one by area and the other by population, were both governed by communists. Wars were raging in Indo-China which resulted in several more communist-led countries joining the group. Wartime prestige, especially as leaders of anti-Nazi resistance, had led to the expansion of communist influence in western Europe, especially France and Italy. While a wave of post-war popular fronts had fizzled out, radical groups were growing in Latin America, culminating later on in the Cuban revolution. This supposed communist 'camp' or 'bloc', in Cold War terminology, was blown apart by Khrushchev's speech. Mao and the Chinese leadership increasingly criticized Khrushchev for 'revisionism' – a cardinal sin in the Marxist tradition – and the uneasy relationship turned into a split in 1959–1961. In eastern Europe, protests, which had first emerged in Berlin in 1953, produced a full-scale uprising in Hungary in 1956. In the West, many communists were shocked by the extent to which they had been lied to by their party and they left in droves, many joining groups in the Trotsky tradition since Khrushchev seemed to have confirmed key points of Trotsky's critique of Stalin. In some ways, it seems ironic that they would leave at the point the party was trying to change itself; but the deception had been so thorough that they had lost all trust in it. Nonetheless, the French and Italian parties weathered the storm and remained influential, especially in labour unions. Despite the turbulence, Khrushchev held his course and even deepened it. Town names with Stalinist associations were changed. Even the great hero city of Stalingrad was renamed Volgograd. Statues of the fallen Great Leader were removed. In 1961 Stalin's embalmed body was taken out of the Lenin Mausoleum in Red Square and buried in the Kremlin cemetery with a modest bust similar to that of the other significant figures buried there. More practically, Khrushchev continued with structural reforms intended to ameliorate the most dysfunctional elements of the system Stalin had set up.[2] It is most likely that Khrushchev believed the changes might lead to an end of Cold War confrontation and he proposed, in place of Stalin's assumption of the inevitability of war between capitalism and communism, the doctrine of 'peaceful coexistence', meaning that the systems could survive alongside each other and whichever proved itself the more successful would replace the other. There was a slim chance that the Cold War might have ended in 1954–1955 but by 1956 and the violent suppression of the Hungarian Uprising the moment had passed and the next decade was one of Cold War max, characterized by the Cuban revolution and missile crisis, the flaring up of the already long-running war in Vietnam and the suppression of the Prague Spring in 1968.

In the West, especially the United States and its predecessor as world leader, Great Britain, the direct political impact of Stalin's death was very limited but it was an opportunity to be exploited in two ways. First, though there were many blinkered politicians who refused to see the splits as real, many opportunities were opened up for playing different factions off and exploiting the political turmoil, especially in the newly christened 'Third World' – that is, that which was neither capitalist nor communist and comprised mainly but not exclusively former colonies of the European imperialists in Asia, the Middle East, Africa and Latin America. For a variety of reasons beyond our scope, the West was not notably successful in these early decades of post-Stalin Cold War. In fact, the Great Powers were as likely to be played by the cannier leaders of some of these emerging states as they were to play the newcomers.

Much more successful was the incorporation of an analysis of Soviet history as a foundation of Cold War ideology. The West, especially the United States, wrapped itself in the banner of a largely undefined 'Freedom' and denounced almost all of its challengers as Marxists whose rule would lead to a Soviet-style tyranny. Helpfully scholars developed a theory of 'totalitarianism', initially based on the study of Stalin's arch-foe, Nazi Germany and its fascist allies and offshoots, which was developed in a way that lumped both left and right together.[3] Going well beyond scholarship, the process became a foundation of US and NATO ideology. In the simplistic personalization of complex issues so beloved of the modern media and sections of the political class, Hitler and Stalin were endlessly 'compared'. A gruesome world championship of evil seemed to be at stake. Was Hitler worse than Stalin or did Stalin take the crown as the world's greatest inflictor of suffering?[4] A 'numbers game' emerged with participants from holocaust deniers to purveyors of impossible exaggerations of the number of Soviet purge victims.[5] The present study has deliberately avoided such a practice as the complexities get ignored, especially the differences between the two individuals and the regimes and states they led. Germany and the Soviet Union were different countries. Stalin was not a racist whereas Nazi ideology was little but racism. Nazism looked to pagan symbolism and the irrational for inspiration. Soviet Communism was built on reason and science (though obviously distorted in ways we have seen). Nazism aimed at world domination by military conquest. Soviet Communism expected to prevail through the contradictions of capitalism, the globally widespread hatred of imperialism and the supposed attractions of the communist alternative. Simplistic comparison of individual with individual have often glossed over these issues.[6] Nonetheless, the simple association of Stalin and Hitler has been a very successful ploy in Cold War thinking and has encouraged a reflex reaction to all forms of radicalism as leading to the gulag along the lines that social experiment will lead to Stalinist tyranny. Stalinist tyranny is worse than Hitler's; therefore, all challenges to the dominance of the ruling elites will lead to terror and genocide.[7]

Setting direct political polemic to one side, the totalitarian thesis has had a long and persistent life. In the 1950s and for much of the 1960s it ruled unchallenged. The founding tomes of 'Sovietology' were mostly written in its spirit. Very influential and highly scholarly works, including *How Russia Is Ruled* by Merle Fainsod, *The Communist Party of the Soviet Union* by Leonard Schapiro and, in terms of Stalin biographies, Adam Ulam's *Stalin: The Man and His Era* were foundations of the discipline. Richard Pipes, who still writes in this vein, produced a range of volumes on late tsarism and the revolutionary years. They did not have it all their own way. Very significant exceptions to the Cold War paradigm included E. H. Carr and R. W. Davies in the UK and Leopold Haimson in the United States. In fact, probably the most influential biography of Stalin of the era was Isaac Deutscher's *Stalin: A Political Biography*, an interpretation which reflected Deutscher's own Trotskyite leanings and which injected that view deeply into the Western Cold War consensus, an irony given the Marxist outlook of Deutscher and the anti-Marxist aims of the cold warriors. It also shows there were no significant 'defenders' of Stalin. On left and right the view of a possibly psychopathic, power-seeking megalomaniac with a barbarous tendency to taunt and torture his associates became a convenient view. This Stalin was crude, provincial, slow-thinking, chauvinistic, deceptive and manipulative. He had, in effect, hijacked the revolution in support of his own power lust. In conformity with the totalitarian thesis he was also deemed to be all-powerful from the early 1930s, ruling like the most ruthless tsars such as Ivan the Terrible or Peter the Great.

By and large, before 1980 most scholarly interest was focused on 1917–1929 rather than the 1930s; but a new revision of Stalin began to emerge. Perhaps two sources were in the forefront. In the Soviet Union, the dissident Marxist Roy Medvedev produced an account of Stalin's life and career entitled *Let History Judge* (1972), which gave new impetus to the notion that, to simplify, there was a 'good' Lenin whose legacy was thwarted by the 'bad'

Stalin. This notion had numerous supporters, perhaps surprisingly including the writer Alexander Solzhenitsyn who, in *The First Circle* (1968), gave a memorable fictional account of a brooding Stalin dividing his time between identical rooms in his suburban *dachas* and in his Kremlin suite. It was also promoted by Stephen Cohen whose biography of Bukharin (1973) was, in part, a biography of Stalin as well in the 1917–1938 period. However, it was J. Arch Getty's writing which began a truly 'revisionist' approach to the Stalin era, notably his book *The Origins of the Great Purges* (1983). Getty argued that Stalin was not in control of everything that happened in the USSR. One might consider this to be an unexceptionable point to make about even the most powerful of leaders; but in the context of Soviet historiography, it was an approach which called down accusations of being a Stalin 'apologist'. Getty has not written a biography of Stalin but he has diminished Stalin's direct role in the purges attributing its features to the ramshackle nature of the Soviet state, the independent action of local mini-dictators (he calls them 'mini-Stalins') and so on. While Getty's ideas were not widely accepted, since that time a much more sophisticated historiography of Stalin and his era has emerged from Western and some important Russian scholarship.

A complete survey of this new landscape is beyond our scope although much of it is represented above within the interpretation of Stalin and his actions in the present study. Nonetheless, a few pointers can be made. In terms of political history, Oleg Khlevniuk has done more to enlighten us about the everyday working of Stalin's government in the 1930s, showing that Stalin relied a great deal on others to get things done. This insight has been expanded by Sheila Fitzpatrick in her 2015 book *On Stalin's Team*, which underlined the importance to Stalin of a close group of loyal colleagues who remained with him from the 1920s to the end, in many cases. A whole host of writing has shown Soviet society to be much more complex than the grey, cowed masses implied in the original totalitarian assumptions. Widespread support for Stalin and his government within the Soviet population has also been detected, initially by Fitzpatrick in *Social Mobility* and more recently from sources such as diaries, the study of which was pioneered by Jochen Hellbeck, to newly opened archives showing even the grim, post-1945 years of austerity and wartime reconstruction were more complex and the society more mobile and even creative than had previously been suspected. Going beyond Cold War era simplifications, a more complex view of Soviet foreign policy was pioneered by Jonathan Haslam, though his more recent work has moved away from his earlier views on the 1930s. Nonetheless, Geoffrey Roberts and others have shown convincingly that Soviet efforts to set up collective security in the 1930s and, more controversially, to share control over Europe rather than exercise a blueprint for takeover, represented genuine initiatives.

Some years ago the Canadian scholar Lars Lih argued the time had come for scholars to write about 'the historical Lenin' – that is, a perspective more closely related to the man himself, to the historical sources and to the context of his life and less to political and ideological pressures and presuppositions. In essence, the same call needed to be made for Stalin and many scholarly works of the last decade and more have been written in that spirit. The ideological myths created by supporters, in the cult of personality, and critics in the Cold War are giving way to a more securely documented, more objective and less preconceived interpretation of the man and his times. Past accusations that such an approach is tantamount to being an apologist for Stalin or a kind of holocaust denier have no place. Establishing exactly what Stalin's crimes and achievements consist of and where, in reality, rather than legend, they came from is the essence of the historian's craft. While historians remain a long way from consensus a more historical Stalin is certainly emerging. What are the main characteristics of this view?

In the first place, the more lurid and unlikely elements – the gangster, the tsarist snitch, the psychopath, the dominator of a continent by pure fear – have been cast aside or reduced in significance. There is more attention to Stalin's early, formative years despite a tantalizing lack of definitive evidence on key issues like his time at the seminary in Tiflis. A picture of a real person with great abilities – how else could he have achieved what he did? – as well as great flaws has begun to form. The testimony of those who worked with him, especially the generals and foreign leaders and diplomats he encountered in wartime, bear this out. He was considered highly competent. No one detected the mental imbalance beloved of Cold War propagandists, though he could be ruthless in the extreme. Increasingly the root of this last characteristic is seen to be his unfailing commitment to his vision of revolution as the driving force of achievements and catastrophes alike. While a simple view of an *Alice in Wonderland* Queen of Hearts-type character able to command 'Off with their heads' to all and sundry can no longer be sustained, the black cruelty of the 1930s and beyond and the personal issues involved in the condemnation of certain people who had been close to him, such as Bukharin and Anna Alliluyeva and the seemingly arbitrary protection of other old friends, family and allies, opens up dark and unfathomable areas. Stalin was first and foremost a ruthless revolutionary but he was also an emotional and sentimental person who could feel love, for his mother, his daughter, his wives, though all these could be suppressed, temporarily or permanently, by massive will power and the primacy of the revolution in his mental universe. Everything was subject to that. He also had a near-invulnerable sense of self-confidence which held up under all but the most extreme circumstances of, apparently, the first hours of the Nazi invasion. He was not simply obeyed through fear by those around him; they idolized him and were lost without him at the height of his powers. However, his last years show signs of growing mental and physical frailty despite his active involvement not only in politics but in setting the scientific, philosophical and ideological agendas for the next generation, a set of initiatives which, in fact, barely survived him. By the time of his death many of his former supporters like Khrushchev were manoeuvring to succeed him.

Perhaps the most surprising element of Stalin's career is its rapid obliteration in the Soviet Union and the disappearance of the personal elements of his legacy in the stampede to take over from him. The cult of his personality vanished rapidly. The vast Stalin museum in his birthplace, Gori, which dated from 1937, of all years, but had been extended massively in the years 1952–1957, became an empty relic, not the place of pilgrimage it was supposed to have been. It remains open today but its annual footfall is claimed to be under 15,000.[8] Across the Soviet Union statues and pictures were removed. References to Stalin in the press quickly reduced to zero. His theoretical guidance through his extensive writings was rarely sought, a feature symbolized by the failure of the authorities to complete the publication of his *Collected Works* which petered out after 13 volumes covering the years to 1934. It was left to Chinese publishers and enthusiasts in the West to extend the coverage to 1952 in several supplementary volumes. Under Brezhnev, active attacks on Stalin wound down to be replaced by silences and elisions from the official record of Soviet history. Unofficial historians like Solzhenitsyn and Roy Medvedev were not matched by any real analysis by the authorities.

The silence was spectacularly broken in November 1987 when Mikhail Gorbachev, in a speech commemorating the seventieth anniversary of the October Revolution, called for the 'blank pages' of Soviet history to be filled in. One of the first fruits was the massive but rather unsystematic account written in four volumes by Dmitrii Volkogonov. It was the first extensive, critical, archive-based account of Stalin's life and career to be published in the USSR. After the collapse in 1991 new archive materials were opened up and there have been extensive publications of documents and, in an unprecedented agreement between the former Communist Party archive and Yale University Press, a great deal of the most important material from Stalin's personal archive has been published online and in print. This has enabled a new generation of Russian historians, led by Oleg Khlevniuk among political historians, to produce a brilliant series of soundly documented and reliable accounts of the period. More broadly, there has been an explosion of scholarship on the cultural, economic, international and political aspects of the Stalin years and of Stalinism, variously defined.

There are pockets of support for Stalin in Russia and elsewhere around the globe. Part of the Russian Communist Party still reveres him and marks significant anniversaries with, usually, small public commemorations. However, what such people seem to be attracted to is not full-blown Stalinism but a rose-tinted nostalgia for Russia/USSR's great power status, a sense of social and political advance, a stability which rarely figured in the real world of Stalin and a sense of collective social action and relative egalitarianism in contrast to the perceived egoism and greedy self-enrichment associated with the kind of bandit capitalism to which Russia (not to mention Ukraine and other parts of the former USSR) have been subject since the fall of the communist system. This is not to say there is not a lurid literature of full-scale apologies for a Stalin who is deemed to have been totally misrepresented by mainstream historians. In this neurotic fantasy world, as two reviewers put it, numerous 'Stalin apologists . . . have . . . been working feverishly to establish the Man of Steel's innocence, in particular for the mass bloodletting of the Great Terror' with 'authors determined to "prove" the utter innocence of the Soviet leader'.[9] More significantly, the Chinese Communist Party has never de-Stalinized and, apart from being a major source of reprints of his work, his image is still part of official Chinese iconography, though little trace of Stalin's ideas and influence can be found in the post-Mao policies of the Chinese leadership.[10]

In a 1975 lecture at the University of Warwick attended by this author, one of the finest 'sovietologists' of his generation, Alec Nove, suggested that the image of Stalin would settle into something like that of Napoleon for France, a great state-builder and embodiment of national power built on a hecatomb of victims. The collapse of that system led to Nove modifying his tone later but the question remains pertinent. For many Russians Stalin is a kind of Napoleon who built the country up irrespective of cost. For others he is nothing but a vicious tyrant. Clearly there is no consensus, even setting the extreme supporters and detractors aside. A new, source-based view of Stalin and his era is emerging and many fine studies have contributed to the new appraisal; but Stalin remains a controversial figure. There are very few who wish to revert to his policies wholesale and his political influence has diminished to near zero but he retains a strong symbolic presence. As we have seen, figures from Jeremy Corbyn to Putin via Gaddaffi and Saddam have been described as 'Stalinist' though none of them shares much with Stalin beyond a commitment to resist American and international capitalist pressure and, in the case of the dictators, a ruthless determination to stay in power for a variety of reasons, from self-preservation and self-enrichment to a more truly 'Stalinist' commitment to a cause. In that sense the term 'Stalinist', though used less frequently, has become an equivalent on the right to the widespread but intellectually lazy left-wing use of the term 'fascist' to a broad swathe of their opponents on the right of the political spectrum. While it is impossible to know what the future will decide about Stalin, it is clear controversy over the man and his legacy will not be over any time soon.

Notes

1 Apart from Trotsky, of course, who was never actually tried and was assassinated unofficially in 1941 in Mexico.

2 It is beyond our brief to pursue these policies. There are numerous volumes which do so including Service, R. (1997), *A History of Twentieth-Century Russia*, Harmondsworth and New York, Penguin: note this book has undergone three changes of title; Sandle, M. (1999) *A Short History of Soviet Socialism*, London and Philadelphia, PA, Pennsylvania State University Press; and Read, C. (2001) *The Making and Breaking of the Soviet System*, London and New York, Macmillan, which interprets the period 1953 to 2000 and beyond as one of continued de-Stalinization.

3 Gleason, A. (1999) *Totalitarianism: The Inner History of the Cold War*, Oxford and New York, Oxford University Press.

4 In fact, it has become a paradigm still in use today. Though the scale differs, the basic depiction of an enemy of the United States or the UK as a murderous tyrant with a repressive regime has been applied to Milosevic in Serbia (but not Tudjman, in Croatia), to Gaddafi and Saddam Hussein despite them, at times, being allies of the United States and, most recently, to Bashar al-Assad, who has gone from wicked enemy and suppressor of freedom to *de facto* ally in a matter of months. Western allies sharing very similar characteristics, such as white South Africa, Mobutu in the Congo, or Pinochet in Chile, had their transgressions overlooked in the name of realpolitik.

5 Writers such as Timothy Snyder have continued the tradition, in his case placing the greater share of blame for the horrors of the interwar period on the Soviet Union. See, in particular, Snyder, T. (2010) *Bloodlands: Europe between Hitler and Stalin*, New York, Basic Books.

6 There are some good examples of the genre: Bullock, A. (1992) *Hitler Stalin: Parallel Lives*, New York and London, Alfred A. Knopf; Kershaw, I. and Lewin, M. (eds) (1997) *Stalinism and Nazism*, Cambridge, Cambridge University Press; and Overy, R. (2004) *The Dictators: Hitler's Germany, Stalin's Russia*, London and New York, W. W. Norton & Co.

7 It has been particularly bizarre to hear people who should know better making the same argument about the mild-mannered, pacifist leader of the British Labour Party, Jeremy Corbyn. Allister Heath in the *Daily Telegraph*, 5 August 2015, recommended: 'Here is a simple corrective for any gullible youngster you know who has fallen for Jeremy Corbyn's socialist siren song. Buy them a copy of *The Great Terror* by Robert Conquest, the wonderful historian of communism who died this week.' While admitting the obvious, that Corbyn and his followers are 'no Stalinists', their policies, Heath argues, will lead to the same tyrannical results. See http://www.telegraph.co.uk/news/politics/labour/11786061/Jeremy-Corbyns-supporters-should-get-off-Twitter-and-read-a-book-instead.html.

8 Ioseb Stalin Museum official website, http://www.georgianmuseums.ge/?lang=eng&id=1_1&th_id=208.

9 Sommer, T. and Chodakiewicz, M. (2011) 'Average Joe: The Return of Stalin Apologists', *World Affairs*, January/February, include summaries of some of the more grotesque examples. See http://www.worldaffairsjournal.org/article/average-joe-return-stalin-apologists.

10 Maoism, of course, did retain key aspects of Stalinism such as anti-imperialism, productionism, forced industrialization, proletarian chauvinism, voluntarism and cultural revolution, though often with a specifically Maoist spin.

Further reading: a brief guide

The recent output of writing on the Stalin era is not only immense, it is, overwhelmingly, of good quality. It has contributed to the ongoing development of a more historical and less polemical view of Stalin and it provides the bedrock on which the present study stands. The following list is highly selective and many of the items have extensive, not to say exhausting if not exhaustive, bibliographies. The first volume of Stephen Kotkin's life of Stalin, has about 50 pages of bibliography comprising well over 1000 items – and that is only on Stalin's life up to 1928! When complete, the bibliography alone will be a great work of scholarship. Given the vastness of the terrain, the selection below is aimed at the serious reader who wishes to pursue aspects of the Stalin story and acquaint herself with up-to-date (though some older items are included as 'classics'), stimulating and reliable additional reading. The research scholar will already be familiar with these items. I have attempted to give a representative sample of key works.

Collections of primary and secondary sources

First off, reference should be made to the ongoing Yale University Press series *Annals of Communism* which has seen the publication of dozens of hefty volumes of documents from the main Russian archives on topics of great importance and sensitivity. A number of them are mentioned in the chapter endnotes; but the full list should be consulted at http://yalebooks.com/search/node/annals

%20of%20communism. The present study has used Getty and Naumov's *Road to Terror*; the volumes of Stalin's correspondence with Kaganovich and Molotov; Katerina Clark, Oleg Naumov and others on *Soviet Culture and Power*; Lewis Siegelbaum and Andrei Sokolov on *Stalinism as a Way of Life*; and Matthew Lenöe on *The Kirov Murder*. There are many other crucial items such as Lynne Viola and others on collectivization, David Shearer on the secret police, which are immensely important to the general history but which reflect less directly on Stalin. The Russian speaker also has a stunning series of no less than 98 volumes on *The History of Stalinism*, combining documentary and secondary studies, published in Moscow by the Rosspen (Russian Political Encyclopaedia) publishing house. The list can be consulted on their website at http://www.rosspen.su/ru/catalog/.briefly/id/56/limit/0.20.1../.

The third major collection on which this study has relied is the extraordinary Marxist Internet Archive, devoted to publishing the main works of major Marxist figures and some supplementary materials. The whole collection can be accessed through its portal at www.marxists.org. The entire content is free to consult and much of it is not copyright. Of particular relevance to this study is the sub-branch entitled Stalin Internet Archive, which includes an extensive but not complete collection of Stalin's major speeches and writings. The index to Stalin's works can be found at https://www.marxists.org/reference/archive/stalin/works/decades-index.htm.

There are a number of edited print volumes which are especially helpful in providing a wide range of key ideas in a single book. Of special note are the studies by Sarah Davies and James Harris (eds) *Stalin: A New History* (Cambridge, 2004) and James Harris (ed) *Anatomy of Terror: Political Violence under Stalin* (Oxford, 2013). J. Arch Getty and Roberta Manning, *Stalinist Terror: New Perspectives* (Cambridge, 1993) remains stimulating. A selection of classic articles on the Soviet era can be found in Chris Ward, *The Stalinist Dictatorship: A Reader* (London and New York, 1998) while a selection of post-Soviet era scholarship can be found in Christopher Read, *The Stalin Years: A Reader* (London and New York, 2002).

Biographies of Stalin

There are two classic biographies of Stalin which still have relevance. They are Isaac Deutscher's *Stalin: A Biography* (Oxford, 1949) and many editions since; and Leon Trotsky's two-volume *Stalin: An Appraisal of the Man and His Influence* (London and New York, 1941) and many other editions including https://www.marxists.org/archive/trotsky/1940/xx/stalin/. It may seem odd to recommend these two Trotskyist interpretations given the insistence that the contemporary reader needs to get the Trotsky interpretation of Stalin into a new and less prominent perspective, but they are of historical importance. Note the Trotsky volumes were extensively edited by an admirer, Charles Malamuth. There is an argument over how extensively he edited the original manuscript. More recent accounts of interest for a variety of reasons include Stephen Kotkin's magisterial *Stalin: Volume 1, Paradoxes of Power 1878–1928* (New York, 2014), though at over 700 pages it is a hefty commitment for even the serious reader. More accessible accounts include Robert Service, *Stalin: A Biography* (Basingstoke, 2004) (also lengthy at 600 pages but at least it covers his whole life and career); and Robert Tucker, *Stalin as Revolutionary: A Study in History and Personality 1879–1929* (New York and London, 1973) and *Stalin in Power: The Revolution from Above 1928–1945* (New York and London, 1990). Kevin McDermott's *Stalin: Revolutionary in an Era of War* (London and New York, 2006) is accessible, readable, up-to-date and reliable. Oleg Khlevniuk, *Stalin: New Biography of a Dictator* (New Haven and London, 2015) is most valuable on Stalin's links to his inner circle, which is also the focus of Sheila Fitzpatrick's *On Stalin's Team: The Years of Living Dangerously in Soviet Politics* (Princeton and Oxford, 2015). Dmitrii Volkogonov, *Stalin: Triumph and Tragedy* (London, 1991) was the first real Soviet-published biography (four vols in Russian, Moscow, 1989) though the *samizdat* (unofficially published) *Let History Judge: The Origins and Consequences of Stalinism* (London, 1971) by the dissident Roy Medvedev poses many questions as do the same authors in *The Unknown Stalin* (London, 2003), written in collaboration with his brother Zhores Medvedev. Also paradoxical, since the present study has deliberately avoided comparing Stalin and Hitler, there are some valuable contributions to this genre, notably Alan Bullock, *Hitler Stalin: Parallel Lives* (New York and London, 1992) (over 1000 pages); Richard Overy, *The Dictators: Hitler's Germany Stalin's Russia* (London and New York, 2004) (over 800 pages) and Ian Kershaw and Moshe Lewin (eds) *Stalinism and Nazism* (Cambridge, 1997).

Specialized studies on key aspects of Stalin's life, career and influence

Beyond this brief selection of broad items there lies a mountain range of superb scholarship on specific aspects and details. It is somewhat invidious to make a small selection from this vast literature but the following authors are especially noteworthy and full details of several of their key works can be found in the chapter endnotes. On the early Stalin, the works by Rieber, Suny and van Ree are indispensable. Tracy Macdonald has made a major impact upon our understanding of the 1920s. Collectivization, industrialization, the economy and everyday life have been brilliantly served by R. W. Davies, Mark Harrison, Lynne Viola and Sheila Fitzpatrick. The mentality of Stalin and the 1930s has been searchingly illuminated by Jochen Hellbeck, David Brandenberger, Katerina Clark and David Hoffmann. On the tangled politics of the purge era, Oleg Khlevniuk, J. Arch Getty, Matthew Lenöe, Arfon Rees, James Harris and Sarah Davies have produced outstanding work. The history of Stalin and the Great Patriotic War has been well served by Geoffrey Roberts, David Glantz, Evan Mawdsley, Richard Overy and Antony Beevor. On the related issues of foreign policy and emerging Cold War, Daniel Yergin, Stephen Ambrose and, once again, Geoffrey Roberts are outstanding. On Stalin's last years, Oleg Khlevniuk and Yoram Gorlizki were pioneers and many younger scholars have followed their footsteps, including Juliane Furst, Benjamin Tromly, Ethan Pollock and Robert Dale.

Apologies to the many additional worthy candidates whom I cannot include here for reasons of space.

Index

Printed in Great Britain
by Amazon

28110650R00201